THE INVENTION OF

The Invention of the Future

A HISTORY OF CITIES
IN THE MODERN WORLD

BRUNO CARVALHO

PRINCETON UNIVERSITY PRESS
PRINCETON & OXFORD

Published by Princeton University Press
41 William Street, Princeton, New Jersey 08540
99 Banbury Road, Oxford OX2 6JX

press.princeton.edu

GPSR Authorized Representative: Easy Access System Europe - Mustamäe tee 50, 10621 Tallinn, Estonia, gpsr.requests@easproject.com

All Rights Reserved

ISBN 9780691246550
ISBN (e-book) 9780691246567

LCCN: 2025933407

British Library Cataloging-in-Publication Data is available

Editorial: Priya Nelson and Emma Wagh
Production Editorial: Natalie Baan
Jacket Design: Katie Osborne
Production: Erin Suydam
Publicity: Carmen Jimenez and Alyssa Sanford
Copyeditor: Jennifer Harris

Jacket image: Courtesy of the Francis Loeb Library / Harvard Graduate School of Design / Special Collections

This book has been composed in Arno

Printed in the United States of America

10 9 8 7 6 5 4 3 2 1

CONTENTS

List of Illustrations ix

Preface xv

Introduction 1
I. No City, No Future? 1
II. Making Plans 10
III. Under a Warmer Sky 15

1

In Pursuit of the Future (1750s–1790s)
Lisbon + Paris, London, St. Petersburg,
Vila Rica, and more. 20
I. Earthquake and Revolutions 20
II. Inside the Grid 29
III. Secular Utopia 42
IV. Resonances 48

2

New Worlds Emerge (1790s–1840s)
New York + London, Washington, DC, Paris, Philadelphia,
Salvador, and more. 55
I. Leaping Ahead 55
II. Outside the Grid 73
III. Gained Illusions and Slavery 86
IV. Between Heaven and Hell 95

3
Everything Seems Possible (1850s–1880s)
Paris + New York, Barcelona, London, Berlin, Vienna,
Boston, and more. 106
I. The Spectacle of Progress and Its Discontents 106
II. Modernity as Rupture and Continuity 115
III. Competing Futures 132
IV. Unplanned Afterlives 152

4
Possibilities and Limits (1870s–1910s)
Rio de Janeiro + Mexico City, New York, Chicago,
Havana, and more. 159
I. Black Streets, White Masks 159
II. Futures Deferred 172
III. How the Other Half Lives 183
IV. Haussmannization Americanizes 193
V. Reinventions 214

5
The Sky Is Not the Limit (1900s–1940s)
Buenos Aires + Garden Cities, New York, Berlin, Rio de Janeiro,
Paris, Rome, and more. 218
I. The World of Tomorrow 218
II. Destructive Torrents and Explosions 232
III. Futures in Transit 237
IV. The Star of the South 266
V. Divided We Stand 280

6
After the Future? (1940s Onward)
Lagos + Brasília, Suburbia, Algiers, Dakar,
the Pacific Rim, and more. 289
I. We Were Never Modernist 289
II. Which Dreams Are Over? 296
III. Endings and Beginnings 313

Epilogue 330
I. Pedestrian Futures 330
II. Where Can the Future Go? 333

Acknowledgments   343
Notes   347
Bibliography   379
Illustration Credits   403
Index   405

ILLUSTRATIONS

o.1. Estimated number of cities among the 20 largest by population, located near the Atlantic, Pacific, or Indian Ocean, between 1750 and 2020.   6

o.2. Estimated number of cities among the 20 largest by population, located in Europe, Asia, the Americas, or Africa, between 1500 and 2020.   6

o.3. Estimated number of cities among the 20 largest by population, located in the "Global North" or "Global South," between 1500 and 2020.   7

1.1. "Plan for the ruined city of Lisbon, also according to its new layout by the architects Eugenio dos Santos de Carvalho and Carlos Mardel," 1758   28

1.2. "Portrait of the Marquis of Pombal" or "The Expulsion of the Jesuits," oil on canvas, Louis-Michel Van Loo and Claude Joseph Vernet, 1766.   40

2.1. "A futuristic vision: technology is over-sophisticated, and the masses devote themselves to intellectual pursuits, while the basic needs of society are neglected," colored etching by W. Heath, using the pseudonym Paul Pry, 1828.   59

2.2. "A futuristic vision: the advance of technology leads to rapid transport, sophisticated tastes among the masses, mechanization, and extravagant building projects," colored etching by W. Heath, using the pseudonym Paul Pry, 1829.   61

2.3. "Plan of the city intended for the permanent seat of the government of t[he] United States," Pierre Charles L'Enfant, 1790–1791, reproduced in 1887.   72

2.4. "The Commissioners Map of the City of New York, 1807," reproduced in 1893.   75

2.5. "The future: perspective of a phalanstery or corporate palace dedicated to humanity," according to the plan of Charles Fourier, signed by Victor Considerant.   97

3.1. "The transept from the Grand Entrance," souvenir of the Great Exhibition, 1851.   113

3.2. "Design for the Great Victorian Way," Joseph Paxton, 1855.   116

3.3. "Les Halles," Central Market in Paris, photograph by Charles Marville, ca. 1867.   119

3.4. "New Monumental Paris: A Practical Guide for Foreigners in Paris," F. Dufour, 1878.   120

3.5. "Official Birdseye View of the Universal Exhibition of 1867," Paris, 1867.   123

3.6. "Avenue de l'Opéra: Morning Sunshine," oil on canvas, Camille Pissarro, 1898.   129

3.7. "Barricade of the Chaussée Ménilmontant, March 18, 1871," unknown photographer.   133

3.8. "Plan for the surroundings of the city of Barcelona, and project for reform and extension," Ildefonso Cerdá, 1859.   139

3.9. "General Plan of Riverside," Olmsted, Vaux & Co. Landscape Architects, 1869.   145

4.1. "En L'An 2000," paper card, attributed to Jean-Marc Côté, ca. 1899.   161

4.2. "Mexico, Centennial Festivities, 5 de Mayo street lights," postcard, ca. 1910.   177

4.3. "Italian Mother and Her Baby in Jersey Street, 1888–1889," photograph by Jacob Riis.   185

4.4. "Holyoke, Mass. in Future," postcard, early 1900s. 186

4.5. Palace of Mechanic Arts, exterior, designed by
Peabody and Stearns, World's Columbian Exposition
in Chicago, 1893. 196

4.6. Palace of Mechanic Arts, exterior loggia, designed
Peabody and Stearns, World's Columbian Exposition
in Chicago, 1893. 196

4.7. "Rio de Janeiro City: Commercial District," map, ca. 1910. 206

4.8. Central Avenue, photograph by Marc Ferrez, ca. 1909. 207

4.9. "How it was, how it is, how it will be," cartoon
by Crispim do Amaral, *A Avenida*, August 19, 1903. 208

4.10. "The Avenue," drawing, *Gazeta de Notícias*,
August 3, 1904. 208

4.11. Central Avenue, photograph by Marc Ferrez, ca. 1910. 210

5.1. "Leaving the Opera in the Year 2000," print,
Albert Robida, ca. 1902. 223

5.2. "An International World Centre, general perspective,
bird's-eye view," Ernest Hébrard and Hendrik Christian
Andersen, heliogravure reproduced in *Creation
of a World Centre of Communication*, 1913. 224

5.3. "Ward and Centre," Ebenezer Howard, *Garden
Cities of To-morrow*, 1902. 229

5.4. Radburn Garden Homes brochure, City Housing
Corporation, late 1920s. 231

5.5. *La Città Nuova* series, ink over pencil drawing,
Antonio Sant'Elia, ca. 1914. 236

5.6. "Buenos Aires in the year 2010," drawing by
Arturo Eusevi, *PBT*, May 25, 1910. 240

5.7. *King's Dream of New York*, drawn by Harry M. Pettit,
ca. 1908. 242

5.8. Cover, *Electrical Experimenter*, July 1920. 244

5.9. "Contemporary city of three million inhabitants," neither signed nor dated, gelatin print on Canson paper, ca. 1922.   250

5.10. Plan Voisin, detail, model of new city with architect's hand, Le Corbusier, ca. 1925–1930.   251

5.11. Still shot from *Metropolis*, directed by Fritz Lang, 1927.   254

5.12. "Study for Maximum Mass Permitted by the 1916 New York Zoning Law," drawing, Hugh Ferriss, first published in the *New York Times* in 1922.   257

5.13. Philadelphia Housing Association pamphlet, 1920s.   259

5.14. "City of the Future," or "The Flying City," Vkhutemas Diploma portfolio, Georgii Krutikov, 1928.   261

5.15. Cover, *Everyday Science and Mechanics*, December 1931.   263

5.16. Shell Motor Oil advertisement campaign, ca. 1937.   265

5.17. "The City of the Future: Hundred Story City in Neo-American Style," drawing and design by Francisco Mujica, reprinted in *History of the Skyscraper*, pl. 134, 1929.   269

5.18. "Plan for the City of Buenos Aires [. . .] following the general layout proposed by Carlos M. Noel," 1924–1925.   273

5.19. Sketch of a plan for Rio de Janeiro, charcoal, pastel on Canson paper, Le Corbusier, 1929.   276

5.20. Radiant City, Zoning, gelatin print on Canson paper, Le Corbusier, undated, ca. 1930–1933.   277

5.21. Master Plan for Buenos Aires, undated photograph, Ferrari Hardoy Archive, Harvard Graduate School of Design.   279

5.22. Model for "World Capital Germania," ca. 1939.   287

6.1. Magazine advertisement, Revere Copper and Brass, Inc., 1943.   293

6.2. Pilot Plan of Brasília, by Lúcio Costa, 1957.   297

6.3. Car traffic in front of the Brazilian National
Congress, designed by Oscar Niemeyer, stock
photograph, 2021.   297

6.4. Magazine advertisement, The Bohn Aluminum
and Brass Corporation, 1946.   302

6.5. Magazine advertisement, Firestone, 1945.   304

6.6. Magazine advertisement, America's Independent
Electric Light and Power Companies, 1958.   305

6.7. Cover, *Mechanix Illustrated*, June 1957.   306

6.8. Plan for Surinameplein, Amsterdam, designed by
David Jokinen, photomontage, 1967.   310

6.9. Makoko in Lagos at midday, stock photograph, 2023.   324

6.10. The National Theater in Lagos, stock photograph, 2024.   325

PREFACE

IN THE 2010S, a question popped up here and there: *where did the future go?* A prominent anarchist anthropologist and a libertarian tech billionaire held a debate with that title.[1] They agreed on a surprising amount. Both lamented that people of their generation, born in the 1960s, had to contend with lowered expectations: flying cars and teleportation devices did not materialize. To them, politicians and bureaucracies stall radical change, which decentralization could unleash. In modernity, cities concentrated innovations and reshaped how humans imagine the future. At the event in Manhattan, the cities of tomorrow came up, but only on Mars. No one acknowledged how decentralization could make it harder to build and maintain infrastructures for the billions of people currently living in urban areas. The debate did, however, point to a perception that our futures are exhausted. At the time, my own work asked related questions, dwelling on disillusionments with urbanization as well as climate change anxieties. The volume of discourse on unfulfilled aspirations and catastrophic scenarios steadily increased in the years since.

The future has gone to seed, it appears. It is also all over the place. While writing this book, I tried to notice references to the future. They were ubiquitous. At the bus stop, a banner for the Kendall Square innovation district declares: *the future is bright.* This is a genre: *the future is female, the future is crypto, the future is now.* A young man strolling around Boston Common wears a t-shirt that snarks: *future corpse.* During an NBA game on television, the broadcaster announces: *free throws for futures.* It was similar wherever travels took me. An advertisement for electric cars at the El Dorado airport in Bogotá promises: *the future arrived.*[2] Every trip to the bookstore reveals new releases with future in the title. The future is scary, it is seductive, and apparently it still sells. My email inbox can resemble a fortune-teller's placard. Events tout insights into the future of energy, healthcare, the gig economy, sustainable meat, literary criticism, higher education, climate activism, artificial intelligence, the international order, etc. And of course, cities. Maybe we can agree with a "precog" who transmits visions of what is to come in the science fiction *The Minority Report*: "I'm tired of the future."[3]

In 2011, I attended a conference on urban studies in the town of Prato, Italy. The country was mired in a debt crisis and political dysfunction. My presentation was called "The Future Revisited: Cities of Tomorrow in Retrospect." It focused on failures of twentieth-century urban planning, and argued against the narrowing ambitions of cities, given the large-scale approaches needed to tackle social and environmental challenges. I also walked around Prato. In a postindustrial neighborhood, a graffitied slogan on a wall seemed to speak directly to the ruling classes that my talk criticized: "You stole our future, we take back the city."[4] The boldness echoed the language of advertisements down the block. The veiled threat conjured revolutionary histories. Later that year, I thought about the Italian motto as I joined Occupy Wall Street protests. At the time, it was easy for me to choose sides, but I still wondered: *what's the plan?*

That basic question animated much of my research for this book, leading me to the 1700s and back to the present with revised intuitions. For one, prospects are seldom fixed or given. We should be cautious about maximalist claims, and open to the ability of urbanites to continuously reinvent themselves and the built environment. Though some moments seem especially full of uncertainties, startling shifts recur in modern history. Meanwhile, there is a lot that we can know about what works well in cities. On the one hand, good urban design often requires not being too possessive about the future. And on the other, bottom-up approaches are not necessarily less authoritarian than top-down. Planning can play a vital role in renewing possibilities for our urban planet—for better or worse.

Cities are places where things happen, but they also make things happen. In retrospect, this book became part of my life long before there was ever a plan to write it. I grew up in Brazil. In the 1980s, the country felt stuck, outside the story of progress, locked into an eternal present.

My family moved from Rio de Janeiro to Brasília, which had been envisioned as a modern utopia. There was talk about the future but couched in mystical or religious terms. One afternoon, my mother stocked up on water and candles. She had heard the world was going to end, but Brasília would be spared. We had to prepare to receive relatives from Rio. Just in case. Prophecies seemed closer-to-home than the modernist city, which I only learned about much later as a scholar. Brasília was a place where car crashes killed dear friends. It was at the edge of a world centered in Rio. We returned every summer. For a kid prone to introspection, Rio could be liberating. Bumming around downtown, scouring used bookstores, record shops, or pick-up soccer games, life always seemed to be happening: a man falling to the ground with a heart attack; an exchange of glances in a bus ride; intimate conversations with strangers. The urban world was intricate and full of possibilities. It hooked me.

When I was ten, Rio hosted the United Nations Earth Summit, which we knew as Eco '92. It felt like Brazil mattered on the global stage, even more than during World Cups. My stomach curled with news of deforestation in the Amazon. I was losing faith in religion but still prayed at night for the birds and plants. Sometimes I looked at the open skies, searching for holes in the ozone layer. (Banning CFC emissions is a success story of transnational cooperation and environmental progress, but in the thirty years after Eco '92, humans added as much carbon as in the previous 30,000 years.) As the world got bigger and more intense, daydreaming about migration became an outlet. I have now lived most of my life in the United States. Perhaps the migrant condition (or disposition) is necessarily future-oriented? My scholarship, at any rate, has focused on history, with an eye toward how the past converges with the present. Those early preoccupations with cities and the environment, meanwhile, carried over to my profession.

As a professor, I have taught or co-taught several courses connected with different facets of this book, and served in capacities that exposed me to myriad fields of knowledge. *The Invention of the Future* results from years of accumulated readings, collaborations, and experiences. Some characteristics of urban life might come across in this book's style: diverse, peripatetic, hopefully exciting. Like our cities, it was shaped by serendipity as much as preconceived plans. It also demanded methodical and steadfast work. As I wrote, on many nights I put my daughter Lola to bed. Ruminating on love and turmoil, being tired of the future was always an impossibility. We know some of what is coming: urbanization and climate change, life and death. Between all that, there is a lot of space for reinvention. And if we must reinvent, there might be no better place to look than the history of the future.

THE INVENTION OF THE FUTURE

Introduction

I. No City, No Future?

On September 11, 2001, Bob Dylan released a highly anticipated album. In the song "Bye and Bye," we hear a wistful voice: "Well the future for me is already a thing of the past." That morning, New Yorkers had good reasons to expect just another Tuesday. It was a time of relative peace and stability. As two airplanes crashed into the World Trade Center, the future changed in ways no one could have predicted. Terrorists killed nearly 3,000 people. The US response caused hundreds of thousands of casualties. Dylan's song was not about geopolitics and offered no guidance or consolation. Taken together with the events of that day, it can remind us of a recurring tendency in modern life: our ability to foresee cannot keep up with developments.

In Manhattan's history, as in other booming cities, the future was more often something to be built than a thing of the past. On 9/11, technologies that drove urban transformations collided: the steel beams supporting the towers, the glass enveloping the façades, and the explosive fossil fuels powering flight. Between the activities of office workers and the beliefs of suicidal pilots, we have long-standing forces that shaped the course of urbanization: trade, religion, war. Dylan's verse could be interpreted as either foolish or premonitory. It actually meant to express commitment: the singer's first love would be the last. He was reacting to a world where changes might be taken for granted, when relationships come and go, like airplanes or buildings, dreams or money.

The Invention of the Future tells a story about how ever-changing modern cities defied predictions and remade the destinies of humanity. It opens with another catastrophe that captured mass media, the 1755 Lisbon earthquake, and the reconstruction that followed. Around then, the expectation that the future would be radically different from the past began to emerge as a defining trait in modern life. Cities became expressions of self-determination and collective aspirations. They promised material improvements in this world rather than redemption in an afterlife. This book recasts urbanization within almost three centuries of competing visions. It traces the shifting perspectives of planners and city dwellers across the Atlantic. Whether they vied for liberating potentials or entrenching hierarchies, salvation or survival, countless people experienced and imagined cities as places of possibilities. Forward-looking habits of mind, institutions, and technological innovations changed how they dressed, worshipped, labored, loved, built, organized, moved around, cared for their health, had fun, made money, created art, and told stories. How did ideas about the future matter in their worlds—and to ours?

Throughout history, human beings mostly assumed that divine forces determined the future. During the eighteenth century, lettered Europeans and Americans began to wonder how they could transform human society and the environment. Urban planning was premised on an understanding of progress as achievable and desirable. Few, however, agreed about what that meant. Dreams for cities of tomorrow contemplated sewage systems, flying vehicles, and anything in between, from egalitarian utopias to exclusive enclaves. Projects multiplied, from zoning ordinances and poetry to transit infrastructures and science fictions. More recently, climate change created another condition: calamity seems inevitable. With curtailed powers, urban planning has become more engaged in adaptation and mitigation than making new worlds. Myriad narratives present the future as something to be prevented rather than built. Meanwhile, we continue to learn about how improved living standards and sustainability can coexist in compact urbanization. When we account for the simultaneous forces colliding and converging over the past several decades, it is hard to discern any single arc. One global pattern, however, continues unabated: more and more people moving to cities.

As we look back, this book will move between detailed focus and panoramic scales, revealing connections across continents, sites, and lives. Each chapter homes in on particular cities where modern cultures flourished, during major turning points in urban planning: the rebuilding of Lisbon as a secular imperial capital after the 1755 natural disaster; the gridded Commissioners' Plan of 1811 for Manhattan, catalyzing a radically open-ended relationship to development; the comprehensive reconstruction of Paris from 1853 to 1870, which became a global model; reforms to modernize Rio de Janeiro between 1903 and 1906, in the wake of the abolition of slavery; dueling proposals from the 1920s and 1930s for Buenos Aires by local planners and modernist icon Le Corbusier, with different approaches to emergent transportation modes and growing metropolitan scales; the unprecedented expansion of Lagos since the 1950s. Other major cities reappear throughout or provide counterpoints, including London, Barcelona, Chicago, Algiers, Berlin, Mexico City, and Brasília. As we get closer to our century, urban futures move from the Atlantic world to the Pacific. A book on more contemporary urbanization would have to focus on a very different set of cities, largely in Asia. The epilogue reflects on today's viable futures, on the limits of learning from the past, and on how we can draw wrong lessons or inspiration from history.

––––––

Hunter-gatherers and medieval Parisians did not walk around imagining that their surroundings would look unrecognizable to the next generation. Our more recent trajectory as a species, building and destroying at a breathtaking pace, defies credulity. Yet futures, of course, existed before. Some psychologists call us *homo prospectus*, primed for "nexting."[1] Even in societies with cyclical cosmologies, there is still a sense of time behind and ahead. Humans lived nomadically for most of our time on earth. Doing so required anticipating seasonal patterns. Agriculture would demand significant planning, including systems for irrigation, storage, and recordkeeping. As urban societies developed, it became common to project forward through planning or building with intergenerational horizons. Long before modernity, people designed settlements in anticipation of growth or potential disasters. They planned wide streets to prevent fires from spreading, managed woodlands to ensure water supply, or devised antiseismic structures. Stone temples and marble forums presupposed a relationship to a future beyond a single lifetime, if not eternity. In both ancient and early modern Rome, for example, the monetary value of fines for vandalism or infractions would sometimes be carved into walls or marble plaques, with no apparent consideration of inflation or changing conventions. The future, we could say, was set in stone.

In modernity, clocks, calendars, and other forms of timekeeping became standardized and prevalent, organizing temporality. Expectations of change became a constant, and people increasingly imagined radical departures from known circumstances. Inventions and reinventions took place in growing cities. From the 1750s to the 1950s, they largely concentrated in the Atlantic world. As transformations accelerated, a sentiment voiced in Vienna amid the revolutions of 1848 becomes widespread: "what was scarcely conceivable yesterday is reality today and history tomorrow!"[2] Originally, this evoked political volatility. In retrospect, it could apply to infrastructural progress and expanded rights, but also to violence and imperialism. Attributing the origins of "the invention of the future" to cities of the North Atlantic is not meant to be a compliment. Nor is it necessarily an indictment. A crucial aim here is to trace how certain ideas and practices that emerged in Europe became rendered as universal, often through imposition. At the same time, working with or against power differentials, throughout the Atlantic people mobilized future-oriented planning with a variety of goals in sight: democracy, dictatorship, colonization, reform, revolution, and so on.

In this book, besides serving as a chronological marker, *modern* suggests a sensibility toward the present and the future that assumes a break with the past. Needless to say, not everyone embraced such mindsets. As the chapters advance, the boundaries of who had a desire and an ability to shape the future (or a city) will widen in many cases, and contract in some. Who could even afford to be modern? Who and what would be left behind? How about those that wanted to be left behind? Modernity was never absolute. It was characterized by an ongoing interplay between continuity and rupture, fixity and flux, limits and possibilities. As we address the changing contours of these relationships, variants like *modernism* or *modernization* will gain more precise meanings based on their uses at a given moment and place.

Planning is also to be understood somewhat loosely, and contextually. It will comprise attempts to organize urbanization that predated the consolidation of the planner as a professional. References to *design* encompass a more deliberate and specific concern with the formal or architectural dimensions of planning. And *urbanization* suggests the city, but also how flows of resources, peoples and ideas extended beyond its boundaries. Urban development upended lives and ecosystems in the countryside and hinterlands. Our focus lies on cities but recognizes how their growth intertwined the destinies of landscapes and peoples, often across faraway shores.

During the period covered here, the relative role of transatlantic connections to the global history of urbanization went through a rise and fall. The choices of case studies reflect large-scale demographic patterns. The Atlantic world's share of the twenty largest cities on the planet began to increase dramatically in the eighteenth century, and then dropped even more sharply after the 1940s, as urbanization accelerated across the Pacific region (see figure 0.1).[3] A graph of the most populous cities by continent, over a longer span of time, adds some nuances (see figure 0.2). Asian dominance among major cities waned as the European share peaked around the 1850s, followed by the Americas a century later (first North, then South). By the latter decades of the 1900s, the urban boom was mostly in Asia, and then increasingly in Africa in the 2000s. In the twenty-first century, the locations of the world's largest cities once again reflect the distribution of global populations, after a century and a half of exceptional urbanization in the North Atlantic (see figure 0.3).[4] This does not, however, represent a return to some kind of historical norm, as cities in China, for example, increasingly become leading high-tech hubs. And urban growth in the so-called Global South

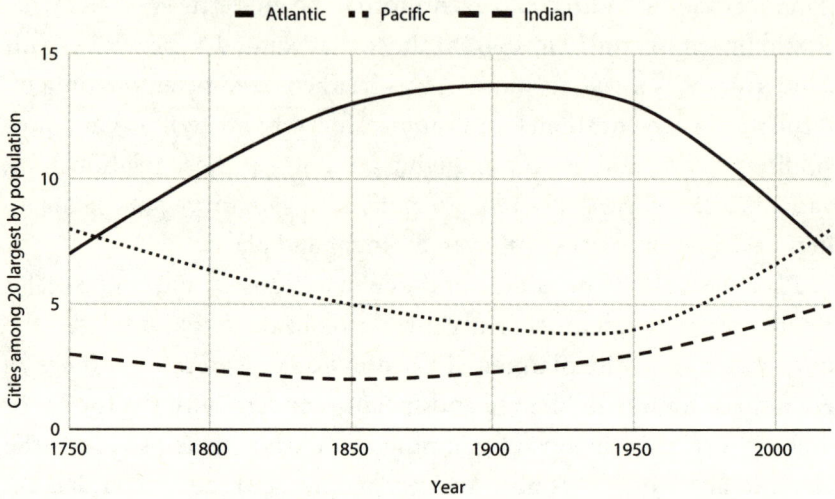

FIGURE 0.1. Estimated number of cities among the 20 largest by population, located near the Atlantic, Pacific, or Indian Ocean, between 1750 and 2020.

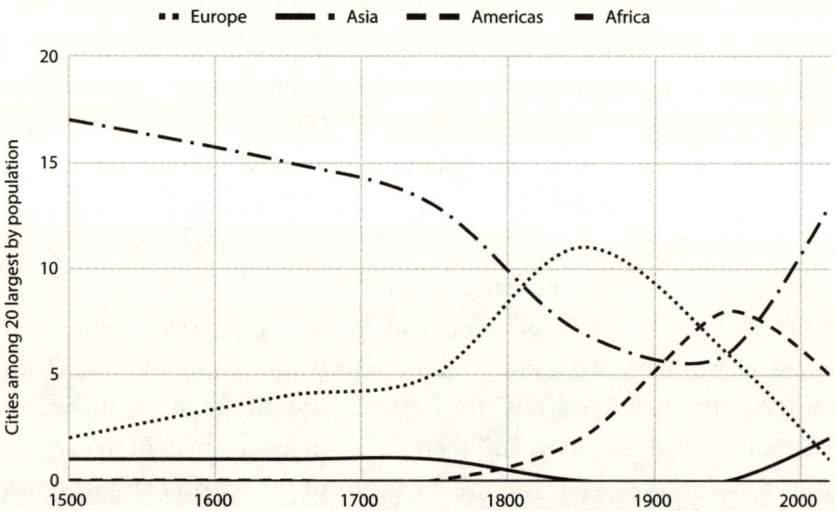

FIGURE 0.2. Estimated number of cities among the 20 largest by population, located in Europe, Asia, the Americas, or Africa, between 1500 and 2020.

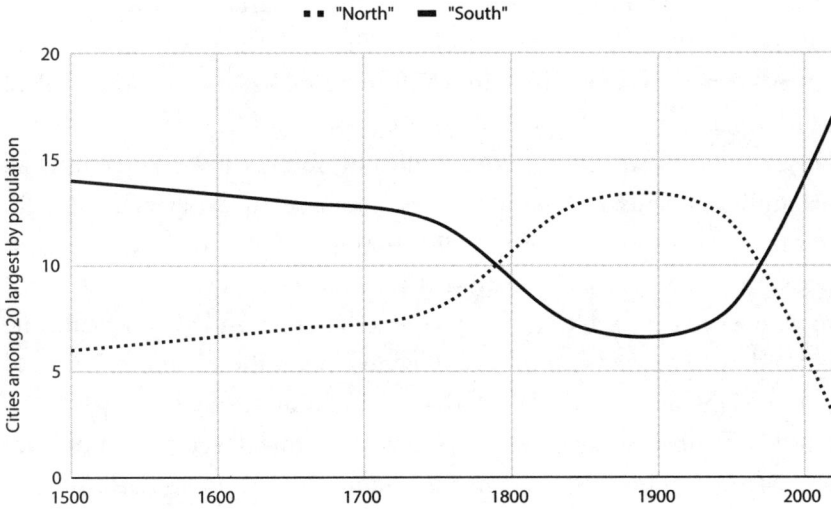

FIGURE 0.3. Estimated number of cities among the 20 largest by population, located in the "Global North" or "Global South," between 1500 and 2020.

has had greater orders of magnitude: the number of people moving to a metropolis like Lagos every month is comparable to the entire population of Manhattan in 1800.

Survey histories of modern architecture and planning used to have a basic diffusionist plot: "first the West, then the rest."[5] More recent scholars unsettle Eurocentric and North Atlantic perspectives. Studies map the circulations of capital and ideas across national boundaries, demonstrating how the marginalized did not merely imitate models and resisted exploitation. They compel us to follow threads connecting cotton plantations in the Americas to textile manufacturing in Europe, and to consider how legacies of the transatlantic slave trade endure. This book builds on transnational scholarly efforts. Yet, while national and regional dynamics loom large, the urban scale remains the key category of analysis here. A comparative framing foregrounding cities rather than fault lines like the West or the South can help us draw out similarities between urban dwellers and lettered elites across the Atlantic. An engineer in Rio de Janeiro could have a lot in common with another in Paris. Factory workers in both cities might also share hardships and yearnings.

Zooming in will allow us to see revealing differences. Stepping back can evince broad historical patterns. Within the span of a generation, for instance, the razing of Seneca Village to make way for Central Park in Manhattan (1850s), the violent suppression of the Paris Commune (1870s), and a war against a messianic community in Brazil (1890s) all exemplify states asserting themselves against urban experiments in self-governance. National governments progressively narrowed the range of possible urban futures. Around the same decades, the movement toward a secular faith that futures could be open-ended and malleable peaked, with a rapid succession of techno-scientific advances. It is only in hindsight, after World War I, that we can draw an arc leading to fore-closed imaginations. No two stories of economic development or tran-sit history are the same. But in the twentieth century, as nation-states further strengthened and cities morphed into unwieldy metropolitan areas, planners became hamstrung by the dominance of cars and sub-urbanization (whether through high-income single-family houses or poverty-stricken self-built dwellings).

It takes time and appropriate conditions for ideas to coalesce into plans, and for plans to get built. From the mid-nineteenth century on-ward, for example, Charles Darwin and Karl Marx greatly impacted debates. Both devised future-oriented interpretations of change, aban-doning premises that we are inexorably tied to the past. We can imagine how witnessing fast-paced urbanization might have softened any belief in nature and social classes as fixed like the firmament. Marx directly accounted for industrial cities as engines of wealth accumulation for the rising bourgeoisie and immiseration for wage-earners. It took until the twentieth century, however, for Darwinism and Marxism to wield major influence in planning. They inspired theories of evolution and revolu-tion. The social Darwinist concept of *survival of the fittest* fueled justifica-tions for urban inequality and segregation. Marx's work left an imprint in left-leaning politics and projects after the Russian Revolution, re-maining central for some disciplines concerned with urbanization, like critical geography and social theory.

The role of capitalism in urban developments should not be minimized, but here readers will not find an unbridled defense or condemnation. The historian Jonathan Levy describes capital as "a process of valuation, in which assets are expected to yield future pecuniary profits."[6] Capitalism in this definition is structured around prospects, rather than just past accumulation through savings or physical things. Credit and finance often set in motion extractivism and the production of housing, labor markets, infrastructure, etc. But the kinds of pressures that capitalist economies exert on urbanization have varied over time and between places. An investor, for example, might profit from building a new house, or from owning an existing house that appreciates when a city constrains new building.

This book sustains that no totalizing theory of change could resist contact with empirical realities. Today, computational modeling helps us forecast and track trends in climate, traffic, markets, energy, infectious diseases, and more. Planning can stand to benefit from available tools. But urbanization is more than the sum of its parts and cannot be reduced to any single set of variables. Understanding cities requires attention to statistics as well as stories, data as well as deities. Throughout modernity, diviners and futurists overestimated the predictive uses of precedents, and downplayed the political power of predictions. More recently, scholars have researched how expectations can propel capitalist dynamics, shape political participation, influence policy decisions, engender modern forms of subjecthood, and create self-fulfilling prophecies.[7] Fictional futures, one critic argues, widen the range of behaviors "by new wishes, demands, and goals."[8] In urban design, bold proposals can stretch the limits of the thinkable, becoming influential even if unrealized.

When Aymara peoples in the Andes allude to the future, they have a custom of gesturing with the hands toward the back, to evoke what cannot be known.[9] The future is not ours to see. Unlike most other cultures, they then motion forward while referring to the past. What already happened is not behind us. It is what can be seen and shown. That might capture the work of history: we can only predict the past. But life is messier. The experience of time is not always so neatly linear. Aspirations can be bound up with recollections, and the past sometimes can be a thing in the future. There was Bob Dylan's lover on 9/11, validating promises of steady devotion with appeals to what had been. And oblivious to his jazzy travails, men with holy certainties hijack advanced tech to renew ancient wars, sending worldly futures up in flames. Articulations of possibilities can shape how we understand records of the past, as well as material developments in the present. The philosopher Walter Benjamin imagined an "angel of history," thrust forward by the storm of progress toward the future, looking back on the wreckage behind.[10]

II. Making Plans

How did people in the past make sense of their futures in a changing world? What are the connections between the imagined cities of tomorrow and how cities actually developed? Who and what belongs in any given vision? Who gets to decide? How is it supposed to materialize? What does it look like? Versions of these fundamental questions will resurface when we get to urban plans. It behooves us to keep in mind that sometimes the big stories are in minor details. Originally aired in 1962–1963, *The Jetsons* formed an indelible mental image of futurism for people across generations and in much of the world. As the cartoon characters zipped through familiar dramas in outer space, dreams of flying cars were already a thing of the past. We will return to *The Jetsons* and this historical moment, but for now, the opening scene can help us see what contemporaries overlooked, and we inherit. The show's first sequence frames planet earth, still there. We then see George Jetson dropping off his kids at school and his wife Jane at the shopping mall before arriving for work at Spacely Space Sprockets, Inc.

Where does George park his flying car? It is easy to miss. He hits a button, and the car becomes a suitcase. Sure, this is a joke about gadgets, an afterthought in a feel-good sitcom. Finding parking in outer space should not be hard. Maybe the point was to spare viewers of any reminders of this real-life stressor. *The Jetsons* re-created in Orbit City the car-centric and sprawling land use patterns taking over the United States at the time. It portrays how cars could streamline mobility. But like many of the visionary car-oriented urban plans that promised speed, it neglected storage. Back on earth, private vehicles spend most of their time parked, and they would require a lot of space.

Life in outer space was probably a more reasonable prediction than what ended up happening: vast swathes of cities razed for highways and surface lots. Eventually, there would be more square footage "dedicated to parking each car than to housing each person" in the United States.[11] The Space Age might have stalled, but *The Jetsons* proved prescient in oblique ways. Only a hefty dosage of magical thinking (or denial) could make parking seem so smooth. Orbit City had no streets. In the actual future materializing as the show aired, nonflying cars turned streets from places where kids played into thoroughfares or parking. A strange metaphor is attributed to then–Senate Majority Leader Lyndon B. Johnson, foretelling Cold War threats: "Soon, the Russians will be dropping bombs on us from space like kids dropping rocks onto cars from freeway overpasses."[12] No bombs dropped, but you would not know that from before and after images of US downtowns. Meanwhile, car drivers became the leading cause of death among children.

What happens is often not part of the plan, for good or for bad. When cars arrived in cities, drivers started parking wherever they could, because it was usually free and convenient. This started as an innocuous story. Once more cars hit the streets, that intractable expectation was harder to match, and snowballed. By the time Jane Jetson went to the shopping mall, the whole sprawling arrangement benefited from tax codes, racial politics, and much more, with cars on their way to becoming one of the biggest stories in the production of urban futures, emissions, and environmental degradation. Today, plans to replace surface parking with housing or with dedicated lanes for buses and bikes suffer the wrath of grassroots revolts, especially in the United States. An overarching moral here is that if for every problem there is a solution, for every solution there is a problem. Exciting innovations like cars or well-meaning correctives like community participation in planning often result in unintended consequences. Sometimes yesterday's solutions are today's problems.

We should not conclude, however, that it is better to forego attempts to improve urban conditions. The best plans proved adaptable to changing technologies and demands, whether intentionally or not. In fact, sometimes yesterday's problems are today's solutions. Dense neighborhoods in nineteenth-century industrial cities exposed people to overcrowding, disease, and pollution. They can now house them in energy-efficient, transit-rich, and healthier environments. Changes can surpass expectations in desirable directions too. The earliest starry-eyed seers imagining fantastic inventions like time machines or spacecrafts would be stunned by news of modern antibiotics and women's rights. *The Jetsons* did not foresee changing norms in gender relations: George went to the office, while Jane spent his money at the mall. Urban history does not provide a consistent verdict about who gets the future right. The stakes are not the same, but from fictional creations to technical reports, any number of approaches can be prescient, lost in the clouds, or even a bit of both.

Reasonable expectations underestimate the range of potential outcomes. Though that usually only becomes apparent in retrospect, drawing on this insight can make us more alert. Understanding how urban transformations have eluded predictions helps to loosen up perceptions of any given prospect as inexorable. Histories of cities might even reinvigorate our capacity to envision and pursue large-scale transformations, rather than succumbing to doom or techno-boosterism. In the least, they serve as humbling reminders for us to accept the limits of what can be known and controlled about the future. The framing of a *climate crisis*, for example, can imply that our current environmental predicaments are only temporary, or a stage in a sequence of events with a resolution in sight. Things worsen or improve, there are endings and beginnings, but history cautions against fantasies of finality, closure, salvation, or permanent solutions.

Since at least the 1750s, inventions of futures in urban planning evolved out of a turn away from religion. Practical concerns overrode divine orders. Many secular planners and designers, however, maintained linear or teleological premises familiar to Judeo-Christian-Islamic traditions. Le Corbusier, for example, envisioned transformations with an end point. His plans would fix problems once and for all, saving the city for posterity. Godless manifestations of faith-based structures of feeling and dogmatic thought can be found in pursuits of silver bullets, economic miracles, or master plans. The anthropologist Fernando Coronil, focusing on Venezuela, wrote about "the magical state" creating "the illusion that instantaneous modernization lay at hand, that torrents of oil money would change the flow of history and launch the country into the future."[13] There is also "magical capitalism," showcasing assets while concealing social or ecological costs, asking us to suspend disbelief like a magical realism novel.[14] And we can think of the designer Norman Bel Geddes, who published a paean to modern car infrastructures called *Magic Motorways* (1940).

———

It may not always look that way in a well-preserved neighborhood with historic architecture, but like all else in the cosmos, cities are in constant flux. At the same time, the experience of change within modernity was always embedded in specific circumstances. As a part of larger processes, urban design evolved within a push-and-pull between agency and contingencies, possibilities and limits. Planning treated cities as key sites for imagining nations and state building. If the nation-state becomes the channel through which imagined futures flow, capital cities in particular could serve as a map for what is achievable through modernization. Often, major urban plans and projects sought to circumscribe or prescribe boundaries of belonging based on status, along lines of class, gender, age, race, ethnicity, citizenship, religion, language, and so on. As we will see, the locations of grandiose opera houses or highways cutting through neighborhoods reflected assumptions about which lives mattered most. Monuments showed off who held power. Neoclassical aesthetics and rectilinear layouts showcased supposedly universal standards of beauty, progress, and civilization.

And yet, the history of urban planning is full of stories about the unplanned, and people making their own plans. Urban-based groups and individuals appealed to ideas of universal values to expand rights. They worked to abolish slavery, extend the voting franchise to women, or enact welfare policies serving the poor. Sometimes, the forms associated with certain values morph: over centuries, an obsession with straight-lined grids as harbingers of order and modernity gave way to sinuous layouts. Other times, design showed and tried to tell, but could not control the message. Skyscrapers functioned as symbols of prosperity or dystopia. The transparency of glass implied openness or surveillance. Dispossessed urbanites appropriated newly built modern boulevards meant for the wealthy. Amid everyday struggles and striving, often taking chances against the odds, myriad people did not accept assigned roles and sought to refashion themselves. To the Brazilian author Clarice Lispector, that defined her condition as a human being: "necessity makes me create a future."[15]

The future could be a project, a destination, a foreign place, even a burden. A range of unenthusiastic reactions to urban modernity unfolded: quiet resignation, capitulation, insurgence, refusal, lament. As transformations rendered familiar cities unrecognizable, nostalgia began to refer less to a place and more to bygone times. The French photographer and journalist Félix Nadar wrote in 1867: "It is no longer Paris, my Paris that I know, where I was born [. . .] I no longer know how to find myself in that which surrounds me."[16] That futuristic modern Paris has become traditional. Meanings and uses of spaces continuously evolve, often in unintended and surprising ways. Planners are not always captive to top-down elitist perspectives, and progressive voices sometimes miss the trees for the forest. Still in 1867 Paris, Émile Zola claimed that "the future belongs to gardeners." He meant that negatively. The writer railed against what he saw as mere "scraps of meadow" and artificial "microscopic parks" recalling modern shop windows, sullied by the loud and crowded city.[17] Landscape architects designing these spaces had aimed to enable "the crowds" to enjoy "the murmur of the birds" and to give their strolls "a magical air."[18] Today, few issues generate more of a consensus than the desirability of tree-lined streets, pocket parks, and green spaces in the urban fabric.

Histories of planning and architecture almost necessarily dwell on designs that never came to fruition, frustrated intentions, and unforeseen outcomes. More broadly, engagements with modern urbanization tend to have some orientation toward the future, even if latent. This book therefore relies on vast amounts of materials. It is indebted to scholarship across fields and languages. If one set of debates asks whether ideological or material forces drive history, we can think of design as where they meet and become inextricably linked. Therefore, though this is not a survey, many canonical references in planning, architecture, and urban studies will be found here.

To parse through shifting experiences from a variety of vantage points, analyses turn to an array of archival sources and media. Plans, diaries, testimonies, memoirs, letters, speeches, reports, laws, newspapers, postcards, magazines, advertisements, drawings, film, music, and literature can all reveal resonances and tensions between planning elites and people on the ground, or between technologies, economics, and cultural narratives. There are fictions in archives, and archives in fiction. Literary texts, for example, will help us grasp transitions in what could be imaginable at a given moment, and its bearings on social life. In each chapter, the choices of highlighted voices to a significant extent reflect the availability of sources. As we get closer to the present, they diversify.

Cities are as diverse as the futures they can nurture. And the futures they can nurture are as diverse as the people that live in them. Heavy-handed ideas about what counts as universal have frequently been used to legitimize inherited hierarchies, subjugation, and exclusion. At the same time, through much of the twentieth century and in our own, urbanization has coincided with a fragmentation of plans and dreams. Utopias lost appeal. To be in an urban world has always meant living among strangers. In the twenty-first century, digital technologies have facilitated connectivity, and the role of space-based common denominators dwindled. It became untenable (and unfashionable) to still believe in universal futures. Yet, we are haunted by planetary ones.

III. Under a Warmer Sky

To understand relationships between ice ages and atmospheric carbon dioxide, the Swedish scientist Svante Arrhenius created a climate model in the 1890s. He estimated that doubling the concentration of CO_2 might lead to increases of up to seven degrees Fahrenheit. Although the calculations were rudimentary by later standards, the results were not far off. Arrhenius thought that people in the future would welcome living "under a warmer sky."[19] He predicted, however, that it was going to take another three thousand years for humans to generate enough emissions. Arrhenius lived amid an urban boom that began in Europe, spread to the Americas, and became global. The growth of cities unfolded along with rising fossil fuel emissions, as well as the transformation of vast territories to sustain industrial and agricultural production. Arrhenius underestimated how rapidly we would alter the composition of the air and reshape our planet. The scientist and his peers could envision climate change. What they failed to imagine was the speed and scale of urban change.

Even in the 1890s, a warmer sky would not have been as welcome in the tropics as in Sweden. Arrhenius was aware of growing emissions in the North Atlantic, but overlooked how "the advances of industry" often relied on exploitation and violence.[20] In 1933, another European, Walter Benjamin, meditated on the experiences of contemporaries: "A generation that had gone to school on a horse-drawn streetcar now stood under the open sky in a countryside in which nothing remained unchanged but the clouds, and beneath these clouds, in a field of force of destructive torrents and explosions, was the tiny, fragile human body." Benjamin was referring to the traumas of the Great War, the ongoing Great Depression, and presciently, "the shadow of the approaching war."[21] He brought to mind landscapes crisscrossed by railroads, perforated by mining, and ravaged by modern warfare. Every generation since, across the planet, has experienced dramatic transformations. We now know that, with greenhouse gases, even the clouds and the open skies are no longer unchanged.

In the North Atlantic, the modern history of environmental futures was marked by "a single-minded expectation of endless growth on a finite planet."[22] That too has changed. Today, dire visions abound in fiction and scientific reports, and they do not spare any corner of earth. Several writers note an exhaustion in the imagination of futures in response to ecological devastation, but not exclusively. Though disputes over memory are nothing new, a focus on the past appears to have intensified in the twenty-first century. Online platforms provide constant fodder for well-grounded and fantasy-fueled takes on history. In the

best option is to drive, and they can afford it, they likely will. Some green activists miss the forest for the trees, or microplastics from EV tires for plastic bags from grocers.[27] Unwittingly, opposition to urban developments can exacerbate housing scarcity and stimulate oil use and pollution. There are, however, emerging efforts to enable more abundant multifamily homes and multimodal mobility. Environmental and urban politics do not need to be at odds.

Looking forward, large-scale changes might seem too daunting. Unimaginable transformations, however, have happened throughout the history of cities. The future was always at a crossroads. Urbanization helped cause climate change. Now, responding to climate change requires urban change. Growing cities can help. Carbon emissions and biodiversity losses are material realities no matter how humans think or talk about them. But narratives matter. Critics stress how terms like Anthropocene obscure the immensely greater contributions to climate change from higher-income countries, and how those at the peripheries of modernization suffer disproportionately from impacts. We can be even more precise and productive by foregrounding metropolitan scales. As climate conversations heat up, leading voices in academia, activism, business, tech, politics, and the arts have paid surprisingly short shrift to how our planet's future largely depends on which pathways urbanization takes. Our counterparts in the past seldom foresaw major transformations around the corner. They could still have a more fertile sense of urban possibilities than we do. How might futures in the past enrich the stories we tell ourselves about the days to come? In the history of urbanization, we find the roots of our present predicaments, but we might also search for seedlings, flowers, and fruits.[28]

1

In Pursuit of the Future
(1750s–1790s)

LISBON + PARIS, LONDON,
ST. PETERSBURG, VILA RICA,
AND MORE.

I. Earthquake and Revolutions

When the sun rose on November 1, 1755, people throughout Europe expected to celebrate All Saints' Day. They had no reason to think the date would usher in a seismic shift in early modernity and represent a turning point in urban planning. Few cared about historical periodization or participated in debates about the future of cities. Most lived as peasants. The experience of time was marked by natural cycles and faith. Seasons, religious festivals, and living beings came and went. One day, the time would arrive for the earthly world to end. In Portugal, a deeply Catholic country, this holiday served as a reminder of Judgment Day. It was meant, after all, to commemorate a spiritual bond with saints departed from earth and triumphant in heaven. That morning one of the most powerful earthquakes to ever hit Europe devastated Lisbon. Many experienced it as a sign of the end of times.[1]

In Europe, it was easier to imagine the end of the world than the radical transformation of a major city. Apocalyptic visions had been recurrent for several centuries. Rooted in the biblical story of Sodom and Gomorrah, prophecies commonly included cities as objects of God's wrath. Other than by divine intervention, it was difficult for people to conceive of how their city might look unrecognizable to a later generation. Cities were constantly changing, sometimes even dramatically, but this tended to be gradual or piecemeal: a cathedral built over several decades; an added well, fountain, or aqueduct; a new thoroughfare cutting through dense quarters. Powerful urban institutions, like guilds and religious orders, worked to ensure continuity and stability.

The Portuguese capital, with around 200,000 inhabitants, was Europe's fourth largest city, after London, Paris, and Naples. A tsunami and fires followed the earthquake. Most of Lisbon's buildings were destroyed, and thousands died. The event became widely known for its aftershocks in European philosophy, inspiring responses by Voltaire, Rousseau, Kant, and others. The philosopher Susan Neiman would posit that "Lisbon proved we cannot understand God's purpose."[2] Why might a benevolent God provoke so much suffering? In a heartfelt poem, Voltaire suggested that only a senseless God could target the Portuguese city, while sparing other European capitals: "Lisbon is destroyed, while people dance in Paris."[3] Intense debates ensued over whether the catastrophe had been the result of divine justice or natural causes, exposing profound rifts in eighteenth-century intellectual and spiritual landscapes. The earthquake helped to crystallize an "awareness that understanding has limits."[4]

Other conceptual shifts away from religiosity were well under way in European thought. Lettered intellectuals began to cultivate an ability to project humanity into the future, conceiving of brighter possibilities for this world. Ideas about the perfectibility of nature and human progress became commonplace. These would not be dictated primarily by divine forces or tradition, but by the guiding lights of reason and knowledge. As the historian Reinhart Koselleck put it, "the future would be different from the past, and better, to boot."[5] A belief that the future could be constructed defined the secular imagination of the Enlightenment.[6] And yet, in the mid-eighteenth century, the expectation that humans had the capacity to make new futures and shape their own destinies was only beginning to take hold. That idea would help to fuel the aspirations of urbanists, urbanites, and revolutionaries.

To see this more clearly, we can fast-forward to the French Revolution. In May of 1793, in a speech during the lead-up to a radically egalitarian constitution, Robespierre claimed that "the time has come to call upon each to realize their true destinies; the progress of human reason laid the basis for this great revolution, and you shall now assume the particular duty of accelerating it." The future was worth pursuing, and it seemed within their power to make the world anew. The French revolutionary told his peers: "to fulfill your mission you must do exactly the opposite of what existed before you."[7] The ambition of breaking with the past and resetting time found a stark expression in the adoption, later that year, of a French Republican Calendar to replace the Christian one.

Cities concentrated social and cultural change. Enlightenment ideals flourished in urban settings like universities, academies, clubs, publishing houses, salons, coffeehouses, and even some churches. Forward-looking habits of mind became widespread, and not just among revolutionaries. They might be expressed in predictions of a happier humanity thousands of years ahead, in the declaration of an unalienable right to the pursuit of happiness, or in self-development and profit-seeking projects.[8] Political aspirations became more projective, less restorative. The US, French, and Haitian revolutions would embrace possibilities for greater equality, freedom, and prosperity. The independence movements of Spanish America in the 1810s and 1820s also moved in that direction. This represented a shift away from a tradition of peasant revolts motivated by a mystical past, and a "latent hatred of anything new."[9] Now, rather than the recovery of a golden age, the prospect of improvements increasingly set the agenda for heated disputes. These often revolved around emerging notions of progress and civilization.[10]

During the urbanization boom of later decades, much like revolutions, cities would become manifestations of new secular visions, enticing throngs of people seeking to rupture with tradition and to fulfill the promises of self-actualization. Reinhart Koselleck argues that in early modernity Europeans experienced the perception of "the compression of time." Radical changes produced "consciousness of difference between traditional experience and coming expectation."[11] We can think of Copernican heliocentrism, the "discoveries" and colonization,

innovations in mobility and print technologies, freer and faster economies, intensifying connections to faraway lands, and of course, growing
urbanization. Koselleck posits that at the outset of the Reformation,
Martin Luther understood the seeming compression of time as "a visible sign that, according to God's will, the Final Judgment is imminent,
that the world is about to end." To the historian, more than 250 years
later Robespierre saw the acceleration of time as "a human task, presag-
ing an epoch of freedom and happiness, the golden future."[12]

In modernity, the idea of a desirable future resulting from human
enterprise rather than salvation would have unforeseen consequences.
The French Republican Calendar intended to rationalize time with features like a ten-day week, freeing society from the oppressive weight of
religion. Not everyone appreciated the overturning of festival cycles,
and the unpopular calendar lasted barely more than a decade.[13] During
"the Terror," with Robespierre's leadership, tens of thousands met with
executions in the name of Republican virtues like justice and public
safety. Yet, conflicts and violence had plagued Europe for over two centuries, amid the various religious wars that followed the Reformation.
Tensions abounded about who got to have a place in the future, whether
it was envisioned in the afterlife or in an ideal political community.

The description of futures to be achieved through human tasks as
golden also contains unintended resonances. The image of a golden age
has been common since classical antiquity. But the use of the adjective
here allows for a transatlantic dimension that will stay with us in the
coming pages. It helps to complicate any easy diffusionist interpretation
of the invention of urban futures. By the time of Robespierre's 1793
speech, the Haitian Revolution's rebellion against slavery had obtained
important victories.[14] And we are reminded, at the same time, that a
significant amount of eighteenth-century European wealth derived
from the enslaved labor of Africans and their descendants working in
gold mines, particularly in the Brazilian captaincy of Minas Gerais.[15]
They helped to create the conditions for newly invented futures in
Europe, but enslavement foreclosed their own.

Some would look back on the 1755 earthquake as an event that ended
a period of optimism.[16] Indeed, in his poem on the Lisbon disaster,

Voltaire famously refuted the axiom that "all is well." Did peasants in Europe or enslaved Africans need this reminder? Voltaire's goal was to ridicule Gottfried Wilhelm Leibniz's "fundamental assumption that God has chosen the best of all possible worlds."[17] Leibniz had kept faith at the center of his worldviews while he pioneered calculus, among other accomplishments. The prominent polymath often remarked that "the present is pregnant with the future."[18] Although this phrase might strike us as banal today, it represented a shift in orientation. Change emerged from existing circumstances without being preordained. The future, like offspring, remained circumscribed and familiar, but could be actively nurtured. If we extend the metaphor, it implies that those with access to power, knowledge, and resources should make decisions about rearing. Even the French revolutionary leaders, despite egalitarian commitments, could not curb their impetus to control outcomes as they sought to father the future.

Most people in the planet carried on with their lives oblivious to brewing transformations in the realm of ideas and earth-shattering historical events in Lisbon or Paris. Nonetheless, forward-looking theories in social engineering, advancements in agronomy, and incipient tools in economic planning played a role in bolstering systems of slavery or coercive labor, managing resources, generating surpluses and trade across the Atlantic and beyond. These developments both originated from and created conditions for growing urbanization in Europe. And yet, in modern cities, the future would escape the control and calculations of anyone, however almighty or learned. That lesson could only be learned in practice.

———

The rebuilding of Lisbon probably constituted the most ambitious experiment in urban design of the Enlightenment, embodying the modern values of rational planning. Although philosophers of the period argued over the meanings of Lisbon's earthquake, they failed to take note of its reconstruction. There was little reason for them to suppose that a country understood as backward and obscurantist might engender new urban futures, by their own standards *enlightened*. Forms of planning that prioritized secular interests accompanied the turn away from governance by clerical institutions and belief in the divine. It took an earthquake, however, for this to be attempted in a comprehensive way, on a major city. Mid-eighteenth-century Portugal was an unlikely candidate. The country had as many as 200,000 clergymen in a population of less than 3 million.[19] Predictably, in the immediate aftermath of the 1755 disaster, Lisbon became the site of religious rather than revolutionary fervor. Priests and the population at large took to the streets with displays of faith. Their reactions framed the destruction as divine punishment for human sins. The city's reconstruction, however, created an opportunity for the state to impose authority.

Portugal in the first half of the eighteenth century was a place of significant riches, largely due to gold from Brazil.[20] Before Lisbon's rebuilding, the Portuguese monarchy was already behind one of the most monumental projects of the period. King João V had vowed to build a convent if Queen Maria Ana of Austria gave birth. What had been intended as a modest Capuchin convent became an extravagant complex, built about twenty miles from Lisbon in the village of Mafra.[21] Drawing inspiration from the Vatican, the palace was designed by a German goldsmith. It rivaled the Escorial, the Winter Palace, Versailles, and any that came before in scale and luxury. The baroque aesthetics, in the mold of these other great palaces, pointed toward the assertion of Portuguese power in a European order. It overlooked, at the same time, the actual cosmopolitan diversity of early modern Lisbon, a global city that struck visitors as reminiscent of Africa and Asia, full of foreigners and transcontinental connections: a place where a shopper might stumble upon ivory from India, raffia cloth from Madagascar, or porcelain from China.[22]

When Mafra remained relatively unscathed by the earthquake, a long poem in *ottava rima*, a form usually reserved for epic themes, attributed it to a miracle. The *Gazeta de Lisboa*, Portugal's main newspaper at the time, concurred.[23] But burgeoning print culture was beginning to mediate people's relationship to politics and the built environment in ways that escaped Church and state control. Pious locals had taken exception to Mafra's expenses. Pamphlets from the period expressed fear that "it be poorly received in God's eyes."[24] Advances in print technologies, at the same time, helped to turn the Lisbon earthquake into an event throughout the Atlantic. Widely circulating pamphlets and engravings set it apart from previous disasters. Mass-produced texts and images caused a revolution in news environments. They also helped to strengthen the relationship between architecture, urban design, and the projection of religious, national, or imperial power. By 1755, Portugal had a new king, José I. It was one of his secretaries, however, who shaped the response to the earthquake and Lisbon's rebuilding: Sebastião José de Carvalho e Melo, later known as the marquis de Pombal.[25] Pombal, who had served as ambassador in London and Vienna for almost a decade, was attuned to the importance of imagery in politics, and to where Europe seemed to be headed.

The Mafra Palace can be seen as a type of swan song to the European baroque, in sharp contrast to the *rational* futures heralded by the Enlightenment. Lisbon's reconstruction would provide an antithesis to Mafra. The two projects, at the same time, shared key elements. Symbolically, both drew on Eurocentric design conventions. Materially, they evinced the growing entanglements of the Atlantic world. The building process implicated lives from at least three continents. Cost demands from these massive projects put pressure on the backs of enslaved Africans mining gold in Brazil, and on tax-paying slaveholders. About Mafra, a French traveler had reputedly quipped that "only in Portugal would a monarch convert gold into stone."[26] Though the funding stream would not change considerably, Pombal attempted to set the Portuguese capital on an entirely different course: it would represent the pursuit of a modern future. The earthquake created an opening for him to take control.

Because of the tsunami and fires, only around one-third of Lisbon's streets and 3,000 of its 20,000 houses remained inhabitable.[27] Contemporary casualty estimates ranged from 6,000 to 90,000. The actual number was probably around 10,000 to 20,000.[28] Displaced people moved to improvised dwellings, including large-scale tents. Pombal is said to have called upon the king to "bury the dead, and feed the

living."[29] He took measures to avoid epidemics, looting, and price goug-
ing. These firm reactions bolstered Pombal's reputation as an enlightened despot.

The scenario was desolate, but work had to be done. A little over a
month after the earthquake, at Pombal's request, the seventy-eight-year-
old Manuel da Maia delivered a document with five possibilities for
Lisbon's reconstruction. Portugal's chief engineer, he was one of the
catastrophe's survivors. Maia had worked on another important architectonic project from Dom João V's reign, a massive aqueduct system
that helped to more than triple Lisbon's water supply. Its arches, reaching a height of 65 meters, survived the earthquake. Maia lived in the
Baixa. This neighborhood, located in the city's low-lying, river-facing
central area, was particularly hard-hit. His own house was burned down,
along with a collection of maps, city plans, and books, many on architecture and engineering.[30] When the tremors struck, Maia spent the day
saving important documents from the archives of the Torre do Tombo,
which he oversaw. While Mafra's project had been entrusted to a goldsmith, experienced engineers designed the new Lisbon.

Maia's outline to Pombal offered a wide range of rebuilding options.[31]
The first plan replicated Lisbon as it had been. The second sought to
reform, introducing broader streets and betterments, while maintaining
property lines. The third offered to reduce, with smaller building heights
that might offer fewer risks in the event of another earthquake. There is
already a secular turn here, imbued in the prediction of another natural
catastrophe as inevitable, regardless of Lisbon's favors before an almighty God. Maia's fourth option was to reinvent Lisbon, razing and
leveling the flood-prone Baixa to rebuild the city with better water management systems. Perhaps even more radically, the fifth proposal was to
reset, moving the city to a new location, less constrained by existing
conditions, and with more flexibility from the perspective of honoring property rights.

Maia amended the document twice in the next four months, carefully weighing pros and cons. He remained sensitive to pushback from
property holders and voiced a preference for regularity and standardization. He prized "some diversity," even if just in the façade colors. Maia

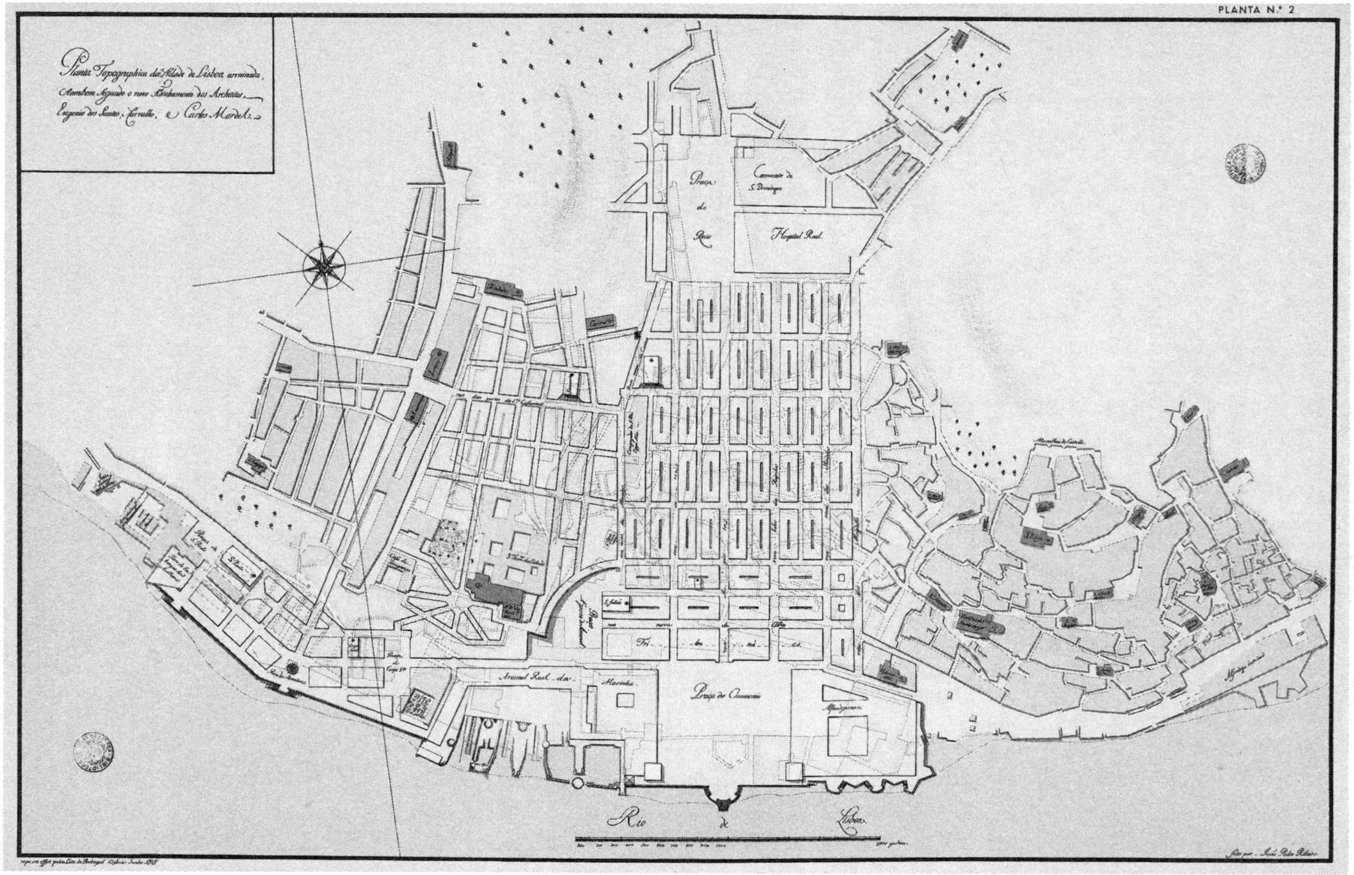

FIGURE 1.1. The Baixa grid emerges from the ruins.

strongly recommended two younger professionals, describing them as "the first" in civil architecture: Eugénio dos Santos and the Hungarian-born Carlos Mardel. Arguing that situations in need of new approaches posed greater challenges, he articulated the importance of balancing "the old and the modern."[32] Both men contributed with a series of six plans and multiple drawings. One of the plans by Santos followed Maia's fourth option, overlaying a grid pattern onto the existing territory. This became the basis for the reinvented Lisbon. Santos, in collaboration with Mardel, developed and refined the plan. In 1758, with Pombal's backing, a royal law officially adopted it.

II. Inside the Grid

Whereas old Lisbon had been characterized by tangled streets and alleyways, the new downtown would be laid out in a regular grid. Straight streets and wide avenues were meant to encourage more efficient traffic flow, prevent the spread of fire, and improve lighting and air circulation. Although theological explanations for the earthquake prevailed, Pombal's city would take no chances on miracles: buildings incorporated an innovative antiseismic framing structure called the "gaiola," or birdcage. To integrate some of the most advanced technical knowledge in waste management, the planners produced the first known representation in section view of a street with buildings, including drainage and cisterns.[33] Façades signaled a rupture from baroque ornamentation. With neoclassical self-restraint, they echoed the increasingly fashionable poetic principles of *inutilia truncat*, cutting out the useless. The plans balanced schemes to compensate prior property owners with novel ideas in housing, like block-long, multifamily buildings of individual apartments, replacing structures that had grown increasingly crowded.[34] The planners attended to issues ranging from sanitation to safety at night. Practical concerns dictated nearly every choice.

By articulating a functional system for the city as a whole, Lisbon's reconstruction anticipated a turning point in European planning theories. There was a growing desire among lettered thinkers for more total and comprehensive urban reforms, rather than for projects restricted to certain sites. Among the latter, we can think of the Colbert plan in seventeenth-century Paris, which resulted in a classicist colonnade for the Louvre. In his seminal *Essay on Architecture* (1753), the French Jesuit Marc-Antoine Laugier rejected a focus on such interventions, arguing that "embellishment" programs should extend themselves "to entire cities."[35] He envisaged a grandiose Paris of wider, straight, and unobstructed avenues. Voltaire had expressed sentiments along similar lines. In an essay from 1748 he praised Colbert's legacies but railed against the "continuous disorder" of Paris. The city had markets in narrow streets, the Louvre hidden behind Gothic buildings, and a center so crowded and "obscure" that it brought to mind "barbarism." The philosopher claimed to be voicing the opinions of "every good citizen." He tried to appeal to the pride and pocketbooks of the wealthy, asking them to support his vision of a Paris with more convenient amenities like public markets, fountains, and performance halls. The capital should be reorganized in a manner befitting its status, he argued, with regular crossroads, widened streets, and unencumbered monuments.[36]

As some of those ideas germinated in France, Portuguese planners put them into practice. Many of the technical solutions adopted in Lisbon, at the same time, dated back to the earlier half of the eighteenth century, and even to the seventeenth century. Some scholars attribute them to the planners' military training.[37] Though Maia lost his collection to the fires and could not study other plans, he cited London and Turin as precedents. Turin's planning in the seventeenth century combined vast straight avenues, a geometric layout, and uniformity in the scale of buildings. As Maia noted, however, the new Turin was added to the existing city. As a work of expansion rather than rebuilding, it was less relevant for Lisbon.

London had more comparable circumstances. Following the Great Fire of 1666, designers generated large-scale plans to reinvent the second largest European city at the time, behind Paris. A few days after the fire subsided, King Charles II expressed a desire for "order and direction" in the reconstruction.[38] His vision included wider streets. A series of proposals by John Evelyn and Christopher Wren opted for regular grid patterns, crossed by angular or diagonal roads. The plans were rejected.

Labor shortages and an unwillingness to confront property rights led to a rebuilding process that largely replicated the previous layout, though with widened streets and more fire-resistant materials like stones and brick instead of wood. The ideas for a new London would not have much of an impact in Lisbon, but they had afterlives across the Atlantic, influencing developments in the Province of Carolina and in Philadelphia.[39]

London and Turin aside, the grid was a preferred form for rebuilding cities struck by disasters in early modern Europe. It was the case in Scandinavian towns in the fifteenth century, and in the northern quarters of Rennes in the 1720s, ravaged by fires.[40] In larger cities, such proposals were more likely to run into opposition. Residents and local authorities of Brussels rejected a grid-like plan to rebuild the city center, destroyed by the French military in 1695. The Russian tsar Peter the Great founded St. Petersburg in 1703 on a site without an existing city, skirting that problem. Envisioned as a modern capital, built in authoritarian fashion, the planning adopted baroque principles of regular streets and canal patterns. It was perhaps the most significant large-scale urban plan carried out in Europe prior to Lisbon's reconstruction.

The Pombaline grid alone does not herald the invention of a new future. It should be understood within larger processes. Rectilinear layouts have been favored in urbanization throughout history, including in Greco-Roman classical sources, some of them known to early modern Europeans. Several planned new towns of the late medieval era adopted the grid. It was not a unanimous choice. Leon Battista Alberti, for example, praised winding streets in his fifteenth-century treatise On the Art of Building. But the straight line could have practical advantages: it was easy to design, implement, and navigate. At the same time, as the art historian Samuel Edgerton wrote, a "synonymy between moral and geometric rectitude" became "ingrained in the Western mind."[41] He notes that Thomas More believed that geometric urban planning freed man from temptation. Lewis Mumford, thinking back on the ancient Greek world, posited that "utopia was nothing more than a new exercise in solid geometry."[42] In early modernity this sometimes took radial or circular shapes: we can think of Filarete's design for the unbuilt Sforzinda (ca. 1457), or Tommaso Campanella's theocratic City of the Sun (1602), both under the influence of astrology and Platonism. Venetians planned the town of Palmanova in a star-shaped polygon in the 1590s.

Expectations of order and rationality as qualities manifested through symmetry, solid geometry, and regularity increasingly inflected transatlantic urban planning. In several Indo-European languages, we get words like *regular, correct, regal,* and *rectify* from the root *reg-,* meaning to move in a straight line. They form an opposition to associations between sinuosity and sin: being straight versus being crooked. Enlightenment-era stadial theories, positing an evolution toward commercial civilization, heightened a temporal dimension: the straight lines of planned streets began to connote efficiency and progress. Grids could render both space and time as linear. In practice, rectangular blocks and straight streets became the privileged forms for pursuing desirable urban futures. In that sense, the reimagined Lisbon was less a reflection of Christian and Platonic ideal forms, and more a metonym of modern aspirations for control, order, and productivity.

In early modernity, the creation of new cities and the reinvention of old ones happened mostly in the Americas. Colonial uses of rectilinear layouts also had material and ideological dimensions. Europeans at once strived to reproduce familiar social orders, and projected desired futures onto the colonies. That process took the shape of the grid throughout the Spanish Americas. As early as the sixteenth century, a set of instructions to be known as the Laws of the Indies attempted to regulate urban life and planning. They dictated how settlements should be ordered from the top down, with spatial organization reflecting hierarchies of functions, as well as the place of social and ethnic groups. A city's form conveyed status and potential. The Spanish ordinances contained guidelines about site selection, governance, and the treatment of natives. They mandated that appropriate spaces should be assigned to common activities like slaughtering, tanning, and grazing. *Order* was a recurrent term in the Laws of the Indies. Ángel Rama, in an important study, argues that the Spanish project "organized people within a repetitive urban landscape," reflecting a rationalized and planned vision of the future to condition them to obey the requirements of colonization.[43] All this led one historian to declare Spanish colonization as responsible for "the real invention of the modern city."[44]

If imperial authorities legislated *ex nihilo* creations with "architectonic unity," realities on the ground involved negotiations that often subverted the intentions of plans.[45] Although some Spanish cities like Mérida and Zaragoza had a grid as part of Roman legacy, most followed the "organic" medieval logic. The form was generally more familiar to natives than to colonizers. It was found in several Mesoamerican settlements, for example, most notably in Tenochtitlan and the ruins of Teotihuacán. The vast central square of Mexico City, the Zócalo, had already been an open space of comparable proportions in the gridded Aztec capital. Lettered Europeans, unsurprisingly, did not acknowledge the extent to which Spanish American cities inherited some of the spatial scales and layouts of the places that they sought to supersede. The main *plazas* of several Spanish American cities, often much larger than what Eurocentric standards required, remain as fragments of indigenous urbanization.

In the Portuguese Americas, the grid only became a preferred colonial template in the years preceding the Lisbon earthquake. A series of new gridded settlements in the Amazonian basin aimed to secure Portuguese sovereignty over territories negotiated with Spain in the Treaty of Madrid, signed in 1750. Amazonia and the Brazilian hinterlands served as a testing ground for principles that animated Lisbon's reconstruction: linearity, uniformity, and a programmed separation of functions.[46] These are key characteristics of what would later be called modern urban planning. In the next chapter, we will see even more innovative iterations of the grid in North America, in cities, in the countryside, and at unprecedented continental scales. Although immersed in the broader currents of a changing Atlantic world, Lisbon's planners also guided their thinking by more immediate horizons. For Pombal, rebuilding a capital city was surely an opportunity to concentrate power. That helps to explain why practicalities and matters of well-being weighed more heavily than ecclesiastical and aristocratic interests, for example. And not by chance, the standardization of construction materials benefited close associates in the commercial classes.[47]

At the same time, the language used in the royal decree that set the plans into law does hint at the broader ideological shifts at play. Pombal signed the decree in the name of King José I in 1758. In some respects, it echoed Charles II's call for "order and direction" in seventeenth-century London. The new Lisbon was to be "regular and decorous."[48] The first adjective can be read as a spatial descriptor. *Decorous* recurred as a keyword in contemporary decrees, and in Pombal's correspondence about the creation of planned settlements in the Amazon.[49] It evoked morality. Presumably, there had been something indecorous about the Amazonian jungles, or the alleyways and jumbled streets of old Lisbon. The royal decree welcomed wider streets, rebuilt "with rectitude," as part of works which are "so useful and necessary to the Common Good."[50] And although decorous shares an etymological root with decorative, it suggests a contrast between the sober façades of the new plan and the exuberance of Mafra. Baroque aesthetics now offended a sense of decorum and the worship of rational efficiency and productivity. It belonged in the past.

———

By the 1750s, a number of debates had moved away from a focus on the end of the world, turning instead to dreams about better ways of inhabiting it. Many channeled those yearnings toward the reform or creation of political communities. Some, as we have seen, imagined potential futures in urbanistic terms. If philosophical responses to the earthquake's devastation challenged the premise that God has a plan for humanity, Lisbon's rebuilding rendered concrete the idea that humans forge their own destinies. That is not to suggest any semblance of democracy. Like other major urban planning projects of the period, the city's reconstruction followed an authoritarian process. But the designs for the central Baixa grid stood apart from transatlantic precedents by seeking to subordinate religion to a new secular order. The Spanish Laws of the Indies had shown great concern with the placement of churches in prominent locations, and specified "preaching the gospel" to natives as the principal goal for new settlements.[51] The rebuilt

London had a Stock Exchange at its heart, yet no other building could compete with the new St. Paul's Cathedral, which replaced a previous Gothic structure. Christopher Wren's monumental masterplan for London was rejected, but he got to design that church with considerable baroque pomp, in the same tradition embraced by the Mafra Palace. St. Petersburg's very name paid homage to Christianity; the new capital developed around cathedrals and palaces in ornate and grandiose baroque style.

Religious language was remarkably absent from Maia's planning treatises. Between the first set of plans in 1756 and the one selected in 1758, the name of Lisbon's main central square changed from Terreiro do Paço (Palace Grounds), as it had been called, to Praça do Comércio (Commerce Square). *Terreiro* etymologically refers to terrain (soil, earth). It was a common term for a churchyard and persists today as a noun to designate places of worship in Afro-Brazilian religions like Candomblé. *Praça*, a cognate of plaza, was a bit more formal. The shift signals a symbolic and material reorganization: the new Portuguese capital would not have a square flanked by a royal palace or church at its center, as had been the norm, but a large riverfront square framed by imposing government buildings. These included the Stock Exchange, and an official name commemorating commercial values. The designs for another major public square, the Praça do Rossio, included a public market. The Praça da Erva (or Nova), now known as the Praça da Figueira, likewise lacked the familiar and commanding presence of an ecclesiastic building. There was no precedent for this conspicuous religious absence in major cities of contemporary Europe, if not the world. Eugénio dos Santos, who led the process of crafting the chosen plan, apparently died full of remorse for his role in short-changing places of worship.[52]

The majority of Lisbon's dozens of churches, convents, and monasteries suffered significant damages due to the earthquake. As historian Timothy Walker has shown, the reconstruction deliberately sought to reduce the visibility of religious buildings by imposing severe constraints on architectural elements like bell towers and façades.[53] Churches would no longer shape Lisbon's skyline and the experience of being on its streets. A walk around old Lisbon would invariably lead to churches. Usually seen from afar, they tended to be framed by open spaces. These served as nodes for spiritual and social life, hosting festivals and gatherings. When incorporated into the grid, churches lost those features. And with the more muted neoclassical style, they no longer showcased the marvel of gothic or baroque designs. The new urban fabric clearly meant to assert secular power over religious institutions. It also undercut landowning aristocracies, composed of influential families that assumed their futures to be secure. The message was clear: (royal) state authority, rationality, and commerce would rule over Lisbon's destiny. The new Portuguese capital was supposed to usher in secular, enlightened values.

The top-down approach clashed with everyday life. Lisbon residents kept referring to the new Commerce Square by its old name. Street toponyms from the pre-earthquake Baixa resurfaced in neighborhoods on the city's outskirts.[54] The disconnect proved to be starkest in terms of Christianity's role. A traveler expressed surprise at how the rebuilt Lisbon looked like a "city of Atheists."[55] People in Lisbon of course continued to be deeply religious. Indifferent to philosophical debates about the earthquake, they still assumed that it resulted from God meddling in human affairs. A popular Jesuit preacher worked tirelessly to press that case. The Italian-born Gabriel Malagrida had been a missionary in Brazil. Before the earthquake, he was well received in the Portuguese court. In its aftermath, he gave sermons and published a book stating that the destruction resulted not from "natural causes," but from divine punishment for "intolerable sins."[56] This was fairly standard fare for the period. A contemporary clergyman in London also exhorted people to "live for the future so religiously," to avoid God's wrath.[57] But in Portugal, Malagrida's position did not just contradict the Pombaline secular outlook. It also represented an affront to the royalty. His explanation for the earthquake implicated them in moral corruption.

In 1758, after an alleged attempt on the life of King José I, authorities accused Malagrida and the aristocratic Távora family of being involved in an assassination plot. Months later, the state sentenced several members of the nobility to public execution. Perhaps this foreshadows the revolution that Robespierre sought to accelerate. Pombal also had

Malagrida and the Jesuits in sight. His campaign against the powerful religious order predated the earthquake. It partly originated in their resistance to abide by the 1750 Treaty of Madrid, delineating Brazil's frontiers. In 1759, Portugal expelled the Jesuits. The state, however, did not have the authority to execute a priest without papal dispensation. Pombal installed one of his brothers as Grand Inquisitor, overseeing the process against Malagrida. In 1761, condemned for crimes like heresy and false prophecies, he burned at the stake.

The execution of the Jesuit mystic brings to mind the idea that "the modern was constituted through a rejection of prophecy."[58] To Malagrida, the end of the world was inevitable. In opposition to that expectation, the argument goes, "the philosophy of the Enlightenment required that time would be open to human achievement." This commitment to the pliability of time could inspire both social progress and despotic actions. Who got to judge achievements and goals as worthwhile? In Portugal, Malagrida's interpretation of the earthquake posed enough of a threat to secular dreams that it had to be violently suppressed. We might say that Pombal paradoxically adopted the tools of religious obscurantism, at the service of the Age of Reason: burning a dissident at the stake, to pursue enlightened aims.

An unusual censorship case embodied these tensions. Dated from 1772, it retroactively addressed Malagrida's book on the "true causes" of the earthquake. The Portuguese censor juxtaposed its "fanatical preoccupations" to the "superior degree of Enlightenment" that Portugal had achieved.[59] The historian Rui Tavares speculates that the censor worked under Pombal's order and sees this as a dialogue between two Portugals.[60] In the Portugal of the past, Malagrida's book had met with censorial approval. In the other, the forward-looking Pombaline vision triumphed. The censor condemned Malagrida's books to be burned in the Commerce Square. It is telling that the style of his text, ornate and circuitous, recalls Malagrida's prophetic writings and the old Lisbon much more than Maia's sober, direct, and decorous prose—and plans.

Scholars have argued that "by bracketing eschatological questions, the Enlightenment effectively 'sealed off' the future from prophetic knowledge."[61] When the Laws of the Indies discarded traditional astrological criteria to determine the location of new settlements, it already moved in that direction. Lisbon represented a dramatic acceleration. It was not just a matter of modern methods. There was already a growing practice, after all, of military engineering treating existing conditions as obstacles to be overcome by efficient straight lines. This impetus, however, generally still obeyed "religious reasoning."[62] The most well-known early modern major urban intervention in Europe was the opening of wide and straight avenues in sixteenth-century Rome, under Pope Sixtus V.[63] These reforms, though conceived as a rationalized system, had in mind the experience of pilgrims. In comparison, the new Lisbon stood apart for creating spatial hierarchies that sought to sideline religious worldviews. But we should be careful not to overstate how much the city's rebuilding breaks from the temporal structure of Christianity.

It might seem paradoxical that efforts to "seal off" the future from a Jesuit prophet resorted to the violent tools of the Catholic Counter-Reformation. But there is some consistency at play here. In a way, Lisbon's urban planning reproduced the teleological expectations of religious mindsets. Designs were oriented toward an end both in the sense of having purposes, and in presuming the possibility of completion. Instead of salvation in the afterlife, the focus is on an urban ideal. Once built, the city's forms are meant to be fixed, and the plan is done. The urban future was still largely conceived in static terms. We should not see the Mafra palace-monastery, prompted by a vow, as an antithesis only. Though the two massive projects aimed to fulfill different promises, there are continuities in the top-down, centralized, and controlling modes of planning. Both had established end goals.

Does Lisbon's rebuilding represent the substitution of a religious *telos* with a secular one? It would be an oversimplification to say so. Here we must more closely discern between the plans and their implementation. Lewis Mumford described how "baroque planners tacitly assumed that their order was eternal."[64] As a theory of the future, Renaissance and baroque urban plans already focused on achievable ideal forms on earth, rather than the end of the world. As an instrument of power, they reflected a despotic vision of an absolute state. The attempt "to congeal

time" underpinned both theory and practice. Lisbon's planners inno-
vated by not gesturing toward a Christian horizon. And they also managed to incorporate some open-ended possibilities. This aligned with
preferences for more dynamic approaches, like those of the French
architect Pierre Patte, who became one of the most influential
Enlightenment-era planning theorists.[65] Lisbon's planners anticipated
some of his insights about how a city's various parts are interconnected,
including its surroundings. They realized, for example, that the city
needed to accommodate outward expansion, because the rebuilt Baixa
would have less capacity for density. The Portuguese planners worked
on blueprints for gridded suburban industrial neighborhoods, peri-
urban rural zones, and extensive new developments.[66] These parts of
the plan were mostly discarded. Pombal did not treat those provisions
with the same zeal that he applied to the central Baixa. He envisioned a
bourgeois and modern urban future, but not a less authoritarian or
more open-ended one.

Pombal gained a reputation as an enlightened despot based on more
than his earthquake response. He abolished slavery in Portugal, and
pushed for secular education, as well as reforms in the tax system and
new economic regulations. His policies sought to stimulate manufacturing and merchant-dominated trade monopolies. In 1766, two wealthy
businessmen, one Swiss and the other English, commissioned a portrait
of him. Presumably, they had benefited from relationships with Pombal.
The hired painter, Louis-Michel van Loo, had been a court painter to
Philip V in Madrid, and made several portraits of Louis XV in France.
He was based in Paris.[67]

Louis-Michel van Loo's painting illustrates the new narrative: the
master planner, supplanting divine will. It had a size befitting the subject.[68] Behind Pombal, to the viewer's left, we see a model of an equestrian statue of King José I, surrounded by allegories of Commerce, Arts,
and Industry. His right arm rests on plans for the new Lisbon. Drawings
of buildings, spread out in the floor and on a stool, suggest a pragmatic
visionary at work on the reconstruction project. He is positioned on a
perch, sitting in an imaginary building with marble floors and classical
columns, removed from the urban hustle-bustle below. The image of the

FIGURE 1.2. Pombal, an Olympian master planner, dictates the future!

masculine planner above the city would have a long tradition in urban discourse.

If we read the painting from left to right, as we tend to in alphabetic cultures, the dark ominous clouds give way to enlightenment, as if responding to Pombal's actions. His left-hand gestures toward the horizon, where the Tagus meets the Atlantic, suggesting bright possibilities ahead. The busy port and the colonies beyond evoke the transatlantic connections funding Lisbon's rebuilding. The plans for the capital showcase the modern values of the Portuguese empire. The painting's three planes tell a related story. Each has a distinct spatial and temporal logic. In the background, beyond the river, the wayward oceans. In the middle ground, the built environment that withstood the earthquake, in grandiose Renaissance style.[69] In the foreground, the linear efficiency of the planned city, brought into being by the powerful statesman. The past,

the present, and the future. Does Pombal's gesture imply that he is taking the light of rational planning to the colonies across the Atlantic?
Could we also read a narrative about the primitive Americas propelled
by the master planner toward civilization, embodied by the enlightened
European capital? Regardless of how we interpret the composition, this
was a painting supremely confident about its place in posterity. Van
Loo's style became dated and obsolete in a matter of decades.

We must, then, also discern between the aspirations of Pombal's
secular dreams, and the actual repercussions of the new Lisbon. In 1775,
on the inauguration of a monumental equestrian statue of King José I
in the center of the Commerce Square, Pombal wrote: "The sumptuous
and well-built edifices of Lisbon demonstrate the flourishing state of
architecture."[70] Parts of the Baixa still lied in ruins, but reconstruction
was well on its way. He continued: "These things abundantly prove to
foreigners that Portugal has no cause to envy them either their drafts-
men, or their painters, or their sculptors." In reality, Lisbon's renewal did
not set off a comparable artistic movement. The modernized Baixa did
not prove to be all that consequential for the development of Portuguese culture or urban planning. We can also surmise that regardless of
the capital, the grid would have remained part of the grammar for "rational" urbanization in Portugal's overseas territories. And against Pombal's wishes, his response to the disaster and the new Lisbon would not
really change perceptions of Portugal among lettered Europeans of the
Enlightenment.

Although the frequency of public executions diminished in the eighteenth century, the Iberian Peninsula was still associated with *autos-
da-fé*—the spectacle of burning heretics at the stake. The otherwise
sympathetic entry for Portugal in the *Encyclopédie* condemned the "still
very severe" inquisition, suggesting *autos-da-fé* as more backward than
Aztec sacrifices.[71] In Voltaire's *Candide* (1759), an international best-
seller at the time, the title character and the optimist Dr. Pangloss survived a shipwreck. They ended up in Lisbon just before All Saints' Day,
1755. After the city's destruction, both got caught up in an *auto-da-fé*.
Two men were burned for refusing pork fat, and Pangloss was hanged:
"It was decided by the University of Coimbra that the burning of a few

people alive by a slow fire, and with great ceremony, is an infallible pre-
ventive of earthquakes." Voltaire's book reminded readers of the brutal
persecution of Jews, and led them to assume that religious zealotry and
irrationality guided Portugal's reactions to the disaster. In fact, Pombal
hired the physician António Ribeiro Sanches, who had left Portugal to
escape the Inquisition and reclaimed his Jewish heritage.[72]

Lisbon residents expressed frustration with what they saw as the exag-
gerated repercussion of the earthquake in Europe.[73] The entry for the
city in a 1765 edition of the *Encyclopédie* lamented "all the beautiful things
that have been erased from the book of life" by the "unforeseen" event.[74]
The author mentioned foreign aid received by the city but offered no
news of its impressive recovery. The Pombaline project viewed Lisbon's
reinvention as a way of asserting Portuguese prominence, diminished
after the 1500s. If news of the urbanistic feats failed to reach Enlightenment circles, that can at least in part be attributed to the twists and turns
of history. In 1781, the eminent natural scientist José Correia da Serra
missed the deadline for an article on Lisbon, commissioned for inclusion
in the *Encyclopédie Méthodique*.[75] In his unpublished entry Correia da
Serra looked ahead, and showed awareness of the potential impact of the
publication. He regretted that the previous article in the *Encyclopédie*
focused only on the destruction, and provided details about how "the
useful sciences" inform the rebuilding. The *nouvelle* capital, he writes, led
by *savants*, has even "gained a lot from the earthquake."[76] The Baixa grid
had minimal repercussions abroad. Instead, news of what became known
as the Távora affair and Malagrida's burning spread across Europe.[77] It
would be the last *auto-da-fé* held in Portugal.

III. Secular Utopia

By the 1770s, it was no longer necessarily easier to imagine the end of
the world than the radical transformation of a great city. Literary fiction
set in the future began to flourish. As Daniel Rosenberg and Susan
Harding explain, the "Enlightenment proscription against traditional
prophetic practices turned out to produce new and intensified imaginative demands on the future and new techniques of narration and

prognosis."[78] To the German critic Lessing, a group of writers emerged that could not wait for the future and wished for it to arrive sooner. Indeed, even if these works used settings in times to come as a device through which to critique their own contemporary societies, they also articulated scenarios worth pursuing. Scholars recognize Louis-Sébastien Mercier's *L'An 2440* (The year 2440), from 1771, as the first known utopia set in the future.[79] Previously, writers projected their ideal societies onto the past or elsewhere in space, like Thomas More's fictional island of Utopia, a milestone of the genre. Mercier situated his fantasy in a transformed version of Paris, his hometown.

Banned in France for criticism of the status quo, the novel was first published anonymously. It became a major success, with over 60,000 copies circulating in various languages.[80] Mercier opened with an epistle paying tribute to the idea of progress. He dedicated it to the year 2440, a time that "shall bring happiness upon earth," and apologized for the oppressive stupidity of his own age.[81] We quickly understand how the book struck people as subversive. In this future, the kings of his day would be no more. Mercier appealed to the judgment of posterity to inspire readers to free themselves from the constraints of the present. That would become a common trope among modern planners and utopians: defending a disruptive vision, with promises of redemption, by asking dissenters to *just wait and see*. Or alternatively, the comforting thought of being *on the right side of history* when oppressive politics prevail. Here, this rhetorical exercise was at the service of Mercier's *telos*-driven vision, shaped by his certainties about what the world ought to be like.

The plot consists of a narrator telling his English friend about waking up from an enchanted sleep in 2440 Paris. This trope of sleeping for hundreds of years was key to the Seven Sleepers tradition in Christianity. In these stories, often set in Ephesus, the built environment differed because of crosses added to buildings, revealing a Christianized future. In Mercier's secular rendition, the narrator noticed that "everything had changed." He was taken around by a philosopher type, a *savant*. The author clearly used this as a strategy to denounce what he saw as wrong in the present. Paris was a place of "disorder," "extreme opulence and excessive misery." Those descriptions also applied to London, and the two friends seemed to agree that "all great cities resemble each other." The French original deemed Paris a "deformed monster," which one contemporary English translation rendered as "most irregular compound."[82] Was this an insinuation that an enlightened city should be made up of straight lines? Indeed, as the narrative begins to outline a model society, it illustrated how the urban fabric of the future Paris would reflect ideal moral values.

Mercier's future Paris shared several characteristics with the plans for Lisbon. Paris of 2440 had "grand and beautiful streets, properly aligned," or "built in straight lines," "strictly regular," and in "perfect order."[83] All houses were of equal height. Street traffic was well-organized, so that carriages no longer crushed pedestrians. Mathematics had been stripped of all that was speculative. It now served engineering and useful aims like the construction of triumphal arches and stately buildings. A secular society, Paris was no longer oriented around churches or monasteries. The narrator's guide decried both astrology and Gothic architecture as "ridiculous." He spoke approvingly of demolitions, as they had made the city safer and more accessible. Mercier doubtlessly endorsed a sentiment voiced by the narrator: "Our age was that of innumerable projects; yours is that of execution." Some changes went further and anticipated later developments, like functional clothing and simpler hairstyles, "speedy" water supply, and widespread lamps.[84]

Mercier, however, took aim at privileges in ways that anyone attached to conventions of the Old Regime would find intolerable. His future Paris was a city of "natural equality," without "destructive luxury." The system of governance served people's interests, with Kings raised to mingle with the public, and exercising power with responsibility and care. This was not an absolute monarchy. Nobles walked around with everyone else. All had become wise to the "horror" of "vain pageantry," and to the fact that "pomp and ostentation are abuses." This extended to urban design. Paris was now endowed with monumental, awe-inspiring public squares and buildings. They served public functions, like a temple hosting the King's Cabinet, a mixture of museum and research facility. Mercier foresaw postrevolutionary changes: the Louvre became part of a public complex largely dedicated to the arts, and the Tuileries royal garden was opened to all. We learn about these developments from the narrator's guide. But Mercier also added a set of footnotes referring to the present. In one of them, he denounced the insult of refusing entrance in those spaces to "common people."[85]

In the Paris of 2440, there was a type of deistic state religion with collective daily prayer, and no hierarchies among the religious. There were no cemeteries, as they cremated the dead. Ancient prejudices and religious divisions had been abolished, and "Europe is no longer the enemy of the other four parts of the globe." The narrator's guide was in fact Chinese, and explained that French was now spoken in Beijing. Mercier's vision was radical, but still imagined enlightened culture emanating out of Paris. Peace reigned among nations, and the colonies of the New World had become independent. The guide denounced how Europeans plundered the Americas, and enslaved Africans. Slavery, he says, had made Europeans infantile and superfluous in their pursuit of "glaring objects" rather than happiness and virtue.[86] Mercier was in fact addressing his contemporaries: you "mistook, at every step, the image for the reality."[87] As the men walked around in 2440, the narrator saw a monument to abolition. On a magnificent pedestal stood "the figure of a negro," with a "noble and commanding stance." Above it, the inscription: "To the avenger of the new world." This commemorated a "renowned legislator," who with "virtuous spirit" led to a reckoning and left no doubts about the insidiousness of slavery.[88]

In this utopian future, access to rights advanced greatly, but only for men. It still excluded women from public life and obligated them to serve as wives and mothers. Mercier's egalitarianism had serious limitations. His ideal Paris was not democratic either. It can seem like a tyranny of productivity. Those deemed by monitors to be rebellious or indolent had to be banished from the city. Mercier, ultimately, articulated transformations already under way, or deemed possible. He reacted against some and delighted in others. The vision shared blind spots with Lisbon's planners, unable to foresee the technological advances ahead. The "extraordinary" inventions detailed in the book are somewhat quaint: malleable glass, transparent stone, purple dyes, inextinguishable lamps. There was nothing that could fundamentally alter urban experience. Mercier, at the same time, boldly envisioned a new secular order, where the city's future had to be different from present and past. It was a central bet for Lisbon's Baixa plan as well. Yet here, if the end of the world no longer monopolized imaginations of the future, the end of almighty institutions suddenly seemed plausible. *L'An 2440* closed with Versailles in ruins.

———

Even before the idea of utopian future cities matured, urbanization had its discontents. During the Enlightenment, Rousseau stood out as the most prominent voice against cities. In a letter after the Lisbon earthquake, he held urbanization responsible for the catastrophe. The tremors had only been a deadly event, after all, because of urban density. His widely read *Emile, or On Education* (1762), declared that "cities are the burial pit of humanity."[89] Rousseau was also not keen on the turn toward future-oriented dispositions, which he associated with urbanity. The treatise warned against the pitfalls of civilization, and those were "the real source of all our troubles." It asks: "How mad it is for so short-lived a creature as man to look forward into a future to which he rarely attains, while he neglects the present which is his?" To Rousseau, it was self-evident that global interconnectedness and economic prosperity would not lead to happiness: "How many princes make themselves miserable for the loss of lands they never saw, and how many merchants lament in Paris over some misfortune in the Indies!"[90]

Rousseau's distrust of cities did mean that he could be an attentive student of their social dynamics. This was apparent in his *Julie; or, The New Heloise* (1761). The epistolary novel might have been the biggest best-seller of the period.[91] It told a story of love between Julie, an aristocratic young woman, and her tutor Saint-Preux, a plebeian young man. They swore this passion would endure for as long as they lived. The lovers parted ways, however, after Julie agreed to a marriage of convenience with a social equal, at the behest of her baron father. Saint-Preux wrote her letters about his travels, including impressions of Paris.

The French capital served as a foil to the sensitive protagonist, who was always authentic to his feelings. He called the city a "vast desert," with a "chaos" that left him unable to make connections with others. Paris was a place of "horrible solitude," where hypocrisy and appearances reigned. Saint-Preux complained that "no one ever says what he thinks." Inadvertently, Rousseau's character spelled out what we might identify as a quality of urbanites: "They have principles for conversation and others for practice." In fact, urban life, or living among strangers, demands that people shift registers, find common denominators, and adapt to fluid circumstances. Modern cities ask people to play roles and to play along, even when events take unforeseen turns. So, although he meant it as a scathing indictment, Saint-Preux came up with a decent definition for how urbanites adopted a new attitude toward the future: "In a word, everything is absurd and nothing shocks, because they are accustomed to it."[92]

Near the end of the novel, Julie died of a fever. On her deathbed, she wrote a letter to Saint-Preux declaring that he was her true love. Plots that revolved around forbidden love across classes helped to challenge the notion that aristocratic futures are fixed. Julie stayed true to her passion, not to her social lineage, and her husband did not get his way. The message seems clear: love and passion are stronger than assigned roles. Yet, the novel can also be interpreted as a reaction against a changing world. The ideal of true and authentic love promised the temporal clarity of Christian teleological thinking. It was everlasting and predictable. You basically knew what you would get in the end. This was not yet a type of modern narrative where the thrill came from not knowing what to expect—the plot twists, the surprise ending, or the unsettling resolution. In *Julie*'s time, it was generally the case that a story about forbidden love implied a limited set of outcomes and fulfilled certain expectations: the lovers are the protagonists, and their love will be consummated, resulting in marriage or tragic death. If it was a relationship across social classes, we could expect death.

Over time, fiction caught up to what cities laid bare: in modernity, predictions underestimate the range of potential outcomes. That is part of what bothered Saint-Preux. But Mercier faced a similar anxiety. In his utopian Paris of 2440, nothing was left to chance (*hasard*, in the original). The word itself was banished.[93] In the actual city, you never really knew what you were going to get. People had to learn to live with a widening sense of possibilities, openness to the unexpected, and constantly negotiated their sense of themselves. They recognized this predicament as absurd, but not shocking. To a moralizing sensibility, the uncertainties and hypocrisies could be unbearable. The idea that anything is possible meant that anything goes. It posed a grave threat to what was most sacred, be it God, love, or authenticity. And indeed, the changing urban world was rife with exploitation, abuse, and hardship. We know that, at the time, the proportion of children born out of wedlock grew considerably in major cities like Paris.[94]

Ultimately, Rousseau and his peers had no idea what was coming. The writer became a cherished reference for revolutionaries, especially Robespierre. If Julie's family and husband had to deal with a blow to their sense of entitlement, a generation later French nobility would face previously unimaginable possibilities: loss of privileges, a tyranny of commoners, and the guillotine.

IV. Resonances

In August of 1789, the French National Assembly issued decrees to abolish ecclesiastical and aristocratic privileges. Days later, they adopted the Declaration of the Rights of Man and of the Citizen, radically expanding the scope of individual liberty and aspirations for democratic governance. Versailles was not in ruins, but neither was its future secure. The new futures opened up during the eighteenth century could be characterized by the speeding up of changes, and the quality of being extremely unpredictable. The accelerated transformations, to Koselleck, "abbreviated the space of experiences, robbed them of their constancy, and continually brought into play new, unknown factors."[95]

That unpredictability bears out in the history of modern revolutions. The range of possible outcomes seemed to widen considerably. After the 1789 Declaration, extending civil rights to women was more easily conceivable. Some called on the National Assembly to do so. A couple months later, in what became known as the October Days, women led a march from Paris to Versailles. Protests included a host of issues, including bread scarcity. They pressured the royal family to relocate to Paris—Versailles, it turns out, would never again be the seat of royal power. Changes came fast and rendered the future as unknown as ever. In 1791, Olympe de Gouges published a Declaration of the Rights of Women and of the Female Citizen. The Revolutionary Tribunal sentenced her to the guillotine in 1793. Robespierre, who had called for a break with the past and an acceleration toward a revolutionary future in May of that year, met the same fate within weeks.

The imponderable permeates modern urban history, though in less conspicuous ways just yet. We can distinguish, nonetheless, between the intentions of the Pombaline plans and some of the consequences. To the historian Jonathan Israel, responses to earthquakes in Peru (1746), Chile (1751), and Portugal evidenced a newfound "transatlantic awareness."[96] Case in point: each revolution in the Atlantic world helped to inspire the next, as well as the spread of counter-revolutionary backlash. In comparison, while the earthquake shook people far and wide, Lisbon's reconstruction produced few reverberations. And even those did not go according to plan. The Portuguese king instituted new taxes to cover the costs of disaster response.[97] These measures fueled discontentment in the mining-rich captaincy of Minas Gerais, culminating in the most significant independence movement in eighteenth-century Brazil. Some of the conspirators, composed mostly of slaveholders and wealthy urbanites from Vila Rica, advocated for abolition. After a rebellion in April of 1789, the movement was suppressed, but it would become a touchstone of Brazilian political history.

We can also think of more local developments that the Lisbon plans could not anticipate. The sewage system proved to be deficient. Designs for the Baixa included buildings of three floors. By the 1900s, they had five. Many became tenements. The construction process emboldened real estate speculators and weakened not just aristocratic families but also the traditional artisan class, as it favored the serial production of parts.[98] And of course, despite being at the forefront of Enlightenment-era innovations, the new capital never became a beacon of new urban futures.

As the historian Maria Helena Barreiros put it, for decades the Baixa remained an "island of modernity" in a city "deprived of water, a sewer system, paving, and public lighting, where stray dogs, chickens, and pigs roamed freely."[99] During much of the twentieth century, the Commerce Square functioned as a parking lot, and eventually, as a tourist hot spot.

There was, however, one unexpected way in which Pombal's reforms had widespread consequences in Europe, and they are reflected in Mercier's narrative. Portugal expelled the Jesuits in 1759. France followed suit in 1764. The religious order had a central role in education, and their absence bolstered the idea that the state should be responsible for it. Mercier served on the Committee for Public Education after the revolution. In *L'An 2440*, he was already clearly concerned with the pedagogical roles of art and architecture. In his utopian Paris, painting was taught in open and accessible academies. These had a utilitarian role, teaching virtue to the general public. Aesthetics is part of education, which in turn is a state matter. There are obvious links between the secular turn in the imagination of urban futures, and the erosion in church control over education. In both, echoing some of the central ideas in Rousseau's *Émile*, children would become less bound to the destinies assigned to them at birth.

By destabilizing the aristocratic and religious hold on the future, figures like Pombal and Mercier assisted in the erosion of Old Regimes. At the same time, of course, the impetus for Atlantic revolutions had very material dimensions: it was about taxation in Boston and Vila Rica, bread prices in Paris, the cruelties of slavery in Le Cap (Cap-Haïtien), and so on. This concerns futurity on a more existential or immediate level, and often escaped the capacities of Enlightenment-era prognostication.[100] It also evinces a gap between popular and lettered cultures. The Atlantic world in the eighteenth century underwent an unprecedented proliferation of printed materials and readers.[101] Booming print cultures could bring writing closer to the masses in urban environments, but it could also distort the views of intellectuals. The primacy of lettered culture in hierarchies of knowledge had been well established by the second half of the eighteenth century. It created the assumption among writers that culture would follow a pathway already discernible to them, with print as the privileged mode of transmission.

For Mercier, literary cultures are at the heart of the urban future. *L'An 2440* becomes an opportunity for him to extol favorites and dish out attacks. Paris is dotted with Academies and statues of enlightened *savants* like Voltaire, Rousseau, Buffon, and Montesquieu. Mercier predicts that children in the future will all read and digest the *Encyclopédie*. It was not such an idiosyncratic opinion. A contemporary reader wrote that the publication, "[nearly] drunk with so much hope for the progress of reason, prophesied a Jerusalem of philosophy that would last more than 1000 years."[102] Interestingly, the metaphor sought to project stability through the proverbial City of God rather than a secular urban reference. In these mindsets the future belonged to the lettered, *le gens de lettres*. Books could therefore also threaten order and progress. Mercier's fantasy confined works of theology to the basement of libraries. People that wrote "bad books" would have to wear a mask as a sign of shame, until they could produce something "more rational and more wise."[103] And we need not resort to fiction. The Portuguese state decided to set Malagrida's books on fire over a decade *after* they burned the author.

There is also a certain lettered condescension about posterity at play here. Mercier's guide to 2440 issued a smug but pointed assessment of the 1700s: "Instead of envisaging an august series of centuries to come, [people in your time] rendered themselves slaves to a momentary taste." Channeling Mercier, he offered a maxim: *"Be severe as the time that flies; be inexorable as posterity."*[104] Literate cultures, including both writers and urban planners, had enormous confidence that their works would withstand time. The project of the *Encyclopedia* in fact represented a shift, showing awareness of the "provisional character" of knowledge, which had to be renewed and updated. Its writers expressed preoccupation with how books became obsolete with growing speed in their time.[105] This anxiety would only become pervasive among urban planners and designers in the next century. In literature, however, more conventional authors often thought that *others* succumbed to momentary tastes, and continued to assume that they wrote for posterity.

In Lisbon, twenty years after the earthquake, more than 600 poets dedicated verses to the inauguration of the equestrian statue of the king in the middle of the Baixa's Commerce Square.[106] Queen Maria I rose to the throne in 1777, unseating Pombal and engaging in a program to rehabilitate the role of ecclesiastical architecture in Lisbon. This included building the monumental Estrela Basilica in baroque and neoclassical style, recalling the Mafra complex. After Pombal's fall from power, a plaque commemorating him on the pedestal of King José's statue was stoned and removed.[107] Memory and its inscription in the city quickly became another aspect of disputes over the future. Some eulogizing poems took Pombal's side. One, from 1786, praised how he gave Portugal "new ideas," securing his honor for posterity.[108]

Despite a backlash against the Pombaline period during Queen Maria I's reign, several ambitious literary works celebrated Lisbon's reconstruction. This included a book-length poem published in 1780, written in *ottava rima*, touting the city's newfound gloriousness. To the poet, Lisbon outmatched classical Ephesus, competed with the Vatican, and compared to Vasco da Gama's journeys to India. Strikingly, the built environment was deemed fit to receive the same epic treatment as overseas colonization. Some verses laud the spare style and uniformity of the grid: "simple architecture, but beautiful / A noble idea of rare equality."[109] An earlier poem had made an association between straightness and justice.[110] There is a glaring contradiction between the functional Baixa and the baroque qualities of these literary works. But they shared a modern concern with capital cities as embodiments of national prowess. Another book-long poem dedicated to the rebuilt city omitted Pombal's role, amid a changed political order. It heralded, nonetheless, the beautiful city that emerged from the ruins, "presenting itself to the world."[111] In 1803, another epic poem covered similar ground.[112] These works showed great confidence in their judgments about what would endure in posterity, conceptualizing the future as both static and shaped by standards of the past. They tended to imagine that the values of the present would endure relatively unchanged. This literature, needless to say, did not appeal to modern tastes, and was soon forgotten.

———

At the outset of the nineteenth century, across the Atlantic, most of the population remained rural and illiterate. Several decades of slave revolts, rebellions and revolutions reflected and created changing sets of expectations among both ruling classes and subordinates, inside and outside of cities. Nonetheless, early secular visions for urban futures largely neglected popular aspirations. Multiple forms of folk religion continued to animate yearnings for justice, daily life, and understandings of the future. Our access to these perceptions and experiences is mediated by writing, which neglected the vast majority of perspectives. Here and there, however, we find hints of urban textures that lettered cultures tended to overlook. Literature by survivors of the Lisbon earthquake was written mostly by white men, many of them neither Portuguese nor Catholic. In passing references, we get inklings of black men as protagonists in rescue efforts, and we can listen to women reacting to the destruction by singing *ladainhas*, a form of call-and-response prayer.[113]

When scholars refer to the eighteenth-century "widespread urge toward invention" they tend to think of new technologies in farming and manufacturing.[114] These would indeed underlie modern urbanization, as we will see in the next chapter. But inventions in cultural forms also shaped the experience of cities. While much of the vast literary production concerned with posterity would find few readers in later periods, emergent musical genres pointed toward modern futures. Domingos Caldas Barbosa could be characterized as a harbinger. Born in Rio de Janeiro, he died in Lisbon. His father was a white Portuguese state official and merchant. His mother, a black Angolan, had been enslaved. Caldas Barbosa studied with Jesuits in Brazil, and at the University of Coimbra after their expulsion. Racism curtailed his prospects. He arrived in the Portuguese capital in the aftermath of the earthquake, when many theaters and opera houses had not reopened. A creator and performer of *modinhas* and *lundús*, Caldas Barbosa became a wild success in the salons and taverns of the Portuguese capital.[115]

Modinha and *lundú* refer to songs and dances with wide formal variation, but marked by cross-rhythms, or syncopation. They combine elements of European and African matrixes, especially Bantu. Polyrhythmic practices, perceived as an irregularity in Eurocentric music, could be understood as challenges to the uniform and symmetrical visual orders of the day. One of Caldas Barbosa's lyrics brought together lexicon derived from African Kimbundu, Amerindian Tupi, Hebrew, and

Brazilian Portuguese.[116] This bewildering linguistic diversity defied Mercier's fantasy of a future world dominated by a *lingua franca*. Lettered contemporaries of Caldas Barbosa assumed his inventions to be a passing fad, unable to survive the *inexorable* judgment of posterity.

Over time, Afro-inflected rhythmic syncopation ceased to be a deviation and became the norm in Brazilian music. Caldas Barbosa was a precursor to some of the most long-lasting cultural creations of the urban Atlantic, such as samba and fado, reorienting the presumed North–South direction of knowledge circulation. Like the philosophical responses to the Lisbon earthquake, his music also challenged the limits of European understanding. The diminutive *modinha* shares etymological roots with the Portuguese word for fashion, *moda*. We should also associate it to *modern*, reflecting transatlantic urbanization as a process shaped by hierarchy, control, and order, but also dynamism, experimentation, and a sense of possibility. Put another way, Caldas Barbosa's art can be interpreted as an example of how something seemingly small can amount to more than the sum of its parts, flowing into ever-changing cultural legacies.

From the perspective of the modern state, urban design became a crucial tool in broader efforts to render territories and populations legible, monitored, manipulable—a process that the scholar James Scott called *seeing like a state*.[117] Moving like Caldas Barbosa was a counterpoint. To him and others in urbanizing milieus, pursuing the future most often meant finding rhythms and making do. In the coming decades, planning and design would involve some measure of dancing too, between the push and pull of rigid forms and shape-shifting realities, modernity and tradition, continuity and rupture, fixity and flux.

2

New Worlds Emerge
(1790s–1840s)

NEW YORK + LONDON, WASHINGTON, DC,
PARIS, PHILADELPHIA, SALVADOR,
AND MORE.

I. Leaping Ahead

In the late 1700s, who could have foreseen that New York would become the world's largest city within a few generations? It was inconceivable that any metropolitan area might one day be home to several million people. That would seem even less likely in the United States. Urban changes, however, outpaced reasonable expectations. While the rebuilt Lisbon stood as a relatively static record of the early ideals of modern planning, the Commissioners' Plan of 1811 for New York City catalyzed a new phase in the invention of urban futures. The Manhattan grid established an even more radically modern relationship between planning and urban life: less religiously charged, and more open-ended. It was oriented toward commerce and capitalism in unprecedented ways. Though the city's layout was fixed in a rigid, rectilinear plan, it ushered in a seemingly perpetual state of flux. New York's transformation in the nineteenth century exemplified transatlantic urbanization as a laboratory for social stratification, identity formation, and creativity. That was not, however, part of the plan. Nor could anyone see it coming.

The commissioners behind the 1811 plan for New York were anything but avant-garde disruptors. They did not envision Manhattan covered in buildings, let alone skyscrapers, within a foreseeable future. How could designs for gradual expansion within a familiar horizon prove to be so adept for a city that would leap ahead in a matter of decades? In the early 1800s, though already the largest city in the United States, New York still paled in comparison to urban centers of the Old World. At around 60,000, it had a population closer to Uruk during the Bronze Age, a single district in contemporary London, or the Woodhaven neighborhood in Queens today. Fast-forwarding to the 1900s, we find New York as the archetype of urban modernity. The Commissioners' Plan took a chance, and the results surpassed the imaginable. Yet, Manhattan's development was not inevitable, nor did it occur in isolation. For one, an inclination toward taking chances inflected planning and everyday life in multiple places, with odds stacked for some and against others, from politicians and businessmen to migrants and mainstream fictional characters. New worlds began to emerge on both sides of the Atlantic. Understanding how this all happened requires stepping back, as well as detours.

Even after major revolutions rocked the political foundations of the Atlantic world, basic daily patterns of agrarian and religious life remained in place. Outside of indigenous societies, chances of surviving war, famine, and disease mostly improved. It became easier to move around, grow crops, and trade efficiently.[1] Population growth largely accelerated.[2] The speed of transformations was not yet as explosive as those of the second half of the nineteenth century, after the take-off in construction, communications, and transportation technologies, especially steamships and trains. For now, slavery remained entrenched. The planet continued to be overwhelmingly nonurban. At the same time, the fixation of modern relationships to space and time, based on stable boundaries and exclusive ownership rights, helped to create conditions for the changes ahead. Yet, no sensible person could have anticipated the major boom in the growth of cities across the Atlantic. And it was certainly not a consensus that urbanization was even desirable.

Despite works like Mercier's *The Year 2440*, cities did not yet dominate visions for the future. The idea of self-sufficient agrarian

communities animated various protosocialist utopias and group experiments, from the nonconforming Diggers in seventeenth-century
England to the egalitarian Gracchus Babeuf in 1790s France.[3] The revolutionary French Republican Calendar celebrated symbols from rural
life, elevating the countryside in a political project that emanated out of
urban settings. Nonurban communities and societies persisted in parts
of all inhabited continents. And followers of the economic theories of
eighteenth-century physiocrats believed a nation's wealth derived from
agricultural production.[4]

An urban versus rural dichotomy, in fact, can be misleading. From
Eurocentric early-modern perspectives, civilizing implied settling land,
which in turn required legible forms of spatial regularity and temporal
stability—whether in the city or countryside. In this vision of civilization, nomadism harked back to the primitive stages of humankind. Nomadic and seminomadic societies tended to rely on more fluctuating
relationships to the land based on usufruct rights and seasonal cycles.
They posed a threat to modern models of citizenship and state-building.
In lettered cultures, nomads belonged in the past. This was a broader
consensus than sympathy for urbanization or even colonization, both
of which sometimes came under attack as antithetical to civilization and
moral progress.[5] Given their interdependence and sedentariness, we
could group urban and rural together in a continuum, with nomadism
at the other end of the spectrum. During this period, fixity versus flux
might be the more salient opposition for the invention of the future.

Urban growth can at least in part be attributed to changes in the
countryside. Great Britain was at the forefront of implementing modern
land management regimes, which would ultimately tie together the fortune of cities and territories across the world. A series of enclosure acts
sought to organize the countryside under more fixed relationships. The
Act of 1773 intensified the imposition of exclusive land rights over traditional open-field systems.[6] Mobile practices like common grazing and
open-field crop rotation lost out. Similarly, land ordinances in the
United States sought to determine allowable uses and ownership rights
(potentially in perpetuity) over vast territories that had been crucial to
the livelihoods of nomadic or seminomadic indigenous peoples. In the

Portuguese Americas, forcing mobile natives into settlements became a way of rendering them as vassals of the Crown, part of a strategy to secure sovereignty of disputed hinterlands.[7] And the French state, as part of scientific approaches to forest management, enacted policies to sedentarize traditional pastoral groups in Europe and North Africa.[8] The impetus to discipline and control itinerance, often with violence, became a hallmark of modernization.

The shift toward spatial fixity enmeshed cities, towns, and rural settlements in interrelated transatlantic systems. It also proved to be disruptive. In Great Britain, enclosures led to higher agricultural productivity and more trade, while displacing peasants who lost access to land. Urban population grew with internal migration from the countryside, especially London. Like Lisbon, the British capital benefited from having both a court and a port.[9] A series of unrivaled enclosed docks built in the early 1800s set it up for bustling trade at an unprecedented scale. Other developments helped: in exchange for support during the Napoleonic wars, Portugal opened Brazilian ports for trade with "friendly nations" in 1808, to the great advantage of the English economy. London played an outsized role in national life and was at the fulcrum of transatlantic markets.[10] It became the first European city since Ancient Rome to have more than a million inhabitants. In the Atlantic world, only Paris also passed the half a million mark at the time. By the late 1820s, London was the largest city in the world and arguably in history, remaining so until New York surpassed it a century later.

Perhaps because it leapt ahead earlier, London's culture reflected unease with the nature of progress. In hindsight, the metaphor of leaping evokes the qualitative and quantitative changes under way. The experience at the time, however, could feel more like a march, and some people asked questions about where this was all going. In satirical engravings during the 1820s, the British artist William Heath would mock "over-sophisticated" technologies and "intellectual pursuits" that overlooked "basic needs." In his futuristic vision, we have multimodal streets with raised sidewalks segregating speeds. A well-dressed man driving a carriage reads *The Times*. In the 1810s, this London newspaper pioneered the steam-powered rotary press, leading to much higher circulations.

FIGURE 2.1. "A futuristic vision" teeming with inventions: sped up or stuck, rich and poor, all caught up in the mix.

All four readers in Heath's scene seem oblivious to the action around them, which includes a child falling on the road, raggedy street performers, and soot-faced chimney sweepers. Meanwhile, two extravagantly dressed women peer into a modern shop window with comically large hats. The future was not evenly distributed.

From an economic perspective, London exemplified the advantages of agglomeration effects and innovations spurring productivity. In Heath's humorous depiction, the intermingling activities and proliferating inventions promised a future where class inequalities and chaos would rule the streets. New technologies served futile or destructive ends. A contraption moves people to the top floor of a building. Up above, a balloon-ship engages in battle. Other vehicles are propelled by birds, kites, and steam engines. The background gestures toward infrastructures at larger scales and geopolitics: a bridge connects Dover in England to Calais in France, and a balloon hovers with an early flag for the fledgling United States. Another futuristic etching was titled "March of Intellect," a recurrent phrase to celebrate or criticize progress. Here, Heath made the connection to colonization, and even more forcefully ridiculed new technologies at the service of rapid transit, showing a pneumatic "grand vacuum tube" with direct service to Bengal. If anyone might doubt whether they were supposed to admire or fear these visions, at the top a caption drips with sarcasm: "Lord how this world improves as we get older." Amid prescient themes, there was a conspicuous absence, to which we will return: the railroad.

As England urbanized, manufacturing innovations sometimes happened outside of cities because of resistance from guilds.[11] City and country continued to evolve interdependently, amid intensifying circulation of goods, peoples, and ideas. But urban economies had more options, as emerging transatlantic networks connected them to far-flung places. Enslaved labor in cotton plantations in the Americas, for example, helped to fuel gains in textile production in England, bolstering the rise of Liverpool as a major port and urban center. These economic linkages did not necessarily find correspondences in the cultural and political realms. It might be tempting to frame an urban and rural divide along familiar lines: cities as progressive, the countryside as

FIGURE 2.2. A satire of "rapid transport" with connections between London and Bengal, New South Wales, Cape Town, and Bath, but missing the actual next big thing: trains!

conservative. Already in the French Revolution, after all, Paris was a hot-bed of leftist politics, against the more religious and reactionary rural France. Similarly, urban abolitionists took on the slaveholding plantation class. But there are too many connections and contradictions for such generalizations to work. Nonetheless, although people from across a wide political spectrum vied for the superiority of agrarian life, cities began to dominate imaginations of the future as radically different from the past.

Cities, even when conceived as part of a civilizing project of fixity, became sites of flux: places where people could go to become someone else and invent new futures. Mass migration and technological innova-tions acted as destabilizing forces. The revolution in the production of textiles, for example, helped to upset a social order where clothing signi-fied station. Cheapened and more accessible items would make it harder for nobles to differentiate themselves. To be sure, the range of possibili-ties opened by urbanization was framed by variables like age, class, gen-der, race, and ethnicity. New mechanisms for distinction also emerged, as bourgeois classes and aristocracies competed or colluded. Urban planning, in tandem with policies targeting nomadic practices, gener-ally prioritized order, control, and spatial hierarchies. And yet, when compared to rural settings, nineteenth-century cities blossomed as sites of change, transience, and indetermination, when not insubordination or insurrection.

The interplay of fixity and flux shaped cities as both lived and imagined spaces. The precise contours varied enormously from place to place. In gold-rich Minas Gerais in Brazil, wealthy, slaveowning urbanites wrote neoclassical Arcadian poetry where they imagined themselves as shep-herds in bucolic Europeanized settings. That placed them squarely within a transatlantic literary community with fixed aesthetic conventions. Out-side of verse, however, escaping urbanity could lead to contact with real and imaginary threats, like maroon communities, thieves, or bellicose natives. Some of these eighteenth-century poets tapped into the epic genre to address local colonization, producing foundational narratives of nomadic tribes and wilderness subjugated by civilizing urban forces, which *they* represented. Bucolic ideals coexisted with a sense that outside of cities, civilization was at peril. From this perspective, rather than agri-cultural or pastoral landscapes, it was the unstable savagery of frontiers and hinterlands that constituted *the other* of urbanity. In much of the Spanish Americas, quite differently, colonization contended with indigenous urban civilizations, creating a set of *mestizo* dynamics.

Authoritarian civilizing projects never proceeded without backlash and dissidence. Those deemed uncivilized often resisted. And if to civilize was to settle, this did not necessarily translate into favoring cities. The historian Thomas Bender argues that, in the United States, the idea of an agrarian republic "transformed what was originally a literary convention," the pastoral, "into a political theory."[12] To people like Thomas Jefferson, the countryside rather than the city provided models of good citizenship. Pastoral here could still imply movement and westward expansion. But it replaced nomadism with a fixed relationship to land through ownership and cultivation, as befit civilization. In the meantime, antiurban sentiments abounded, especially in anglophone lettered cultures. William Blake's "London" found in "every face [. . .] / Marks of weakness, marks of woe." In the United States, comparable recriminations could be listed indefinitely.[13]

There were also those that equated cities to civilization but did not mean it as a compliment. Rousseau remained widely read and influential throughout the Atlantic world. In *Emile*, he had come close to exalting nomadism as a model, arguing that "the savage" is sharper, more alert, and better fit because "he is tied to no one place, he has no prescribed task, no superior to obey, [. . .] he is therefore forced to reason at every step he takes." Here, however, Rousseau left room for ambivalence. Savages are "cruel." His real target, after all, was the "civilized life" of cities, with people in denial about their own forms of cruelty. Moved by self-interest, Rousseau's urbanites "devour" each other: "This is why we all flock to Rome, Paris, and London," he wrote, because "human flesh and blood are always cheapest in the capital cities."[14] Those that stood in the way of violent agrarian expansion would beg to differ.

———

After the thirteen US colonies obtained independence (1776–1783), the new republic expanded its boundaries at a rapid pace and rose above hemispheric neighbors as a geopolitical power.[15] This divergence would probably not have been the safe bet. In early modernity, Spanish vice-royalties in present-day Mexico and Peru occupied the most prominent place in lettered imaginations of the New World. Maps certainly showed South America as more integrated into "enlightened" knowledge systems than North America, with much of its Western lands still uncharted by colonizers. The Aztec and Andean urban civilizations generated great interest, and these regions had ample supplies of silver and other resources. In the early 1700s, the Portuguese Americas experienced their own mining boom. It would have been reasonable to predict Brazil as the future American superpower. A less Eurocentric transatlantic order was also possible. The Haitian Revolution, as Vincent Brown put it, "threatened a remapping of colonial America and African territory."[16] Plausible scenarios at the outset of the nineteenth century began to seem more far-fetched over time, and historical developments eventually gained an air of inevitability.

Prognosis became an important political tool. Koselleck writes that "apocalyptic prophecy destroys time through its fixation on the End," whereas "prognosis produces time."[17] Leading US intellectuals and politicians had an acute sense of how setting up expectations could help to shape their status in hemispheric affairs. During the war for independence, for example, Benjamin Franklin suggested to antislavery European audiences that emancipation was right around the corner, should victory be obtained.[18] Thomas Jefferson mastered the genre. In 1816, the prominent French writer Madame de Staël wrote to him that "if you should succeed in destroying slavery in the south there would be at least one government in the world as perfect as the human mind can conceive."[19] Jefferson ignored this entreaty but replied to an inquiry about the future of South America. Staël supported Spanish American independence movements.

In her letter, Staël expressed admiration for Jefferson's "splendid prophecy" of Napoleon's "overthrow [. . .] by the spirit of liberty." Jefferson's record as a prognosticator conferred him authority, which she couched in the language of religion, as if he were a prophet for a secular age, reliant on rational calculation rather than faith. To paint a picture of Europe's declining fortunes, amid a return of "old despotism" and "superstitions," Staël resorted to an example from medieval Portugal: "Thus Dom Pedro of Portugal has had Inez de Castro exhumed, to crown her after her death." This was likely a legend. Despite the Pombaline reforms, the trope of an obscurantist Portugal lived on. Jefferson's response focused on the future of the hemisphere and evinced his young nation's confidence. In a scribbled map in the letter's margin, he foretold the split of the Spanish Americas into different states after independence. Jefferson's predictions played into her expectations, while also implying that the United States was a hemispheric leader and the future of liberty. He offered that "all will end in military despotism under the Bonaparte of their region," because "the whole southern continent is sunk in the deepest ignorance and bigotry." South Americans, Jefferson allowed, might eventually "go on advancing toward the lights of cultivated reason."

In a letter from 1820 to Correia da Serra, a prominent Portuguese natural scientist, Jefferson adapted his vision to the recipient's own expectations. He wrote that "nothing is so important as that America shall separate herself from the systems of Europe & establish one of her own," and suggested that the United States could lead a new hemispheric order with an American Portugal.[20] The Portuguese court had moved to Rio de Janeiro in 1808, fleeing the Napoleonic Wars. What he probably really wished for was conveyed in a letter to James Monroe, in 1822: "to see no emperors or kings in our hemisphere and that Brazil as well as Mexico will homologize with us."[21]

Racism played a role in the setting of expectations. As president, Jefferson had proven himself a skillful player in geopolitical strategizing. With the Louisiana Purchase (1803), he executed an ambitious move, nearly doubling the country's territory. US negotiators had the French fears of another Haitian Revolution on their side. Koselleck describes modern political prognostication as structured around a "potential repeatability," where a prediction "implies a diagnosis which introduces the past into the future."[22] Indeed, the prospect of a repeat of the uprising in Haiti continued to haunt colonizers and served as a political cudgel well after the country declared independence in 1804. The United States imposed a trade embargo and refused to recognize the new country until 1862. In Eurocentric diplomatic gamesmanship, the agency of enslaved Africans and their liberated descendants was mostly only legible as a threat. They had no right to the future. Black people, however, increasingly shaped cities throughout the Atlantic, including New Orleans, part of the Louisiana Purchase and essential for control of the Mississippi River.[23]

Urbanization, as a process that essentially escaped the control of grand strategists, defied political prognostication. In cities, changes began to happen so rapidly and unexpectedly that you could not infer the future based on past experience. But let us not put the cart before the horse—or the car before the cart.

———

Jefferson's belief that the United States would lead a hemispheric union in the Americas anticipated manifest destiny. In a letter from 1816 to another former president, John Adams, Jefferson decried "Old Europe" and boldly speculated: "what a Colossus shall we be when the Southern continent comes up to our mark!"[24] This is a far cry from the interventionism of his successors, but like them, Jefferson took for granted that the United States was ahead of the curve and should be emulated. He then summed up what we might consider a very modern political philosophy: "I like the dreams of the future better than the history of the past." The United States became positioned as the land of the future from Eurocentric perspectives. But this was not entirely new either.

When the pilgrims left England to escape what they viewed as a corrupt society, it was also a forward-looking break from the past. John Winthrop, first governor of the Massachusetts Bay Colony, sermonized in 1630 that "we shall be as a city upon a hill." The pronoun, nouns, and preposition have garnered more attention, but the verb tense is just as significant. Winthrop's image was metaphoric, and drew on the Sermon on the Mount, when according to the Bible Jesus told his disciples that "a city that is set on a hill cannot be hid." The point was that Christians must serve as examples. Neither the biblical Jesus nor Winthrop meant to evoke an urban community in any modern sense. The Puritan, however, explicitly pointed ahead toward a new society to be made in a New World. He played into a trope of the Americas as a place onto which Europeans could project better futures. This evolved into an ethos, particularly in the United States. One historian refers to the period of Andrew Jackson, president from 1829 to 1837, as being marked by promise and "the spirit of improvement."[25] By 1837, the Bohemian-born Francis Grund would write that "the Americans *love* their country, not, indeed, *as it is*, but *as it will be*." That spirit is to him what set the people of the country apart: "They live in the future, and *make* their country as they go on."[26]

But who makes this future, and belongs in it? What does it look like? It was clear whose aspirations mattered in Jackson's or Grund's worldview: "The Americans have fought for, and acquired their liberty: they have given it *gratis* to their negroes."[27] Grund described African Americans as lacking "a love of freedom" or care for "the fate of their brethren."[28] In this, he echoed the sentiments of many prominent white Americans, including Thomas Jefferson.[29] Attitudes about the humanity and rights of Africans and African Americans thus became a key factor in competing visions for the future. Racism often overlapped with contempt for cities. The latter tended to be more tempered. Though often carrying bigoted undertones, perceptions of cities as morally corrupt are as old as urbanization itself. In the United States, however, urban bashing from people in high places has been practically a national sport. The vice president and soon-to-be president-elect Thomas Jefferson, in a letter to Benjamin Rush from 1800, speculated that "some good" may come out of yellow fever epidemics, as they "will discourage the growth of great cities in our nation." He deemed great cities to be "pestilential to the morals, the health and the liberties of man."[30]

Jefferson was certainly not alone in his antiurban opinions, but he was not voicing a consensus either. His rivals in the Federalist Party, with a stronghold in the Northeast, had a much more sympathetic view of urbanization and industrial development. They vied for a commercial rather than an agrarian nation. These disagreements, however, tended to center on the role of government, slavery, or fiscal policy. Urban planning was not really an important topic. Nor yet was the future imagined as looking radically different from the past. If we had to discern a shape to the desired United States that could appeal across political divides, once again the grid stands out. The Eurocentric correspondence between geometric and moral rectitude also found fertile ground in the young republic. In a letter from 1782 to the Scottish scientist James Hutton, Benjamin Franklin lamented bloodshed in the frontiers between farmers and Indians. Just a few months before the American revolutionary war ended, with biblical overtones, Franklin wrote that he was "convinced of a future State" where "all that here appears to be wrong shall be set right, all that is crooked made straight."[31]

The metaphor gained a material dimension as the United States leapt ahead. The grid, as we have noted, is probably the most recurring form in urban history. It has also been used widely in agrarian settlements.[32] But the United States adopted the grid at unprecedented scales. The Land Ordinance of 1785 standardized the surveying, organizing, and selling of territories to the west of the Appalachian Mountains. It divided land into grids of 6-square-mile townships, subdivided into 1-square-mile sections that land companies could then sell to settlers or investors. Each township had four lots set aside for future sale, and one for public schools. In 1787, under Jefferson's influence, the Northwest Ordinance proposed the creation of new states with rectilinear boundaries, echoing an earlier idea of the Continental Congress. As the country expanded toward the Pacific, the principle largely prevailed. This contrasts with precedents from South America. The 1494 Treaty of Tordesillas split the overseas claims of the Kingdoms of Castille and Portugal with a longitudinal line cutting through South America, a continent still unknown to them. Lands to the east would belong to Portugal. In the 1530s, the borders of captaincies in present-day Brazil were drawn as straight lines parallel to the Equator, from the Tordesillas line to the Atlantic. Over time, however, those gave place to modern boundaries that follow natural features or result from local negotiations.[33] In North America, the straight line ruled. Something similar would occur in European colonization of Africa in the late nineteenth century.

Land ordinances gave the US federal government the means to raise revenue and administer settlements, including the establishment of future navigation and transportation routes. It fixed land ownership rights and boundaries. Indigenous peoples actually inhabited these territories, as well as those purchased from Napoleonic France. In practice, what the US government acquired and sold was the right to preempt or dispossess societies that in many cases lived nomadically or seminomadically. The grid became a tool to impose a rationalized order on colonial expansion, just as it had been elsewhere in the Americas. We can see it as a deadly weapon in the modern war on flux. It is also commonly interpreted as "a blueprint for an egalitarian republic," laying the groundwork for a "post-feudal West" where commodified land is traded easily, avoiding concentration in the hands of a few.[34] The futures that this invention engendered, of course, would present new forms of inequality. The architectural historian Spiro Kostof wrote that with the ordinances "what matters in the long run [. . .] is the luck of first ownership."[35] That was not the only kind of luck. This was still a republic largely premised on restricting rights to white males.

Grids had spatial and temporal implications. From the perspective of surveying and parceling, they provided the most clear-cut and efficient model. Straight lines could also be perceived as more stable and permanent. Flux was not just a problem posed by nomadic peoples, but by ecosystems as well. Rivers, for example, also move around. Rectilinear and standardized patterns facilitated the operations of a centralized state predicated on static boundaries. They helped to unleash the creative and destructive potentials of capitalism. Territories brought under modern systems of organization generally lost in biological and cultural diversity, becoming more homogenous and fungible. But that should not be seen as inherent to the spatial forms. In urban settings, grids proved to be versatile and adaptable.

By the early 1800s, a variety of grid systems could be found throughout the United States, including in the port cities of New Orleans, Savannah, Baltimore, Philadelphia, and Charleston. In some places, like Mobile and St. Louis, orthogonal layouts meant to accommodate expansion. In others, like New Haven and Annapolis, they sought to control it.[36] William Penn's seventeenth-century grid for Philadelphia was the earliest, and perhaps the most comprehensive and ambitious of the colonial period. His instructions from 1681 called for detached houses surrounded by gardens, orchards, or fields, so that Philadelphia "may be a green country town, which will never be burnt, and always be wholesome." The justification brings together a pragmatic solution to the problem of fire, and a moralizing suggestion of density as a corrupting influence. Boston, made up of crowded and winding streets, had quickly become the largest town in the Thirteen Colonies after the arrival of Winthrop and the pilgrims. Philadelphia surpassed it in the mid-1700s. Contrary to Penn's intentions, people subdivided the large green plots, adding narrow alleys and row houses.

As urban historian Dell Upton writes, Penn's plan envisioned a "closed hierarchical community." Upton argues that in the independent United States the grid underwent a revival as part of an "intellectual program for the subordination of landscape to republican life," where "all spaces, all locations must be potentially equal."[37] Agrarian expansion loomed larger, and it took some time for urban planning to catch up. The young republic's most ambitious urban project was the construction of the new capital city of Washington. As with Pombal and the Portuguese planners behind Lisbon's rebuilding, US political leadership understood capital cities as a component of nation-building. But they disagreed about what the city should be like, just like they could not agree about the nation itself. Federalists wanted a grand capital worthy of the nation's ambitions. Secretary of State Thomas Jefferson, opposed to a strong central government as well as great cities, preferred a more modest plan. Washington's location, in a swampy site by the Potomac River, resulted from a compromise between northern and southern states. Its layout resulted from a compromise between a regular grid, which Jefferson pushed for, and a more monumental plan with the addition of diagonals, designed by Pierre Charles L'Enfant.

L'Enfant was a Paris-born military engineer, and had served in the American revolutionary war. In 1789, writing to his friend George Washington, he promised a plan that would match the expectations of "any period however remote."[38] His pitch to the president was oriented toward the future, but assumed that values and tastes would remain static. L'Enfant set off to materialize national ideals in the urban fabric,

L'Enfant was dismissed in 1792. Andrew Ellicott, a land surveyor, revised the plan but kept the basic design. Visiting in 1842, Charles Dickens dubbed Washington a "City of Magnificent Intentions," where "spacious avenues [. . .] begin in nothing and lead nowhere."[45] Alexis de Tocqueville jokingly noted "rooted up trees for 10 miles around, lest they should get in the way of future citizens."[46] Never mind that this was probably to dry up the swamps and prevent malaria. The Frenchman was obviously incredulous about the city's future growth. In 1850, it had a population of around 52,000. L'Enfant's promises remained largely unfulfilled until the twentieth century, when a commission revisited his plans. Eventually, Washington would develop into the hub of a metropolitan area with over 6 million inhabitants, well beyond the wildest dreams of L'Enfant or any of his contemporaries. But the planned capital was not the turning point that made the United States so central to the invention of urban futures. That came with another plan that had less bold intentions and proved to be more fitting for emerging new worlds.

II. Outside the Grid

Ancient Mesopotamia, Egypt, Greece, Rome, Mexico, Inca, Tokugawa Japan, and China all had urban grids with clearly discernible hierarchies embedded in the layout. This might be manifested through a centrally located palace, place of worship, or state building. As we have discussed, gridded cities also proliferated in the Americas and became signs of a New World, but their plans followed that familiar logic. The 1811 Commissioners' Plan for Manhattan quietly broke from this long history.

New York City initially developed into a network of winding streets on the southern tip of Manhattan, previously inhabited by the seminomadic Lenape. The early nineteenth-century city could only expand north. In 1807, the New York state legislature appointed a three-person commission to devise a plan. They laid out a grid starting at the northern edges of the existing city, covering the island with around 2,000 rectangular blocks all the way to 155th Street. The longest avenue planned for Lisbon's Baixa had a length of about half a mile. The Champs-Élysées in Paris was extended in the 1770s to 1.19 miles.

L'Enfant's longest diagonal was to be around 4.5 miles. The Commissioners' Plan imagined new avenues as long as 8 miles. It looked forward with greater freedom from precedents, beyond the daunting scale. The plan did not establish a detailed program besides a commitment to growth and openness to change. In that way, the Manhattan grid resembled the 1785 land ordinance more than previous city plans.

As with Lisbon, practicality was in, grand ornamentation was out. But this goes much further. In their laconic report, the commissioners rejected "supposed improvements" that might "embellish" a city, preferring instead the "convenience and utility" of a regular grid, because "straight-sided and right-angled houses are the most cheap to build and the most convenient to live in."[47] A large square, equivalent to about forty blocks, was dedicated to military exercises. Another, a bit larger than twelve blocks, would host a public market. The plan determined the location of these spaces based on considerations like cost. The plan did not set aside significant green spaces for "fresh air," the reasoning went, because the rivers already served that function. Instead, it suggested accommodations for a large reservoir to provide fresh water.

The commissioners raised the possibility that the reservoir might one day host an observatory, "consecrated to the purposes of science." Religious references in the plan were indirect, and in passing: a mention of the Harlem Church as a geographic marker, and the dating at the bottom of the report, "in the year of our Lord." A verb to describe making spaces sacred was used here toward a secular purpose. We should not assume any grand intentions, but in light of the role that some modernist planners ascribed to themselves a century or so later, it is striking that the language implicitly placed the authors in a kind of sacerdotal, God-like role. In fact, the Commissioners' Plan was even more radical than Lisbon in effacing the urban tradition of centering religion. Scholars tend to underestimate this aspect of the plan. Maybe we take it for granted in a city associated with tolerance of religious diversity, or find the shift unremarkable in comparison to later modern planning. But when viewed against known grid precedents, Manhattan's stood out for ignoring the divine. We no longer seem to be in a world where an

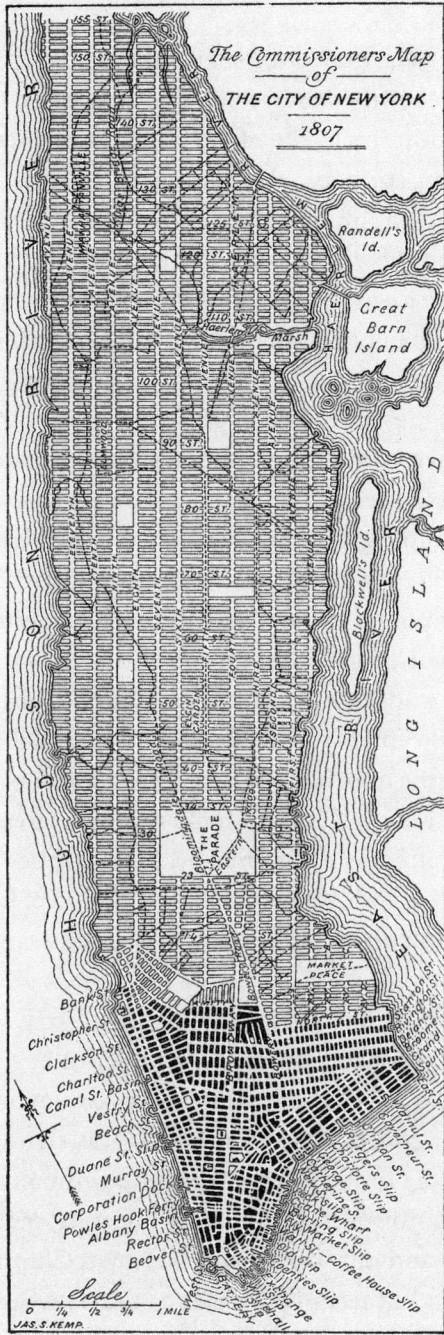

FIGURE 2.4. Like the borders between US states, Manhattan's layout would progress toward rectilinearity.

omnipotent God determined the shape of the future, or where the spatial organization of cities manifested religious truths.

Many contemporaries would of course disagree with those premises. Also in 1811, a prophetic pamphlet by Nimrod Hughes, a Virginian from the Appalachian Mountains, claimed that one-third of humankind would perish the following year, "as foretold in the Scriptures." There was no inquisition to go after Hughes, but newspapers bashed him as a false prophet. The pamphlet became a best-seller. That same year, riding the wave, Nicodemus Havens imagined New York City struck by an earthquake and a "devouring tide," provoked by God's ire. Lower Manhattan was destroyed: "[Urban] fabrics which had stood the test of ages, were no longer to be seen." We can surmise that this was not yet a city teeming with confidence. In the prophecy, having learned their lesson, Manhattan's survivors heeded God's warning and built more than 19,000 "places of public worship in the short space of three weeks."[48] The impact was worldwide. London and Paris nearly vanished. The historian Max Page reads this as the beginnings of recurring tropes: New York as a global epicenter, "the necessary place that will illustrate a larger apocalypse." And the hopeful note that "disaster is a necessary precondition for the city's renewal."[49] Nicodemus Havens, presumably a pseudonym, self-identified as a shoemaker. His prophecy of Manhattan rebuilt in tribute to God also suggested a disconnect between the aspirations of elitist planners, and those of at least some sectors of the broader population.[50]

The three commissioners were all older than sixty, with long careers in public life.[51] None had substantial experience in engineering or architecture. Simeon De Witt came closest, as surveyor general of New York state. Washington had recommended him as a top surveyor to Jefferson, but he was not involved in the land ordinances. De Witt had adopted the grid, however, throughout the state, including for street layouts in Albany and Ithaca. His cousin DeWitt Clinton was New York City's mayor. John Rutherfurd, the Manhattan native of the group, lived in the city for only three years as an adult. He worked as a lawyer. Rutherfurd was an heir to a wealthy family and amassed enough property to become the largest landowner in New Jersey, where he spent most of his time on an estate. As a Federalist, he served as New Jersey's senator from 1791 to 1798. Rutherfurd was an ally of the most prominent commissioner, Gouverneur Morris. Likewise hailing from a powerful landowning family, Morris wrote the preamble to the US Constitution. He had also been a Federalist in the US Senate, serving as New York state's representative between 1800 and 1803.

Generally, planning for national capitals brought added scrutiny. In New York, the commission was given considerable autonomy to design a plan "most conducive to public good," within four years.[52] They seemed to prioritize getting the job done and relied on previous proposals. Their plan detailed the form of the street layouts but had very little to say about what would go where. Where would buildings with specialized functions go? What would the city look like? Maybe the absence of answers came from the fact that none of them had a background in engineering or design-oriented fields. The result, to the historian and theorist Manfredo Tafuri, is that "urban planning and architecture are finally separated."[53]

Planning for Lisbon's reconstruction had involved the design and regulation of façades and construction methods. The commissioners, in contrast, provided no outline for the city's architectural style. Tafuri attributes this novelty to the "geometric character" of American plans. Because planning did not seek "an architectural correspondence," design becomes "free to explore the most diverse expressions."[54] That is not quite as true in his other two examples, Penn's Philadelphia and L'Enfant's Washington. Both had plans prescribing or suggesting buildings of a certain type, and grids that attempted to imbue specific sites with greater value. Anyone looking at these plans could guess where the most important buildings would go. And those buildings were expected to conform to Eurocentric architectural traditions. The Commissioners' Plan, however, neglected to predetermine a spatial hierarchy. As a result, if you ask people where they think New York's heart or center is located, you will get a lot less agreement than in most other cities. It is an unusually polycentric place. The commissioners naturally assumed that buildings of two or three floors would end up filling the grid. Though it was not their intention, the attempt to neutralize differences between sites paradoxically created a grid with unusual flexibility to accommodate a variety of developments and expressions—including, eventually, the vertical grid of skyscrapers.

In his *Delirious New York*, the architect Rem Koolhaas calls the Commissioners' Plan "the most courageous act of prediction in Western civilization."[55] The planners themselves were not aiming quite that high. There was no calendar or budget attached to the grid. Their report speculated that within fifty years New York's buildings might extend to around 34th Street, with the population reaching 400,000. It was deemed "improbable" that north of Harlem could be built up with houses "for centuries to come." Morris only imagined a bridge over the Harlem River as viable.[56] The report conceded that "it may be a subject of merriment that the Commissioners have provided space for a greater population than is collected at any spot on this side of China." By 1860, around 813,000 people lived in Manhattan, which already had clusters of buildings spread throughout its grid. A century after the plan, with over 2.3 million, Manhattan's population was comparable to Beijing's. Harlem was one of its densest neighborhoods. By then, New York City had consolidated into five interconnected boroughs totaling nearly 4.8 million residents and was on its way to surpass London as the world's largest urban center. If anything, the commissioners' predictions vastly undershot.

Two of the planners were in fact partly responsible for New York's rapid ascent. In 1810, the New York state legislature appointed Simeon De Witt and Morris to a commission for building the Erie Canal. Morris chaired it. In 1825, DeWitt Clinton, then governor of New York, marked the canal's inauguration by pouring water from Lake Erie on the ocean. A 363-mile waterway now connected the Great Lakes to New York City, giving its port an insurmountable comparative advantage. The new infrastructure, in a sense, also extended the Atlantic inland. It brought upstate New York and the Midwest closer to the transatlantic orbit, which was consequential to the whole region's urbanization. But nowhere would the impact be felt more than in Manhattan.

New York City's harbor had a lot going for it. Less prone to freezing than more northern or riverine ports, it also had depth, proximity to the ocean, and a connection to the navigable Hudson River. New York was also relatively central on the Eastern seaboard. Access to the Great Lakes ensured its dominance. The city's ports benefited from larger ships, which more than doubled the average weight of cargo carried between the 1830s and the 1860s. It made more sense to centralize operations in a single place. During the same period, the number of vessel arrivals just about doubled. Cargo was delivered from throughout the country to be shipped abroad, and from abroad to be distributed to other states.[57]

New York's role as a trade and transportation hub helped its manufacturing to boom. Major industries all relied on location. Sugar from the West Indies was refined and sold domestically or exported. The latest novels from Europe landed first in New York, giving its publishers a head start in commercializing them, before copyright laws regulated the literary market. And garment production, the biggest employer, innovatively turned incoming textiles into ready-to-wear clothing for local and national markets, including slave plantations in the southern states. It is a classic case of agglomeration and scale economies, illustrating "the tendency of people to attract more people."[58] The New York area also became an immigration center, especially in the second half of the century. In 1860, Manhattan had nearly a quarter million more inhabitants than Philadelphia's 565,000. Brooklyn, at nearly 260,000 people, became the third largest city in the United States, with a population that surpassed all other cities in the Americas, ahead of Rio de Janeiro and Mexico City.

One of the main proponents of earlier gridded plans for Manhattan, the French architect and surveyor Joseph François Mangin, predicted in 1796 that New York appeared "to be designed as the future center and metropolis of the commercial world," due to its location at the mouth of two rivers, with access to the Atlantic.[59] We can interpret this as yet another instance of prognostication as a self-promotion strategy. Mangin had settled in Manhattan after fleeing the Haitian Revolution. He was pitching the municipal Common Council on a plan to develop the area around the Collect Pond (in present-day Chinatown), by connecting it to the harbor through canals. This proposal did not go forward, but his later work influenced the Commissioners' Plan. Mangin's prescience about New York's role as a trade center affirms the notion that geography is destiny, at least in part. And he certainly did not foresee the Erie Canal, which only sped up and intensified the city's spectacular growth.

The planned grid was probably not a direct factor in New York's rise, but gave it shape. Opinions on the work of the commissioners have remained sharply divided. James Kent, an esteemed jurist, wrote in 1836 that the plan "laid out the highways on the island upon so magnificent a scale, and with so bold a hand, and with such prophetic views, in respect to the future growth and extension of the city, that it will form an everlasting monument to the stability and wisdom of the measure."[60] Yet, in the decades following the statement, it became common to raze and rebuild the fabric of Manhattan, in pursuit of greater profits, and in accordance with the latest styles. We have to wonder whether Kent would still speak of stability. Nearly a century after the plan's publication, the influential critic Montgomery Schuyler attacked the commissioners as "public malefactors of high degree" in the pages of the *Architecture Record*.[61] A defender of modern architecture, he thought the planners "incapable of taking thought for the morrow, [. . .] of imagining what a city was like." Schuyler lamented the lack of an "unquestionable center" to the city and argued that adding two diagonal avenues from 14th to 59th Street could help to give it some "dignity and stateliness." These are qualities he found in Washington, which had been planned "with an eye to beauty as well as to convenience."

It is incontrovertible that Manhattan was planned with more of an eye to profit and convenience than to beauty. But beauty is of course in the eye of the beholder, and the commissioners probably had aspirations that their report did not make explicit. In 1816, Morris gave a speech to the New York Historical Society casting himself in a prophetic role, and the city as an imperial beacon. And De Witt, aligned with his early modern European predecessors, published a book on how rectilinear designs could have "a wholesome influence on [. . .] morality and happiness."[62] Instead of the crooked traditional cities of "idleness and dissipation," the grid would discipline urbanites with the virtues of Cartesian rationality and calculability, leading to "frugality, temperance and economy."[63] Ultimately, the choices of planners reflected contemporary ideas and left a lasting mark beyond anyone's imagination, even as wayward urbanites or the vagaries of history subverted their intentions.

Scholars like Spiro Kostof and Peter Marcuse have interpreted grid systems as either closed or open. The first are bounded by firm limits like walls or greenbelts, with a "definite design."[64] The second are geared toward "expansion and reduplication," typical of capitalist economies.[65] We can also draw out temporal differences. Closed grids assume the future is stable and constant, while open ones embrace the possibility of change, and leave a lot to chance. They can also set the city up for rampant real estate speculation. New York's grid clearly fit the open category. It has long been identified with burgeoning capitalism. Tafuri suggests that the fact that plans did not dictate the forms of buildings created conditions for an "ethic of free trade" alongside "the pioneering spirit."[66] We might also recall the critique proposed by the sociologist Richard Sennett. As the land ordinances had begun to do in the frontiers, the homogenizing Manhattan grid tried "to deny that complexity and difference existed in the environment."[67]

Sennett associates the grid's neutralizing efforts to Max Weber's argument about a Protestant ethic, the "rational" organization of society, and the spirit of capitalism. Part of the idea is that competing for wealth became an expression of self-worth, whereas pleasure could signal vice. Sennett writes that the Puritans strived "to deny the present so as to be deserving of the future; to compete ruthlessly against others so as to prove one's worth; [. . .] to live in a *state of endless becoming*."[68] Protestants, after all, remained unsure of whether they would be saved or not. To Weber, these traits survived outside the religion. They can help to explain why the wealthiest competed for capital accumulation beyond the capacity for enjoyment.

New York City's real estate became a machine for profit. By standardizing lot sizes and neglecting to assign greater value to particular places, the Commissioners' Plan facilitated investment and speculation. Mumford thought that laissez-faire ideologies were also about freedom from town planning and urban regulations.[69] Manhattan's grid catalyzed a broader spirit of the times. In France, the July Revolution of 1830 led to the end of the Bourbon restoration and a constitutional monarchy under the more liberal Louis-Philippe I. His administration introduced strict demands on the vote based on tax payments and favored the bourgeois classes. Their response to those dissatisfied could be a slogan for the times: *enrichissez-vous,* enrich yourselves. Surely, the Commissioners' Plan produced an open grid. But open for who? Definitely for those with capital.

New York's evolution, however, did not proceed in a neat and straight line. A Lenape walking trail intersected the gridded plan, in what became known as Broadway Avenue. Some owners of farmland, unable to foresee how much money they stood to make from urbanization, greeted surveyors by throwing cabbages at them. Others managed to control the uses of properties, and their family names survived in the neighborhoods of Kips Bay and Murray Hill, outlasting the actual geographic features. Real estate interests added Lexington and Madison Avenues to the original plan. The commissioners dedicated only about 5 percent of the grid to public squares, over half of which was taken up by the Parade Ground. By 1815, this space was cut down to a third of the planned size, before being eliminated in 1829. The space allotted to the public market was similarly reduced. In the late 1850s, as we will see in the next chapter, Central Park became a corrective and a site for other visions.

Investors and speculators did not always have their way. John Jacob Astor, a migrant from Walldorf, in present-day Germany, started to buy up land in New York, after making a fortune in the fur trade. In 1819, he tried to influence street layouts, but a more assertive city government pushed back.[70] Amid an emergent bourgeois and political class, there was a loosening grip of aristocratic landowners on power, and on the city's fortunes. Astor, unlike Morris and Rutherfurd, bought his lands rather than inherit them. By the 1840s, he was the richest man in the United States, and perhaps the first modern real estate mogul.[71] He was also, for what it is worth, a Protestant. His name and legacy lived on in Gilded Age monuments like the Waldorf-Astoria Hotel, but contemporary portraits of Astor were invariably austere.

———

A city always amounts to more than the sum of its parts. We can say the same of religious communities, or really anything made up of people.

To put it another way, urban life can never be reduced to a set of discrete variables. In New York City, *a state of endless becoming* gained meanings very different from what Puritans might have lived through, or what the commissioners envisioned. The methodical and ruthless John Jacob Astor placed a bet that continuous urban growth would increase the value of land. Not all moneyed elites understood the changing dynamics or chose to play along. And New York was just the most extreme case in processes happening throughout the Atlantic. In 1819, Rebecca Gratz, an heir from one of Philadelphia's wealthiest Jewish families, reflected in a letter to her younger brother Benjamin about "the ideal good" pursued by men of his generation: buying up land, and then "waiting till it should grow into a populous city." She believed this method for building wealth was "too chimerical for realization," and admonished Benjamin not to waste his time "in such vain experiments."[72]

Her prediction was off, from the perspective of financial advice. But Rebecca Gratz had different priorities from men like Astor. In her own way, she was an agent of change. Gratz was active in philanthropic initiatives like a relief association for women and children impacted by the revolutionary war, and an asylum for orphans in Philadelphia. In the year of the letter to Benjamin, she helped to create the Female Hebrew Benevolent Society. Rebecca Gratz understood a good deal about what it might mean to live amid the destabilizing transformations of modernity. In 1828, she sent news of the "bustling city" to her sister Maria, in rural Kentucky. In her hometown of Philadelphia, she wrote, "every day casualties alarm agitate or change the destiny of some portion." Gratz was sickened by "oft repeated" stories of loss, and how "it all ends in the stale truism that we are all to take our turns in the ups and downs of life."[73] In 1840, she complained to her sister about how "living in large cities" entailed wasting time with "trifling pursuits" like "walking about the street and exchanging uninteresting visits."[74] By 1863, in her eighties, Rebecca Gratz seemed incredulous that anyone would like to move into a city at all: Philadelphia is "full of idle people," with crowded streets and shops.[75]

Yet of course, people were moving to urban areas like never before. A city, after all, is made up of individuals with a wild variety of backstories, motives, and yearnings. For migrants, it was not so much about the future of the city but finding a future in the city. Samuel Rosenbaum, a twenty-five-year-old Jewish man from a small town in Bohemia, described in his diary what it felt like to arrive in "magnificent New York," in 1848: "I forget all pains, all discomforts. I have seen America, my wishes are fulfilled and are now experienced." He had grown up in a religious family of some means. In New York, he quickly found a job as a window shades painter, earning "nice money." But part of the allure was the excitement of the shiny, surprising city: "In brief, here is a life that I never suspected," he wrote.[76]

Rosenbaum was a forerunner to millions of European migrants to the urban Americas, and could never have anticipated the horrors that lay ahead for Jews in his homeland. Around 1855 he moved to Allentown, Pennsylvania, where he raised a family. The town, like many in the region, boomed with the construction of a waterway, the Lehigh Canal, completed in 1829. It had a population of around 8,000 in 1860. Rosenbaum's excited description of his arrival in New York was the last diary entry from 1848. He added a postscript, probably fifty years later, reflecting on the sacrifices of leaving family behind, and reassessing the decision to migrate. His high hopes "to go to free America" led to a life of peddling, sweating on crowded streets to make sales, "buried alive." Financially, Rosenbaum did well. Tafuri writes of the "bourgeois anguish" arising from the "'free' contemplation of destiny."[77] It is part of the continuous drama of modern urbanization. Rosenbaum, faced with unfulfilled expectations, laments: "Oh, if I had been able to see into the future, how different it would be with me now." Maybe life would have been better in the "discreet and secluded" small town of Lamstedt, he wondered. Even if embittered and regretful, the migrant settles: "Still, things that have happened cannot be undone," he wrote, resigned to the march of time.[78]

In a way, the furious process of building and rebuilding cities tried to challenge that very premise. The idea of *a state of endless becoming* could be extended to the urban fabric. Though no longer holding much of a plausible relationship to any single religious ethos, it certainly encapsulated the spirit of capitalism. In New York City, new generations would set off to undo work done by the previous. The site of the Waldorf-Astoria Hotel is a good example. Formerly Lenape land, it was settled as a farm, and was bought by John Jacob Astor in 1826.[79] He and his son both had houses built there. John Jacob Astor's great-grandson replaced them with a mansion. His son razed that to build a palatial hotel, in the German Renaissance style, named after John Jacob's hometown. It opened in 1893. A feuding cousin built the Astoria Hotel on an adjacent site. The two hotels consolidated. In the 1920s, developers bought the Waldorf-Astoria, and razed it to build the Empire State Building. The Art Deco skyscraper remained the tallest in the world from 1931 until 1970, longer than any before or since.

In a single Manhattan site, there may have been as many as four generations of buildings within a span of a century or so. The future was no longer determined by divine forces, nor by rational ideals or the judgment of posterity. New York City was at the forefront of urbanization driven by the pursuit of profit and a compulsion to reinvent the built environment in conformity with the latest version of the modern. In 1857, the E. V. Haughwout Building pioneered the passenger elevator. That technology, along with steel frames, allowed new architectural experiments to transform the urban fabric, verticalizing the grid. The conditions were set, but scales now familiar to us would have to wait. In 1850, the Great Pyramid of Giza stood as one of the tallest human-built structures on the planet, along with a few cathedral towers. It was surpassed by the Washington Monument (1884) and the Eiffel Tower (1889). The first commercial building taller than the pyramids only opened in 1908, with the Singer Manufacturing Company headquarters in lower Manhattan. The island's streak of having the world's tallest skyscraper lasted until Chicago's Sears Tower in 1973.

As a rule, skyscrapers took the place of relatively new buildings. This cycle of undoing and outdoing became characteristic of New York in the decades following the Commissioners' Plan. It was only well into the twentieth century that preservationist politics slowed down or stalled the process. In nineteenth-century Europe, a series of building acts limited heights, reducing incentives to replace existing structures.[80] The expectation that built environments would be constantly redesigned to meet future demands shaped urbanization throughout the Atlantic, but especially in the Americas. In a letter to family from 1853, the Prussian migrant Frank Lecouvreur wrote about how "a temporary city had sprung up," asking in what by then was a kind of refrain: "Where in the world can you see anything like this, except in America?"[81] Lecouvreur was relaying his impressions of Marysville in California, during the Gold Rush. In the United States, the makeshift, making-anew ethos described by Francis Grund now extended from coast to coast.

III. Gained Illusions and Slavery

Many of the observers most impressed with booming urbanization in the Americas did not hail from Europe's major cities. Paris and London continued to loom large. During the 1850s, the French capital passed Beijing as the world's second most populous city, behind London. In Honoré de Balzac's *Lost Illusions*, the narrator referred to an "old town" in southwestern France as a place that condemned people to "the most fatal immobility."[82] The converse works as a definition for Paris: a place of vital mobility. The novel's protagonist is Lucien Chardon, a young man from a mother of aristocratic descent, whose "devotion for his future knew no bounds."[83] But they had little money. He moved to Paris as an aspiring poet, longing to be accepted into high society. Lucien eventually adopted his mother's surname, de Rubempré. It was a story of love affairs, disenchantment, shifting allegiances, and social climbing. Lucien ended up hanging himself with a tie, in a Parisian prison, accused of a crime he did not commit. The city could also be fatal.

The basic setup became a staple of early realist fiction: young men moving from small towns to the big city, full of illusions. Countless novels, especially English and French, tell the stories of urban characters obsessed with their futures. Lucien, while struggling in a Parisian slum, projected confidence in his abilities to sell a historical novel. He wrote to his penniless and caring sister: "If the present is cold and bare and poverty-stricken, the blue distant future is rich and splendid; most great men have known the vicissitudes which depress but cannot overwhelm me." Posturing around predictions of fame and success abounded, especially among men. Social life mirrored the stock market, trading on future contracts. The possibility that someone could ascend gave them power. Urban dramas often revolved around maintaining that illusion, and it could be a matter of life or death.

A vast body of nineteenth-century urban fiction conveyed the lesson that people cannot control their destinies. Yet, in these works, fates are not preordained either, as in Greek or Christian myths. In the modern city, developments appeared to be ruled by the same force that Mercier had banished from the rational Paris of 2440: *le hasard*, chance. Balzac's Lucien, intoxicated by the city's atmosphere, deemed Paris "the capital of chance," and for a moment believed that fortune would favor him.[84] The element of chance made plots thrilling. Just as in the city, amid ups and downs, you never quite knew what you were going to get. In urban fictions, the range of possibilities proved to be wider than rational expectations could envision. Literature assimilated that lesson before modern urban planning.

The metropolis frustrated expectations, but it did not always crush hopes. Even when a protagonist failed, another might succeed. Popular rags-to-riches narratives also emerged, in which characters often found good fortune through chance encounters. It was as if by moving to the city, one took a gamble. In Charles Dickens's *Oliver Twist* (1838), the orphaned title character moved to London, where he unwittingly fell in with a gang of petty thieves. He meets Mr. Brownlow after being wrongfully accused of picking the man's pockets. Later in the novel, the poor boy spotted the man again in London, setting off events that lead to a happy ending: the kind and well-off Mr. Brownlow adopted Oliver as a son, saving him from the mean streets.[85]

Dickens was probably the most famous and well-regarded person in mid-nineteenth century England.[86] His novels, like those of Balzac, form a lasting literary canon. But a more popular contemporary genre tapped into working class urban experiences, anxieties, and yearnings. Eugène Sue's best-selling serial novel *The Mysteries of Paris* (1842–1843) inspired versions in Berlin, Madrid, Barcelona, London, Amsterdam, Philadelphia, Buenos Aires, Boston, New York, Hamburg, and Lisbon—all within just a few years of publication. City mysteries, as the genre became known, foregrounded identities in flux, class tensions, and the miseries of urbanization.[87] If in the theological sense mysteries referred to hidden mystical truths, in these novels' titles they promised to reveal the underworld of working classes, rogues, and vice.

Sue's protagonist could be a prototype for modern superheroes. Born into the nobility, Rodolphe becomes a savior to prostitutes, former inmates, and others subjugated by powerful commercial classes or unfair legal systems. Rather than stay in Paris, Sue's hero returned to his native town to live out the status assigned to him at birth. George Reynolds's *The Mysteries of London* (1844–1845) was hugely successful too. Also concerned with injustices against the poor, it portrayed criminal behavior as an inevitable symptom of despair and exploitation. In keeping with his leftist inclinations, as well as a desire to appeal to working-class readers, Reynolds offered trenchant denunciations of aristocratic villains and socioeconomic inequalities. Some of the characters found redemption, and even social mobility. The virtuous protagonist became the "Grand Duke" of a progressive republican state in Italy.[88]

The first known city mystery written in the Global South and by a woman, Juana Manso's *Los Misterios del Plata* (1846), was less attuned to questions of class and life in a crowded city. Argentina's major urban boom had not quite happened yet. But she was equally concerned with literature's potentials to shape national futures, and her book forcefully denounced the dictatorial Juan Manuel de Rosas. In a very gendered genre, which framed agency and the ability to make a political difference as male traits, one of Manso's protagonists was a conscientious and fearless heroine, Adelaida de Avellaneda. A model republican citizen, she actively challenged Rosas, and the narrator expressed confidence that a "future historian" will recognize her role.[89]

The genre also took off in the United States, where more than elsewhere it reveled in antiurban sentiment. Ned Buntline's *The Mysteries and Miseries of New York* (1847) presented itself as more muckraking "real life" reporting than fiction. He catered to rural and small-town readers, many of whom had never set foot in a big city. The book depicted a city segregated along ethnic and racial lines, and seemed to take delight in antiblack, anti-immigrant bigotry. Like other city mysteries, it also went after the wealthy, and targeted a group directly engaged in the invention of futures: fortune-tellers. Frequently associated with minorities, they are accused of duping "credulous sewing-girls, servants, and others."[90] Readers would have identified them as yet another trap in the deceptive city. The overall tone echoed the Jeffersonian idea of urbanization as a threat to the republic. It is as if these novels worked to validate the statesman's prediction from the 1780s: after "[Americans] get piled up upon one another in large cities [...] they will become corrupt as in Europe."[91] Compared to European counterparts, immensely popular with an urban public, US city mysteries resonated less with those living in the places that they purported to describe.[92]

City mysteries are not set in the future, but they register changing expectations about the built environment, sometimes in prosaic but revealing ways. In Reynolds's novel, two burglars are overheard in their hiding spot, an old house in a working-class ward in Central London. One commented: "I've heard it said that the City is going to make great alterations in this quarter." That meant they would have to find a new place. The other is less worried: "They always talks of improvements long afore they begins 'em." There was recent precedent: Regent Street had cut through dense parts of London in the 1810s and 1820s. The men hated the thought of seeing their "lovely old crib" torn down.[93] Readers knew, of course, that the house contributed to crime. But many could probably relate. Top-down reforms appeared arbitrary, and disrupted people's sense of attachment to familiar places.

Critics have tended to emphasize the melodramatic clichés of city mysteries, when not outright dismissing their importance.[94] Though these novels lack the psychological depth of works by Balzac or Dickens, they also have much to say about social complexities, and the expectations that being in a city could generate for the destitute. One the one hand, city mysteries reinforced dichotomies between good and evil, men and women, rich and poor. On the other, they showed how the fates of people with little in common could be interconnected, often in ways that disadvantaged the working classes and did not flatter the wealthy. It is easy for us to look down on their reliance on formulas like cliff-hangers, mistaken identities, and plot twists. Heavy on dialogue and light on inner lives, these novels gripped an array of readers. People found them electrifying. Repetitive structures evoked the routines of working-class urban life, punctuated by occasional disruptions or variations, and animated by the possibility of a sudden transformation. These forms could play into the hopes, fears, or vanities of readers that felt stuck in menial jobs and grimy neighborhoods. Like some of these characters, maybe they too were the chosen ones, to be noticed by just the person who could alter their destinies. Or maybe it was better to avoid risk. A chance encounter or an overheard conversation might lead to love, fortune, or murder.

Regardless of the genre, urban fictions alerted readers to how in the city, anything could happen. In them, the urban drama played itself out through individuals trying to differentiate themselves among strangers. You could never quite know who was who, so it sometimes became easier to project, to swindle, or to bluff. This was still a world where clothing set people apart, but sartorial codes and stable signs of class or occupation waned. Literature could act as a manual for deciphering urban norms and offered cautionary tales. The man dressed like a gentleman might be a crook.

Novels often encouraged skeptical attitudes toward the types of success that characters normally sought—wealth, power, and status. If the future seemed open, literature asked readers to carefully consider which goals were worth pursuing. Obsessively looking to get ahead might mean missing what stood right before your eyes. Balzac's fiction could teach you that. In the moments before his suicide, Lucien took stock of the medieval architecture outside his prison window and wondered how "this marvel existed unknown in Paris." The narrator described this late realization as a "poetic goodbye from civilized creation."[95] It conjured not nostalgia, but a sense of the missed opportunities for the poet who could have been. There was also something symptomatic in Lucien's obliviousness. The urban marvel remained unknown, but for who? Does the fixation on desired futures, the novel seems to ask, render past and present invisible? And what outward signs are we readers missing in our own lives?

Literature from the period paid extremely close attention to clothing. Lucien, always on top of the latest fashions, hanged himself with his long black silk tie, while wearing a redingote and a gilet waistcoat. This was in May of 1830, weeks before the July Revolution overthrew the Bourbon monarch. Setting the novel in a past decade still familiar to most contemporary readers meant that they were aware of futures unknown to characters. This was true for clothing and culture as much as for politics. The redingote had fallen out of favor. Readers were advised: all that is fashionable will become passé.

———

While writers like Balzac minutely described fabrics in their fiction, there was a transatlantic revolution in textile manufacturing under way. England displaced Mughal India as the major producer. "King Cotton" overtook other materials. We even learn through Balzac's narrator that the traditional way of making paper in Angoulême, the main economic activity of Lucien's hometown, was threatened by competitors adding cotton to the pulp. It is no wonder that decades later the world's tallest building would belong to the Singer Company, makers of sewing machines. Textile industries drove urban growth, and their products reshaped urban cultures. Ultimately, fashion-forward modern cultures in the urban centers of the Atlantic originated in plantations. Circulating commodities and manufactured goods animated a culture of flux and impermanence. But they often depended on fixed property relationships to land and forced labor. It became harder to keep track of where things came from, and to see their connections to faraway places and people.

In the mid-1800s, there were many more people enslaved than living in major cities of the Atlantic world. Nearly 4 million inhabited the southern United States, where their work on cotton fields drove the regional economy and had global impact. Around 430,000 lived in Cuba, ensuring the island's status as the main sugar exporter in the globe.[96] Brazil had a population of around 1.5 million enslaved people, many working on coffee fields to supply that other fuel of modern cities.[97] Even greater shares of West African populations endured some form of slavery.[98] The right to a future expanded with urbanization, or at least the illusion of it. Working-class or bourgeois urban dramas and dreams, however, remained out of reach for many. As aristocratic futures entered a state of flux in parts of Western Europe and the Americas, systems of chattel slavery meant to fixate in perpetuity the destinies of the enslaved—and their children.

The relationship between transatlantic slavery and urban prosperity was not exactly a secret. Already in the eighteenth century, a famous actor snapped back at a hostile Liverpool crowd: "I have not come here to be insulted by a set of wretches, every brick in whose infernal town is cemented with an African's blood."[99] Abolitionists often understood the fates of civilization and the enslaved as intertwined. They obtained important victories in the early 1800s. Haiti banned slavery in 1804. The UK abolished the slave trade in 1807. Other countries followed suit: the United States in 1808, the Netherlands in 1814, Spain in 1816, Portugal and France in 1818. Newly independent South American republics began to outlaw slavery in the 1820s, and the British Empire gradually did the same overseas after an 1833 parliamentary act. Defenders of slavery similarly viewed the fates of civilization and the enslaved as intertwined. The institution permeated most aspects of the Brazilian economy. In 1843, a prominent conservative political figure spoke in the Senate on behalf of the slave trade. He argued that the United States owed its economic growth to slavery, and that Brazil would fall behind if it succumbed to abolitionist pressures: "wealth is synonymous to civilization in our century, therefore Africa has been civilizing America."[100]

Indeed, between 40 and 45 percent of all humans trafficked from Africa arrived in Brazilian ports. The slave trade become illegal in Brazil in 1831 but continued throughout the 1840s. Brazil would be the last country in the hemisphere to abolish slavery, in 1888. Although a comparable percentage of their populations were enslaved in the mid-1800s, there were important differences between the two largest countries in the Atlantic. In the 1850s, the vast majority of African Americans in the United States lived in bondage, whereas Brazil had white-minority rule, and a majority of people with African descent, most of whom were not enslaved (especially among those of mixed race).[101] The United States had lower importation and manumission rates. Most African Americans were born into bondage and remained in it until death. Unlike Brazil's more widespread slavery and Afro-descendant populations, the United States was divided between Northern and Southern states. Their economies and politics remained interconnected, but the regional tensions loosely mapped into the divergent visions for an agrarian or an urban-industrial nation.

In 1845, the Anti-Slavery Office in Boston published the *Narrative of the Life of Frederick Douglass, an American Slave.* William Lloyd Garrison, a famous white abolitionist and women's rights advocate, wrote a preface framing the memoir as evidence of how the enslaved condition "filled the future with terror and gloom." Douglass recalled being taken in his youth to Baltimore, which he had "the strongest desire to see." It struck him as a place of some hope, and greater possibilities: "A city slave is almost a freeman, compared with a slave on the plantation." Douglass argued that in urban areas, the "atrocious cruelty" of slaveholders might hurt their reputations with nonslaveholding neighbors.[102] He anticipated an insight dear to later urbanists, the notion that eyes on the street can curb crime and violence.

The narrative is far from a paean to the city, however. Returning to Baltimore years later, Douglass suffered brutal discrimination while working in a shipyard, including being beaten up. His writing illustrated a key conflict of modern urbanization. On the one hand, cities can have transformative and liberating potentials. On the other, they are sites for the exercise of power seeking to foreclose possibilities for change. In the decades ahead, urban planning would navigate the two. Douglass vied for a chance at the first and suffered with the second. Later, he proposed paying his master for the right to work independently, with the goal of saving enough money to afford an escape. The slaveholder refused, and warned of the pain he would inflict if Douglass attempted to run away: "He told me, if I would be happy, I must lay out no plans [...], if I behaved myself properly, he would take care of me." Of course, the slaveholder reserved the right to decide what proper and care meant. Both men understood how new expectations of rights and freedom posed a threat to the status quo. The slaveholder, Douglass wrote, advised him to have "complete thoughtlessness of the future."[103]

Douglass succeeded in fleeing to the north. He described his arrival in New York: "There I was in the midst of thousands, and yet a perfect stranger; without home and without friends, in the midst of thousands of my own brethren."[104] We might find these lines in any narrative about the modern urban experience. But being among strangers and chance encounters contained a possibility unique to an African American in the United States. Douglass described the fear of speaking to the wrong person and being kidnapped back into slavery in the south. Instead, his *Narrative* became one of the most influential abolitionist texts in the world, and he found fame. Douglass traveled to cities in Scotland, Ireland, and England, where he felt freer from discrimination, and was appalled by the poverty.[105] Supporters helped to buy his emancipation. He returned to the United States in 1847, settling in Rochester, which had boomed due to its location near the Erie Canal. Douglass started an antislavery newspaper and continued changing the future.

Douglass was both representative and exceptional. For many, freedom remained outside the realm of possibility. At the age of 100, Delia Garlic looked back on her time as a slave in a plantation as a hopeless hell: "Us jest prayed fer strength to endure it to de end." She adds: "We didn't 'spect nothin' but to stay in bondage 'till we died."[106] More often than not, the future in these narratives was conceived in terms of religious salvation. But communities of faith and the divine could also serve as an impulse for insurrection. In 1835, a group of mostly Muslim men led one of the main urban slave revolts of the period, in the port city of Salvador in Brazil.[107] Unlike counterparts in plantations, they had some ability to circulate in the city, and thus to plot and strategize. The Malês, as they were known, used outward symbols to identify themselves, dressing in white-colored *abadás* for example. The Haitian Revolution inspired hope among them, and fear in slaveholders. Authorities violently suppressed the revolt. Anxieties about African-led insurrections strengthened arguments for ending the semiclandestine slave trade. In Brazil and Cuba, during the gradual emancipation process, enslaved women also played a key role by appealing to courts.[108]

Whether in slave narratives or city mysteries, however, mobility remained far more accessible for men. In much of the Americas, the majority of enslaved people in cities were women, at least partly because
slaveholders perceived men as more likely to rebel. Several narratives
told stories of women's domestic confinement and sexual exploitation.
The movement to obtain full rights for women, in the meantime, gained
ground in several cities. Two pioneers in the struggles for both abolitionism and women's rights seized on chances to transform their
societies. The idea that stability could no longer be taken for granted
inspired them to step out of their assigned social stations. Sarah Moore
Grimké and Angelina Emily Grimké were born to a wealthy, slaveholding father. He was a prominent jurist, politician, and cotton plantation
owner in South Carolina. The Grimké sisters had half-siblings from enslaved women.

After their father's death, Sarah met Quakers in Philadelphia. They
deeply influenced her views. Both sisters eventually moved to the city
and converted to the faith. Despite opposition from Quakers who saw
them as too radical, they became tireless advocates of abolitionism and
gender equality, drawing a large following for their public speeches and
writings from the 1830s onward. Their extensive correspondence captured a mixture of excitement and trepidation. In 1836, Angelina Grimké
wrote to her older sister from Philadelphia: "I feel strangely released,
and am sure I know not what is to become of me." She felt stagnated,
and wanted to have a greater impact on social causes. Angelina Grimké
understood that change was in the air, but showed a kind of restraint
and wisdom that was rare among grand strategists and fellow radicals
alike: "I am perfectly blind as to the future."[109]

IV. Between Heaven and Hell

The opening up of urban futures had different meanings. It might manifest in the flexibility of buildings and functions in New York's plan, the
intensifying circulation of goods and peoples, or a sense of possibility
in the experience of cities. Not everyone desired dynamism. To some,
the right to a future could be about aspirations for permanence or

stability. They might have moved to cities for the ability to worship and more food security. Others saw promise in volatility. The expectation that everything is possible, combined with dire social conditions, helped to generate urgency in theory and action. Whereas democrats, republicans, liberals, and even some monarchists sought change through reforms, utopian socialists pushed for more radical departures from the status quo. If Mercier imagined that his utopian Paris would take centuries to materialize, now ideal societies seemed to be attainable within a lifetime.

Visionary programs had a variety of forms. The Welsh-born Robert Owen, after gaining wealth through textile manufacturing, tried creating organizations that were not just about maximizing profit. He ran a factory in Scotland with significantly better working conditions than the norm for the period. Like many contemporaries and several city mystery novelists, Owen believed environments shaped behavior. Akin to Rousseau, he thought children's education was key to social improvement. His proposals included secular co-ed education, child labor laws, shortened working hours, recreational opportunities, and decent housing. Owen had "confidence equal to certainty itself" that such measures would transform society.[110] In the 1820s, Owen moved to the United States and founded the cooperation-based New Harmony community in Indiana. Suffering from a lack of skilled workers, housing shortages, and mismanagement, it lasted only a couple of years. Owenite principles, however, became an inspiration for other utopian experiments as well as legislation benefiting workers.[111] He remained influential in the trade union movement and in socialist thought.

Radical ideas and communitarian experiments flourished. Rather than imagining urban revolutions and transformed cities, many proto-socialists seemed much more invested in planning new societies from scratch. In France, Henri de Saint-Simon renounced his aristocratic station, and advocated for an industrial society with merit-based hierarchies. Saint-Simonianists of many political stripes would take on his mantle for decades. Charles Fourier, born into a well-off family of textile merchants, came to detest industrialization and the types of rationality prized by contemporary political economists. His vision for the future

L'AVENIR.

Perspective d'un Phalanstère ou Palai ...iétaire dédié à l'humanité.

François Marie Charles FOURIER né à Besançon le 7 Avril 1772, mort à Paris le 10 Octobre 1837.

FIGURE 2.5. "The Future!" Phalansteries promised to leave the "filthy" city behind for life ordered within geometric designs; utopia as an island.

included sexual liberation, women's rights, and pleasure as the foundation of work. Fourier, echoing Rousseau, called for not sacrificing "today's happiness in the name of future happiness."[112] Fourier's utopias had a fleshed-out architecture and plan. His self-sufficient *phalanstères*, as he called them, consisted of monastery-like buildings with wings for specific purposes: collective dining, quiet study, manual labor, and so on. Hundreds of these utopian communities took shape throughout the Atlantic, especially in North and South America. They tended to only last a few years, falling apart because of rapid growth, lack of funding, or social engineering gone awry. Fourier's political impact outlived the *phalanstères*.[113]

Emerging dreams of futures outside the city cut across political, class, and spiritual differences. Though they often retained a relationship to the divine, utopian socialists by and large rejected organized religion and recast the pursuit of justice and hope in secular terms.[114] Their ideas were still largely confined to lettered sectors. The perception that progress was both vital and fatal, however, became unavoidable. Cities were polluted, loud, dirty, and disease-prone. Even breathing could be hard in places with coal-fueled manufacturing. Benjamin Disraeli reputedly stated in 1844 that "what Manchester does today, the rest of the world does tomorrow." This was usually quoted in celebration of the city's leading role in industrialization. Indeed, Manchester became known as Cottonopolis, and hosted the world's first intercity steam-powered train service with Liverpool, opened in 1830. At the same time, a six-year-old might work sixteen hours a day. Mortality rates tended to be even higher than in rural areas: in Manchester, around half of children died before they turned five.[115] The average age of death was twenty-six. Manchester was often described as hell. Its conditions spurred the research and revolutionary politics of a young Friedrich Engels, who stressed that the industrial age reserved similar miseries and oppression for his native Germany and other countries, unless they adopted a whole new social system.[116]

Living conditions tended to be worse in fast-growing places like Manchester, Lyon, and Chicago. It is easy to understand how some people in the mid-1800s might find urbanization hopeless. But for the poor, life in the countryside could also be hellish. The interconnectedness of rural and urban dynamics only intensified. In the United Kingdom, urban demand for livestock products put pressure on land and food availability in Ireland. Enclosures had left peasants with fewer options, when not dispossessed altogether. Once a potato blight hit, vulnerable crop monocultures and laissez-faire policies resulted in the Great Hunger of the 1840s. Historians estimate that around one million Irish died, and another million migrated across the Atlantic. They would reshape cities like Boston and New York.

In the typical urban experience, there was no escaping health risks. Cholera epidemics killed tens of thousands in several European and American cities during the 1830s and the 1840s. Other long-standing threats increased with overcrowded, unsanitary conditions: tuberculosis, measles, whooping cough, typhoid, smallpox, scarlet fever, diphtheria. In the warmer climates, you could add yellow fever. Miasma theories, prevalent until at least the 1880s, blamed disease transmission on "bad air" (from which we got the term *malaria*). As a result, planning often focused on sanitation. Most nineteenth-century urban reforms had health-related justifications, such as widening streets to increase

NEW WORLDS EMERGE   99

ventilation. In London, with unusual state capacity for the period, the civil engineer Joseph Bazalgette pioneered sewage systems with pipes wider than seemed necessary, presciently aware of how it was impossible to predict the needs of the future metropolis.[117]

————

Even the most optimistic mid-nineteenth-century imaginations of urban futures could not have anticipated the medical advances of the decades ahead. This was still not a time, after all, where you would necessarily associate scientific innovations with improved quality of life. Rather than liberating, new technologies were often perceived as destabilizing and oppressive, like the dangerous machinery of factories. The anglophone world experienced early industrialization, and as we have seen, also had a deeply ingrained pastoral tradition. That combination underscored the emergence of anticity utopias. The architectural historian Nathaniel Walker shows how a fear of cities and a desire for "abandoning Babylon" in North America could be tied to a long history of science and Christian prophecies converging. In the United States, the self-image of a city on a hill would in effect be expressed in dreams of a "sprawling fabric of suburban dispersal [. . .] united only by high-tech transportation networks."[118] Heaven might be in a future version of this world, but it would be a radical departure from dominant urban patterns. In such visions, scientific progress was seemingly preordained. One example was John Etzler's fictional utopia of Lithconia, "the paradise within the reach of all men" (1833). The book echoed the Jeffersonian spirit of the land ordinances and a rejection of density. It imagined extensive canals and iron railroads, in a landscape of "gardens as far as the eye can see."[119] With limitless resources and government-owned "mighty engines," Americans could have the "power to become within ten years a nation to rule the world."[120] Other technological utopias of dispersal followed in the 1830s, envisioning mechanized transport, hot running water, elevators, gas light, and crystal palaces.[121]

There might have been a maturing transatlantic consensus of the United States as the country of the future, but internal differences of opinion over what this should be like only sharpened. Not all utopians promised a retreat from the city. Mary Griffith's *Three Hundred Years Hence* (1836) recycled Mercier's plot device. As the title suggests, her protagonist wakes up centuries in the future. He found that urbanization extended into his own property, called Hamilton. The name alluded to the Federalist leader, invoking the vision rivaling Jefferson's.[122] In Griffith's future, cities are beautiful. Men and women have roles "assigned to them by the Creator," but equal rights. Slavery has been abolished, and "the negro population" was moved to colonies like Liberia. New technologies are benign, including air travel in balloon-like vehicles, safe and fast water vessels, and "locomotion cars" that resemble automobiles, but were part of a public system.[123] Philadelphia and New York City were largely rebuilt. The height of new constructions was capped for safety, due to the risk of fire. Streets are wider and more orderly, kept cool and clean by abundant water fountains.

Outside of fiction, US cities continued to grow at a faster rate than ever before. In the press, reflections about the immediate consequences of rapid urbanization raised more concern than hope. One newspaper column in 1836 noted that while there was not yet a London in America, New York was on its way. The author worried for the lack of green spaces in the Commissioners' Plan: "The whole of [Manhattan] is already laid out, in anticipation of the future greatness of the city [...] but where is the reservation for even one great park [...]?"[124] Alexis de Tocqueville, during his stay in the United States also grew concerned, but for different reasons. He was worried about the "rabble" of freed blacks and poor European migrants: "I look upon the size of certain American cities, and especially on the nature of their population, as a real danger which threatens the future security of the democratic republics of the New World."[125]

Cities across the Atlantic were rife with turbulence and unrest. De Tocqueville offered a similar admonishment to Europeans, in January of 1848. In a famous speech to the French Chamber of Deputies, he told his peers: "I believe that we are at this moment sleeping on a volcano." De Tocqueville was in the liberal Movement Party. He thought that France was divided between a ruling class marked by "languor, impotence, stagnation, and boredom," and the "feverish" lower classes, awakening to new social and political possibilities. The most relevant tensions were no longer between the aristocracy and the bourgeoisie, but between property-holders, with a stake in continuity, and those struggling, "destined not only to upset this or that law, ministry, or even form of government, but society itself."[126]

In February, Karl Marx and Friedrich Engels published the Communist Manifesto. It also hinged on divisions grounded on ownership and temporality: the proletariat sold their time in the form of wage labor; bourgeois capitalists exploited it for profit. The manifesto argued that the "bourgeois epoch" was marked by a "constant revolutionizing of production" and an "uninterrupted disturbance of all social conditions," which swept away "all fixed, fast-frozen relations." Though their primary aim was revolutionary change, Marx and Engels also theorized about modern urbanization. A lyrical passage could work as a kind of epithet or epitaph for mighty industrial cities: "All that is solid melts into air, all that is holy is profaned, and man is at last compelled to face with sober senses his real conditions of life, and his relations with his kind." To Marx and Engels, the massive cities of industrialization "rescued" people from the stupor of rural life. The metaphor of sobriety might sit a little awkwardly, when alcohol permeated the social realities of the proletariat, but it could evoke connections between temperance movements and progressive causes.[127] More importantly, Marx and Engels overestimated the extent of urbanization in 1848 and underestimated the appeal of nascent nationalism. But the manifesto is presciently attuned to shifting dynamics, including the interconnectedness of modern economies: "In place of the old wants, satisfied by the production of the country, we find new wants, requiring for their satisfaction the products of distant lands and climes."

The Communist Manifesto did not invite much of a reaction at first. And Tocqueville's prediction was greeted with irony. They all operated under a premise underlying the scale of the Commissioners' Plan, and the experience of urbanization: times were changing fast, and the world would never be the same. In late February of 1848, Paris erupted. As news circulated in mass print media, revolution spread to cities throughout Europe. Reportedly, urban spaces became suffused with a sense of freedom and collective energy.[128] Marx and Engels had deemed the workers of the world as "the revolutionary class, the class that holds the future in its hands." In revolutionary streets and squares from Milan to Budapest, people felt like actors in a historical turning point. But the aftereffects defied initial expectations.[129] A diffuse set of motivations, from discontentment with inflation to toppling monarchies, had sparked the insurrections. A broad coalition included democratic radicals and middle classes composed of an assortment of skilled professionals, such as butchers and tailors, as well as doctors and lawyers. They either vied for greater power, or to preserve ways of life under decline. Rather than the overthrow of the bourgeoisie, the events of 1848 largely led to their political dominance.

In France, the fall of the king was followed by a provisional government and a period of turmoil, with measures like the abolition of slavery in the colonies.[130] In June, the government suppressed a leftist workers' uprising in Paris, killing thousands. An alliance between liberals and conservatives prevailed. Tocqueville, for example, joined the right-leaning Party of Order. Marx looked back on the "so-called revolutions" not yet as the hoped for volcano eruption, but as "small fractures and fissures in the dry crust of European society."[131] On the one hand, we might think of a line from Tomasi di Lampedusa's novel *The Leopard*, set during the decades-long process of Italian unification, which also involved revolts in 1848. Tancredi, a prince who joined the rebels, famously states: "If we want everything to stay as it is, it is necessary that everything change."[132] On the other hand, as the historian J. B. Bury would see it, 1848 marked the inflection point when the idea of progress "was definitely enthroned as the regnant principle."[133] Scholars continue to disagree about the revolution's impact. Some even connect it to the development of social welfare and democratic systems decades later. More immediately, in the first elections of the newly established French Second Republic, Napoleon Bonaparte's nephew won in a landslide. Louis Napoleon received overwhelming support from rural areas. As we will see in the next chapter, the future Emperor Napoleon III would prove to be enormously consequential for modern planning in Paris, and for urbanization throughout the globe.

The revolutions became known as the springtime of the peoples, or springtime of nations. We might say that of the available imagined futures, the imagined community of the nation emerged as the one most capable of mobilizing a sense of belonging among the masses.[134] Or, alternatively, that nationalism contained the potentials of revolutionary change to the benefit of conservative forces. In effect, 1848 represents a marker for the establishment of constitutional governments, with a greater role for self-rule by the people, rather than absolute monarchs. Who gets to count and speak for the people would of course remain a major point of contention. At the beginning of the century, the recognition of open futures and exercises of prediction largely reflected the views and agendas of grand strategists like Jefferson and Madame de Staël. As the decades advanced, urbanization and social change exceeded expectations. A lot more people, representing multiple perspectives, staked claims on the destiny of the world around them. The stage was now set for the development of urban planning as a more professionalized practice, with the city as a battleground for the competing visions of radicals, reformists, and reactionaries.

In retrospect, there are specific ways in which the Commissioners' Plan for Manhattan was neither representative nor ahead of its time, but rather emerged as a historical anomaly. After 1848, planners could no longer minimize programming. They had to more directly attend to popular demands and social issues. On the one hand, city governance became increasingly subsumed to national or imperial interests. On the other, as the historian Christopher Clark argues, the revolutions "shifted the balance of power between the state and the municipal authorities, enabling the former to override the entrenched opposition of municipal elites to major public expenditures."[135] In 1848, protesters throughout Europe resorted to a form of insurrectionary planning, the building of barricades. Going against the goals of better-connected streets and faster-moving traffic, barricades sought to create dead-ends, in order to protect insurgents and corner armies. As popular movements vied for control of the city, reactionaries would strike back. They backed military responses and rebuilding the city to facilitate them. But the dire conditions of cities and fear of another 1848 also pushed conservatives to be more open to social reforms. Some progressive urbanists seized on the opportunities. The implementation of centralized and top-down planning, nonetheless, continued to require proximity to wealth and power. Even when aligned with or pressured by revolutionary politics, planning as a state-sanctioned practice had to operate within the constraints of authoritarian nationalism and incremental reforms.

The upheavals also resonated across the Atlantic. In their wake, Colombians elected a liberal president who pushed for agrarian reforms, the abolition of slavery, separation of church and state, and freedom of the press. In Mexico, news of 1848 arrived as the country lost half of its territory to an increasingly imperialist United States, emboldening nationalist reformists. In Argentina, the dictatorial Rosas, the villain of a city mystery, used the threat of revolution to persecute dissenters.[136] In northeast Brazil, opening of the ports for trade with Great Britain had disrupted local sugar economies, by creating demand for cotton. The events of 1848 influenced the Praieira Revolt in the neighboring cities of Olinda and Recife. Rebels rose against landed aristocracies, calling for civil rights like expanded voting and freedom of the press.[137] It was a key year for the expansion of imagined futures and voting franchises in the United States as well. Seneca Falls famously hosted the first women's rights convention. Supporters of the 1848 revolutions, especially from the German states, emigrated to the Americas. Many were refugees. In Brazil, they impacted urbanization in the south. In the United States, they became known as Forty-Eighters. Their progressive politics bolstered union organizing and antislavery movements.

Urban politics in the Americas was entangled in both transatlantic and local dynamics. US cities had been experiencing nearly two decades of almost constant turmoil, including violent riots, gangs, and mobs.[138] In 1849, the Astor Place riots broke out in New York City, at a popular opera house named after the real estate magnate. The event left twenty-two dead and more injured.[139] Ostensibly, it was provoked by the rivalry between an American and an English Shakespearean actor. But the two sides of the conflict spoke to growing tensions involving migration, nativism, and nationalism. Ned Buntline, who had written *The Mysteries and Miseries of New York*, kindled xenophobic passions. He was behind a flyer asking, "Working men / shall Americans or English rule in this city," signed by an "American Committee."[140] The uprisings in Recife also involved violence against immigrants, especially from Portugal.

In the decades ahead, race, gender, nationality, and ethnicity played central roles in shaping the contours of imagined communities—of who counted as *the people*. Urban planning continued to serve as an instrument of power, and a tool to enact or suppress change. Visions for urban futures would take different directions in each continent, at the same time as transatlantic connections intensified. Amid dramatic technological innovations, unprecedented migratory diasporas, and rapid urban growth, the experiences and expectations generated by cities would make it seem like everything was possible.

3

Everything Seems Possible (1850s–1880s)

PARIS + NEW YORK, BARCELONA, LONDON, BERLIN, VIENNA, BOSTON, AND MORE.

I. The Spectacle of Progress and Its Discontents

The revolutionary fervors of 1848 proved to be less consequential to urbanization than steel and steam. In the aftermath of the upheavals, states invested more actively in infrastructure. Several European cities underwent reforms aiming to improve public health and economic conditions.[1] Yet, even amid widespread transformations, no one could foresee the extent to which technological progress would reshape the planet. Steamships and railways enabled unprecedented diasporas. Within a few decades, tens of millions of people would move from Europe to the Americas, and from rural to urban settings. Cable telegraphy revolutionized the operations of transportation networks, financial markets, warfare, and news media. Messages that used to take days or even months now traveled in a matter of minutes. The speed of innovations in mobility, construction, and communications took off. They stretched the limits of the buildable and the thinkable. In the mid-1800s, the Egyptian pyramids and cathedral towers still vied for status as the tallest human-built structures. By 1889, the metal-made Eiffel Tower nearly doubled their height. From its top, inventors conducted experiments in wireless telegraphy. As the pace of change accelerated in major cities, the reality of a wide-open future became more apparent than ever.

For growing numbers of urbanites, the past no longer served as a yardstick for what seemed possible. At the same time, in an increasingly connected world, ambitious reforms in imperial Paris would set the standards for urban futures. French planners no longer wanted cities to develop "without foresight" and "by chance."[2] To them, urban design needed to apply the latest "conquests" in both science and art.[3] They assumed that the city's population would grow to millions, and sought to rebuild it as a hub of burgeoning transportation and communication systems.[4] The modernized French capital was also conceived as definitive. Its reinvention should be understood both as a reaction to ongoing changes, and as a projection of contemporary Eurocentric assumptions. What could possibly surpass trains or telegraphs, after all? In this implied future, the civilized world was to be more like Paris, while the city itself would remain congealed as a beacon of progress. Paris became a model.

Throughout the Atlantic and beyond, planners and politicians emulated Georges-Eugène Haussmann (1809–1891), the heavy-handed official behind the Parisian reforms. Other foundational planners emerged in the period. We will focus on two with less autocratic approaches: Ildefons Cerdá (1815–1876) in Barcelona, and Frederick Law Olmsted (1822–1903) in the United States. All three left lasting marks on our built environments. Paradoxically, this relied just as much on their abilities as visionaries as on their blind spots. Attempting to devise far-reaching designs required some degree of unawareness about what lay ahead. Social and political conditions empowered planning, but as a rule, these men overestimated their predictive capacities. They underestimated how much cities would evolve within a couple generations and planned for posterity. Not knowing the future imbued them with confidence to conceive large-scale designs for the long term. Before returning to their projects and legacies, it will be helpful to start with how others outside of policy-making or planning circles sometimes more acutely perceived impending changes that would escape anyone's control, and from which there was no turning back.

Herman Melville's "Bartleby, the Scrivener," published in 1853, might not be an obvious source for powerful intuitions about urban futures. The short story did not make all that deep of an impression among contemporaries but captivated the imaginations of many later readers. Melville disassembled urban clichés as they became widely mobilized. His cities are places of imposition and compromise instead of opportunity and self-actualization. Yet, this was by no means an antiurban diatribe. Melville's story explored what it meant to be human in a modernizing world. How could people reconcile the expectations of wide-open futures with the regimented realities of everyday life? The subtitle revealed the setting: "A Story of Wall Street." Readers quickly learned that Bartleby's tale took place around the time of publication: the first-person narrator bragged about a professional connection to "the late" John Jacob Astor. Astor had died in 1848.

In the opening line, the narrator identified as "a rather elderly man." His legal business involved real estate transactions: mortgages, title deeds, and so on. We get an image of his office amid a compact downtown, with windows facing the walls of a new "lofty" building. Wall Street was being rebuilt as a business center. The obstructed view evoked a modern temporal order, less dictated by the cycles of seasons or daylight. In the confines of the work environment, time needed to be regular and controllable, rather than negotiable and porous. Natural rhythms only surfaced through references to eating. And yet, meals had set times—twelve o'clock, meridian. During the second half of the century, as the historian Vanessa Ogle writes, time assumed "more abstract qualities, a grid to be grafted onto natural rhythms."[5] The timetables of industrial capitalism, transportation, and communications required a standardization of calendars and clocks. As long-term futures came to seem increasingly unwieldy and unpredictable, in everyday life schedules and routines became more uniform and accountable.

Melville's characters did not adjust seamlessly to the new demands of office life. Bureaucratic labor might be alienating, but the workers' humanity remained irreducible. They are quirky and eccentric. The titular man was hired as a copyist. At first Bartleby was "cheerfully industrious." But then, he reacted to a request with a now iconic line: *I would prefer not to.* Though the story preceded the widespread adoption of

scientific management, it evinced some basic principles: efficient capitalist production depended on separation of functions, repetitive tasks,
and vertically integrated workflows. When Bartleby does not follow his
superior's instructions, it threatens the whole system. One coworker
deems him "loony." The plot then revolves around attempts to deal with
Bartleby's repeated refusal to comply. Like many contemporary planners and urban elites, the narrator understood the flaws of his employees as intrinsic, not as a product of workplace conditions for which he
had responsibility. He avoided, nonetheless, approaching the situation
as a ruthless capitalist.

The narrator tried different methods, each with an analogue in planning culture. Seeing Bartleby's soul as afflicted by an "innate and incur-
able disorder," he suggested collecting bills in the countryside. Echoing
the urban parks movement, he supposed that "wholesome exercise" in
nature could lead to better health and performance. The scrivener, however, seemed impervious to what Raymond Williams calls "morality of
improvement."[6] Proud of his "masterly management," the narrator
shifted strategies. He told the insubordinate worker to leave, with extra
money to avoid any loud scenes, recalling a ruler that seeks to buy off
or appease potential revolutionaries. The scrivener stuck around. His
boss then appealed to inexorable rules about who can claim a place in
the modern city: "What earthly right have you to stay here? Do you pay
any rent? Do you pay my taxes? Or is this property yours?" Scholars
note that this language brought to mind political battles over reforms
against land monopolies, as magnates like Astor concentrated ownership.[7] The scrivener, again, stayed.

Medical, financial, and rhetorical appeals all fell short. The narrator
became convinced that just letting the scrivener be in the office was his
"mission in this world," a "predestinated purpose." Those comfortable in
their positions can always find relief in assigned roles. The narrator had
introduced himself as someone who, from his youth, had a "profound con-
viction that the easiest way of life is the best." Critics have argued that he
unconsciously identified with Bartleby's refusal to go along. Did Bartleby's
inaction produce doubts about whether the successes in Wall Street had
been worthwhile? Did the narrator secretly envy the clerk? We cannot
know. But the story lays bare that there was an obvious incongruity

between a pursuit of the easy life and this métier, described as energetic, nervous, useful, combative, hurried, mechanical. The lawyer's professional life demanded productivity and future-oriented actions.

Modern subjects could try to resist exploitation or opt in and strive to move up in society. The basic idea that human destinies are not predetermined made space for a wide range of phenomena: revolutionary utopias, migrant dreams, progressive movements, and capitalism. Bartleby's defiance is never portrayed as heroic. For the narrator, it was a means without an end. Nonetheless, the clerk's insubordination, however inscrutable his motivations, destabilized the status of the aging narrator and the office hierarchies. He compared Bartleby to "the last column of some ruined temple." Perhaps he too felt like a relic, amid intensifying changes to the built environment and an increasingly secular milieu? Bartleby exposed the flimsiness of certainties, generating anxiety about the security of established positions. He acted as an unwelcome reminder that Manhattan might rise, but eventually all turns to dust.

Eventually, the narrator moved his office, leaving the scrivener behind. Bartleby was then, ironically, jailed as a vagrant. Throughout the Atlantic, vagrancy laws represented another moment in the modern war of fixity against flux. They were often abused to keep the poor and propertyless in check. Bartleby died in jail. The narrator concluded with two exclamations: "Ah Bartleby! Ah humanity!" By offering no clear resolution, the ambivalent ending defied teleological expectations of closure or redemption, common to linear narratives of progress and religion alike. Just like the future, the story remains open-ended. It points to the limits of understanding, and to our only possible certainty about what is ahead—that we will each die one day. Melville's enigmatic story speaks to dilemmas of modernity. Others took sides, and made an impact. He lacks answers, but suggests a prescient and enduring question: where will this urban vortex lead us?

———

Starting in the 1820s, wrought-iron rail and steam engines facilitated the circulation of goods and peoples. Trains sped ahead, often in a straight line, cutting through geographic barriers and impervious to the natural rhythms of weather or animal-powered travel. To those that first witnessed locomotive engines in action, they "almost annihilated time and space."[8] The first half of "Bartleby, the Scrivener" came out in *Putnam's Monthly*, in November of 1853. That same issue opened with a headline about the Pacific Railroad. The magazine presented the project as "rivaling in grandeur and surpassing in usefulness any work that the genius of man has hitherto undertaken," including the Egyptian pyramids.[9] Railroads to the Pacific would promote trade with Asia and serve cities, becoming a vector for urbanization. This, the authors insisted, should be a private enterprise led by capitalists rather than the government. They had confidence that naysayers would be proved wrong, just like those that had doubted the feasibility of the Erie Canal. Thomas Jefferson was mentioned among the latter: even this secular seer, with a "hopeful and springing confidence in the future," mistakenly thought that the canal had been "a century ahead" of its day. As the march of progress rolled through, those standing in the way could join it, step aside, or be removed. Prefer not to? Tough luck.

Railroads reorganized urban territories and their relationships to hinterlands. Soon enough, someone in New York would be able to buy strawberries grown in California in the middle of winter. Mainstream publications like *Putnam's Monthly* excluded from optimistic narratives the violence committed against indigenous societies.[10] The logics of efficient productivity acted as blinders. Compartmentalization occurred at every scale. It permeated infrastructure planning as well as the experiences of city dwellers. In his history of railroads in Baltimore, David Schley argues that "the rise of the private corporation as an economic agent and the spatial configuration of the industrial metropolis were structurally intertwined."[11] The distribution of infrastructure, buildings and bodies privileged profits. It also offered a spectacle. Some Native Americans called trains the "great steel horse."[12] Another material manifested a shiny and alluring facet to the compartmentalization of time and space: glass. New methods for mass producing sturdy and polished glass sheets led to myriad applications, including in train sheds and windows. Melville described glass folding-doors dividing up the

Wall Street office. Later theorists focused on relationships between glass and surveillance. To many contemporaries, glass invoked the sleek and modern future.[13]

The second half of Melville's short story was published in December of 1853. That same volume of *Putnam's Monthly* opened with an article on the Great Exhibition in the New York Crystal Palace. Inspired by London's 1851 Crystal Palace, it was built in iron and glass, to showcase the "climaxes of Art, Industry, and Invention."[14] This was where, to much fanfare, Elisha Otis introduced elevator technologies. Along with the structural use of cast iron, helping to pave the way for steel frames, they enabled skyscrapers. In the space, *Putnam's* writers announced, visitors could find "the dawn of thought that will one day shine out over the land." At first, the gas-lit spaces dazzled with "sparkles and rainbows." And then, "the eyes settled, order emerging here and there." Months earlier the magazine had described the original Crystal Palace as an "exhalation of the dawn."[15] It was as if the sun shone first in London. New York's Crystal Palace would be but one among others built for exhibitions in Cork (1852), Dublin (1853), Munich (1854), Paris (1855), and later in cities like Toronto, Amsterdam, Montreal, Madrid, Porto, Sydney, Curitiba, and Petrópolis. The buildings and the events they hosted stood as spectacles of progress.

The 1851 Great Exhibition in London's Crystal Palace set the tone. Comparable events had taken place since the 1790s, most regularly in Paris. This one represented a watershed due to the size, architecture, and international reach. The Crystal Palace was around three times more spacious than the monumental St. Paul's Cathedral. With as many as ten miles of galleries, the exhibit received more than 6 million visitors, the equivalent of around a third of England's population. *Putnam's Monthly* had voiced commonplace reactions: the building, designed by Joseph Paxton, was "the first original piece of architecture in modern times."[16] They praised him for not looking to the past for inspiration. The Crystal Palace lacked the load-bearing walls that constrained designers. Iron pillars supported the glass enclosure. People perceived the building as both sturdy and ethereal: one material suggested fixity, the other flux.

THE GREAT INDUSTRIAL EXHIBITION OF 1851.

FIGURE 3.1. At the Crystal Palace, nature under control, and nations in "the line of progress."

Joseph Paxton's own trajectory exemplified a sense of urban possibilities. Hailing from a rural background, he ascended socially working as a gardener. With the surprising success of the Crystal Palace, Paxton was knighted by Queen Victoria. He eventually became a liberal member of Parliament, amassing wealth through investments in railroads. In 1850, Paxton seized on an opportunity to innovate. Major buildings were entrusted to designers with more experience and higher station, but the Crystal Palace was meant to be ephemeral. Construction adopted an unprecedented combination of experimental architectural forms, cutting-edge materials, and modular techniques. Because it was in Hyde Park, Paxton had to avoid cutting down full-grown elms. His design incorporated the trees into the barrel-vaulted transept. This also signaled nature under control, aligned with narratives of industrial progress. In a reminder that some would prefer not to go along, pesky sparrows stuck around the interior.

Exhibits for dozens of countries put on display a future where everything seemed possible, but within clear ethnic and geopolitical hierarchies. Nations of the urbanizing North Atlantic showcased spectacular inventions: precision surveying instruments, Colt revolvers, vulcanized rubber goods, steam engines, microscopes, telescopes, hydraulic presses, a barometer billed as a "Tempest Prognosticator," and precursors to photography, calculators, fax machines, and bicycles. Meanwhile, exhibits from the Global South focused on primary resources and traditional products: furs, hand-woven baskets, silk goods, pottery, ivory, precious stones, ores.[17]

In the United States, *Putnam's* writers were unconcerned with imitation but self-conscious about competition. Attempting something comparable to London's Crystal Palace in New York, the magazine argued, became a matter of "honor and pride" for "the whole [national] community."[18] They bristled with confidence about the country's ascendance. Even this monumental architectonic feat would fall short in conveying "what American industry and American energy have achieved." The article added some local touches, but extolled US progress within Eurocentric standards, celebrating the electric telegraph, steam vessels, railroads, the Erie canal, wilderness "redeemed" for agriculture, educated children, hungry migrants made rich, and interconnected cities "rising everywhere." No mention of slavery. The implication is of a race among nations, with world's fairs and architecture as the appropriate standards to measure the "place which each [. . .] occupied in the line of progress." The image of a line suggests a shared and singular idea of what the future ought to be like.

Some found Crystal Palaces irresistible, others hated what they stood for. Charles Dickens reputedly wrote the novel *Bleak House* (1852–1853) in response to this triumphalist spectacle. He championed an England with fewer imperial pretensions and better off for it. Fyodor Dostoevsky also preferred not to be swept up by the march of progress. In *Notes from*

Underground, with a sense of foreboding, the Crystal Palace embodied a process where "new economic relations will be established, all ready-made and worked out with mathematical exactitude," ushering in a predictable and "frightfully dull" future.[19]

II. Modernity as Rupture and Continuity

To many in Victorian England, predictable and dull would certainly beat dirty and dangerous. London remained a central node in increasingly global commercial networks, and the capital of a financial empire. The city attracted wealthy and destitute people from all corners of the planet.[20] It pioneered a host of urban improvements in health and engineering, from ambitious sewage systems to smoother pavements that made it easier to clean horse manure. London had a fair share of spectacular proposals, including Joseph Paxton's unbuilt Great Victorian Way. In 1855, he proposed a 10-mile "girdle" to relieve congestion and improve connections between districts. It was partly inspired by Christopher Wren's plans after the Great Fire, but the futuristic style and scale drew from the Crystal Palace. The project envisioned a monumental system of arcades, elevated at some points, lined with shops, residences, and pneumatic railways. This enclosed boulevard, built with iron and glass, would protect people from urban filth, pollution, and inclement weather. It meant to emulate the countryside, providing working classes with a respite from crowded neighborhoods. Paxton argued that his plans, the "greatest novelty" anywhere, would make London "the grandest city in the world."[21]

The most significant self-consciously modern approach to urban planning would take place in Paris instead, through a set of bold reforms from 1853 to 1870. Victorian London would see the world's very first underground mass transit system in 1863, built by Metropolitan Railway, a private company. Yet, in its most symbolic public projects, the "invention of tradition" prevailed. The historian Eric Hobsbawm used the expression to describe the attempt to imply continuity with an idealized past.[22] To illustrate it, he gave the example of the British parliament's reconstruction in Gothic style, after a fire in 1834. The massive Palace of

FIGURE. 3.2. Paxton's palatial "novelty": an unbuilt precursor for mixed-use urbanism with segregated speeds, and for London's Circle Line.

Westminster, rebuilt again after World War II, still stands—unlike the Crystal Palace, which succumbed to fire in the 1930s. When Paxton presented his monumental project in the 1850s, members of parliament were aware of the rebuilding in Paris. The architect tried to appeal to their competitive spirits, to no avail.

By remaking the French capital, the anglophile emperor Napoleon III helped to catapult the nation to the front of "the line of progress." The vision for Paris had elements of the invention of tradition, but more so, relied on a myth of rupture with the past, a key component of modernity.[23] Even before its transformation, Paris already occupied a prime place in transatlantic urban imaginations. In an aforementioned issue of *Putnam's Monthly*, which seems to unwittingly offer a map for the period's lettered mentalities, an article opened with a rhetorical question: "Tut! Tut! Tut! Paris empty? Paris dull?"[24] Dullness, it turns out, was in the eyes of the beholder. The authors found in Parisian boulevards a sense of history, vitality, and consumer experiences (champagne! cafés!) that aroused a "taste for life." They expressed enchantment with the city as a "reservoir of hope." In a classist tone, the article evinced social spaces segregated by income and culture: there was on the one hand an effusive "gilded Paris," and on the other a working-class "Kingdom of Rags," where "discontent oppresses the air."

Alluding to a history of political turbulence, the article described France as a country in which "Nothing is permanent but what is temporary."[25] We are not far from Charles Baudelaire's seminal definition in "The Painter of Modern Life" (1863): "Modernity is the transient, the fleeting, the contingent; it is one half of art, the other being the eternal and the immovable."[26] This interplay between fixity and flux is crucial to understand the process that became known as Haussmannization. Politics, economics, and aesthetics come together under the term, which became synonymous with large-scale demolition and rebuilding. It derives from Haussmann, who Napoleon III appointed as Prefect of the Seine in 1853. Elected president in 1848, Louis-Napoleón Bonaparte had installed himself as emperor in 1852, after a coup and two undemocratic plebiscites. His prefect, more a bureaucrat than an urban visionary, led the imperious reforms of the French capital until 1870.

The reforms stood apart from precedents for imposing a modern fabric on an existing major city. A system of wide and straight avenues, framed by corridors of uniform buildings, cut through maze-like neighborhoods. The modernized Paris attempted to exemplify capitalist dynamism and hasten mobility, while also enshrining age-old values of order and beauty—for posterity. It enacted a vision for the future based on both continuity and rupture. As early as 1842, Napoleon III wrote that he wanted to be a second Augustus, because the first had made Rome "a city of marbles."[27] The desire to remodel and modernize the city was not new, dating at least to the eighteenth century, as we have seen. Several plans from the first half of the nineteenth century stayed on paper, including one modeled on L'Enfant's Washington. But interventions picked up after the 1830 July Revolution, among them new public water fountains, trees, sidewalks, and the Arc de Triomphe.

Napoleon III also harkened back to his uncle's expressed desires. Decades earlier, Napoleon Bonaparte dreamt of a "fabulous" and "colossal" capital of 2–4 million people, like none before it, in place of the "old Paris."[28] Haussmann, who yearned for aqueducts and sewage systems that might recall the Romans, spoke frequently of "the conquest of old Paris."[29]

In both rhetoric and in practice, the reforms blended an attachment to the past with an embrace of change. In the tangled maze of the city's historic center, not far from the Notre Dame cathedral, the addition of "the great cross" (la grande croisée) at once represented tradition and disruption: two major thoroughfares intersected at a right angle, functioning as an axis for the entire city.[30] This invoked the symbolic power and modern valence of the grid, as well as a religious affiliation. Haussmann opted for well-established gas lamps for street lighting, rather than experimental electric technologies. Les Halles market also embodied a compromise between innovation and tradition: the cast-iron, glass-paneled structure, influenced by the Crystal Palace, housed longstanding popular vending practices in the heart of the city. Sometimes the appearance of rupture concealed continuities.

Until then, top-down projects of comparable scope relied on an ability to treat territories as blank slates for development, either as part of peri-urban expansion, rebuilding after involuntary destruction, or from scratch. Haussmann had authority to expropriate and engineer the reselling of land adjoining new streets to private developers. The process destroyed around 27,500 dwellings, creating another 102,000 or so.[31] Haussmannian architecture had an eclectic style composing a cohesive whole: generally, five- or six-story apartments with façades in limestone shared walls along a boulevard. The reforms updated infrastructure, including in sanitation, water supply, transportation networks, open spaces, government buildings, and cultural institutions.

The redevelopment of Paris operated at various scales, from the local to the global. Within the city, wider thoroughfares meant to take air and sunlight into crowded quarters. They eased the circulation of goods, people, and military forces, with smoother paving allowing for higher speeds. The new network of boulevards integrated insular

FIGURE 3.3. Traditional vendors in Victor Baltard's modern building, with on-going construction in the foreground.

neighborhoods, and created hubs around stations, squares, or monuments. Haussmann and his team pushed for the consolidation of gas provision and coordination between the various horse-drawn omnibus lines. Dozens of miles of new or widened roads helped to incorporate suburbs into mobility systems, especially after 1860, when annexations more than doubled the city's extension and increased its population from around 400,000 to 1.6 million. This metropolitan scale allowed the reorganization of Paris to anticipate aspects of modern zoning, placing heavy industries away from the urban core to avoid pollution and the presence of poor workers.[32]

During the two decades prior to the reforms, Paris had already been experiencing massive growth, mostly due to migration from rural areas. Thousands arrived each year. The capital increasingly concentrated both

FIGURE 3.4. A new monumental Paris of boulevards and park systems for posterity—and the masses.

the French population and national power.[33] In 1841, it had been made by law the fulcrum of the French railroad system. Significant railway expansion under the Second Empire, from around 2,000 to 12,000 miles, reinforced that role.[34] It was easier, of course, for planners to be more deliberate about the location of rail infrastructure than ports and canals. Rail routes, with telegraph lines frequently running beside them, linked French regions through Paris. The reforms placed train stations as key interconnected nodes within the city. They acted as gateways to the nation and the world.

France needed a capital befitting its imperial ambitions. Preparations for the 1855 Universal Exhibition helped to generate pressure for the first set of interventions.[35] *Universal* here of course presumed particular modern values, which the new city aimed to manifest: beauty, order, and progress expressed through symmetrical geometries, efficiency, and productivity. Napoleon III's version of authoritarian and state-sponsored industrial capitalism resulted in economic growth of around 5 percent per year. In 1860, marking a liberal turn for the regime, France and Great Britain signed a free trade agreement, the Cobden-Chevalier Treaty. The restructuring of Paris also coincided with infrastructural investments laying the groundwork for colonial expansion; foremost, in the construction of the Suez Canal (1859–1869), a French-led venture. This set off Haussmannian reforms in Cairo.[36] In global affairs, the French emperor sought to assert a leading role. Napoleon III aggressively advanced colonial efforts in New Caledonia, Cambodia, and present-day Vietnam. In Senegal, this included a new port.[37] As early as 1853, the French government had begun to attempt telegraph connections to Algeria, with an eye toward competing British efforts.[38] By 1855, the Universal Exhibition showcased electric submarine cables crossing the Atlantic to the United States. Closer to home, France fought on the winning side of the Crimean War (1853–1856) and meddled in the Italian wars of independence, siding against republicans. Napoleon III's designs also extended to the Americas with a failed effort to forcibly install an allied emperor in Mexico (1864–1867).

The Parisian reforms occurred within a dynamic global landscape, steeped in the idea of future-oriented urbanization. The march of progress in the metropolis, in a sense, built on colonization in North Africa, after the invasion and conquest of Algiers in 1830. There, the Ottoman past and Islamic present became obstacles. As the historian Zeynep Çelik sees it, the French rulers promoted "the cutting and slicing of the old fabric," prefiguring "a Hausmannian operation before Haussmann."[39] She argues that "the army was the main conduit of modernity in Algeria."[40] Over the course of subsequent decades they would target dissenters with violence, killing hundreds of thousands. During the Second Empire, at the same time, urban design largely preserved the old town, due to a mixture of respect and condescension. In the dominant view, locals lacked the modern customs and lifestyles of Europeans. Napoleon III's state visits to Algiers in 1860 and 1865 coincided with construction of the grandiose Boulevard de l'Impératrice, which replaced Ottoman-era houses and fortifications but had minor impact on the casbah. He called on colonists to "have faith in the future," cultivating their relationship to this "new fatherland" while treating the less-civilized natives with "peace" and "charity."[41]

In 1867, in a blow to the French project of a "Latin" empire, Mexicans executed Emperor Maximilian. That year, however, Paris shined on the global stage. An even larger Universal Exhibition hosted over 9 million visitors in an oblong-shaped metal and glass building in the Champ de Mars. An official publication mused: "more than a city, it is a world, and this world breathes the same air and lives a common life in a unique center."[42] France acted as the convenor of modern civilization. That same year, the capital held the inaugural gatherings of the International Congress of Architects, the International Telegraph Conference, and the International Monetary Conference. Paris aspired to set standards for beauty, communications, and commerce. We should not, however, infer the spread of Haussmannization as inevitable. Haussmann probably owed part of his great influence to the fact that the reforms associated to him lacked a single guiding blueprint. That way, others could borrow and adapt as they saw fit.

Like other autocratic planners before him, Haussmann had no training in design or engineering. Contemporaries compared his work to Pombal's in Lisbon.[43] In both cities, unlike the more minimalist

FIGURE 3.5. Paris in 1867: a city to encapsulate the world, leading the march toward progress.

Manhattan grid, plans brought together urban form, architecture, and programming. The Pombaline and Haussmannian projects had a sense of totality and carried on a vision that foreclosed other possibilities. In the fifteenth century, Leon Battista Alberti theorized that the architect, different from the builder, operates with the whole in mind. The architect designs, and construction fulfills that vision. The Parisian rebuilding deviated from Alberti's perspective more than Lisbon's. Like the Commissioners' Plan, it left a lot to the initiative of private investors. And although so closely associated with Haussmann, political contingencies and improvisation continuously shaped the process of planning and implementation.

Historians have pored over the relationship between the prefect and Napoleon III, sometimes disagreeing over the roles played by each. Haussmann remarked in his memoirs that urban development "ordinarily results from the confluence of circumstances that are beyond prediction, beyond calculation, and which, most often, no human will can direct."[44] If this was an admission to which he arrived in retrospect, even then, it is qualified. In his writings, the planner left the door open for himself as an exception. But he recognized that planners must contend with imponderables, and that urban futures could escape anyone's grip. Napoleon III was thinking of politics, not cities, when he wrote to his cousin in 1859 that "nothing lasts forever."[45] Family history certainly taught him that. We can imagine that such awareness of the vagaries of power presented one more reason to turn Paris into a centerpiece of his legacy, like Rome had been for Augustus.

———

How did Paris residents experience transformations that reflected the aspirations and actions of powerful men? A much greater share of the population benefited from access to fresh water and a sewer system that quadrupled in extension. Living conditions, nonetheless, continued to be dismal for working classes and the poor. They can still be understood as protagonists in the renovations, even if their visions for the future did not shape the planning process. In the least, they posed a threat to elitist dreams of order and progress. The historian David Jordan states that "the year 1848 made modern Paris possible."[46] Indeed, making it easier to mount military operations against barricaded insurrectionaries was an important motivation for the ruling classes. An opponent of Napoleon III's regime, in what became a truism, claimed that the boulevard's straight lines owed to how "bullets don't know how to take the first turn to the right."[47] Many of the new boulevards had the width of a cavalry company.

Fear of popular uprisings coupled with the visible plight of the dispossessed made some authorities sensitive to the need for improvements, especially in water management, sanitation, and amenities. Workers also began to organize more effectively. Leftist groups receded after the backlash to 1848 but began to coalesce again. In 1864, activists from throughout the continent met in London and founded the

International Working-Men's Association. It would become known as the First International. In France, labor movements and strikes grew over the course of the Second Empire. Well-positioned Parisians, at the same time, conflated discourses on urban hygiene and "the dangerous classes."[48] They often framed rural migrants, vagrants, and dissidents as prone to deviant behavior. A book from a prominent lawyer, for example, argued that these potential enemies to public morality and safety had to be contained.[49] These concerns shaped designs like the new Gare du Nord train station. Architects created compartmentalized spaces to enforce physical separation, rather than open halls that might allow for social mixing and rowdy gatherings.

Overall, by easing circulation between formerly tight-knit quarters, the reforms led to greater social diversity in shared spaces, which made some wealthier Parisians unhappy. The process, nonetheless, disproportionately disrupted the lives of the poor. Around 15,000 people lost their homes in the Île de la Cité alone.[50] They had to move from the centrally located island in the Seine to other precarious housing nearby or in the fast-growing outskirts. The future planned for Paris envisioned much more of a hierarchical than an egalitarian society. Haussmannization helped establish what increasingly become a transatlantic pattern: wealthier centers surrounded by lower-income peripheries. Haussmann had the habit of calling the urban poor "nomadic."[51] The underlying suggestion was that their displacement should not raise alarm, or that the natural condition of the poor was to be unrooted and antithetical to urban civilization. They are not granted a right to shape the city's future. Haussmann was against expanding suffrage, rent control, and subsidized housing for workers. Napoleon III disagreed on the latter and promoted charity-funded affordable units.[52] He learned that popular pressures could be enlisted in his own political battles, or alternatively, to help overturn governments. Heads of state ignored the poor at their own peril. Not for nothing, France recorded the last famine in its history in 1855.

Haussmann was generally unpopular, so having him as a lightning rod served the emperor's interests. Even early on people accused the prefect of "megalomania."[53] Napoleon III, in turn, oversaw an authoritarian regime that suppressed the opposition, curtailing freedoms of speech and assembly. Although initially elected with broad support, the list of his prominent detractors only grew over time. It counted among them the exiled Victor Hugo and Eugène Sue. The popular author of *The Mysteries of Paris* had been elected to the legislature in 1850, and left France after Napoleon's coup. The roll call of critics included some of the now most esteemed writers and artists of the nineteenth century, like Édouard Manet, Claude Monet, Émile Zola, and Gustave Flaubert. Even if they disliked the emperor, there was often ambivalence in the attitudes of artists toward modern Paris. Pushback, however, increased in the press and legislature as the regime moved toward liberalization in the late 1850s.

For one, the reforms proved to be expensive. Under Haussmann, the prefect's budget increased by 500 percent, amounting to two times Belgium's and one-half Prussia's.[54] The city drew on revenue from bonds and duties on goods like construction materials. But most of the resources came from a mix of deficit-financed state funds and private investment. We might think of it as a kind of financial architecture predicated on an understanding of a dynamic urban future. At the time, there was a justifiable perception that state authorities and private speculators engaged in impropriety and collusion. Those with insider information could purchase undervalued land in anticipation of public investments, amassing significant profits. Developers and property owners also benefited from demand by construction workers to rent units close to their jobs. Housing was generally only available in the unregulated open market.

Budgets throughout the 1860s surpassed expectations, inviting criticism from lawmakers.[55] Costs, delays, and disruptions created frustration. Yet, viewed from the vantage point of our century, it is impressive how the Second Empire left Paris with a generous system of green parks, tree-lined sidewalks, and open spaces. Public amenities, even when intended for the wealthy, attracted a motley crew of urbanites.[56] Credit for foresight, where it is due, tends to lag. Early in his government, Napoleon III set his eyes on a vast area on the western edge of the city for the Bois de Boulogne, partly modeled on London's Hyde Park, but more than six times larger. The landscape served as a playground for the social life of the well-to-do. It also became dedicated to mass entertainment for the working classes, holding a zoo, aquarium, botanic garden, amusement park, and racecourse. Napoleon III wished for a rough equivalent in the more impoverished eastern Paris, the Bois de Vincennes.

Modern cities assigned different spaces for labor and leisure. Compartmentalization and the separation of functions extended to urban administration, with different offices assuming specific responsibilities. Haussmann created a promenade and gardens department, headed by the civil engineer Adolphe Alphand.[57] They helped to invert some expectations about how urban parks should be designed. Early modern French gardens had been composed of geometrical symmetries, prizing rigid formal compositions. Along comparable lines, the modern city introduced straightened thoroughfares for efficient mobility. Departing from this rectilinear tradition, these modern parks privileged meandering pathways. Part of the idea was that leisure and nature should be contained, but that at the same time, within these landscapes, built forms might foster exploration and a less regimented experience of time.

Forested parks had another specialized function. The Bois de Boulogne was conceived as the "lungs" of the city. This increasingly prevalent bodily metaphor to describe cities reminds us of how much health concerns shaped modern planning. It also points to the dissonance between the city of planners, often understood as a whole and from the top down, and the contingent experiences of urbanites. In fact, many of those that lived through the reforms cared more about what they lost. Many Parisians fumed over the reduction of the beloved Luxembourg Garden, to accommodate rectilinear street layouts. Furious pamphlets and newspaper articles decried it. More than two decades later, an obituary for Haussmann disparaged his legacy as "vandalism," highlighting his "mutilation" of the Luxembourg Garden.[58] Anatomic metaphors could go both ways. A narrator in a novel by Zola, in another example, lamented seeing Paris with "its veins opened."[59]

People voiced a sense of bereavement as they saw their surroundings radically change. The city's fabric lost much of its morphological diversity. In many cases, rules established a correspondence between the width of streets and heights of buildings. Unlike in Pombaline Lisbon, architectural uniformity was not strictly legislated. Standardization, however, offered economic advantages for developers. One contemporary journalist called new buildings "lamentable in their regularity."[60] Another writer mourned the "monotony of the architecture."[61] Edmond and Jules de Goncourt wrote that "without sinuousness, without the unexpected perspective, implacably straight," the new boulevards brought to mind London or "some American Babylon of the future."[62] Théophile Gautier echoed them: "This is no longer the Paris I used to know, [...] it's Philadelphia, St. Petersburg, anything you like, but not Paris."[63]

The writers touched on anxieties about the ascendancy of the United States, and the risk that rampant commercial values posed to a notion of French cultural superiority. The reference to an American Babylon suggested that capitalist modernity substitutes a divine God for a worldly one. By locating this in the future, the Goncourt brothers evoked Babylon's downfall. The United States was a rival, and no model. This geopolitical antagonism also helps to explain France's attempt to found a Catholic empire in Mexico, taking advantage of the US Civil War. Although the intervention largely failed at expanding France's sphere of influence in the region, Haussmannization would provide an unintentional source of soft power in the years after Napoleon III. Rather than generically American or futuristic, over time the new boulevard system and architecture would be seen throughout the globe as quintessentially Parisian: modern, civilized, and fashionable.

Of course, many in France perceived the rebuilt city as a major achievement. They knew that the "old Paris" could no longer attend to the social and economic needs of a modern capital. On the one hand, the accelerated pace and seeming finality or definitiveness of the reforms caused discomfort even among enthusiasts. A prominent writer remarked that they should "leave something" for the twentieth century to do.[64] On the other, there was often an unexamined confidence about the judgment of posterity. Like in Lisbon and New York City before it, the futures invented for Paris represented a turn from religious to secular values. More than elsewhere, spatial hierarchies meant to reflect the aspirations of rising bourgeois elites. Tellingly, by far the costliest

FIGURE 3.6. The futuristic and modern became traditional and historical.

architectural project of the Second Empire was an opera house, intended to be the most grandiose in the world.

Charles Garnier won the commission to design the opera in a competition announced in 1860. He was until then a relatively unknown architect. The state rather than the city ran the project. Napoleon III remained involved, but Haussmann did not control it. He in fact preferred a different location. Throughout Paris, new boulevards connected insular neighborhoods, and converged on prominent sites, creating vistas that highlighted impressive train stations or historical monuments, like the Arc de Triomphe. The opera occupied one of these central places, framed by the urban fabric. There was an obvious cultural hierarchy at work in this elevation of a favored upper-class pastime. Access to the opera, however, was no longer a privilege people were born into, as in an aristocratic order. It was sold. A bourgeois commercial logic now reigned. This celebration of upward mobility instead of inherited rank can be understood in terms of both rupture and continuity. Even as the contours of class changed, we can still interpret the opera as fulfilling elite desires for segregation. The future was more open and dynamic. But it would be a variation of the past.

The design reflected this interplay. Innovative uses of cast iron supported the structure, but unlike in the Crystal Palaces or Les Halles, remained invisible. In that regard, the appearance of continuity concealed rupture. The opulent exterior can evoke both the invention of tradition and modernity as a myth of rupture. It combined classicist and Beaux-Arts elements. One prominent contemporary architect wrote that Eclecticism in design, by departing from religious and aristocratic models, sampled the best from the "ruins of the past" as a form of "research and preparation for the future."[65] Any passerby untrained in architecture would find familiar tropes like columns, and still know that a façade in such eclectic style could only be the *nouvel* opera—as it was first named. Inside, an enormous hallway defied precedents for theaters, and unlike the new Gare du Nord, encouraged mingling—a safe space, for those that could afford it.

When Charles Garnier entered the competition to design the opera, each submission needed to contain a motto. He chose to paraphrase the Italian poet Torquato Tasso: "I yearn for much, [but] expect little."[66] The sixteenth-century verse had biblical undertones. But coming from an ambitious thirty-five-year-old in 1860, the verse could be interpreted as a reference to secular aspirations. The architect's father worked as a blacksmith, and later in the carriage industry. Partly through a more open public school system, Garnier ascended from working-class origins. To modern mentalities, hope for the future had become an ideal with a force of its own, in spite of any actual promises materializing or not. Expectations mattered as much as their fulfillment. In this case, against the odds, Garnier indeed became the architect of the grand project.

The building became known as the Palais Garnier. Crystal Palace was also an unofficial moniker that caught on. The fact that people used the descriptor *palace* for buildings with semipublic purposes already signaled a shift from a naming practice that dated back to Rome's Palatine Hill, the residence of Augustus. London's most spectacular nineteenth-century construction was privately funded but served as a relatively popular and accessible attraction. The Palais Garnier reflected the elitist ambitions of an imperial–bourgeois society. In the new Paris, other prestigious and key urban sites hosted transportation infrastructure that pointed toward the future, or architectural markers that commemorated national glories of the past. The opera gained a similarly elevated status in the city's fabric. This building would stand both as a temple and a palace, but for high culture—and those that could afford it.

The opera's completion came only in 1875, under the Third Republic. As it turned out, cultural developments did not conform to expectations. The bet on posterity was at least partly off. In effect, the creators canonized by modernity often found greater vitality in the dirty and rowdy playhouses and taverns of the working classes than in the dazzling hallways of the dull upper classes. In modern culture, technocratic and literary writing would be increasingly at odds. The Paris of Impressionist painters and experimental "damned poets" had more to say to the twentieth century. Already during the reforms, vagabonds, artists, and writers began to flout mores and rewrite scripts assigned to them based on gender and class. George Sand, pen name of Aurore Dupin, incarnated some of that rebellious spirit. In an essay tied to the 1867 Universal Exhibition, the novelist showed how people defied the implied modern futures of Haussmannization. While imperial–bourgeois social life sought interior spaces like the opera, open spaces acquired unintended functions. Besides regimentation and efficient circulation, boulevards also allowed for idleness and exploration. A new term even had to be coined for those reveling in the experience: the *boulevardier*.

Sand wrote that she knew no other city where "itinerant daydreaming" (*rêverie ambulatoire*) provided greater pleasure: "in Paris, life is everywhere, and everything seems more alive than elsewhere."[67] The United States surfaced as ahead in the line of progress here too. After depicting a man's cart causing congestion, she describes how those that had become ensnared in traffic might react: "people now say, in Paris as in America, 'Time is money!'" using the expression in English. Sand ascribed the modern commodification of time to the entire United States, whereas in France it might be understood as an urban phenomenon. Other geopolitical hierarchies can be gleaned. Sand predicted a future where technologies like underground heating systems would allow "exotic" plants to flourish in the North Atlantic. There is something of the extractive colonizer's imagination at work, with European naturalists taking "treasures" home. The insubordinate meanderings of Sand and others, we might say, had been afforded by the subordination of peoples and territories elsewhere in the planet. But Sand also dreams of public education and knows that not everyone could go on a leisurely stroll. This required free time, and the ability to be safe. Sand was well-off and wore men's clothes.

Her essay made clear that in Paris, despite transformations, modern life remained manifold. And the invention of the future contained fissures. She conferred agency to urban spaces, and celebrated being "lulled by the movement and the murmur peculiar to this mad and wise city, where the unexpected has always reigned." We have, again, continuity and rupture at work. Planning cannot quite reduce urbanization to a set of manageable variables. Impermanence is a constant. Some things disappear, only for others to remain the same. Charles Baudelaire, another partisan of "itinerant daydreaming," put it differently: "Paris may change; my melancholy is fixed."[68]

III. Competing Futures

Napoleon III was correct: nothing lasts forever. Under pressure from an emboldened opposition and increasingly unpopular in the capital, he dismissed Haussmann in 1870. A few months later, the Franco-Prussian War led to the collapse of the Second Empire, and the declaration of a Republic. Prussian forces kept Paris under siege for over four months, until January of 1871. The grand gardens of the new city gained unimaginable functions. Desperately hungry and cold, Parisians cut down the Bois de Boulogne for firewood, and ate zoo animals.

In March of 1871, just a few days after France surrendered to Prussia, revolutionary upheaval led to the creation of the Paris Commune.

FIGURE 3.7. Seizing the city and the future?

Disaffected National Guard soldiers and workers seized control of the city. Within days, they ran an election. On March 28, Commune Council representatives were announced to a crowd of tens of thousands in front of the Hôtel de Ville, the centrally located City Hall where Haussmann worked for seventeen years. A red flag now flew atop the imposing building. In the French Renaissance style, it had survived Haussmann unscathed. But the reforms opened up the surrounding areas and left them better able to accommodate massive gatherings. If boulevards had been conceived as a strategy to suppress insurrections, this appeared to have failed—for now. The Communards made ample use of barricades and appropriated the new spaces. From the Hôtel de Ville, the day after being elected, the Council addressed citizens. Their language spoke directly to a right to the future: "You are masters of your destiny."[69]

An iconic photograph from that month captured competing modern futures at stake. In the foreground, triumphant National Guard members and insurrectionists pose in a barricaded boulevard. They appear to celebrate the beginnings of an age of revolution and self-governance. Two men hold a sign that reads: "Long Live the Republic." Behind them, a prominent advertisement painted on the side of a building addressed other aspirations. It read, in big and bold capital letters: "novelties for workers / exceptional deals."[70] The store was in a boulevard named after an aristocrat from the *ancien régime*, Prince Eugene. Its sales strategy adopted the language of class identity, making a promise specifically to workers. But the appeal was to their agency and self-interest as consumers, not citizens. At this establishment, they would find the latest products at great prices. Capitalist modernity, the advertisement suggested, should be for workers too—if they could afford it.

Most Communards were wage earners and manual laborers. When they ran the election for the Council, many socially conservative and upper-class Parisians abstained. Tens of thousands had already left the city. A little less than half of eligible male voters elected a set of representatives hailing largely from the working classes.[71] This was probably the first time that a successful revolutionary takeover did not have leadership dominated by lettered professionals. The Council had many more clerks than lawyers, and several participants of the First International. It included an array of political currents and tendencies: democrats, communists, neo-Jacobins, anarchists, socialists, republicans, and a group of "Independent Revolutionaries."

The diversity of visions about what it meant to exercise control over one's destiny reflected tensions that would shape both leftist politics and urbanization over the subsequent decades. Not everyone set their eyes on the future. Some vied to resurrect the days of the authoritarian Committee for Public Safety of the French Revolution, and even brought back its Republican Calendar. Others more closely aligned with proto-socialists. Anarchists, for example, often preferred not to engage with centralized government and discarded teleological expectations of progress. They aimed to build worker-managed collectives and make the city into an alternative to capitalism and the nation-state. It could then become an example to be emulated in the pursuit of better futures. A few French cities indeed declared Communes inspired by Paris.

No consensus could be built around toppling the national state or appropriating banks, but opposition to the Church was a common denominator. Though religious activities remained legal, the Commune targeted Church properties, clergy, and their role in education. The new government abolished child labor, the death penalty, military conscription, and rental debts from the period of the siege. People set up co-op canteens, bakeries, newspapers, orphanages, and makeshift hospitals, sometimes with women in prominent roles. A public event in May centered on tearing down a prominent statue of Napoleon atop the Vendôme Column. Partly in response to threats and violence from the Versailles-based national government, the Commune moved from decentralized self-governance toward more dictatorial policies. This included surveillance and rushed military tribunals. It was the defenders of the established order, however, who unleashed what became known as Bloody Week, in May of 1871.

Under conservative Republican leadership, the French military executed thousands of people.[72] The Commune killed hostages, including the archbishop of Paris. Generals, some of them veterans of colonial warfare in Africa, attacked the domestic dissidents "with unrestrained ferocity."[73] They imprisoned tens of thousands of Communards, sending several hundred to New Caledonia. Haussmann, in a letter to a friend, had described the Commune as a sign of the "menacing audacity of international socialism," but predicted that it would survive no longer than a day.[74] The Commune lasted nearly three months. Karl Marx, in an address to the International Working-Men's Association, concluded: "Working men's Paris, with its Commune, will be forever celebrated as the glorious harbinger of a new society."[75] The "martyrs are enshrined" in the hearts of workers, he argued, while "its exterminators" would incur "eternal pillory from which all the prayers of their priest will not avail to redeem them." The judgment of posterity could be used as a tool by left or right alike, regardless of the end goal. Marx's prediction about the Commune's legacy positions him as a type of secular seer, imbued with indignation as well as faith in a future that would be different—and more just—than the present.

People have debated the Paris Commune ever since. The Goncourt brothers thought that Bloody Week would serve as a lesson, forestalling the next revolution for a couple decades.[76] Paris only had comparable barricades again in 1968. Flaubert, in a letter to George Sand, described the Commune as a leftover from the medieval era, rather than a harbinger of a new society.[77] Fears of urban masses and proletariat revolutions animated protodystopian narratives set in the future.[78] Meanwhile, thinkers on the left intensely focused on the experiment as a model and cautionary tale. We can also understand it as an important turning point in the invention of urban futures, as much for the possibilities that it opened as for those that it foreclosed.

Some recent scholarship contends that the reforms and the experiences of displacement helped to generate the animus behind the insurrection.[79] As the Commune fell, mobs did go after symbols of Haussmann's works, even if attacks focused on older symbolic buildings like the Tuileries Palace and the Hôtel de Ville.[80] Others maintain that the Commune teaches us that workers do not need to be told what to do, and that there are alternatives to systems of exploitation.[81] Surely that is true, but any takeaways must also recognize the violent suppression as a sign of how established powers do not respond kindly to threats to the social order.[82] Opposition to the Commune ranged from criticism of its dictatorial turn to the French Republic's mass killings. Bloody Week might be interpreted as a watershed in the nation-state's assertion of its power over urban sovereignty and self-governance. The French Republic's response to this urban experiment made it harder to envision futures for a sovereign social collective outside the national state.

———

Napoleon III died in exile in England in 1873. He would not witness the completion of the new opera. Paris never quite fulfilled the Second Empire's visions of an ordered modern future. The city's built and social fabric bore scars from 1871. Wealthier areas had buildings in ruins. Working-class neighborhoods lost considerable population. A small business might have been left without their plumber. A child, without their uncle. Amid foreclosed futures, the Third Republic gave continuity to several of the reforms. Adolphe Alphand stayed on, as director of Public Works. Planning and urban design would continue to serve entrenched interests and rely on state capacity. At the same time, not all resistance to authoritarian modern projects came from revolutionary quarters. Even during the Second Empire, civil society in other French cities began to organize against the Parisian model, arguing that the traditional urban forms of narrow and crooked streets made up an important part of their identity.[83] In subsequent decades, Haussmannization would serve a variety of agendas across the world, while also inviting pushback. Elsewhere in contemporary Europe, its scale and basic principles began to inspire or at least inform a series of ambitious plans.

Berlin was also undergoing rapid growth and industrialization. In what became known as the Hobrecht Plan, approved in 1862, a group of engineers devised a program "intentionally conceived to adapt to an uncertain future."[84] Their plan for the city focused not on demolitions but on expansion in largely greenfield surroundings. James Hobrecht had visited several English cities and Paris in 1860. Akin to the Haussmannian approach, the Berlin planners provided a comprehensive framework for development that prized uniformity, spatial hierarchies, and interconnected neighborhoods, with ample use of the straight line. Elaboration of this program preceded the Franco-Prussian War, which was instrumental for the unification of German states under Prussian dominance, with Berlin as the capital. In 1875, the Prussian Planning Act gave cities expropriation powers to add infrastructure. Despite national rivalries, the renovation of Paris continued to serve as an important source. Geopolitics and urban planning do not always align in predictable ways.

Other European cities also experimented with a reconfiguration of their urban fabric. They often measured themselves against Paris, even if guided by different ideals and solutions.[85] In 1865, Vienna opened the first section of its monumental Ringstrasse, the result of a competition for a ring road to replace obsolete fortification walls. And the process known as Risanamento began to introduce a network of wider streets in Florence, which served as capital of a newly united Italy until 1871. Vienna would become emblematic of modernity with its centrality to

Fin-de-Siècle European culture.[86] But in terms of urban design, the boulevard-like Ringstrasse was less invested in projecting an image of the future, and more bound to the past. It arose out of a late medieval guild model of upper-class beneficence, and the earliest significant construction on it was a votive church with Gothic elements. The first major state-funded building in the project, a new opera house, would be built in a Renaissance Revival style during the 1860s.

Historians of science recognize a shift in the late nineteenth century—rather than just being additive, scientific progress involved a reorganization of knowledge into new disciplines. We might think of a comparable change occurring in urban planning. Whether they focused on expanding into open spaces or demolishing and rebuilding, plans intended to reconfigure the existing urban order. Two contemporaries of the Haussmannian reforms offered competing visions which also proved to be hugely consequential in transatlantic urbanization: Ildefons Cerdá and Frederick Law Olmsted. Like Haussmann and Napoleon III, they sought to address the relationships between urban growth and socioeconomic change. Both Cerdá and Olmsted, however, envisioned planning at the service of more egalitarian futures.

Barcelona's rising bourgeois elites were attuned to the remaking of the French capital. The Mediterranean hub was growing rapidly, and accumulating wealth on the strength of its manufacturing industries, especially in textiles. Its population increased from around 115,000 in 1802 to 187,000 in 1850. As in Vienna, areas dedicated to obsolete fortifications surrounding the city became available for development. A competition run by the municipality in 1859 chose a radial plan, but the Spanish government reserved the right to opt for an alternative devised by the engineer Ildefons Cerdá—he had worked with national authorities on surveys of the city. His plan was chosen in 1860.[87] Barcelona's Eixample (expansion in Catalan) adopted a regular orthogonal grid, with square blocks cut at an angle. These chamfered corners allowed vehicles to make turns more easily, or to load and unload without causing congestion.[88] But it was not just about efficient mobility. The now iconic design also created space for street corners to host social life, including services and businesses—food vendors, shoe shiners, kiosks,

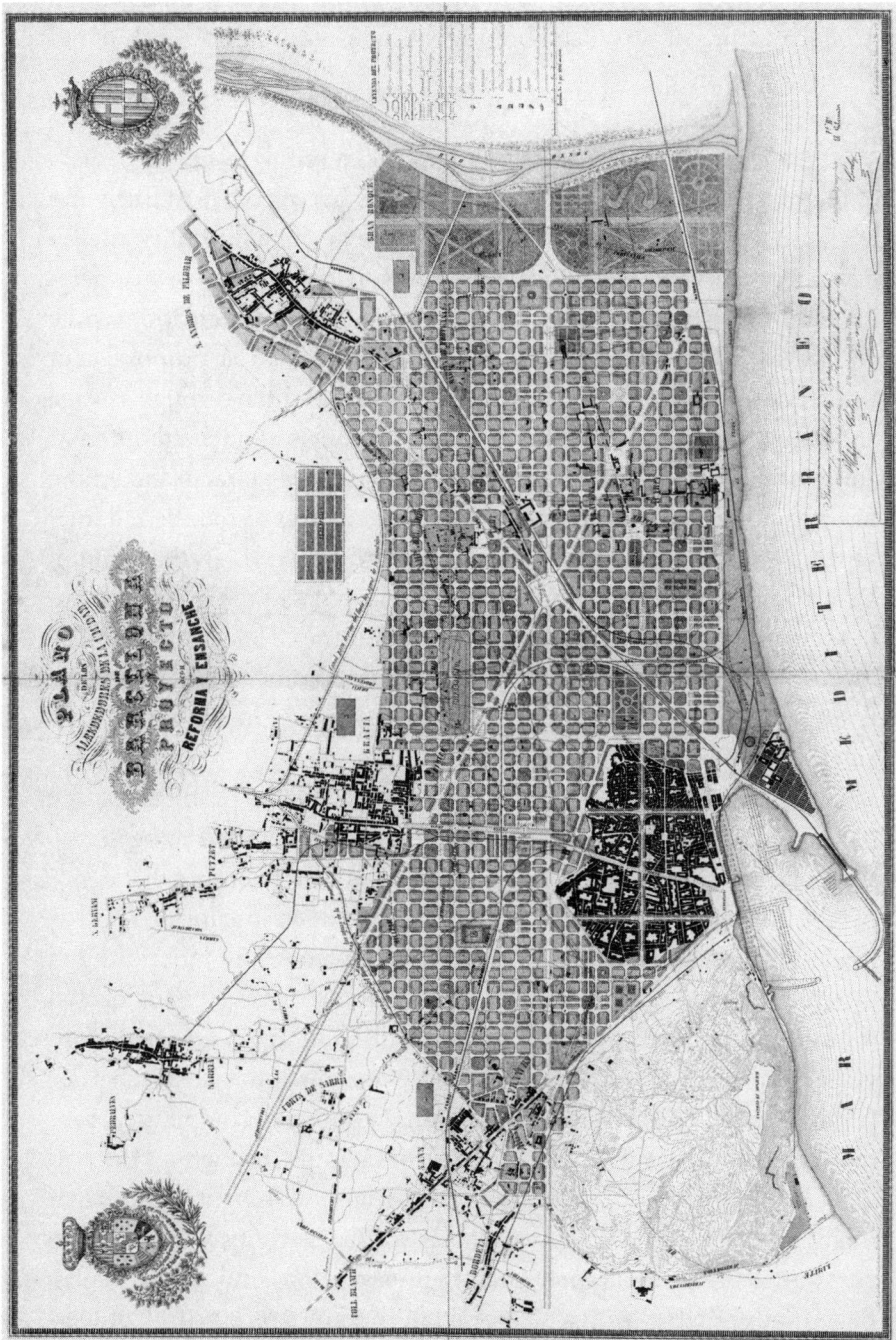

FIGURE 3.8. From a compact and egalitarian template, an iconic city emerged.

or benches. Cerdá's vision was not just about speeding up toward a modern future. It was also about creating a sense of citizenship and belonging in the modern city.   .

Barcelona's residents suffered from the same dire conditions as those of larger cities. Crowded quarters experienced yellow fever and cholera epidemics. Cerdá studied the relationships between urban form and health indicators, documenting for example the high mortality rates in dense working-class neighborhoods. His work contributed to an emerging modern planning consensus about sanitation and circulation, while also developing a series of novel solutions. The Eixample proposal kept the dense urban core but addressed the city as a whole through sewage and water management systems. Major diagonals connected different zones of the city, and the widest one, the Passeig de Gràcia, linked the historic center to new developments. The engineer also designed for a separation of speeds on thoroughfares, with raised sidewalks and rail infrastructure. He wanted both the street layout and the urban form to have regularity. New constructions in the Eixample had set height limits. An average building was supposed to host commerce on the ground floor, bourgeois residents above it, and workers on the top floors. Orientation favored southern exposure.

Cerdá proposed another innovation for the familiar problems of lack of sunlight and ventilation: the plan generally intended to keep two sides of each square block unbuilt. This also meant to ensure that dense neighborhoods could have plenty of flexible open lots for recreation, including gardening. The plan prescribed separation of functions and programming. Districts of twenty blocks would have spaces dedicated for uses like markets, hospitals, and schools. Four main diagonals converged in a new major square. But like the commissioners in Manhattan, Cerdá avoided prioritizing clear religious, commercial, or political centers. He deliberately distributed nodes for civic life throughout the city.

In Madrid, authorities found appeal in wide and straight avenues that might make it easier to suppress riots in the Catalan city.[89] Ironically, in part due to the national government's intervention in municipal affairs, Barcelona ended up with a plan characterized by a relative lack of hierarchies, decentralization, and an antiauthoritarian ethos. The proposal that won the municipal competition, in contrast, had shown an explicit commitment to class-based segregation, with lower-income residents relegated to the outskirts. Many in Barcelona's upper classes pushed back against the adopted plan. They preferred Paris or Washington, DC, as a model. Some accused Cerdá of socialism or communism.[90] Under myriad pressures, the city only partially implemented the plan, which underwent significant changes. Real estate interests led to all four sides of the Eixample blocks being built up. Their interiors gained private uses, including for enclosed malls or parking. And as the wealthy moved from the old center to new constructions, especially around the Passeig de Gràcia, they reasserted stratification.

The plan was nonetheless pioneering in its attempt to address what contemporaries called the "social question" through an egalitarian vision of urban futures. Cerdá's intellectual lineage and political aspirations positioned him closer to the Paris Commune than to the Second Empire. On the one hand, he shared with Napoleon III a prescient sense of the transformational impact of new modes of transportation and urbanization in the modern world. On the other, they diverged in both goals and methods. The very term *urbanización* is widely attributed to Cerdá. His theories shifted the focus toward the city as part of a process rather than an object. They recognized that urbanization extended beyond a city's limits, and that the built environment should be understood in terms of evolving forces, not as a static reflection of ideals. As a consequence, urban planning could not be restricted to buildings, budgets, and the ambitions of the powerful. Shaping urbanization was about social needs and humanity's collective future in a rapidly changing world.

Cerdá, born in a rural town, was exposed to the industrial revolution in Barcelona. His 1867 *Teoría general de la urbanizacion* (General Theory of Urbanization) opens with the deep impression caused by steam and steel technologies. He described riding a steamship as a kid, noticing how the motor and parts moved together. Though the machine was fixed in place, this resulted in locomotion. Cerdá theorized about this as a "complete system," and thought that it presented a contrast to the society of his youth, which appeared "immobile."[91] The uses of steel and steam, culminating in trains, signaled to him the beginning of a new epoch, a state of transition shaped by the relationships between the forces of the traditional past, the interests of the present, and "the future with its noble aspirations and acceleration [*arranque*]."[92] *Arranque* denoted the starting mechanism in a machine, suggesting that technologies had set society on a process of speeding toward the future. There was no turning back. To Cerdá, a "new civilization" was inevitable and could already be felt in urbanization. Cities were the "operational fields" for the "titanic struggles" of civilizational models competing for world domination.

It is clear that for Cerdá the stakes could not have been any higher. His trajectory was the inverse of Paxton's and Garnier's, who ascended socially by catering to the desires of the rich and powerful. The Catalan planner inherited some wealth but died with modest means. He devoted much of his life to reflecting about how to prepare cities and societies for the futures catalyzed by the "gigantic march" of the industrial revolution, marked by "movement and communicativeness."[93] Cerdá saw the present as a straitjacket, constrained by needs that had "not been foreseen nor dreamed in earlier times."[94] Planning was therefore crucial for possibilities of freedom and well-being in modernity.[95] *Teoría general* skirted mentions of Haussmann's Paris, preferring to situate itself within a long historical arc. The book defined urbanization as the occupation and remaking of land: thus, the process started with the first human, and would continue until the last of us disappears from the face of the earth. To Cerdá, forms of development should adapt to the specificities of period, place, and culture. Cities change, but satisfying human needs is a constant.[96]

Cerdá, at the same time, was not just interested in diagnosis. He also wanted to make new worlds. In that sense, he should be placed alongside utopian predecessors. His plans bore the influence of seminal figures like Robert Owen and Henri de Saint-Simon, as well as Étienne Cabet, from a second generation of these thinkers. Cabet's widely read *Voyage en Icarie* (1840) inspired the transatlantic Icarian movement.[97] Its adherents preferred not to go along with the logic of capitalist production, recalling Bartleby. But they went further than the scrivener and tried to create communities modeled after the fictional Icaria. Cabet structured his book as a travel narrative to this urban utopia. It had many of the same formal characteristics as other modern plans, including a gridded layout: "see the streets," the narrator says, "all straight and wide."[98] A river, walled in order to flow in a straight line, divided the symmetrical city, which had a circular shape. Architectural uniformity characterized the urban fabric. Resembling aspects of Cerdá's plan, each quarter had a school, hospital, and temple, as well as factories, shops, and places for public gathering. Squares had trees "like the boulevards of Paris."[99] The design ensured air circulation, which along with water drainage systems, promoted good health. There was public illumination, and streets had iron tracks and lanes to separate speeds. Omnibus and carriage drivers were state employees.

Cabet championed reason—it was a keyword in his book, and a point in common with discourses of protosocialist utopians. Reason was not a deterrent to an exorbitant imagination, but a requirement.[100] This constellation of ideas informed planning. Saint-Simonian engineers and architects in France, for example, had helped to create the conditions for Haussmannization.[101] They all converged around a deep faith that the future could be scientifically perfected. But goals and methods varied greatly, even more so in fiction and in utopian movements. Cabet's Icaria was a place without prisons, almshouses, or aristocratic mansions, where "all the palaces are dedicated to public purposes." It followed a rigid political system. Advertisements, lotteries, games of chance, and the stock exchange were not allowed. Icaria had no "vice." This ideal city banned cabarets, smoking joints, and cafés, as well as a host of other "shameful or culpable pleasures." It was ultimately a totalitarian society. Planners would have faced too much backlash if they ever tried to implement this on a major city. Most Icarian communities lasted only a few years.

Cerdá shared with Icarians a sense of possibility, and egalitarian inclinations. But unlike many utopians, his vision for the future was predicated on transforming existing cities, rather than escaping them. The latter could only be an impossible fantasy, given the social, economic, and technological currents already under way in the modern world.

Perhaps no place was urbanizing quicker than the United States, where Cabet migrated in 1848. Cerdá's theorizations, though they covered an astonishing amount of ground, largely avoided the Americas. He briefly criticized the Commissioners' Plan for creating a hierarchy among public ways, expressed in their numeric addresses as well as in the relationship between streets and avenues, favoring the latter. From the perspective of "reason and science," these ought to be equal, he argued.[102]

With the dawn of the Gilded Age in Manhattan, other much more explicit hierarchies became manifested in the grid, as the wealthy moved uptown. In North America, at the same time, a relatively independent planning tradition arose in response to rapid urban growth, with ideas both about transforming and fleeing the city. Some planners sought to introduce the virtues of the countryside into the city, through democratic-minded urban designs. Others envisioned utopian suburban futures—for those that could afford it.

The Parisian model had early echoes in the United States, in New York City and elsewhere. By the mid-nineteenth century, Boston had become consolidated as a key port, manufacturing base, and railroad hub, with connections far and wide. Tens of thousands of immigrants, most of them escaping the Irish famine, arrived in the city between 1845 and 1855. In 1859, the state granted the crowded city a right to build landfills on the tidal Back Bay. Steam and steel technologies for moving sand and gravel would allow for the creation of a roughly 200-acre neighborhood.[103] For a sense of perspective, this was comparable to the area of the Eixample built within the first two decades of the Plan Cerdá.[104] The new Back Bay, full of Haussmannian (and Victorian) echoes, had a gridded layout with boulevards lined by rows of grand brownstones for the upper classes. The neighborhood was adjacent to the maze-like historic center and integrated into it. Over time, this more Eurocentric approach to planning proved to be less dominant in the United States than in Latin America.

In North America, Frederick Law Olmsted rises above any other name in nineteenth-century planning. His career straddled two major currents in the United States. He worked on great city parks, and on planned suburbs. Alex Krieger inscribed "the romance of the suburb"

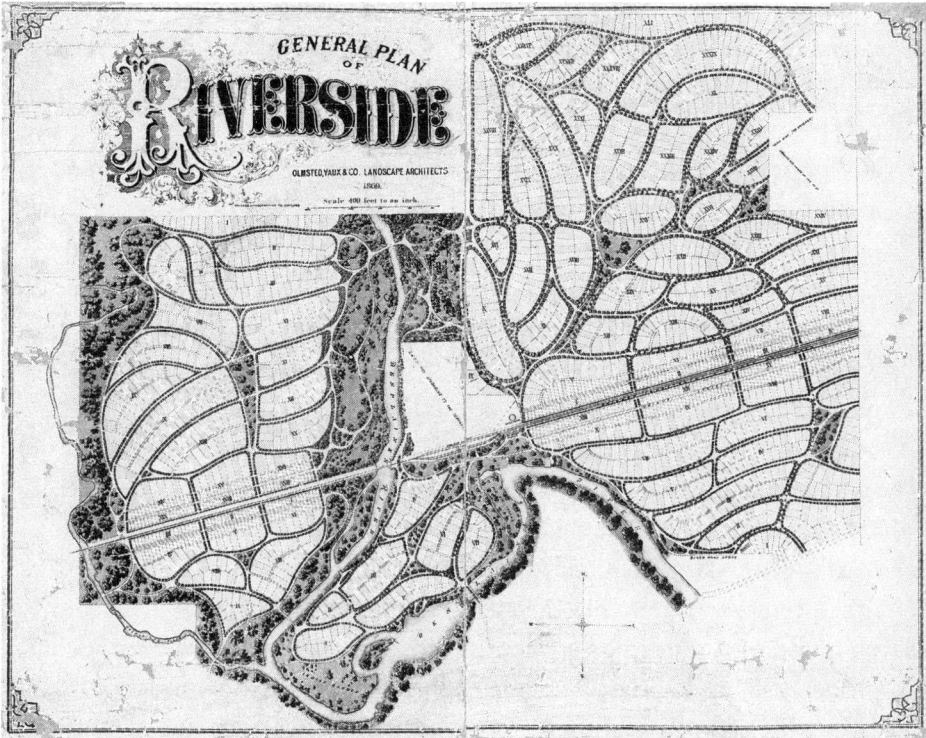

FIGURE 3.9. The promise of nature, dependent on Chicago but not of it.

within a story of American utopian urban idealism. He quotes Olmsted describing suburbs, in 1869, as "the best application of the arts of civilization to which mankind has yet attained."[105] There was of course a long-standing history of the rich living in villas outside cities, and of suburbs as slums. But for Olmsted's generation, planned suburbs provided a solution to the problems of dense contemporary cities, including congestion, pollution, and disease. They became especially prevalent in industrial English cities and in the United States. In the 1860s, Olmsted worked on perhaps the earliest such development in the country, Riverside, about 9 miles from Chicago's downtown. Instead of the grid, his suburb had a meandering layout.

The nineteenth-century suburb might have been utopian, and even egalitarian for those within, but it was also exclusive. Unlike the model communities of socialist radicals, these private developments had few qualms about leaving behind poorer urbanites in crowded downtowns. Already, geographies of stratification in the United States began to depart from the more common transatlantic patterns of wealthier centers and poorer peripheries. We can interpret this in light of Jeffersonian antiurban worldviews, which had many heirs. A saying from the period exemplified what became known as Manifest Destiny: "Go West, young man, go West and grow up with the country." It is commonly attributed to the journalist and politician Horace Greeley, who praised farm living and claimed that "Washington is not a nice place to live in" due to "deplorable" morals, high rent, bad food, and "disgusting" dust.[106] The dream of fleeing the city was tied to agrarian and colonial visions, mostly reserved for white men. Suburbanization tapped into it, but planned suburbs also recognized that cities were there to stay. Most developments in a city's outskirts assumed, after all, that residents would commute to urban centers. Whether in the city or countryside, planning depended on modern relationships to time and space as categories fixed through property rights. Land made available through colonization underlay the idea of the country's future being in the march toward the West—or in the move to spacious suburbs outside an established urban hub. This became increasingly feasible with railroad expansion to the Pacific and a proliferation of streetcar lines.[107] Suburbs might emulate proximity to nature, but they had no room for wilderness. Trains, meanwhile, acted as drivers of urbanization and environmental destruction at unforeseen scales.[108] The romance of the suburbs also constituted a response to these intertwined conditions.

The pursuit of a domesticated nature was manifested in suburbanization and in the construction of major city parks. Olmsted played an oversized role in both. It is not an accident that he became better-known as a landscape architect than as an urban planner. Some even deem him an environmental planner.[109] In Boston, Olmsted designed perhaps his most ambitious intervention, starting in the 1870s. The Emerald Necklace park system now covers well over 1,000 acres around the city, connecting green spaces and waterways. His signal achievement, however, was New York City's Central Park, with his long-standing collaborator

Calvert Vaux. After at least a decade of lobbying from well-connected residents, the state legislature approved the project in 1853, the same year as Haussmann's appointment as prefect. In New York, the process would be subjected to a design competition, which Olmsted and Vaux won in 1858, for what ended up as an over 800-acre park in the heart of Manhattan. Their proposal stood apart from others by creating well-defined separations from the existing urban fabric, through both boundaries and sunken roads.

The new space reshaped the Commissioners' Plan, as growth continued to surpass expectations. By the time of Central Park's completion in 1876, Manhattan's population likely reached 1 million, around ten times larger than when the grid was adopted. It was only in the 1870s, however, that more people lived above than below 14th Street. Even then, around 40,000 lots remained available for development.[110] Central Park's very name placed a bet on future growth. From the perspective of most residents, after all, it was on the outer edges of the city. The site would only become *central* once the uptown grid filled in. In the 1850s, geographical centrality depended on a view of the island as a whole—in other words, from the bird's-eye perspective of a plan.

Like his European counterparts, Olmsted could foresee that planning had to address relentless transformations with an eye toward the long term. Future appears much more frequently as a keyword in his writings, however, than in those of Haussmann or Cerdá. He often appealed to the judgment of posterity. Olmsted defended his large-scale project by telling the Board of Commissioners of Central Park, in 1858: "I shall steadfastly regard the distant future, when alone it can be fully seen how far I am worthy of it."[111] This rhetorical device reenacted what Daniel Rosenberg calls the "proleptic imagination of Christian prophecy." The historian posits that the typical proleptic statement is: "in the end, this will have had meaning."[112] The planner's version came with a secular twist: this will have had meaning once future generations see it.

Olmsted wrote to the board that "the future of the Park" depended on design elements capable of creating a "rural and natural character," and of regulations to ensure the "good order and harmony in its use."[113] Indeed, there would be a long list of ordinances forbidding activities like hawking, fortune telling, and "indecent language."[114] But appealing to the future was not just part of a strategy for exerting pressure on decision makers. This also helped Olmsted to paint a positive and inclusive vision. To him, the democratic ethos could be forward-looking, encompassing those not-yet born.

A contemporary article in the *New York Times* prompted a comparable view. On questions of budgeting, we read, "it must be remembered that the New York for which the Park is being made is not alone the New York of either 1857 or of 1860, but the New York of the next hundred or two hundred years."[115] Despite the "monstrous injustice" of making people pay for a Park that only future generations would enjoy in "its prime," the article concluded that the investment was worthwhile: "They will not only have a keener relish for outdoor amusements than their ancestors, but more leisure to enjoy them." Contemporary taxpayers had a duty to those that would inherit their city. Along similar lines, Olmsted defended the necessity of the Park by dramatically invoking "the expectation that the whole of the island of New York would [...] before many years be occupied by buildings and paved streets, [and] that millions upon millions of men were to live their lives upon this island."[116] Planning therefore had an existential dimension: "the lives of women and children too poor to be sent to the country can now be saved in thousands of instances, by making them go to the Park."[117]

As the park's construction advanced during the Civil War, between 1861 and 1863, Olmsted served in the US Sanitary Commission. Before then, he had become critical of slavery while traveling in the South. After the war he managed a gold mining estate in California that went bankrupt. These experiences only seemed to reinforce Olmsted's commitments to environmental conservation, and to parks as crucial to the future of democracy. His thinking about cities lacked Cerdá's generalizing pretensions, but they had more theoretical heft than Haussmann's. Olmsted had also traveled in Europe and perceived the global dimensions of urbanization. He referred to the project for Brooklyn's Prospect Park, which he would also design with Vaux, as interconnected to Central Park, and crucial to "the metropolis and their customers and guests from all parts of the world for centuries to come."[118] His horizons, however, remained firmly grounded in the United States. Olmsted, for example, contrasted Central Park to European precedents catering to aristocrats.[119]

Reflecting on how dispersion in the United States had reached limits, Olmsted focused instead on planning for the inevitability of urban growth, especially as agriculture became less labor intensive. Phrases like "townward drift" and "townward flood" recur in his writings. In an 1870 address to the American Social Science Convention in Boston, Olmsted's language resonated with widespread negative attitudes toward urbanization. His alarmism, however, served to bolster the case for city planning: "every evil to which men are especially liable when living in towns, is likely to be aggravated in the future, unless means are devised and adapted in advance to prevent it."[120] Parks played a prophylactic role. Those means should result not from "the preservation of legacies from early colonial days but by some conscious effort of a democratic body of citizens to meet a proven need."[121] As in Paris, we have a modern approach combining continuity and rupture. But the elements are different. Planning could be a tool of, by, and for democratic change.

Early in the process of envisioning the Park, Olmsted evoked an image of a future "when New York will be built up," full of "rows of monotonous straight streets" and "angular buildings."[122] Rectilinear modernity, however, was not the selling point. In this scenario, Central Park alone preserved aspects of the island's "varied surface." Olmsted proposed to design "landscape effects" that would maintain a relationship to the existing "picturesque" rocky formations and "undulating outlines." His version of planning for a democracy was still fundamentally top-down in practice. The vision for Central Park's landscape selectively embraced a geological past, but also erased part of its social present. To prepare the territory, the city evicted around 1,600 people. Demographically this is arguably minor, considering the creation of an over 800-acre public park. Culturally it represented a foreclosing of futures. Obvious differences aside, the narrowing of possibilities for self-governance and collective organization in the modern city invite comparisons with the suppression of the Paris Commune. Before the park's development, the area was home to a variety of communities, ranging from Irish livestock farmers to Seneca Village.[123]

Begun in the 1820s, Seneca Village brought together a black-majority community of around 300 people with churches, gardens, and a school, located on what became the Upper West Side range of Central Park. It has been called a Black utopia.[124] In a way, the enclave shared more characteristics with maroon communities than with protosocialist utopias, taking in those that fled slavery in the South. Frederick Douglass visited. At the same time, many of its residents owned property, and the very name Seneca might be a reference to a classical tradition prized by abolitionists. The inhabitants did not flee the industrial city for the same reasons as suburbanites either. Racism marked their urban experiences. New York abolished slavery gradually, with emancipation only in 1827. African Americans, however, continued to be banned from better-paying jobs and faced a higher bar for voting. Antiblack terrorism targeted their churches, schools, and businesses, along with those of white abolitionist allies.[125]

The community remained well-connected to the rest of Manhattan, with residents hailing from institutions like the African Free School, engaging in public speaking on behalf of civil rights, and commuting to work downtown. Seneca Village was home to a hugely disproportionate number of African American voters in the city, because property ownership allowed them to overcome racist restrictions.[126] Though twentieth-century displacement and segregation occurred at a much vaster scale, the destruction of this community could be interpreted as an omen of things to come. Its history only began to be more widely recovered to the public eye in the 1990s.[127] We may argue that a US focus on discourses about the future, including in Olmsted, served to deflect attention from less noble realities, such as violent settler-colonialism in Western expansion. Yet, denials of the past and present could also coexist with evolving democratic aspirations.

The US Civil War expanded the boundaries of freedom. More modestly, New York's Central Park created a space where various urbanites could forge a sense of belonging. We can return to that same set of 1853 issues from *Putnam's Monthly*—where, a few months later, Olmsted began to work as an editor and then publisher. One article told a story of an encounter with a German migrant on a ship to Europe. According to the author, this man had purchased a farm in the United States, making a small fortune after a railroad opened near it, and property prices spiked. The migrant was returning to convince others in his native village to join him in America. There, he said, they could have freedom, while in the Old World, conditions were "not better than that of a slave."[128] Many transatlantic threads come together in this story: the commodification of land, railroads, steamships, diasporas out of rural Europe, and of course, a New York-based publication. In the land of opportunity, the story suggests, the real estate bonanza did not produce just Astor. Indeed, property owners in Seneca Village also profited as real estate appreciated. Socioeconomic mobility was available for capable or lucky newcomers. This was a powerful narrative for contemporary urban readers.

If possibilities for freedom became more fluid in the United States, this had a lot to do with conditions created by migration and urbanization. Over time, representative democracy provided channels for some social changes. With expanded franchise, elections allowed for vested interests to take turns in power, and at times, for initially marginalized groups to ascend. We can think of the rise of the Irish in municipal politics in Boston and New York, for example. Olmsted, who suggested that women were more drawn to cities than men, envisioned Parks as places to be enjoyed regardless of gender, class, or ethnic origin.[129] But there were no African Americans or women working in Central Park.[130] The nation itself moved toward the promise of fuller rights after the Union's victory and the abolition of slavery. But as we will see in the next chapters, virulent racist reactions, with consequences to urbanization, followed the Civil War and Reconstruction. The fate of Seneca Village showed that while new political configurations seemed possible in urban America, entrenched hierarchies kept reasserting themselves, and gained new contours. The German man quoted in *Putnam's Monthly* wanted his compatriots to escape slave-like conditions in the land of opportunity. Their skin color helped immeasurably. Race shaped possibilities of freedom, and urban futures. America was not the land of equal opportunities.

IV. Unplanned Afterlives

Haussmann, Cerdá, and Olmsted approached interplays between fixity and flux with different objectives. Haussmannian Paris meant to fixate urban form for a future defined by flux: the reforms would give definite shape to a modern city fueled by the circulation of bodies, goods, and capital. Cerdá's plan juxtaposed the countryside and the dense city. By incorporating gardens into mixed-use blocks, he sought to "ruralize the city and urbanize the countryside."[131] In his vision for Barcelona, the built form would be fixed, while green spaces remained flexible and open to change. Olmsted took the opposite approach. Though his parks intended to be dynamic social spaces, their landscaped forms remained fixed, while the growing city grew vertiginously around them. Amid the frenzy of booming New York, urbanites could find solace in the park.

The planners could not foresee the major infrastructural updates needed in subsequent decades. Imagined urban futures of the mid-nineteenth century largely underestimated the widespread uses of electricity, including in the rapid growth of streetcars after the 1870s. Paris, Barcelona, and New York City managed to adapt, while still keeping the imprint of the competing visions we have outlined. This is not necessarily to the credit of pioneering planners. All three cities invested heavily in subways during the early twentieth century. Underground transportation alternatives allowed their nineteenth-century fabric to better survive the onslaught of cars than many other places.

Later generations would mostly revere Cerdá and Olmsted. In Barcelona's case, this happened even though the Eixample's development continued to diverge significantly from the planner's ideals. City blocks lost their green spaces to new buildings and became more stratified than intended. In the wake of the 1888 Exposición Universal, the architecture of Catalan modernism thrived, through idiosyncratic architects like Antoni Gaudí. Some hailed Barcelona as "the new Paris of the south."[132] The city also turned into a hotbed of radical politics, including anarchism. Cerdá's building homogeneity restricted choices when social and economic demands shifted. Over time, the plan managed to accommodate much more density than anticipated. By 1958, the built volume of city blocks was more than four times greater than what Cerdá designed.[133] The Eixample extends for over 1,800 acres. Spaces created by chamfered corners have kept gaining new uses, including as public plazas. In 2009, Barcelona commemorated the 150th anniversary of the Plan Cerdá with a cycle of events, including a time capsule for people to leave their visions for the Catalan capital another 150 years into the future.[134] Presumably, this exercise does not contemplate drastic changes to Cerdá's now iconic layout. There is perhaps no major city in Europe with a built form as unique and recognizable.

The Manhattan grid, in the meantime, has become unimaginable without Central Park. Olmsted's landscapes helped to assuage what the writer Edith Wharton saw as the "deadly uniformity of mean ugliness" dominating the "cramped" and "rectangular" city.[135] New York would evolve as a place of migrant dreams and nightmares, with displays of wealth and inequality that challenged anyone's belief in the viability of a democratic future. The great parks designed by Olmsted helped to set off waves of what we now call gentrification, but they also stand as vital to a diverse set of urbanites, and to the promises of a republican system. People could not always take such spaces for granted. As late as 1909, the *New York Times* reminded readers that the future of Central Park was not assured. Given the land's value, it needed to be protected from the "invasion" of development.[136] A satirical piece in 2000 imagined a future Central Park disfigured by privatization, with closed playgrounds, barriers to circulation, and fenced-in lawns.[137]

The Haussmannian vision has been perhaps the most durable of the three. In 1970, a survey estimated that 60 percent of buildings in Paris dated from the reforms.[138] It is also the most divisive. In fact, probably no other topic in urban history has garnered more attention and elicited as much heated debate. In Paris, Haussmann's name is still evoked as a hero for the right, and a villain for the left.[139] The reinvention of Paris has been a kind of Rorschach test for scholars, planners, and politicians. In the next chapter, we will focus on the transatlantic afterlives of Haussmannization. Though that remains a minor story in Eurocentric histories, part of the discourse on the reforms does focus on implications beyond Paris. Esther da Costa Meyer, for example, argues that the idea of Paris as "the capital of modernity" should be reevaluated in light of the expansion of France's overseas empire. An earlier line of comparative interpretations suggested an affinity with Lisbon's reconstruction, through a connection to baroque principles. It may be captured in a formulation, by Lewis Mumford, that planning moved from "order [as an] instrument of life," to a more controlling idea of "life as an instrument of order."[140] Modern Paris thus embodied both a secular and a martial turn, as an expression of central authority in a strong national state. One historian posited that the reforms marked the height of "government control of architecture and urbanism," unmatched before or since.[141] After Haussmann's tenure and the Paris Commune, the city was the site of "the largest building boom of the century."[142] The process, often uncoordinated, empowered private developers.

Even when critical of the reform's means, for decades most assessments tended to commend the results. Many highlighted the successful and large-scale modernization of a capital that used to be filthy, crowded, and unhealthy.[143] After the 1960s or so, a critical tone prevailed. Scholars and commentators criticize the reforms for dividing the city, displacing the poor to the peripheries. Some more recent studies further that critique, while others question the assumption that segregation was new or intentional.[144] The roles of Napoleon III and Haussmann have also been subject to constant revision. Applying the lenses of Marxist economic geography, David Harvey argued for investments in infrastructure and property as an opportunity for surplus capital to find new sources of accumulation.[145] Instead of state power, that perspective foregrounds the consolidation of private property, financial speculation, and wealth concentration.

Several historians emphasize how conditions remained dire for those in lower-income neighborhoods.[146] For some, that was the plan all along, to push the working classes out of the center in order to make way for bourgeois futures.[147] Others allow for a more charitable interpretation, even if actions to benefit workers acted as prophylactic measures against socialist threats.[148] An empirically grounded spatial analysis by a team of researchers has found validation for most of the major scholarly interpretations: yes, there was rampant displacement, but "demographic patterns attest to the presence of investments in neighborhoods both wealthy and poor, both developed and green-field."[149] Though faced with prejudice, the working classes also moved to Haussmannian buildings.[150]

Cultural historians and literary scholars also view the modern spectacles of central Paris with a critical lens.[151] They tend to explore how myths of order and reason function as driving forces in Haussmanniza-tion, while analyzing relationships between modern art, consumerism, and shifting aspirations among lettered classes. In politics, many of the afterlives of the Paris reforms are less concerned with the historical stakes, and more interested in their potential uses to shape the future. At least three generations of authoritarian planners claimed the mantle of Haussmann, as we will see.[152] Others, when the automobile began to rule planning, admired the nineteenth-century ability to assemble public spaces in a compact city. More recently, planners have returned to this historical moment for strategies to design more sustainably, or for similarly ambitious approaches to problems like housing shortages.[153]

––––––

Writers and artists by and large understood urbanization during the Second Empire in France as a watershed. Siegfried Giedion wrote in the 1940s that "in the nineteenth century the paths of science and the arts diverged: the connection between methods of thinking and methods of feeling was broken."[154] People, however, did not necessarily experience urban transformations as guinea pigs of techno-scientific experiments. They of course noticed when buildings went up or down, wars or epidemics broke out, and infrastructure or sanitation improved. Some might have felt as pawns in real estate or geopolitical chessboards. A general perception that the future would be better pervaded in Parisian culture. Victor Hugo's popular Les Misérables (1862) asked readers to entertain "city streets flooded with light [...] nations [as] sisters [...] no more events." In this sort of progression toward the end of history, "the nineteenth century is great, but the twentieth century will be happy."[155]

Several artists and intellectuals, however, developed increasingly antagonistic sentiments toward the invention of the future, and sometimes, directly confrontational attitudes. Romanticist challenges to reason and science are also an offshoot of modern lettered culture. Bohemian lifestyles subverted the expectations of urban civilization, embracing a nomadic ethos—at least in the realm of feeling. Henri Murger's *Scenes of Bohemian Life* (1851) already focused on those that "abruptly turn their backs on an honorable future to pursue the adventures of an existence based on chance [*hasard*]."[156] *Hasard*, a threat in Mercier and a risk in Balzac's Paris, now gained an irresistible allure. The city saw the rise of cabaret culture and myriad eccentric artistic movements. And many urbanites rejected the order and discipline of planning without embracing political revolution.

In a novel from 1863, Jules Verne predicted that the French capital would be nothing like what his contemporaries expected. His *Paris in the Twentieth Century* remained unpublished until a great-grandson found the manuscript in 1989. Set in the 1960s, it imagined a city radically changed by techno-scientific innovations, and with a very different cultural landscape. Verne's first published novel, *Five Weeks in a Balloon*, captivated European readers with a voyage to "unexplored" Africa. That same year, the author's foray into the French future led the publisher to conclude that no one would believe Verne's "prophecy." It was indeed a bold book. As the Parisian reforms unfolded, in an environment of censorship, not many dared to directly criticize the Second Empire. Situating stories in a fictional future afforded a certain amount of license. Some earlier works foretold a bright future for Paris. Others imagined the city as a ruin.[157] A more vocal opponent of Napoléon III, Tony Moilin, published *Paris in the Year 2000* (1869) as a veiled attack on the present, and a rather explicit proposal for a utopian socialist future. He was executed after taking part in the Paris Commune.

Verne's future in several ways seemed like a reaction to the present. Paris had a controlling government, in cahoots with real estate corporations. A Baron calls the shots, and a Napoleon rules. The Île de la Cité, cleared of inhabitants, hosted public buildings. Poorer people, "reluctant to live far from the center of town," rented apartments on the higher floors of new constructions, reproducing a form of vertical segregation typical of the period (in Haussmannian buildings, servants inhabited the top floor).[158] The recently built Saint-Michel fountain is called "hideous."[159] Boulevards are wide and lined with lamps. Railroads encircle the city and connect an expansive metropolitan region. France had colonized "Cochin China," Vietnam.

Verne, like the visionary planners of his generation, perceived that contemporary techno-scientific revolutions would create new worlds. Other writers were not so prescient: Moilin imagined his ideal Paris in the year 2000 relatively unchanged by technological innovations. Verne's narrator, in contrast, quickly announced: "what the previous century called Progress had undergone enormous developments."[160] Several predictions panned out, or nearly so. The city had electricity in every home, locomotives with gas combustion engines, electric telegraph, high-rise apartment buildings (twelve floors), and 5 million residents (about 2.5 short). It suffered from pollution. Tropical vegetables now grew in France, and there are hints of the United States as a major power. Some trains run underground, others elevated, in systems of compressed air and electromagnetic force.

Other predictions turned out to be off. Executions still take place in public, and wars had been relegated to distant memory. Paris had a seaport, compared to Liverpool's, connected by canals to the Atlantic and beyond through the Suez and Panama canals. For Verne's characters, high-tech industrial and architecture marvels generated a mixture of attraction and repulsion. In the site where the Eiffel Tower would go, Verne located an electric lighthouse, the world's tallest construction in his fictional future. France in 1889, when the Eiffel Tower was built for an Exposition Universelle, and in the 1960s, had become more democratic than Verne envisaged. And in reality, during the 1960s the tallest buildings in the world would be Manhattan skyscrapers.

Verne reproduced a common prejudice among science fiction writers. His women characters lacked agency, and their subjectivities are reduced to their relations with men. In this case the plot revolves around Michel, and his love for Lucy. An aspiring poet, he struggled with dilemmas about his own future. This was a privilege of those born into some means, but also a very modern condition. A wealthy and ruthless uncle took the young protagonist, an orphan, under his wing. He thinks the only fitting professions are financier, businessman, and industrialist, and looks down on the arts. Lucy is the niece of Michel's beloved former schoolteacher, who has a heroic attachment to Latin poetry, and very few interested students left. Verne's fiction is fundamentally dystopian. Like Mercier in the eighteenth century, he used the future as a device to lament cultural changes of the present, and to mount a defense of rather conservative aesthetic norms. When characters speak about the possibility that "a revolution will be made against Progress," the stakes are more artistic than political.[161]

In Verne's future, a society obsessed with productivity has no capacity to enjoy the arts and becomes hopelessly "accursed."[162] In atypical fashion for Verne, the novel ends tragically. Michel leaves his uncle's shadow. Jobless and destitute, his dreams as a poet and lover are shattered. The young man's final words, echoing Bartleby's, suggest the city as a source of unfulfilled promises: "O Paris!" "O Lucy!" The disappointment with Paris clearly concerned the author's own anxieties with modernity and capitalism, as Haussmannization unfolded. Unlike Mercier, Garnier, and many utopians, Verne was prescient about how cultural values would evolve along with everything else. But he was too pessimistic about the implications. Music, art and poetry took directions unimaginable for Verne, and underwent their own renewal, often challenging futures imposed from above.

At the same time, Verne had an intuition that eluded visionary planners of his generation. He foresaw how future technologies and tastes would again reshape the built environment. *Paris in the Twentieth Century* assumed that the definitive modern Paris of the Second Empire had been largely rebuilt within a hundred years. As it turns out, Verne was wrong about Paris. The city still preserved much of its nineteenth-century fabric in the 1960s, and beyond. But he was right about many other cities of the modern world. Reformed with Haussmannian Paris as a model, they would go through another cycle of demolitions and rebuilding in the twentieth century. The urban vortex was only just beginning.

4

Possibilities and Limits (1870s–1910s)

RIO DE JANEIRO + MEXICO CITY,
NEW YORK, CHICAGO, HAVANA,
AND MORE.

I. Black Streets, White Masks

In the latter decades of the nineteenth century, technological advances unsettled known patterns and enabled experts to map out prospects with greater confidence. Telegraph networks allowed data to be collected from far afield. Forecasters attempted to predict the weather and financial markets. Prognostication became increasingly understood as a scientific enterprise.[1] At the same time, the future continued to be perceived as open-ended. If social station was not predetermined, then individuals and groups could try to control their destinies. Self-help literature extolled the virtues of "sacrificing [. . .] a present gratification for a future good."[2] Popular utopian fictions devised perfect societies, where humanity's problems would be solved once and for all. Politicians, philosophers, and planners envisaged sweeping improvements through rational and pragmatic approaches. Offshoots of Marxism, Darwinism, and Positivism fueled imaginations and organized actions. And of course, more and more people joined the ranks of urban dwellers.

Cities concentrated a growing range of backgrounds, means, and dreams. Some pursued more exciting lives or even changing the world. Others simply wanted the ability to make a living. Some tried to systematically plan ahead. Others took a plunge "toward the broad sea of the future."[3] Not everyone embraced ideas of secular progress, and religion continued to structure many people's lives. Material change, nonetheless, became a given. Someone born in the 1870s would grow up in a world where incredible inventions kept accumulating: electric lights, combustion engines, generators, typewriters, telephones, phonographs, photography, film. The experience of drastic technological transformations led people to expect more of it, especially in the urban centers of the North Atlantic.

In 1899, a French illustrator made a series of images titled "In the Year 2000."[4] From our vantage point, the scenes range from prescient to silly. They envision devices for hearing the news, dictating and reading letters, automated farming, heating with radium, tailoring clothes, shaving beards, turning meals into pills, microbe hunting, and electric floor scrubbing. Innovations promised to save time and make more spaces accessible. There are flying vehicles for firemen, policing, and postal delivery to rural areas, as well as for aerial races. People ride on submarine liners, and have an underwater croquet party. An electric train connects Paris and Beijing. Gender roles, however, remain the same. And in backgrounds, the architectonic scale and style resemble the contemporary modern city after Haussmannian reforms. One shows the Palais Garnier opera house, with attendees arriving by flight. Another depicts an Aero-Cab station, with an elevator ensuring minimum effort for passengers. Below, they could buy newspapers from a kiosk amid car-free streets, storefront windows, and spacious sidewalks.

These futuristic cards were meant to be sold as inserts in cigarette boxes. This very product had resulted from a recent technology: in Virginia, an inventor patented a cigarette-rolling machine in the 1880s. For much of its history, the tobacco industry relied on enslaved labor in plantations. By the end of the century, most countries in the Atlantic abolished slavery. European colonization, however, expanded and intensified in Africa and Asia. Steel, steam, and mechanization also

FIGURE 4.1. Despite elevators and steel frames, no skyscrapers yet.

revolutionized military operations, with machine guns, barbed wire, and warships. One of the futuristic cards showed a white explorer flying over stereotyped drawings of half-naked black natives. French smokers could contrast their fanciful high-tech devices to the spears of "savages." Though rapid changes left virtually no one untouched, there was a general understanding that an individual's or a city's starting points determined their relationships to the future. How did planners and urbanites, then, conceive of the possibilities and limits of modernization from its margins?

In 1900, Rio de Janeiro was Latin America's largest city with around 811,000 residents. More Afro-descendants lived in Brazil's capital than in any Western African city. It underwent arguably the most dramatic Haussmannization process anywhere outside Paris. This culminated in widescale reforms between 1903 and 1906. In Rio, perhaps more evidently but not exceptionally, modern urban forms and façades sought to mask popular street life and Afro-Brazilian cultures, while showcasing Eurocentric aspirations. As elsewhere, a single figure got much of the glory and the blame: Pereira Passos, a civil engineer appointed mayor. Rio's reforms followed a basic pattern. State-led investment in infrastructure incentivized the growth of national economies. At the municipal level, incipient professionalized bureaucracies remodeled urban spaces with focus on aesthetics, sanitation, and circulation.

Haussmannian-inspired reforms often aimed to both improve living conditions and entrench social hierarchies. On the ground and in printed pages, overlapping and conflicting futures proliferated. Some dreamed of gadgets, others of justice. For urban planners, particularly in the Americas, having an orientation toward the future also implied a reinvention of the past. This often meant whitewashing the legacies of slavery. The contours of these dynamics varied across places and between groups. In Rio's case, the pivotal reforms occurred relatively late. Yet, they also anticipated a twentieth-century turn toward more totalizing plans, aiming for economic progress and cultural advancement along Eurocentric lines. Rio's actual development, at the same time, evidenced how local conditions, rhythms and logics could impose themselves on overbearing models, even as city planning became increasingly subsumed under national interests. But before returning to Rio's version of Haussmannization, we will attend to comparable developments in other cities, and a fuller transatlantic panorama.

———

In South America, not everyone foresaw radical change. In his memoir, published in 1900, the white statesman Joaquim Nabuco expected continuity: "Slavery will remain for a long time as the national characteristic of Brazil."[5] He had been a key supporter of emancipation. In 2000, the musician Caetano Veloso turned that passage from Nabuco's writing into song verses. It was a way of saying that this prediction had come true and remained timely for the twenty-first century. Then and now, legacies of slavery shape Brazil's relationships to the future. Its history stands apart in some ways. Around 45 percent of Africans taken as captives to the Americas arrived in Brazil, many through Rio de Janeiro's port.[6] After the Portuguese royal court fled Lisbon due to the Napoleonic invasion, the colonial city became the seat of the Kingdom of Portugal, and the capital of an empire that included Angola and Mozambique. While the

Spanish Americas split into various independent Republics, Brazil became an independent Empire in 1822 and maintained territorial integrity. It has had no successful revolutions. In 1888, the country was the last in the Americas to abolish slavery. Brazil was different. Nabuco's suggestion of a future enmeshed with the enslaved past, at the same time, finds resonances throughout the Atlantic.

In much of the urban South Atlantic, urbanization and planning unfolded amid the aspirations of subordinate groups and the racist hierarchies of lettered elites. By the 1850s, Western Europe and the US Northeast had among the highest rates of urbanization in the world. Following a century of stagnation, Latin America also began to undergo explosive urban growth. Between 1830 and 1930, major metropolitan areas multiplied populations by at least five times (Mexico City), and as many as thirty-six times (Buenos Aires). Rio de Janeiro's grew more than twelvefold. Cities emerged as arenas for disputes over who and what belonged in national futures. The decline of slavery posed a problem for production. Demands for labor, along with new ocean liners, created conditions for mass migration from Europe. For ruling classes, this provided a strategy to "whiten" societies after abolition. In a similar vein, Eurocentric urban design became a tool for non-European nation-states to catch up in the global race toward modern futures. Elites largely perceived blackness and Africa as signs of backwardness. From that perspective, the presence of former slaves and their descendants hindered the project of progress.

Joaquim Nabuco was born on a sugar plantation owned by his family some 20 miles outside Recife, in 1849. The Praieira rebellion, discussed in chapter 2, was taking place. He studied law and rose through the ranks of the Brazilian Empire, serving in the national legislature. The well-traveled Nabuco knew which way the winds blew and saw slavery as incompatible with modern civilization. In a speech in 1884, he advocated for salaried labor, "without differences among races," and surmised: "What's the worker [today]? Nothing. What will he be? Everything." To him, Brazil's "future, expansion, and growth" relied on paid workers, not slaves.[7] His writings suggest that correspondences between race and progress could be more ambivalent than they might appear at first. Yet even an abolitionist like Nabuco had sentiments tinged by racism.

When Nabuco wrote that slavery would endure as "the national characteristic of Brazil," he did not mean it as an entirely bad thing. He recognized the horrors of bondage but reminisced about plantation life with fondness. To Nabuco, slavery spread throughout Brazil's "vast solitudes a great suavity," leaving the country's "virgin nature" with "myths, legends, enchantments," and a "child-like soul."[8] He partly meant this as a compliment. In effect, the text effaced black and indigenous pasts, and the abilities of their descendants to make new futures. To him, Afro-Brazilians belonged in a constant present, in "their sadness without remorse" and "their happiness without tomorrow." A sense of loss permeated Nabuco's memory. He lamented a growing "mercenary instinct" in the modern world. Embracing progress implied forsaking an easier, sweeter life in the countryside. The child of the master and of the slave had destinies assigned to them at birth. Both presumed a relationship with a fixed future. Unlike aristocrats, the bourgeois had to make their own future. And of course, the aristocratic order that Nabuco cherished depended on chattel slavery.

Nabuco praised older rural properties for creating stable relations between the enslaved and their owners over several generations, supposedly guided by a "spirit of humanity" rather than profit-seeking. When he returned to visit the sugar plantation of his youth, then mostly run through paid laborers and steam power, the nostalgic tone betrayed a revealing description of the workings of modern slavery: "the sacrifice of poor blacks, who had incorporated their lives to the future of that property, no longer existed except perhaps in my recollection."[9] Nabuco meant to ascribe nobility to the enslaved of his childhood memories, writing about them as "saints" who blessed Brazil with "love." They were the "generous race" that he served as an abolitionist. It was not the author's primary intention, but the text evokes how slavery robbed people of their futures by *incorporating* them into the plantation, and shows that even abolitionists could fail to contemplate the rights of freed persons to shape their own destinies.

At the same time, Nabuco understood the contingencies of history. He wrote that slavery would define Brazil "for a long time," not forever.

We can think of this as a modern form of reticence toward the idea of anything as eternal. And of course, as a reflection of faith in progress. Nabuco knew that Brazil was not impervious to global changes. Commercial classes continued to ascend, eroding the status of heirs and the nobility. Broadly, their interests could be reconciled with chattel slavery, which sought to fixate people as property. And to the general property-holding classes, emancipation constituted a threat. But it also opened new economic possibilities. Nabuco argued in 1883, for example, that Brazil had to catch up in the industrial era. This required characteristics that he found to be incompatible with slavery, like individual initiative and "confidence in the future."[10] Yet, even as he sharply criticized bondage, inherited privileges and an attachment to racial hierarchies limited his worldviews.

Other contemporaries pursued the end of slavery with a more energetic sense of justice. The Afro-Brazilian abolitionist Luís Gama found no nostalgic appeal in the country's past and saw emancipation as a struggle for the right to the future. A prominent jurist and poet, Gama spent his childhood in a more dynamic environment than Nabuco. He was born in Salvador da Bahia, in 1830. Brazil's capital until 1763, the port city might have concentrated more ethnic and linguistic diversity than anywhere else in the Atlantic. It had a population of around 65,000 in 1835, comparable to Boston's. About 42 percent were enslaved, over 60 percent of which had been born in Africa. Free Africans comprised another 7 percent or so of the population, and self-declared whites about 20 percent. Salvador was a kaleidoscope of cultures: its residents worshipped Christian or Muslim deities, as well as the Jeje Voduns, the Yoruba Orishas, or the Angolan Nkisis.[11]

Gama described his mother, Luísa Mahin, as a free African of the Nagô nation, a hard-working street food vendor, and a "pagan" who "always refused baptism and the Christian doctrine."[12] He wrote that she participated in insurrections against slavery and the empire. Mahin raised her son immersed in an urban milieu of West African religions, and there is evidence that he learned African languages. By 1840, she was no longer able to raise him. Gama's father, a mixed-race man of Portuguese descent and aristocratic lineage, sold his son as a slave at the age of ten, to pay off debts. As Gama recalled it, slaveowners avoided

Bahians, due to their rebellious reputation. Like Mahin, Gama became unyielding in the pursuit of justice. He satirized the Catholic Church and its role in Brazilian society. On the one hand, his future was in his mother's past. On the other, he sought alternative paths. Gama would fight with legal methods.

Few former slaves became leading lettered intellectuals. Gama was not alone but is exceptional in Brazil's history. Some aspects of his trajectory can also be seen as representative. Like Brazil's capital and Nabuco, Gama moved from the northeast to the southeast. This followed a geographic shift from economies centered on sugar, to gold in Minas Gerais, and then coffee. At first, the enslaved young Gama lived in a town in the interior of São Paulo, and then in the state's capital. The São Paulo region was beginning to rapidly urbanize as coffee production increased. This commodity was much more integrated into the world economy than sugar in the colony had been. The added value in coffee supply chains fueled urban economies. Ancillary activities like insurance, banking, and commercial offices grew. In this burgeoning environment, Gama toiled as an *escravo de ganho* or earning slave, hired to make shoes or fix clothes. It was a common arrangement in urban Brazil. He had to pay a set sum to the owner, probably on a weekly basis, but could keep the rest of his earnings. This generally afforded greater autonomy than life on a plantation and provided a pathway to freedom. Urban slaves sometimes saved for more than a decade of hard labor to buy their manumission.[13] The future-oriented mindset and discipline that this required might have provoked envy or admiration in an Enlightenment figure like Benjamin Franklin, had they been of the right color.

In his late teens, Gama befriended a student who taught him to read and write. Armed with that ability, in 1848 he obtained papers proving his enslavement to have been illegal. As a freedman, he worked as a scrivener. If this was a dead-end career for Bartleby, it afforded Gama the ability to ascend to various positions in São Paulo's police forces. After a conservative administration took over, he was dismissed in 1854, supposedly for insubordination. It could not have helped that Gama was associated with liberals and worked toward freeing people from slavery. Throughout these years, he searched for his mother. In Rio de Janeiro,

West Africans (*pretos minas*) told him that she was jailed and likely deported for playing a role in insurrections.

Experiences in the police and learning about his mother's fate reinforced how the racial terror of a slave-based society included brutal treatment of free Africans. Gama collaborated with a range of people to enact change, including reformists and freemasons. As a self-taught lawyer, he helped hundreds obtain manumission through the court system. As a journalist and political theorist, he proposed a radically expanded scope for liberalism, with public and secular education provided for everyone in Brazil, including free Africans who were not citizens. In 1867, Gama introduced a universal education program in a newspaper called *Democracia* (Democracy), where he signed with the pseudonym Afro. Like his mother before him, he suffered threats of deportation. Ten years later, in a letter to the editors of another São Paulo newspaper, he concluded a defense of the Republic and emancipation with a powerful rallying cry: "We are men, and at last, we have a future."[14] Luís Gama's horizons were equal rights and freedom. He conceived of them in terms of an ability to pursue a better life. To him, full personhood was nothing short of that.

In the 1870s, Gama expressed growing frustration with Brazil's slow pace of change. The empire and Church, committed to fixed futures that did not upset the status quo, stood on the way of liberty and education for all. Gama criticized Republican contemporaries for hiding behind the banner of progress without pushing hard enough for equal rights. Now, he embraced more revolutionary approaches, calling for a shift in the means but not the ends of activism. He was open to violence toward slaveowners as a form of self-defense for the enslaved. Yet, a turn of phrase reveals an enduring pragmatism. In 1880, he wrote that Luísa Mahin's insurrection plans against slavery "had no effect."[15] In a way this reflected the historical record, since those insurgencies failed to topple governments. And there is, of course, the counterargument that abolition movements could build on prior struggles. Gama seemed to be pressing a finer point about strategy. Like his mother, he wanted a new future for Brazil. He also wanted a different destiny for himself. At the same time, Gama knew the threats of state racial terror in Brazil.

Counter-revolutionary responses in Europe left impressions across the Atlantic. His work focused on freeing individuals through the courts and building abolitionism in the lettered public sphere. The goal was to maximize effectiveness.

Luís Gama's life exemplifies a sense of urban possibilities and limits. He faced crossroads and dilemmas of the Atlantic world, making a unique and exceptional pathway in the Brazilian city. We could also understand him as a child of Africa and of the Enlightenment. As a lawyer, rather than appeal to authority, he argued for natural law as irreconcilable with bondage. As a prolific writer in newspapers, he denounced slavery in prose and verse—some of it read aloud in street corners, reaching the illiterate. Gama had awareness of Brazil's place within the hemisphere, following debates abroad. He admired "our brothers" in the United States, where Reconstruction provided inspiration. We might even compare Gama's legacy to Frederick Douglass's, though his work was less celebrated in the twentieth century. Given the vision of education as a vehicle for a "desire to rise" among Afro-descendants, we could also see him as a more radical predecessor to Booker T. Washington.[16] None of these men necessarily sought to subvert a socioeconomic order based on productivity. Yet they all desired change.

Luís Gama did not live long enough to see slavery abolished in his native country. The process in Brazil differed from hemispheric neighbors. In the Spanish Americas, Republican governments emancipated slaves in the wake of wars of independence. Brazil, after declaring independence in 1822, became an empire ruled by the Portuguese monarch's son, and then grandson, for nearly seven decades. Unlike in the United States, which emancipated around 3.5 million African Americans during the Civil War, in Brazil this happened much more gradually. In 1850, around 1.5 million enslaved people comprised roughly a quarter of the country's population.[17] A major turning point took place that year with a ban on the transnational slave trade. It was followed by an 1871 law freeing children born to enslaved mothers. By 1888, when the princess and heir apparent to the throne signed a law ending all slavery, around 700,000 people still lived in bondage. The following year an authoritarian coalition, including former slaveowners, declared Brazil a Republic.

We might think of two common denominators across the Americas, from the last quarter of the nineteenth century onward: rapid urbanization, and a betrayal of the promises of emancipation. As we will see, these are interconnected histories. At the outset, the United States stood somewhat apart for its persistent dreams of an agrarian republic. Booker T. Washington, like his contemporaries, could not have predicted the Great Migration of Afro-descendants from the rural Jim Crow south to cities of the north in the twentieth century. And he probably would not have supported it. In *The Future of the American Negro* (1899), he argued on behalf of policies that "tend to keep the Negro in the country and smaller towns, where he succeeds best, and stop the influx into the large cities, where he does not succeed so well."[18] To him, agriculture was the industry of the future. He wanted African Americans to stay in "the farming districts of the South, where they make the best living and where their services are of greatest value to the country," rather than in "the already overcrowded cities."[19]

In much of Latin America and the Caribbean, the starting point was a bit different. Notions of cities as evil or sources of degeneracy also existed. But the key trope in the nineteenth century was the opposition between civilization and barbarism.[20] The former implied the city and the future, the latter the countryside and the past. Latin American governments generally incentivized urbanization. Exports originating in the hinterlands required the development of infrastructures like telegraph cables, steam engines, railroads, and ports. Urbanites coordinated these processes, and cities benefited from them. Amid this modernization, we can identify some cultural and political continuities with earlier periods. The city was not where you went to be free, but to become civilized—if you could afford it and looked the part. Germán Pavony, a historian of Colombia, captures a near-consensus about Latin America: "the capital city is the site from which the history of the nation-state has been written."[21] Urban centers concentrated key institutions and power. We might add: capitals were also the sites onto which lettered elites projected national futures. And where, against the odds, those deemed undesirable or inferior found ways to appropriate spaces meant to exclude them, subverting authoritarian plans.

In the United States, Washington, DC, was built from scratch as part of a political compromise. In Latin America, capitals tended to be much more vital to the nation as an imagined community. They tended to loom over discourses and the management of territories. As Pavony frames it, struggles between unitarians and federalists in the nineteenth century played themselves out amid a movement "from republican cities to republics of cities."[22] Capitals maintained a central status as several countries adopted variations of the US model: Mexico added Estados Unidos to its name after independence, in 1824; Colombia, did so after a civil war, in 1863; Venezuela, in 1864; Brazil, under the Republic in 1889. Argentina went from the title of United Provinces and Confederation to Argentine Republic in 1860, a switch that happened elsewhere in the twentieth century. Yet, even as citizenship developed within the framework of the nation-state, capital cities maintained a hold on how people imagined national futures.

In the Americas, especially in the port cities of the Atlantic, Africans and Afro-descendants shaped urban life long before industrialization and mass domestic migration. For ruling classes, slavery had presented infrastructural solutions. Why build a sewage system when somebody could move waste on their backs? Why invest in transportation, when free or cheap labor could shoulder the burden of moving goods and even people? Enslaved and freepersons, at the same time, vied to make spaces for themselves. Visitors to cities like Salvador, Rio de Janeiro, and Havana often remarked that they sounded and felt African, given who occupied the streets.[23] Black women dominated food vending, selling in stalls, or moving around. In urban Brazil, free Africans and enslaved men congregated along trade and ethnic lines in groups called *cantos*, which can mean either songs or street corners and alleys in Portuguese.[24] The sound of workers singing African or Afro-inflected music was a staple of the landscape. Fears of African autonomy underlay Nabuco's memoirs because black urbanites made themselves present as a potential future in Brazilian cities, even under slavery.

As demands from domestic consumers and export markets increased, that generated pressure for investments in infrastructures.

Slave societies tended to lag in the modernization of ports, for example. From lettered perspectives, Africans and their descendants became perceived less as the backbone of productive systems, or as potential instigators of insurrections. Instead, economic and governing elites increasingly saw them as an impediment to modernity. Latin Americans wrestled with how to reconcile slavery and its legacies with the pursuit of progress. Luís Gama managed to combine multiple traditions into a forward-looking egalitarian political project. Contemporary planners would not do the same. Their view of modernization tended to be predicated on reproducing hierarchies. There were the same practical justifications nearly everywhere. The circulation of goods to and from ports or railroads had to be more effective. Deadly epidemics required better sanitation systems. Planning also made frequent use of aesthetic norms, foregrounding the language of beautification or embellishment. Prevalent throughout the Atlantic, these keywords echoed Enlightenment-era urban visions, as we saw in Voltaire's writings. But they would gain new meanings. Latin American planners and their lettered circles assimilated antiblack scientific racism and European beauty standards. Associations between Afro-descended cultures and ugliness, dirtiness, and backwardness tightened. The City Beautiful movement in the United States had comparably racist and classist overtones.

State-sponsored urban design and architecture strove to look European—more specifically, Parisian. We can think of beautification reforms as white masks to cover up black pasts, in pursuit of civilization in a North Atlantic mold. That does not mean Latin American planning and lettered cultures were merely imitative. They adapted models, as we will see, to local circumstances. Afro-descendants would also mobilize the language of beauty against technocrats, with some success. And of course, many social undesirables, including an array of poor European migrants, shaped popular urban cultures and national identities, defying the designs of top-down planning. Maybe the preponderance of ethnic mixtures made this inevitable for Latin American urban futures. Some masks fit better than others.

II. Futures Deferred

Ahead of other capitals in the region, Havana and Rio de Janeiro began to exceed national growth rates in the 1840s and 1850s. Scholars draw attention to how, at the time, commodities exports further integrated the US South (cotton), Cuba (sugar), and Brazil (coffee) into the capitalist global economy. Havana received enslaved West Africans later than anywhere else in the Americas, until 1867. By then, more than one million people had been forced to make the crossing to the Caribbean Island.[25] Cuba abolished bondage nearly as late as Brazil, in 1886. Toward the second half of the century, while plantation systems modernized, it became increasingly clear that the future was urban. The Brazilian and Cuban capitals engaged in planning premised on an expectation of growth. In Rio de Janeiro, a proposal from the early 1840s sought to rationalize the city's layout. It proposed the addition of straightened streets and a canal to the existing colonial fabric, as well as to guide outward expansion.[26]

Between 1830 and 1900, Havana's population nearly tripled to around 280,000. Cuba remained a Spanish colony until 1898. In the mid-nineteenth century, its capital was the largest city both in the Caribbean and under European rule in the Americas. In 1859, the same year as Cerdá's plan for Barcelona, Havana's administration approved a comparable extension project, for what became known as the Vedado neighborhood.[27] The civil engineer Luís Yboleon Bosque created an orthogonal plan with square blocks. Widened streets contrasted with Old Havana's density. While the layout may recall the grid of Spanish colonization, like other contemporaries, Bosque departed from tradition. His plan privileged markets, a hospital, and a school over religious and military buildings. The vision included steel railways for animal-powered transport and ample green spaces, with a central *parque* instead of a plaza. Bosque's plan promised a development that would have no equal "in beauty and salubriousness."[28]

The Vedado attracted whiter and wealthier residents. Cuba remained a largely rural country, but the plans represented a shift to a more bourgeois order. They added vistas to secular monuments and the ocean, extending a city already endowed with an iconic modern boulevard, the Paseo del Prado. *Paseo* in Spanish refers to a leisurely stroll, akin to what Parisians would call *flânerie*. This thoroughfare divided the old city from the more expansive new neighborhoods. It would be redesigned in the 1920s by the French landscape architect Jean-Claude Nicolas Forestier, who trained under Haussmann-associate Adolphe Alphand.[29] The Vedado became the site of iconic modernist buildings in the twentieth century, and a bustling gay scene in the twenty-first. When first approved, the plans anticipated the Haussmannian turn toward ambitious scales, spaces for the collective, and cohesion. They lacked the speed in implementation, and the rebuilding of an existing urban fabric.

———

Back in 1830, Mexico City was the largest city in Latin America. Mexico was a lot less integrated into slave economies, enacting full abolition in 1837. Rio and Buenos Aires surpassed the Mexican capital's population by 1900, even after its population more than doubled to around 345,000. In 1864, under the Hapsburg emperor backed by Napoleon III and Mexican conservatives, a team of designers proposed a series of six radial boulevards converging on the capital's main plaza, the Zócalo. This plan, which required razing substantial areas of the center, would be discarded. Instead, a major thoroughfare was added to the edge of the city, connecting the National Palace and the imperial residences in Chapultepec Castle. The Paseo de la Reforma, as it became known, introduced a diagonal to the colonial grid, extending for about 3.5 miles. At 200–230 feet, it was significantly wider than modern avenues in New York City or Paris. Like Broadway in Manhattan, the Paseo partly followed an existing pathway. In practice and symbolically, the inspirations were largely Haussmannian, drawing from Adolphe Alphand's landscaped gardens and a Parisian sense of modernity.[30] But here, as in Havana, the reforms did not require razing swathes of the old city.

The historian Mauricio Tenorio compares Haussmannization in Mexico to frontier expansion, with the ideal city "conceived as a conquest not only over tradition, chaos, and backwardness, but also over nature."[31] Laying out modern avenues as far as the eye could see was a way of blurring the lines between the city and the "uncivilized" countryside. The process preserved the urban core, but it displaced peasants and indigenous communities in Mexico City's outskirts. The new neighborhoods that developed in the adjacencies of the Paseo, catering to richer and whiter residents, had gridded layouts and more green spaces. Revealingly, they are called *colonias*. We might see here a parallel to land ordinances and early suburbs in North America. When we get to car-driven sprawl, the pattern will be even clearer: state-sanctioned planning extends urbanization outwardly, serving the interests of those desiring to be within reach of the urban center but apart from the urban poor, and wealthy enough to afford it.

Behind the scenes, urban reforms involved laws, bureaucracies, and financing schemes. The historian Jürgen Osterhammel points out that the big cities of the nineteenth century might have been mightier than nation-states. They served "to gather and distribute capital" as part of international systems.[32] Indeed, national governments often did not control or coordinate the flow of money, information, and people driving urbanization. At the same time, a capital city's transformation resulted from state capacity and performed it too. Urban reforms worked as a spectacle. They could provide an experience of a country's progress. Architecture and urban design made visible the disparities between the development of cities and rural areas, as well as between capitals and regional hubs or provincial towns.

This was not entirely exclusive to the period. Early modern and baroque urban design in Europe had introduced a monumentality that dwarfed medieval towns, aside from cathedral towers. As we have seen, the massive scale of royal palaces represented a shift from a divine to an absolutist order, ruled by monarchs. In some places, factory towers had signaled a new order. And now, civic monuments and public buildings like city halls and railway stations surpassed previous grandeur. Eventually, skyscrapers would embody the rise of corporations and capitalism. As commercial and working classes ascended, the secular nineteenth-century city negotiated public and private interests. This took different forms depending on local conditions. But more-or-less throughout the world, urban reforms of capitals became expressions of national aspirations.

In modernity, we might say, the manifestation of power through monumentality was not just about stability but also about possibility. To witness spectacular spaces built as if from scratch over a single life-time made clear who could control the future. It showed who called the shots, who could deliver, or who could crush people. In nineteenth-century Latin America, this was mostly the nation-state. In Mexico City, built on top of the Aztec capital of Tenochtitlan, the monumental scale had preceded the early modern or colonial period. This could still be felt in the Zócalo, which retained the vast proportions of the indigenous city. As the Paseo de la Reforma introduced a new large-scale vector to urbanization, nearby pyramids in Teotihuacan began to be surveyed and excavated. Visions for the future would make use of precedents.

Mexico reestablished republican rule in 1867 under the reformist Benito Juárez. The Paseo, initially restricted for imperial uses, opened to the public. A decade later, another president of indigenous descent, Porfirio Díaz, took over. Over the next three decades or so, in what became known as the Porfiriato, he aggressively pursued moderniza-tion, including through investments in railroads and urban infrastruc-ture, with Mexico City as the central hub of the national railroad system. Porfirio Díaz also incentivized European migration. Symptomatically, he tried to whiten the appearance of his skin.[33] As Tenorio argues, the authoritarian Porfirian regime attempted to turn the Paseo de la Re-forma into "the representation of the course of the nation toward su-preme order and progress."[34] Official attitudes to indigenous legacies in Latin America tended to be more positive than to African ones. In Mexico, where slavery had played a smaller role, most had Native ances-try. Planners, the historian Carol Reese writes, wanted "a modern capital whose character would be both international and Mexican."[35]

Beginning in the 1870s, the Paseo's monumental statues were promi-nently placed in the middle of roundabouts. They told a story about progress. Someone walking from the historic center would encounter among others, in chronological order: Columbus, the last Mexica ruler

Cuauhtémoc, and the liberal stalwart Benito Juarez. The former president, son of a Zapotec-speaking mother, was represented in a monument reminiscent of classical Greece. And, overshadowing all others, a monument deemed the Angel of Independence was erected in the early 1900s. It similarly blended modernity with tradition, but in even more Eurocentric fashion. On an ornate pedestal, the steel-made, Corinthian-style victory column is topped with a sculpture of Nike, designed by an Italian native. In gold-covered bronze, the winged deity represents the permanent victory of the Olympian gods against their lawless challengers. She faces the historic center. On her back, the Paseo would extend into a highway during the twentieth century.[36]

The angel might be oriented toward the Mexico City of the past, but she appears to overcome it, headed toward a bright future of freedom, prosperity, order, and progress. The sculpture hovered nearly 150 feet above pedestrians and surrounding buildings. In 1910, the new monument was a focal point of celebrations marking the centennial of the beginning of the Mexican Wars of Independence. The event showcased electricity, turning streets into a public tableau of lights. This was a moment when technocrats and planners, like the angel, increasingly assumed an Olympian perspective on the city, confident about their ability to achieve permanent victory against urban challenges. Mexican and foreign dignitaries attended the celebratory events, Porfirio Díaz among them. Soldiers, trade organizations, workers, students, and indigenous groups paraded down modern avenues.

On a stage set under the new monument, authorities and poets delivered speeches for the occasion. The director of the National School of Fine Arts, an engineer, highlighted independence as "the basis of the progress that Mexico has achieved."[37] Miguel Macedo, the subsecretary of government, contended that Mexicans "must never allow the past, not even the parts that we cherish, to be a chain [that] makes us go backward or slows down our march forward." To him, the column stood toward the sky like "the eternal aspiration of men toward the superior forms of life."[38] Nike aside, these were nearly all men. They seemed to have an unshakable faith in their capacity to shape society. Two months later, the Mexican Revolution began, leading to the downfall of the

FIGURE 4.2. Lights! Cities became stages for a nation-led performance of progress.

Porfiriato. Macedo would go on to a successful career as a businessman and real estate magnate, becoming a key figure behind Mexico City's Torre Latinoamericana in the 1950s. The headquarters of an insurance company, it was the world's tallest privately owned skyscraper outside the United States at the time.

Scholars of Mexico tend to agree that planning during those pivotal decades combined a desire for continuity with the past, and rupture toward modern futures. Porfirian elites adopted (and adapted) old and new symbols. As elsewhere in the Atlantic, they embraced hygienism and social stratification. At the same time, Mexico City preserved its colonial core more than other major metropolises of the Americas, including Rio de Janeiro, Buenos Aires, and New York. Across the Atlantic, intellectual circles and political figures wrestled in different ways with how to position themselves and their nations in relation to possible futures. In Latin America, some now saw the United States as the harbinger of things to come, framed positively or negatively. The efficient powerhouse to the north could be seen as heartless and imperialist, or as a beacon of Pan-American hope. Many looked toward Europe as closer in culture and sensibility, elevating Paris as the capital of modern civilization, to be emulated. Others celebrated Latin America itself as the leading light, often imagined as an amalgam of worlds. Macedo, for example, spoke of Mexico as "the fusion of all the races, of all the faiths and all of the aspirations of the inhabitants of this earth."[39] Few considered Africa as the future.

Amid debates about the merits of autochthonous versus imported models, we might underline two connecting threads in Latin America. Both proved to be enormously consequential to planning. One was the prominence of positivism among the urban ruling classes. In the Porfiriato, technocrats influenced by this philosophy became known as *Los Científicos*, an expression often used ironically. Miguel Macedo was one of them. His 1910 speech at the Angel of Independence praised how scientific knowledge made "the men of today" vastly superior and set up those of tomorrow for even greater advancements. Like Nike had battled the mythical monster Typhon, scientific elites would fight typhoid epidemics.[40] It is again a story of rupture and continuity. Latin American positivists might have imagined themselves as bold pioneers, but many inherited political capital and social standing. Macedo's father, for example, had been the dean of a law school in Mexico City.

Auguste Comte, the philosopher behind positivism, had studied and worked in Paris under Henri de Saint-Simon. He died in the early years of Haussmannization and did not seem to pay too much attention to urbanization. Comte's extensive writings, however, revolved around concepts and terms that were also dear to planners: renovation, rationality, efficacy, order, systematization, practical operations, and modernization. The phrase "future progress" recurs in his work, animating his philosophy.[41] Comte argued that society's evolution began with religion, followed by a transitional "metaphysical stage" after the French Revolution, and culminating with a positive stage guided by scientific methods. Empirical data would render society controllable and predictable: view to preview, as one slogan went.[42] Positivists believed their social science to be as final as some planners thought their designs would be. Their doctrines influenced planning throughout the Atlantic, including the anglophone world.

It is hard to overstate the impact of positivism in Latin America. We see it emblazoned on Brazil's republican flag: Order and Progress. In practice, oligarchic elites mobilized secular notions about the perfectibility of society to serve their own interests. Governing classes combined elements from Comte's ideas and Herbert Spencer's racist social evolutionary theories, drawn from Darwinism. They naturalized inequalities, by positing some groups as more meritorious than others. Racial, social, and gender hierarchies stood at the heart of nineteenth-century scientific philosophies. Positivism held sway over engineering and military circles. Not coincidentally, the dictatorial Porfírio Díaz had a military background. So did the first two authoritarian presidents of the Brazilian republic. Their views of progress underlay not just domestic policies, but also their perception of foreign countries. The latter leads us to a second common denominator with consequences to urban planning throughout Latin America: the expectation of capital cities as embodiments of national prowess in a global battle-field—or marketplace.

Mexico City's name was already an example of capitals as metonymic of nations. More subtly, we can see how this lens inflected Nabuco's writing about experiences abroad. He took each city as a part that stood for the national whole. London struck him as "imperial" and mighty like ancient Rome, with a "gigantic mass." He described it as the center of global trade, with people in crowds "indifferent to each other," unwilling to waste a single minute. The "endless perspectives" of avenues and the immensity of parks and squares created the impression of being in the countryside, while the architectural scale gave the city an "eternal solidity." London embodied England's vigorous and "undentable individuality," which could "degenerate into brutality and selfishness." Paris, in contrast, was an "immortally beautiful" work of art, with urban spaces like theater stages. Nabuco developed a relationship with illustrious locals, including George Sand. As he saw it, the Haussmannian capital exuded the imagination and "aesthetic rays" of France's national character.[43]

In contrast, the Americas lacked the "historical imagination" that came with the Old World's built environments.[44] The New World had a future and a past to build. During an extended stay in New York in 1877, Nabuco wrote in his diary that "the moral temperature of the future, judging by the U.S., must be very low."[45] New York seemed like the capital of the US economy. He again took the city for the nation. The United States was "the practical country *par excellence*," where "everything fulfilled some material end." He called its inhabitants positive, averse to metaphysics and sentimentalism, focused above all on the dollar, "always [moving] ahead like a locomotive."[46] Nabuco thought the United States would become the world's most powerful and wealthy nation, if it was not already. To him, though Americans ignored hierarchies as well as inherited privileges, their commitment to equality excluded blacks, Asians, illiterate migrants, neighboring Mexico, and Cuba.[47] His memoir quoted an interview with Herbert Spencer, where the English social Darwinist predicted that "the mixture of Aryan races" would produce the "most powerful" people in the United States. The influential thinker argued that this more adaptable and evolved white race could make "the most grandiose civilization" in history.[48] Nabuco was skeptical.

The energy of Manhattan convinced Nabuco that Americans were "inventing life" at a large scale, suggesting "great future innovations." But the US "mission in History" remained an enigma, and he had misgivings about its contributions to "human destiny." To him, slavery in Brazil had been "a fusion of races," whereas in the United States it represented "a war between them."[49] Fusion was also the term used by Macedo to describe Mexico.

Nabuco's writings are both personal travelogue and a vehicle for comparing national reputations. Contingent experiences in capital cities could be interpreted as signs of a country's shared attributes, confirming stereotypes. This was a bit of a nineteenth-century sport, and a popular one among well-traveled Latin Americans. International competition in the form of World's Fairs and urban design, as we have seen, helped give life to the imagined communities of the nation. In this transatlantic playing field, Nabuco felt humiliated by Brazil's status as "the last slave[-owning] nation."[50] In 1910, Macedo would express pride at how Mexico had ended slavery relatively early.[51]

————

Focusing on national differences can obscure connections. Across the Atlantic, lettered elites and planners shared references and biases. Meanwhile working classes faced comparable challenges whether in Brazil or England. Surely there was a pecking order among nations, but in any given city the future seemed to arrive for some, while to others it was deferred. The Afro-Brazilian writer Machado de Assis wrote a story about the illusions and realities of progress through a dialogue between donkeys. It could be read as a universal fable, or as a very local critique, set in Rio de Janeiro. Machado de Assis grew up in a working-class hillside neighborhood, and never traveled outside his native city. A friend of Joaquim Nabuco's, he circulated among Brazilian lettered elites, but was not of them. His paternal grandparents had been enslaved, and his mother migrated from the Azores. In time, Machado de Assis became Brazil's most highly regarded nineteenth-century author.

Published in a newspaper, the story in question ostensibly addressed the arrival of electric streetcars to Brazil's capital in 1892. This was a major event. As the historian Kenneth Jackson wrote, they "represented progress and technological achievement; no community that thought well of its future could afford to be thought as backward and unpromising."[52] Electric streetcars were beginning to sweep through cities, and Machado de Assis's narrator described the first one he ever saw. What caught his attention was not the modern invention, but the driver's "great air of superiority," looking down on the older animal-drawn vehicles. The technological innovation increased speeds, and solved the problem of how to dispose of manure and carcasses. But for every solution there is a problem, and Machado de Assis imagined how this would impact two donkeys who might become obsolete as a source of labor. The narrator listened to their conversation. The one to his left was optimistic: "As long as electricity extends to all streetcars, it seems clear that we are free."[53] The one to his right responded: "Between seeming and being there is a great difference." He understood how power reconstitutes itself amid change. This second donkey was under no illusions about the imminence of liberty. Instead of retirement or being rewarded for services rendered, they would just end up mistreated and exploited by someone else—another "senhor," which could be translated as either lord or sir, a term commonly applied to slaveholders. Brazilian contemporaries would have interpreted this as a parable about emancipation and deferred justice.

Luís Gama had already suggested that slogans like "order and progress" might create the appearance of transformation, while inequalities remained in place. In Brazil, Machado agreed, promises of freedom and equal rights after abolition proved to be a mirage. Instead of reparations for enslavement, policies favored appeasing slaveowners and whitening society through European migration. This tale could have taken place elsewhere. Reconstruction in the United States met with a fierce backlash to black enfranchisement, ending in the rise of Jim Crow discrimination and violent segregation. Machado de Assis closed the story with a question that seldom finds good answers, and does not seem to age: "Where is there justice in this world?" The donkey realized that some things change so they can stay the same. Streetcars, for example, set off familiar forms of real estate speculation. Wealthy people with insider knowledge bought land on the cheap in a given location before the arrival of streetcar lines, and had their investments quickly gain in value once plans for transit concessions and improvements became public.

The donkeys underestimated impending technologies. Machado de Assis, however, seemed attuned to how in modern cities there was always the next thing. The proud electric streetcar driver in his story probably assumed that the future had arrived, and he was in control. The automobile would supersede his ride. In the North Atlantic, some had already begun to get around in underground subways. The New York–based railroad magnate Russell Sage predicted that "people would go below ground only once in their lifetime—and that was after death."[54] But urbanites kept adapting. There would always be the next invention, the next fashion, the next iteration of the modern. Contrary to the settled ideals of religion or secular utopias, modern life was incomplete by design. Futures would neither be in heaven nor attainable on earth. They are always deferred in urban modernity. No new technology fulfilled an existing need without generating unintended ones.

Arguably, the expectation of progression toward a moving target was already part of the dynamics of World's Fairs, which showcased (and accelerated) innovations in society and production. Urban reforms began to follow a similar logic. A city might be stuck with a new avenue and layout for the foreseeable future, but these spaces often became sites of experimentation and renewal. As circulation sped up, so did the pace of changes in architectural style. Streetcars, cars, and subways all arrived in Rio de Janeiro, and to the Paseo de la Reforma. And more recently, bicycle infrastructure. The twentieth-century Paseo has very few nineteenth-century constructions left, aside from monuments. It is now the location of many of Mexico City's tallest skyscrapers and corporate offices. First-generation modern avenues had comparable fates in Rio, Buenos Aires, New York City, and other metropolises. Haussmannization in the Americas was never just derivative and would take unforeseen directions.

III. How the Other Half Lives

In 1870, a young Danish man named Jacob Riis made the journey across the Atlantic to New York, in search of better opportunities. He was one among millions, and it showed. US cities were undergoing a building boom and becoming increasingly overcrowded. Riis struggled to make a living. An aspiring writer, he tried his hand at jobs like carpentry, farming, and mining throughout the Northeast. Back in New York, he secured a position in a newspaper after successfully covering an upscale event at a hotel—the Astor House. Riis cut his teeth as a police reporter in the city's most impoverished quarters. That experience, coupled with his own firsthand knowledge of destitution, led to a series of articles and lectures, which formed the basis for the seminal *How the Other Half Lives: Studies among the Tenements of New York*. Published in 1890, the book denounced the dire conditions of Manhattan's migrant neighborhoods, helping to set off a reformist response.

The title gives away the audience. It presumed that middle- and upper-class readers had little knowledge of *the other half*. Riis estimated that three-quarters of New York's population lived in tenements, most of them south of the gridded expansion laid out by the Commissioners' Plan.[55] Regardless of where people lived, technological progress was visible. Like other migrants, including to rural America, Riis traveled on a modern steamer and first landed in a major city. Signs of modernization reached far and wide through trains and cables. And many journeyed from the countryside to urban hubs to visit, work, or shop. People witnessed the rise of the first skyscrapers with steel frames and dodged electric trolleys. They bought, fancied, or peddled new consumer products—Riis, for example, had a career selling flatirons. But the workers behind much of this production often remained in the shadows of the great metropolis—and not just metaphorically.

By the turn of the century, as many as 300,000 lived just in the Lower East Side. Every corner seemed inhabited: cellars, attics, dumps. Entire families shared small, partitioned rooms, lacking ventilation, basic sanitation, or sunlight. To capture this reality, Riis used another new technology that would alter the course of cities: photography. Riis experimented with flash photography, shedding light on scenes of gangs in filthy alleys, multiple lodgers sharing bunk beds amid cooking ware, damp stale-beer dives, children toiling in sweat shops or making cigars. Akin to city mysteries decades earlier, these photographs represented the underside of urbanization. Riis anticipated the rise of muckraking journalism. His work played into a voyeuristic gaze, but also informed a broader public—and touched a nerve.

Photography was quickly turning into a tool of reformists and planners. Riis, for instance, went on to capture images of towns pouring sewage into New York's water supply. Scientists had already developed an understanding of how this could cause cholera epidemics. The exposé, published in 1891, helped pressure officials to develop a safer reservoir system.[56] Photographs also helped to disseminate the brightest facets of cities. The next couple of decades were a golden age for postcards, which became a dominant form for the circulation of urban images before the emergence of competing media like the illustrated press

FIGURE 4.3. Riis captures a mother with her baby. Pursuing futures.

and amateur photography. Postcards often featured modern avenues, new civic buildings, and an overall optimistic view of urbanization. There was even a genre of futuristic postcards, imagining how cities might become in an age of flying contraptions and widespread mass transit. Collages, juxtaposing photographs, showed large and small towns bustling with elevated trains and many forms of air travel.

Even *How the Other Half Lives* was not just doom and gloom. Some images held the promise of better days: a rag-picker holding a baby, a boy learning to write, a kid concealing a smile. The book covers drunkards, thieves, and opium addicts. But Riis also recognized that the metropolis could be a beacon. He likened migrants to moths attracted to a lighted candle. They are ignorant "about the city and its pitfalls," but arrived "in search of crowds, of 'life,'" nurturing the expectation "that

FIGURE 4.4. Holyoke, Massachusetts, is not like this today.

something is bound to turn up among so many."[57] On the one hand, the book portrays New York's slums as a "hopeless desert." On the other, it is animated by an unshakeable faith in the possibility of improvement. There are echoes of Christianity, as well as appeals to technical solutions. In the opening pages, after outlining the misery, Riis asks readers: "What are you going to do about it?"[58] Toward the end, drawing on precedents and attentive to the interests of investors, he provided answers. The book proposed legal measures against rapacious absentee landlords, incentives to remodel existing buildings, and the large-scale construction of "model tenements." These would have apartments with natural light, individual entrances, nearby parks, and could return a share of the profits to "good tenants."

Riis's work in fact influenced urban reforms. President Theodore Roosevelt, a former New York police commissioner, would call him the city's "most useful citizen."[59] Partly because of the book's denunciations, in 1895 the city outlawed rear tenements. In 1901, it began to establish standards for lighting, ventilation, fire safety, and room size. We can understand why scholars call this period in US history the Gilded Age and the Progressive Era. The first stresses the excesses of capitalism and wealth, in cities marked by divides between the haves and the have-nots. The latter places weight on the belief that moral corruption could be redeemed, and society improved not just for the rich. Both the monied elites and reformers assumed the future to be malleable. At times, so did working-class migrants.

How the Other Half Lives quoted a prominent landlord who reputedly claimed that his tenants were "not fit to live in a nice house."[60] The book disagreed, countering the prejudices of educated readers. It rejected social Darwinist notions of squalid conditions as a consequence of individual shortcomings and the inherent inferiority of residents. Riis pushed back on the language of natural selection. He wrote of the Bowery in Lower Manhattan as "the great democratic highway of the city," and admired the "purpose and ambition" of the migrants that wanted to make the most out of opportunities to better themselves.[61] The *other half* was not depicted as homogeneous. At the same time, this study was steeped in contemporary taxonomic thinking, framing the analyses within hierarchies among ethnicities, races, nationalities, religions, and genders. We read about "the contentious Irishman," "the order-loving German," the "hot-headed," "light-hearted," and "swarthy Italian." The gambling and opium-loving Chinaman had "scrupulous neatness," and thus dominated the laundry trade. For the Jews, "money is their God." He criticized how landlords charged African Americans more money. Proud of their "new-found citizenship," blacks are "at least as easily molded for good as for evil," and superior to "the lowest of the whites" (Italians and Polish Jews) in cleanliness, but have a "natural love of ease." The book reveled in stereotypes, and essentialized groups at every turn.

An allusion in the title invites further comparisons, at scales beyond the metropolis. It cited a famous line from *Pantagruel* (1532) by the French writer François Rabelais: "one half of the world does not know how the other lives." Indeed, the end of the nineteenth century was also a period when North Atlantic powers asserted geopolitical hierarchies with a sense of superiority emboldened by scientific racism. A more imperialist United States intervened in Cuba and the Philippines. European countries aggressively colonized Africa and parts of Asia.

Even if indirectly, this exploitation of peoples and territories underwrote urbanization in the North Atlantic. Cities reflected that in the spectacle of progress. The zoo in the Parisian Bois de Boulogne, part of the legacy of Haussmannization to the working classes, began in 1877 to host "anthropological" exhibits displaying individuals from *other* societies, mostly African. In the grounds of London's Crystal Palace, an African Exhibition in 1895 did the same with dozens of people from the Sahil region of Somalia.[62] They were not perceived as worthy of a right to the future.

If the city was a stage, here the script was predetermined: event organizers forced the representatives from the "dark continent" to perform native dances and sports, build huts, cook, and mimic warfare. Implicitly, these exhibits' purported demonstration of the other half meant to dramatize the primitive past as a foil to modern urban civilization. Though they had their critics, human zoos became a popular attraction in major cities throughout the North Atlantic. For Riis's readers, destitute urban migrants constituted the other half. But from the perspective of overworked urbanites, this was how the other half lived. The exhibits could be a way of communicating to the subordinate classes that at least they were not stuck in *that* half of the world.

Many of these global divides came together in Brazil's capital, home to both Eurocentric and Afrocentric cultures. There too, the lives of the urban poor became a key object of interest among the lettered. In the same year as Riis's book, Aluísio Azevedo published the novel *O Cortiço*, which has been translated both as *The Slum* and *A Brazilian Tenement*. The term, used to describe crowded lodgings, means beehive. In the book, drawing on French naturalist writers like Émile Zola, the narrator frequently used zoomorphic language to describe characters, especially Afro-descendants. Azevedo hailed from Maranhão, in Brazil's Northeast. His mother escaped marriage to an abusive man. His father, the Portuguese vice-consul, was a widow. They never remarried, which scandalized local society. As an adult, Azevedo migrated to Rio, where he joined abolitionist circles and became a successful writer. In twentieth-century Brazil, his novel about the life of a tenement building became standard assigned reading in schools.

Azevedo focused on the trajectories of poor migrants and Afro-Brazilians in the period preceding abolition. The Portuguese protagonist, João Romão, toiled tirelessly in a "dirty and dark tavern," dreaming of becoming rich.[63] He invested his savings on building the lodgings of the title, where the story unfolds. Portuguese migrants indeed owned more than half of Rio's tenements.[64] Not all ascended socially. Another character from Portugal, Jerônimo, initially moved to rural Brazil, where he "worked like a Moor." Racial hierarchies defined labor markets and the sense of possibilities. To stay in the countryside meant being among the enslaved in a "degrading milieu, cornered like a beast, without aspirations nor future."[65] In the city, by contrast, Jerônimo's efforts in the construction industry were rewarded. He was a model worker, father, and husband, until meeting Rita Bahiana, the sensual and "devilish mulatta" who threw the best parties in the neighborhood. One Portuguese migrant moved up through his industriousness, the other succumbed to the temptations of the tropical city and gave up on discipline. But there is more to the story.

The narrative is also about urban modernity. João Romão renovated his lodgings to attract higher-income tenants. He renamed the expanded development Avenue, adopting the preferred term for the widened and straight streets of the modern city. Another foil, a wealthy Portuguese neighbor, obsessed over nobility titles. We could thus interpret João Romão as the ambitious upstart outdoing the aristocrat. He was, however, no hero. Azevedo might have written a rags-to-riches tale, but it was not about a self-made man. From the get-go, the landlord partnered with Bertoleza, an enslaved woman, and relied on her savings and labor. Just as a modern city rejected blackness, Romão betrayed Bertoleza. He had forged her manumission letter. In one of the book's final scenes, Romão turned Bertoleza over to her slaveowner. Faced with this destiny, Bertoleza committed suicide. The message was clear: autonomy and the right to the future directly correlated with degree of whiteness. Azevedo's fiction tapped into the broken promises of abolition. And he was prescient about how modernization would bind together urban reform and scientific racism.

Race mattered to the destinies of Azevedo's characters. So did gender. Modern citizenship often relied upon the exclusion of women. This also applied to modern planning. The city of avenues and regulated commerce had less space for the black women who had dominated street vending in Rio, for example. In Azevedo's novel, following a typical storyline of the period, the gradual decline of arranged marriages opened up a slim pathway for female mobility. Women continued to work in domestic-bound jobs as servants, or in textiles, clothing, and laundry. Though largely still under the supervision of men, they could have more autonomy in emerging urban professions, ranging from food processing to department stores. Urbanization could naturalize inequalities, but it also unsettled expectations about who should have the freedom to escape assigned roles. Throughout the broader Atlantic, but most prominently in the United States, women led reformist movements.

The US Progressive Era received the name due to the creation of regulatory agencies, the break-up of monopolies, and challenges to corruption in political machines. It resonated with positivism in Latin America through a deep faith in the promises of scientific approaches to social policy. A transatlantic "efficiency movement" stood at the heart of reformist agendas, much of it concentrated on the municipal scale. In the United States, these efforts became influential in mass media and electoral participation. Although women still vied for the right to vote, they advocated for policies through municipal and national organizations. Often making appeals grounded on gender, they pushed for causes including temperance, public health, maternal care, and ending child labor and prostitution. For the historian Kathryn Kish Sklar, in the United States gender consciousness shaped a "public culture" through which women helped to foster the early welfare state: "gender-specific legislation became a surrogate for class legislation."[66]

We could think of women as a facet in "the other half" formulation. From the perspective of male-dominated circles of power, they became impossible to ignore. Leading social reformers tended to come from prosperous families. The Philadelphia native Florence Kelley, for example, had an abolitionist father who served in the US Congress. This does not make her trajectory less remarkable. Kelley did not settle for assigned roles for herself, nor for others. She graduated from Cornell, one of the first universities to accept women. Back in Philadelphia, she helped build the suggestively named New Century Guild, founded in 1882, to support working women with education and lobbying for humane labor laws. Later in the decade Kelley mobilized in Chicago to insert women into factory inspection roles. In 1891, she divorced, no trivial matter at the time. The following year, she joined a federal study, surveying overcrowded neighborhoods where residents toiled to exhaustion, including women and young children, in return for meager earnings. She worked in the state bureaucracy and pressured politicians to regulate workplaces. In 1898, Kelley became the founding general secretary of the National Consumers League and moved to the Lower East Side in New York City. She would go on to also help establish the National Association for the Advancement of Colored People (NAACP).

We might compare Florence Kelley to Luís Gama, for using the law and institutions in the pursuit of justice. Or to Jacob Riis, for leveraging an emergent media-fueled public opinion to exert pressure on decision makers. She would bridge transatlantic leftist politics and the US reformist movement. In her memoirs, Kelley recalled attending her first Socialist meeting in Zurich in the early 1880s. It seemed to be the "World of the Future!"[67] But this was written in the 1920s, amid the first Red Scare, and she downplayed socialist connections (the FBI kept a file on her). In 1887, when her translation of Engels came out, she had declared that "the future rests with the working class."[68] Like many socialists at the time, she used the language of wage-slavery to denounce labor exploitation, approximating it to abolitionist struggles. To her, inspired by Marx and Engels, the organization of labor offered hope for "a peaceful transition" from the "class-rule of today to that true democracy of the future when all shall be free."[69] We hear echoes of socialist utopians. But Kelley, not unlike Latin American positivists and planners, began to see cities as the locus of change. Although she was on the other side of powerful "profit-plunder" capitalists, Kelley preferred reform to revolution or starting from scratch.[70] If that path might seem timid or less brave, we must remember the daunting challenges facing urban dwellers as well as the suppression of radicals (especially anarchists) when Kelley and her peers started out working toward better conditions. There were, after all, lives on the line.

The United States had its own rough equivalent to Azevedo's *O Cor-tiço* in Stephen Crane's *Maggie: A Girl of the Streets*, published in 1893. The subtitle's indefinite article might suggest an all-encompassing narrative, but the setting is precise: the lower Manhattan of crowded tenements and Irish migrants—close to where Kelley lived. Crane's original title called it *A Story of New York*. He was a twenty-two-year-old white Newark native, born into a progressive Methodist family, committed to women's suffrage and prohibition. His plot covered the perceived pathologies of urban slums: street gangs, derelict parenting, petty crimes, prostitution, and drunkenness. As in Azevedo's novel, the characters mostly shunned religion. The narrator treats the ethnic Irish with the deterministic frame of scientific racism, condemning their children to a role among the dangerous classes: "On their small, convulsed faces shone the grins of true assassins."[71] The hierarchies of social desirability are not quite as black-and-white as they would become.

Being in the city could teach people to dream. At work, Maggie had "imagined herself, in an exasperating future, as a scrawny woman with an eternal grievance."[72] Her brother drove horse-drawn vehicles through the city's crowded streets. She became enamored with one of his friends, who introduced her to New York's bohemian nightlife. In the theater, she wondered whether that sparkling culture "could be acquired by a girl who lived in a tenement house and worked in a shirt factory."[73] She "imagined a future, rose-tinted, because of its distance from all that she had experienced before."[74] It seemed possible to marry or work her way out of the dismal tenements, and even shine on the urban stage. The women performers had certainly done it. But unlike in melodramas, there are no happy endings. Maggie, it is implied, ended up working as a prostitute, and died young. The right to the future turned out to be an illusion, as it had been for Bertoleza. At the same time, both novels came out amid the rise of the New Woman, an expression that would describe a freer and more independent relationship to both the city and the future—for those that could afford it. For these male writers, however, the criticism of patriarchal violence and grand illusions still assumed a world with gendered limits, where women could only imagine otherwise.

Maggie stood out for formal innovations. It was part of a realist turn in literature, like *O Cortiço*. Both departed from Romanticist prose with their terse descriptions of material realities and a resistance to sentimental closure. But whereas the Brazilian counterpart drew on French Naturalist literature, *Maggie* brought fiction closer to reportage. We might say that Crane's novel was to modern literature what Riis's book was to modern journalism. Like a reporter, he tried to capture urban dialogues with phonetic precision, as if they were overheard and jotted down. Streets in the book's subtitle meant to evoke prostitution. But the reference can also speak to how these urban spaces animated cultural modernity. Rather than finding vitality in the artistic glories of the past, or seeking a place in posterity, modern writers turned to their urban surroundings. As with Baudelaire in Paris, nothing in the city could be beneath them as a source of literary inspiration.

From the perspective of planning, order and progress required organization through separation of functions and peoples. Contemporary architects and urban designers were largely averse to popular street cultures. To many of them, there would be a city for the rich, another for the poor. In contrast, we might argue that in the works we have been discussing there was a conflation of sides. We must of course acknowledge their opportunistic use of depictions of poverty for commercial gain. But by being instructive without providing a sentimental sense of superiority, these representations could bring urban denizens closer to realities other than their own. The Rio de Janeiro of slums and avenues, or the New York City of Gilded Age mansions and Bowery tenements, were in fact the same city. As wildly different as individual experiences and fortunes might be, urban futures would in some sense be shared by all. The question remained: who should get to shape the cities of tomorrow?

IV. Haussmannization Americanizes

Joaquim Nabuco was on firm ground when he imagined that the United States would rise above competing powers. Amid stark inequalities, turmoil, and financial panics, its economy boomed between the 1860s and the 1900s: urban wages, steel production, and agricultural output increased at impressive rates.[75] The railroad network expanded nearly sixfold, becoming the world's most extensive by far. This acceleration and a sense of possibility might help to explain the popularity of precursors to science fiction. In 1887, Edward Bellamy published *Looking Backward*. Over the next decade, it became a best-selling sensation in the United States, and eventually abroad.

The basic plot recalls Mercier and Verne. Through hypnosis, the first-person narrator sleeps for over a hundred years. He wakes up in an ideal Boston. In the city of the 1880s, he explained, there was class-based segregation and exploitation. The protagonist was rich like his forebears and expected the same for his descendants. In the year 2000, he learns that all production had been nationalized, and people enjoyed the benefits of a socialistic society: goods are plentiful and distributed according to need. Money is obsolete, and workers retire at forty-five.

Within twelve years of the publication of *Looking Backward*, over 190 literary utopias appeared in the United States.[76] Bellamy's novel inspired dozens of clubs devoted to its political ideals. His book presented a program disguised as fiction, with egalitarian principles implemented in top-down fashion rather than through a proletarian revolution. The means of Haussmannization, toward different ends. The site of the transformed urban landscape convinced the narrator that he had woken up in the future. Aside from a "few old landmarks," the urban fabric of the past had vanished. In this great Boston, he found "miles of broad streets, shaded by trees and lined with fine buildings, for the most part not in continuous blocks but set in larger or smaller enclosures." Each quarter had green squares, statues, fountains, and public buildings of "colossal size" and "architectural grandeur."[77] We have seen this formula before, but there are twists. Social life largely took place outside the home. Public spaces were marked by "splendor," private ones by "simplicity." Cities had sidewalk coverings for when it rained. The problem of pollution was solved. Pneumatic tubes delivered goods. Live music played in halls broadcast through telephones to homes, and people appreciated Bach. Like earlier utopians, Bellamy imagined a future where cultural values stayed relatively constant, while institutions and politics were radically transformed.

Bellamy's utopia attended to gender. The narrator saw women as "hopeless" and weak in the Boston of the present. In the future, they are part of society's "industrial army" and enjoy its benefits. The book, however, mostly skirted ethnic tensions and racism, confining such references to descriptions of Boston in the 1880s. It compared the "sultry stenches" of streets and alleys to "a slave ship's between-decks," and the "swarms" of impoverished children to the "mongrel curs that infest [. . .] Moslem towns."[78] These too seemed to have vanished in the year 2000. Joaquim Nabuco hailed from a country where futuristic fiction had not yet taken off. But his perception of racial "war" in the United States gave him a prescient intuition about how dominant visions for the future would treat blackness as a threat.

The most ambitious event showcasing the country's progress would become known as the White City. In 1893, the Columbian Exposition in Chicago surpassed all previous World's Fairs in scale and spectacle. The nickname derived not from the racial make-up of planners, but from the white façades of the Classical Revival buildings. Some interiors had steel structures encased in glass. But while the Paris World's Fair in 1889 had debuted the bold Eiffel Tower, Chicago's fairgrounds designers adopted the ornamental Beaux-Arts aesthetics of Haussmannian Paris. In a city that was pioneering the development of skyscrapers, they drew heavily from references to Greco-Roman motifs. The plans privileged symmetry and monumentality. Commemorating Columbus, it was as if they sought to signal the New World outdoing the Old, by traditionally Eurocentric standards of "universal" beauty.

The World's Fair grounded the future of the United States in the image of a European past, and placed whiteness at the top of the hierarchies of progress.[79] In a pamphlet distributed during the event, Ida B. Wells noted that the labor of African Americans afforded to white Americans the leisure to pursue achievements in the arts and sciences. Fredrick Douglass wrote that the "splendid display of wealth and power" excluded the colored people of America because it continued the legacy of slavery.[80] They did not quite challenge the premise of technological

FIGURE 4.5. The Palace of Mechanic Arts: a future in the mold of the Old World.

FIGURE 4.6. Inside, functional machinery. Outside, a grand loggia. Both open to the masses. What do these men see or seek?

and socioeconomic productivity as desirable and attainable. But in the White City, as the United States extolled its virtues, the pamphlet publicized to visitors the realities of racism, like lynching and the Ku Klux Klan.

Several major cities in the United States vied to host the World's Fair. Congress voted for Chicago. It was a fitting site for a society hoping to whitewash the legacies of slavery. African Americans comprised around 1 percent of the city's population, compared to about 12 percent of the United States. Nearly 80 percent of Chicago's residents were either foreign-born or the children of migrants, the vast majority from Europe. Chicago represented the modern future for several reasons. It was undergoing extraordinary growth. Doubling in a decade, the population reached over one million in 1890. By 1900, Chicago was probably the world's fifth largest city, and the second in the Americas. It brought to the table private funders, available space, and need, as the city was still recovering from the 1871 fire. Being in the Midwest also carried symbolic power. Linking Columbus to western development, the event set up a narrative of progress beginning with transatlantic colonization and pointing toward the Pacific as the next frontier.[81]

As an affordable attraction, the Columbian Exposition cut across class. It drew over 27 million visitors. Most arrived by train to the grounds, which covered almost 700 acres, an area almost as large as Central Park. Attendees witnessed the latest innovations, including moving walkways, refrigerators, air conditioners, guns, and precursors to cinema. Electric lights made the white façades gleam at night. Florence Kelley, impressed with how the fair "gloriously celebrated [...] the coming of age of American industry," lamented how it did not improve the lives of Chicago residents. She looked back on it as a spectacular missed opportunity: "A lovely vision, an entrancing mirage had come and gone."[82]

The White City was built to be temporary, but it did launch lasting trends in urban planning. An aging Frederick Law Olmsted was behind the layout, which combined sinuous paths, grand boulevards, and picturesque views. The fair enabled a changing of the guards with the rise of its director of works, Daniel Burnham. He would design the

Flatiron Building in Manhattan, Union Station in Washington, and the Ford building in Detroit, as well as iconic department stores throughout the United States and in London. Burnham also became a key figure in the City Beautiful movement, bringing together Eurocentric aesthetics and the social concerns of the Progressive Era. As in the Enlightenment mindset, he tended to equate order with rectilinearity. Consonant with Haussmannization, he placed monumental civic design at the center of his urban visions.

The Chicago World's Fair helped to catalyze efforts to finally turn Washington, DC, into a suitable expression of the ambitious nation. Along with Olmsted's son, Burnham joined a commission in 1901 to create a plan for the capital. They revisited L'Enfant's grand vision, which had remained unfulfilled until then. Burnham looked back on this moment as the origins of professional city planning in the United States. He complained about opposition from "those who regard only the present, and take no thought for future advancement."[83] Burnham went on to devise plans for Manila (1904), San Francisco (1905), and Chicago (1909). The latter plan contended that Haussmannization transformed Paris into "the capital not only of the state, but also of civilization."[84] But it did not merely try to create a Paris in the Prairies. It speculated Chicago might grow into the world's largest city and sought to anticipate needs. Burnham became associated with a slogan that captured the ethos of the new generation of modern planners: "Make no little plans; they have no magic to stir mens' blood [. . .]."[85] It could have been said by Haussmann, Napoleon III, or any number of later designers in the new century.

———

In the early 1900s, Rio de Janeiro finally got its own big plans, though they did not stir men's blood in all the ways intended by planners. The city was not growing nearly as fast as Chicago, or São Paulo, but stood as the capital of the largest republic in the Global South. About half of its residents were migrants, split almost evenly between Brazilians and Europeans. The latter came mostly from Portugal, and they began to

change Rio's demographics. The percentages of Afro-descendants declined and would continue to do so in the twentieth century. But Rio
remained considerably less European and more African than other
major cities of the Americas. In 1890, around 12 percent of its residents
identified as black, and another 25 percent as *pardo* or brown.[86] It would
not be as easy as in Chicago to whitewash the legacies of slavery.

Rio's port had played a key role since the colonial period. In the republic, nearly half of all federal revenue originated from taxes on imports that arrived through it.[87] But as transatlantic trade evolved after
slavery, Rio's port lagged competitors. By the early twentieth century,
ships could be ten times larger than in the 1820s. Ports needed to be
modernized.[88] Rio's main rival was not the port city of New York, the
railroad hub of Chicago, nor the national capital of DC, but another
place that brought together all those functions: Buenos Aires. Transportation and communication technologies allowed it to concentrate the
management of resources across vast territories, with commodities
originating in the countryside supporting a large service sector. During
the second half of the nineteenth century, that drove rapid growth even
more than manufacturing, similarly to Chicago and São Paulo (which
had railroad connections to the modern port of Santos).[89] Buenos Aires
became Argentina's federal capital in 1880, and gained about 5.5 miles of
cement quays with hydraulic cranes along the River Plate in the 1890s.[90]
It was the second largest city in the South Atlantic behind Rio. Like the
Brazilian capital, the Argentine metropolis had over 800,000 residents,
but with a much greater share from Europe and white. For business
interests and lettered elites, it was more modern and civilized. Rio was
behind.

At the end of the nineteenth century, many Brazilians going about
their lives would be surprised to learn that a geopolitical race was even
taking place. They had other aspirations. In the backlands, a popular
movement challenged the young republic, rejecting the invention of a
modern future. In 1893, a messianic pilgrim called Antônio Conselheiro
and his followers founded a city in a semiarid region of the Northeast.
Belo Monte, or Beautiful Hill, brought together peasants and believers,
including formerly enslaved and indigenous peoples. It rapidly grew to

around 25,000. This egalitarian Christian community existed outside formal institutions and against official authorities. Their millenarian expectations rejected the modern faith in order and progress. There was no private property. Conselheiro believed the republic incarnated the antichrist. Machado de Assis, in 1894, described them as a "legion of gallant and audacious adventurers [...] who hate calendars, clocks, taxes, obeisance, anything that mandates, aligns, and embellishes."[91] Aligning in Portuguese can refer both to being straightened, or dressed up. It was used in the press to praise urban reforms.

Like maroon communities or the Paris Commune, Belo Monte represented a threat to state authority, landholding oligarchs, and clergy. Rumors began to circulate about the intentions of Conselheiro's followers to attack nearby towns, and eventually, the federal capital itself. A media campaign painted them as fanatics supported by monarchists set on overturning the government. It became a major story in urban Brazil. Between 1896 and 1897, in the War of Canudos, a series of military expeditions attempted to crush Belo Monte. In 1897, Machado de Assis wrote that no matter how much Rio residents tried, they could never match the "celebrity" of Conselheiro. As proof, he cited "New York and London, where the name of Antônio Conselheiro lowers our stocks."[92] By implying the financial interests at stake, Machado ironically called out the hypocrisy of framing the attack on Belo Monte as a war on behalf of civilization. That same year, the republican military forces destroyed the town, killing tens of thousands of people. They cut off the head of Conselheiro and donated it to scientists.

Machado de Assis seemed to realize there was a conflict between visions of the future taking place. On the one hand, Conselheiro represented a horizon of Christian redemption: life on earth, with the end of the world and salvation beyond it. On the other, his opponents stood not just for positivist-inflected secular ideologies, but also for an experience of time exemplified by the financial markets: short-term, openended, and money-oriented. Machado de Assis expected his readers to understand that if Conselheiro caused a perception of instability in Brazil, it could impact the country's credit abroad. Like other contemporary writers, he noted how the stock market caused a kind of frenzied fever in Rio, mixing oppressive anxiety and high hopes of quick profits. Not by coincidence, informal gambling also took hold in the streets.

At the same time, Belo Monte and Rio de Janeiro shared some attributes that made the upper classes uncomfortable. Prior to abolition, Brazil's capital had quarters that constituted a "hideaway city," or a "Black city."[93] As impoverished migrants arrived from Europe and the countryside, Rio continued to be a place where people sought to find cracks through which to experience relative freedom. They lived in tough conditions, making spaces for folk religiosity and profane festivities. What happened in the self-sufficient messianic town was brought into the urban and capitalist folds through modern news media. But much of urban Latin America remained culturally rural. The visual record of the period reveals the dress codes of city dwellers changing toward the late 1800s. Earlier photographs of urban sites show many people wore traditional or peasant clothing. There was a lot of heterogeneity, both within and across cities. Over time, clothing became increasingly standardized and coded as European or modern in style. This happened amid a growth in mass-produced textile manufacturing and illustrated magazines. Aesthetic uniformity following Eurocentric norms was of course also a central feature of Haussmannization.

The violence against Belo Monte, like the Bloody Week that ended the Paris Commune, showed the modern state asserting itself. It represented a warning against future dissenters, and the inevitability of getting in line. In Brazil's case this preceded urban reforms and took place in the countryside. But we may view it as a rehearsal for Haussmannization. Between 1903 and 1906, Rio residents felt the full force of the republic in what became known as the *bota abaixo*, or putting down. Planners brought about the demolition of as many as 3,000 buildings and the displacement of more than 37,000 residents.[94] In their place, a modern boulevard cut through the colonial fabric. The historian Sidney Chalhoub writes that by razing tenements, modifying layouts, and persecuting popular street practices, the republican regime "attacked the historical memory" of the fights against slavery. The streets and homes that vanished with the reforms had been imbued with meaning, "painstakingly built" during the pursuit of freedom.[95]

This was a moment of rupture with the past, but it also concealed continuities. Some of the veterans of the War on Canudos had moved to the Brazilian capital instead of returning to the countryside. There, they discovered the republic was not exactly on their side. Without access to housing, these migrants adopted architectural techniques from rural settings to build on the city's hillsides. Former tenement dwellers joined them. Displaced during the reforms, they used materials from torn-down constructions to make shacks. These were the beginnings of the self-built communities known as *favelas*. We could view them as the other side of modernization, and another expression of the interplay between old and new.[96] To some, poor people were not supposed to be at the center of the beautified Rio, but they too sought to shape the city, albeit at a more micro scale and from the bottom up.

Political and economic elites shared a vision where progress entailed integration into global markets. And civilization meant catching up to French-inspired urban models. From that perspective, by the early twentieth century many major cities had earned a right to see their futures in the reflection of the City of Light: Havana as a Tropical Paris, Mexico City as the Paris of America, Santiago as a Latin American Paris, and Buenos Aires as the Paris of La Plata.[97] Rio's turn was long overdue. But Brazil's capital lacked a modern boulevard. It was as if irregular, narrow, and aging streets curtailed ambitions. The local press assumed familiarity with francophone references and framed urban planning as a form of global positioning. One newspaper lamented that Rio had "for a long time waited for its Haussmann, who made Paris modern; for its Alvear, who made Buenos Aires [. . .] one of the most enchanting Latin metropoles; and for an Antonio Prado, who metamorphosed São Paulo [. . .] from a colonial city to a piece of Europe planted in Brazil."[98]

Rio de Janeiro would have its own "Tropical Haussmann" in Francisco Pereira Passos.[99] In 1902, he was appointed mayor by President Rodrigues Alves. Both men had made their careers under the empire. Alves studied with Joaquim Nabuco in Rio's most prestigious secondary school, and in São Paulo's Law School. He joined an abolitionist organization with Luís Gama. Twelve years older, Passos came from a family of wealthy landowners and moved as a teenager to Rio, where he attended military schools. Assigned to a diplomatic post in Paris, he witnessed the Haussmannian public works and studied the modernization of French infrastructure from 1857 to 1860.[100] Back in Brazil, Passos worked on railway construction, and joined a commission that created comprehensive plans for Rio in the 1870s. He then worked as a businessman in construction industries. Alves had campaigned on reforming the capital and chose the experienced Passos to lead the process. Both inhabited circles steeped in positivist doctrines. Breaking from constitutional norms, the mayor was given powers to act without legislative approval, unilaterally. That allowed demolitions and construction to proceed at a pace that would make even Haussmann envious. The new boulevard, the Avenida Central, was inaugurated in 1905—on the sixteenth anniversary of the republic.

In 1903, as the reforms began to take shape, a column in a prominent newspaper appealed to Paris as a precedent to argue that property owners and commercial tenants in razed blocks deserved compensation.[101] Tenement dwellers would have to fend for themselves. Months later, the same publication framed the remodeling as a necessity for Brazil's image abroad. It was a requirement for "the progress and development" of the nation. To them, Passos appeared to be "following the footsteps" of Haussmann, turning Rio from an "ugly colonial chrysalis" into a "beautiful, hygienic, and majestic metropolis." They quoted Paulo de Frontin, the engineer responsible for the construction of a grand Central Avenue. He predicted that the public works "will be followed by a zenith from which fertile rays would spread out to the entire territory" of Brazil.[102] All the organic metaphors hinted at a sense of the urban disruptions as part of a natural order. Forecasting was an effective strategy to neutralize criticism. Who could dare to oppose such a brilliant outcome?

The Parisian reforms had also built on momentum and deliberate goals, but their novelty can justify the characterization of Haussmann "gambling on the future."[103] On that basis, decades later, Passos was merely following suit. No planner, however, operates in a vacuum. In Rio, as elsewhere, the reforms reflected a host of conditions and forces, ideological as well as material. Brazil, unlike Napoleon III's France, was a semidemocratic Republic. Federal and municipal administrations assumed responsibility for different projects. This foreshadowed growing tensions in the evolution of cities, with competing interests across spheres of governance. Technically, federal authorities carried out work in the port and built the major avenues leading to it, while the municipality handled much of the rest. The bulk of public commissions went to well-connected men centered around the private Engineering Club, presided from 1903 to 1933 by the aforementioned Paulo de Frontin. Unsentimental toward the past, most engineers favored razing the existing urban fabric. Passos opted to save buildings on one side of new thoroughfares under his control, as well as a few landmarks with religious or colonial connections. The historian André de Azevedo argues that whereas the mayor cared about civilization, the federal government prioritized progress. One vision of the future focused on culture, the other on economics.[104]

Varied motivations converged to enable what became known, somewhat deceptively, as the Passos reforms. Renovating and better integrating the port within transportation networks earned the support of powerful stakeholders, providing a major impetus for the larger-scale plans. At the time, as Osterhammel writes, "merchants tended to regard city planning with skepticism and to recoil from investment in infrastructure other than port facilities."[105] After the demise of forced labor, the Brazilian capital could only help the country meet the international demand for products like coffee by undergoing the transition from a manual to a steam-powered urban economy.[106] This served the interests of landowning planter oligarchies even more than the urban bourgeoisie. Originally, the Republic had acquired loans from London banks to invest in all of Brazil's ports.[107] But resources and attention would flow to Rio. Financing included a mixture of debt, bonds, and import duties. Future property tax revenue partly guaranteed loans. The reforms mobilized a sizable chunk of the national budget, and the press regularly published estimates of the costs.

Everyone knew that Rio would never be the same. The planners assumed continuing development, seeking to stimulate growth in a controlled manner. Though railroads connected the port to the suburbs and countryside, Rio's reforms largely neglected investment in train systems, unlike other cities. Early cars had begun to arrive, but the consensus was that urban mobility would continue to consist of streetcars and carriages. Widened and straightened roads promised to improve circulation. Asphalted pavements, used for the first time in Rio, enabled vehicles to move faster. New avenues radiated out of central areas. An expanded canal addressed drainage toward the north. Infrastructure was extended to the largely unbuilt south, laying the groundwork for the now famous beachfront neighborhoods of Copacabana and Ipanema. From a practical perspective, the Central Avenue eased circulation to and from the port. But as the name suggested, it was also the symbolic centerpiece of the reforms. The Central Avenue would leave the city with a postcard worthy of status as Brazil's capital, and signal to residents that the modern future had arrived. The avenue was about 110 feet wide, comparable to Haussmannian precedents, and over a mile in length. It would be lined with façades designed in the Eclectic French Second Empire style, following regulations to ensure some level of uniformity.[108]

Passos attempted to dictate what a civilized future should be like. He wanted to reform the city and its population. Compared to precedents, the state took a more direct role in programming the Central Avenue. The plan for Rio sought to assign specific roles and functions to different sections, with a nearly all-encompassing zeal that anticipated modernist urbanism. The city's central areas had long hosted hotels, publishers, cafés, clubs, and shops catering to the monied classes. In the new boulevard, buildings closer to the port hosted financial and commercial institutions. Civil society occupied the middle: newspapers, religious associations, labor organizations, and of course, the Engineering Club. At the other end, toward the bay, the avenue culminated in a spectacle of Beaux-Arts aesthetics. A major square concentrated cultural institutions, giving prominence to the Museum of Fine Arts, the National Library, and the Municipal Theater. The latter was inspired by the Opera

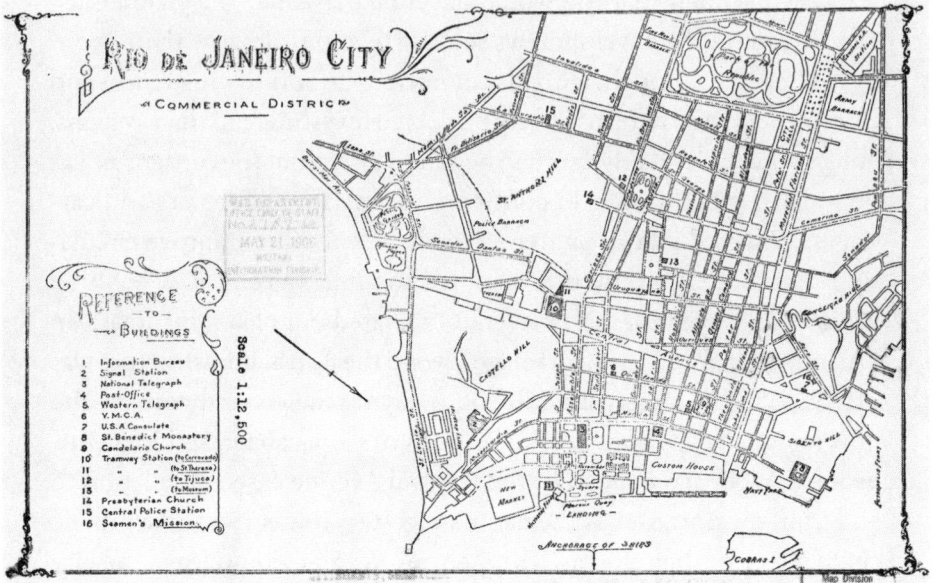

FIGURE 4.7. A modern Central Avenue cut through Rio de Janeiro's colonial fabric, connecting the port and the "commercial district."

Garnier. Fawning articles detailed the building's modern details, like the artificial ventilation system and electric lighting.[109] It was designed by the mayor's son.

The Central Avenue was also framed by an obelisk commemorating its inauguration, donated by a businessman behind the construction. If this monument evoked the Roman and Napoleonic appropriation of Egyptian architecture, then the whole reform could stand for a kind of civilizing mission. André de Azevedo uses the expression "conservative integration." Rather than exclude the working classes, the reforms would elevate them. Access to an iconic museum, library, and boulevard could give the poor an education in traditionally Eurocentric cultural values. This narrow conception of culture was already somewhat out-dated, but the idea that urban design shaped cities and citizenship alike brought together older and newer tropes. In a speech to his peers at the Engineering Club, a contemporary supporter of the plans rhapsodized: "the straight line is not just the pathway through which light propagates

FIGURE 4.8. Another Tropical Paris. Avenue vistas with the Municipal Theater to the side, and the Sugar Loaf mountains if you turned around.

to reach our eyes but also the way to our spirits."[110] This echoed the early modern equivalence between geometric and moral rectitude. At the same time, a commitment to social evolution put the reforms in line with increasingly influential Darwinist theories.

In 1903, a series of cartoons published in the weekly *A Avenida* showed the desired progression. A woman embodied the past, present, and future after the new Avenue. Rather than monkey-to-man, the evolution here is from shabby to chic. The artist, Crispim do Amaral, satirized the whitening and Europeanizing delusions of Rio's planners. A drawing in a newspaper showed men in top hats leading the way, flanked by soldiers and debris. Others pressed the critique further: more men in top hats, holding on to a pole, praising the view from above. Below, again, debris. In the sweltering tropics, they look dressed for the opera. All this trouble, the cartoons seem to imply, so that rich people can

Como foi.

Como sera

FIGURE 4.9. Evolution versus revolution. "How it was, how it is, how it will be."

A AVENIDA

Para diante!...

FIGURE 4.10. The avenue plows ahead, leaving tropical standards and debris behind.

pretend to be in Europe. After the late 1970s, Passos became vilified as the architect of a plan to kick the poor out of Rio's center. More recent scholarship has added nuance. Passos was elitist, but not glib. His administration opened public schools in lower-income suburbs, gave 700 percent raises for teachers, created an ambulance service, improved public squares, and built housing for municipal workers. In private letters, Passos expressed concerns with how the other half lived, claiming he wished the city could have built more centrally located residences for the working classes.[111]

The press generally covered the reforms with excitement. An issue of the illustrated magazine *A Renascença*, with Machado de Assis on the cover, referred to "dreamed improvements" that would leave Rio as "the first" among South American cities. And, if more remained to be done, even better: "let us leave something for the future generations."[112] Although they described Passos as "our Haussmann," that did not imply that Rio would simply imitate foreign models. It had a more irregular layout than Spanish American cities. One writer addressed the criticism that too many streets were left crooked by pointing out the "abuse of the straight line" in the Parisian reforms, leading to "monotonous" and "tiring" experiences.[113] But the embrace of sinuous lines and perspectives oriented around natural landscapes was not just accidental. The 3.2-mile Beiramar Avenue followed the contours of the shoreline with deliberate curves.

Rio's topography was on display in the Avenida Central too. The Municipal Theater was placed at one of its extremes. But it stood adjacent to the boulevard, at an odd angle, rather than at the end of an expansive vista. As a result, instead of foregrounding the monumental building, the avenue opened up a view of the Sugar Loaf Mountain on the horizon. This diverged from the urban hierarchies of Haussmannization, which valued civic architecture over natural landscapes. In Rio, it is as if the picturesque mountains became the monument. Some could interpret this as recognition that Brazil's role in the global economy depended on natural resources. It is a sign, regardless, that people in the Americas had their own visions about what the urban future ought to be like—and that this entailed adapting rather than merely imitating Eurocentric models.

FIGURE 4.11. A postcard showcases the modern boulevard. The topography imposes itself, but Castelo Hill to the left would be leveled in the 1920s.

Brazil was also experiencing advances in modern medicine, with local health professionals conducting cutting-edge work. In the early nineteenth century, when miasma theories of airborne contagion dominated, hygienists had proposed leveling the Sugar Loaf Mountain. In early 1902, some supported tackling yellow fever and smallpox through de-densification, which involved demolishing more centrally located hills. A newspaper columnist complained about these "utopian" whims, which seemed unfeasible "not because we lack a Haussmann," but for a lack of funds.[114] When the resources materialized, it was partly due to sanitation concerns. Modern sewage and water systems connected to homes had been introduced relatively early in Rio.[115] But the infrastructure could not keep up with growth, and disproportionately served the wealthy. Cities in Latin America had even higher mortality rates than those in the North Atlantic.[116] This presented a health as well as an image problem: Rio de Janeiro had been known as a "foreigner's grave" due to epidemics. Sanitation also provided solutions to what planners viewed as a social problem—they saw an opportunity to discipline and constrain urban dwellers like Luísa Mahin.

Public health helped to provide pretexts for planners to target practices and places associated with the supposedly barbaric countryside and dangerous classes. Now, it was illegal to spit in public or walk around barefoot. As the historian Nicolau Sevcenko put it, Passos used his "tyrannical powers" to prohibit anything that was not "stable, fixed, immediately controllable."[117] This included cow herding, stray dogs, vagrants, peddling, fireworks, and balloon lanterns. Federal decrees empowered officials to force people to vacate "unsanitary" properties, which was often followed by their demolition. Some sued, using photographs to document how authorities abused their mandate. Further, the reforms went after spaces where various social, ethnic, and racial groups intermingled, like bars and cabarets. The mayor's regime attempted to ban forms of street commerce that had allowed Africans and their descendants to make a space for themselves in the city. Public outcry led to some flexibility, with restrictions against open trays and limited vending hours. Strict building codes constrained the housing supply, making units less affordable. This indirectly encouraged unregulated and precarious self-built communities on Rio's hills, where people could still live near the renovated downtown.[118]

In much of the press and in some quarters, a stock phrase celebrated the changes: "Rio civilizes itself." Magazine articles and advertisements were peppered with phrases in French. The model was Haussmannian, but some signs pointed to the future having crossed the Atlantic. In 1904, the winner of the architecture prize for foreign pavilions at the St. Louis World's Fair was Brazil's Monroe Palace, in the Beaux-Arts style. After the event, this building was moved to the Central Avenue, where it eventually hosted the national senate. The design might have recalled France, but the name honored James Monroe, a US president notorious for his opposition to European influence in American affairs. The St. Louis event, coinciding with the Olympics, made the US imperial pretensions even more explicit. It displayed Filipinos in "villages" akin to human zoos, portraying them as backward people to be redeemed by civilization. The following year, a shift toward the Americas as a paragon of progress in the new century could be heard in speeches during the Central Avenue's inauguration. A congressman and hygienist doctor enthusiastically praised Brazil overcoming its colonial legacies: "the country penetrates, courageously, the road to the future, creating a nation individualized, enterprising, American."[119]

In Rio, those considered to be backward were not a small minority, nor halfway across the continent or planet. And they could speak back. The speech above was booed by "shady types," a newspaper complained. Press coverage had made sure to create an appearance of buy-in from the general population. During the reforms, articles highlighted the distribution of flyers with information about the plans, to submit them to "public discussion."[120] A newspaper column in 1903 praised the lack of opposition to the reforms, in contrast to Paris and Buenos Aires.[121] It celebrated Rio's alliance of "the Portuguese race," seen as "prudent, full of fertile love of work and peace," with "the black race," framed as "good, resigned, martyr." Six years later, reporting on the now former mayor's birthday upon his return to Rio after living in Europe, the same publication hailed the "Brazilian Haussmann," whose great works received "general acclaim." They flaunted how it took the Paris mayor fifteen years to achieve his great works, and that Passos even had to defeat the "staunch conservatism" of critics. The paper reproduced the former mayor's speech, where he thanked the cooperation of "all social classes."[122] An anarchist paper, in turn, described the avenue's inauguration as a sign of the "miserable exploitation of passive and unconscious workers."[123]

Since the late 1970s, historians have focused on how many of Rio's residents resisted the plans. Indeed, some people referred to the "Passos dictatorship."[124] Insubordination came to a head in November of 1904, in what became known as the Revolt of the Vaccine. Urban dwellers built barricades, burning and destroying streetcars, streetlights, train infrastructure, and construction sites. Supporters of Rio's modernization interpreted the uprising as a backlash of obscurantist antiscience mobs against forced vaccinations. After all, why would anyone oppose solutions to the smallpox epidemics that afflicted the city? They failed to ask themselves why disaffected (and presumably uninfected) urbanites should trust an arbitrary and violent government to fumigate their homes at will, and insert syringes in their bodies. It is not that authorities lacked genuine intentions to combat diseases. It is that they seemed oblivious to the big picture. The Passos project equated civilization with a symbolic remodeling of the city that shored up hierarchies. It championed Beaux-Arts façades while the poor suffered from hunger. Insurrectionists chanted "Death to the Police" and "Down with forced vaccination." But they attacked sites associated with the reforms, rather than public health institutions. Nonetheless, vaccination was suspended. In 1908, more than six thousand people died in a smallpox epidemic.

It might be tempting for us to judge this rebellion in light of our twenty-first century experiences with antivax movements. Rather, we can think of this uprising in 1904 as another clash between visions for the future, as the War of Canudos had been. But the terms were different. Historian Teresa Meade notes that Latin American urban protests of the period often revolved around consumption ("fare hikes, food costs, housing problems") rather than production ("wages, working conditions, union recognition").[125] This implies a more short-term imagination of political possibilities. And in Brazil the different sides of conflicts were not balanced, given the relatively united elites. On one side, the reforms attended to the interests of the state bureaucracy, the urban bourgeoisie, rural oligarchs, and global finance. On the other, protestors consisted of marginalized urban dwellers including the unemployed, proletariats, gig workers, small shopkeepers, hustlers, maids, peddlers, prostitutes, and so on. They had few weapons and chose to disrupt everyday life in the city through destruction—what had been done to them during the reforms. To Nicolau Sevcenko, "the uprising did not seek power, nor did it intend to win." Instead, it was a radical gesture of "horror and indignation." Asserting their dignities, people fought back against "everything that humiliated them, subordinated them, and reduced their humanity."[126] Too uncertain about their destinies, we could say that these mostly disenfranchised urbanites were not out to invent a new world, but rather to deny a future where they did not belong.

V. Reinventions

Police squashed the Revolt of the Vaccine with brutality. They jailed suspects indiscriminately and without trial, sending them to Amazonian rubber plantations in prison-like boats that recalled slave ships. The style of repression under the Republic and slavery differed, however. Appearances mattered, so violence became more hidden.[127] The Passos interventions sought to give an urban form to the positivist ideals of "order and progress" enshrined in the Brazilian flag. To do so, Beaux-Arts façades had to act like white masks, hiding continuities with the enslaved past and projecting a modern bourgeois society. Newspapers and organizations throughout the North Atlantic praised the impressive results.[128]

In the Brazilian press, an article in 1908 described the visit of two assimilated indigenous people from the countryside, arriving in the federal capital to ask for protection. In the "inelegant" city of the past, lacking in monuments and lights, the indigenous would have been met with "some sympathy." Now, the author stated with pride, "the city changed and we changed with it." When the "savages" appear, they are treated "like an embarrassing family member."[129] There was no place for them in the new Rio. The reforms improved sanitation and circulation but left the city more segregated. The latter was by design. To modernize meant to compartmentalize and organize by function, at all scales of operation. Some spaces were demarcated for work, others for leisure or consumption. Restaurants separated kitchens from eating rooms. Streetcars isolated the drivers. In Brazil, suburbs contained the poor. In the United States, African Americans had to ride trains in their own wagons, closer to smokestacks.[130] Spaces like the Central Avenue and the opera house served those that could afford them. Rational plans could render the future as predictable, calculable, and controllable. But as it so often happens in the history of planning, the unexpected prevailed.

We might think of the Passos reforms as both a latecomer and a swan song to Haussmannization. The dreams of a tropical civilization in the Parisian mold waned, as a more relaxed dress code culture attests. Only a handful of Beaux-Arts buildings remain in the Central Avenue, which was renamed. Even the Monroe Palace was demolished. In the meantime, much of Rio's compact colonial fabric, marked by varied and jumbled street life, survived. Automobiles quickly took over the new avenues and helped stretch development to the beachfront. In the twenty-first century, high-tech streetcars and pedestrian-oriented spaces have returned to the city center. The reforms succeeded, to some degree, in pushing the poor to the suburbs. But the public spaces of Rio de Janeiro's downtown, envisioned by some as playgrounds for the elites, became sites of social mixture and gatherings. Periodically, a motley crew of carnival revelers, political protesters, and social movements occupy the square in front of the Garnier-like Municipal Theater.

The Brazilian Republic continued to exclude Afro-descendants from power structures. Nine out of the first ten presidents either had backgrounds tied to landowning oligarchies or married into them.[131] Continuities with slave-based economies persisted. But it proved harder to marginalize Afro-Brazilians from being cultural protagonists. As we will see, many Latin American societies selectively embraced a self-image based on miscegenation. This was a way of changing so some things could stay the same: celebrations of cultural mixture coexisted with racial hierarchies. Between 1890 and 1930, Afro-descendants experienced far less improvement in living conditions than European migrants and their descendants.[132] At the same time, groups relegated to subordinate roles in plans for political and economic futures gained prominence in the cultural sphere. Foreign capital did not shape music to the same extent as other industries. The flow of money reflected racial prejudices, but new urban genres like samba proved to be exceptionally porous, allowing the marginalized to take center stage. It was not the society for which Luiz Gama had fought, but Afro-descendants had a dominant place in Brazilian cultural modernity, particularly through musical innovations.

Like Domingos Caldas Barbosa in early modern Lisbon, samba musicians blended various traditions to produce something new. In the radio era, rural Brazil was brought into the urban fold culturally. Samba became the quintessential national expression both domestically and abroad in the 1920s and 1930s. By then, disillusioned Europeans frequently looked not just to the Americas, but also to its inhabitants for pathways forward. Yet these urban cultures should not be reduced to a bit part in transatlantic history. They heralded an alternative civilization, with a different kind of relationship to space and time. One of its invented percussive instruments has a style of playing sometimes known as the *surdo de Exu*.[133] Surdo, the same word for deaf, refers to a large drum. Exu is a divinity in Afro-Brazilian religions and popular cosmogonies. Christians often mistake it as devilish. Exu, however, embodies the spaces to be made, just like the countermetric syncopated drumming of the *surdo* leaves a beat to be filled by the dancing bodies. There is an analogue in urbanization. City life produces indeterminate spaces that cannot be computed, previewed, or predicted. They remain to be filled in, as people's backgrounds and aspirations rub off on and bump against those of myriad others making their ways.

Knowledge that rational understanding has its limits pervaded modern popular culture in early twentieth-century Rio. We can think of a popular song by samba composers Noel Rosa and Orestes Barbosa, called "Positivism."[134] They sang that "the truth lives inside a well," according to "Pilate from the Bible." The lyrics poke fun at secular faith in empirical observation: there is more to life than what meets the eye. The bottom of the well in Portuguese also connotes a sense of being in the dumps: positivism did not fulfill promises to solve problems. But the choice of reference, the disbelieving Pilate, hardly sides with religious revelations either. The next verses slyly imply that for every solution there is a problem, a lesson that could serve revolutionaries, messianic groups, and techno-boosters alike: "and, because he had a neck / the creator of the Paris guillotine died." Here, Paris is not the place of sophisticated civilization, but a source of innovative violent methods. The song then uses Auguste Comte slogans to mourn a woman who moved on: she rejected order and progress toward their loving relationship. Positivist precepts proved useless. And in the "uncertain trades of life," the lyrics go, the heart trumps the pound currency. The heartless woman makes him hurt, just like those positivist technocrats left the country heavily indebted.

The economic references make clear social critiques. There is an obvious male frustration with women's agency. But the song remains enigmatic and open-ended. To avoid her poison, the rejected and for-lorn singer would poison himself. Yet, we are far removed from familiar stories of tragic lovers choosing death over assigned social roles that keep them apart. This is no longer the world of Julie and Saint-Preux in Rousseau's fiction, where class determines marriage and true love is for-ever. Here, the modern woman made her choice and rejected the man. The poison metaphor flirts with the idea of suicide as a fitting response to modern challenges. But it appears to be a tactic of last resort, with the scorned singer claiming he will ignore the woman back. The last verses allude to "intrigue" over who gets to pick up the tab at a café. Urban relationships are transactional and subject to multiple variations.

Life will go on, and this singer and listeners alike should expect to meet new partners after recovering from being dumped. Love, like the stock market, is both cyclical and fickle. Positivist aspirations, mean-while, became a joke. By the time this song came around, Haussman-nian Rio was already in the past. A new modernist city emerged in bits and pieces. An Afro-Brazilian cultural fabric remained dominant. Maybe we can think of the Pereira Passos plans as a requiem to the notion that reforms might last forever. The world might have felt expanded and more interconnected than before. But the samba composers prefer to dwell in short-term and contingent micro-futures rather than in poster-ity or the universal. Disillusionments and an intimate sense of urban possibilities as being uncontrollable made it harder to imagine an ideal future society for all. In societies shaped by slavery, those very illusions could never really take root. This was perhaps a lesson that samba musi-cians learned before planners: not everything was possible. And yet, to throw one's lot in the city meant embracing adventure, the inability to predict, and a loss of control. Even if some dreams might not be attain-able, any given set of unimaginable things could take place—for good or for bad.

5

The Sky Is Not the Limit
(1900s–1940s)

BUENOS AIRES + GARDEN CITIES,
NEW YORK, BERLIN, RIO DE JANEIRO,
PARIS, ROME, AND MORE.

I. The World of Tomorrow

In 1911, the Brazilian writer João do Rio prophesied "the era of the automobile."[1] At the time, the "novelty" still came from France. It was a
foul-smelling "death machine" that belonged as much in the city as a
Martian. But the seductive powers were irresistible. Cars made people
pity the past and rush toward the future: the "tomorrow that can be
attained right now." Broadly embracing it, he realized, required destroying streets, neighborhoods, and natural landscapes. João do Rio tried to
write with "a language of the future" that could keep up: fast-paced, full
of acronyms, simplified, and direct. In another text, he envisioned Rio
de Janeiro a decade later, in 1920, full of skyscrapers.[2] In his future city,
a "Superior Man" had walls of transparent crystal, gadgets for shaving
and making coffee, instant news and access to global communication
networks. Unable to rest or slow down, he was consumed by ambitions
for more money, power, and efficiency. An "unconscious" desire to end
it all took over this man. Afro-descendant and queer, João do Rio created literature inspired by strolling through streets and serendipitous

conversations. He imagined an urban future that valued neither. Even an incandescent mind like his could not foresee what would happen.

In João do Rio's vision, the "aerobus" would dominate urban transportation in 1920. Given the staggering advances in powered flights during the early 1900s, that scenario seemed more plausible than reengineering entire metropolitan areas for car traffic. Flying cars did not arrive, but aviation played a role in a Great War (1914–1918) that devastated Europe and shook much of the world to the core. The future shifted from Paris to New York. At the same time, modern warfare and automobiles helped to change the stakes of debates on urban density versus dispersion. The latter became more desirable and feasible. Ebenezer Howard's garden cities and Le Corbusier's car-centric utopias became touchstones. As we face the period's crossroads, focusing on plans for Buenos Aires during the 1920s and 1930s will allow us to better understand what could have been, as well as dynamics underlying actual developments. It would still take decades, and another World War, for "the era of the automobile." Earlier in the century, planners operated with faith in the future and in their technical ability to control it. Though unaware of the transit technologies, revolutionary upheavals, and unfathomable wars ahead, they realized that urban growth required systematic attention to metropolitan scales. The writing was not on the wall, but on the pages of specialized publications.

On both sides of the Atlantic, planners began to look to Germany, where the discipline consolidated. We can find in *Städtebau*, or city building, precursors to key modernist principles. A series of codes set height limits and lot coverages for different zones within urban areas and their surroundings. They contemplated land taxation and rail-based public transportation networks. In 1909, at the first meeting of the National Conference on City Planning in the United States, Olmsted Jr. praised the comprehensive nature of planning in Germany.[3] At the time, a competition for Greater Berlin was taking place. It called for plans that connected Berlin and its suburbs, anticipating population growth from 2 to at least 5 million. The scholar Katharina Borsi argues that for the first time the city was seen as "a set of linked and dispersed urban components distributed across the region."[4] The competition led to an international exhibit in 1910. It made news across the Atlantic. The press was eager to report on the cities of the future. By then, experts seemed to agree on a basic recipe: a "rational" division of quarters, with "bothersome and dangerous" establishments kept apart; a hierarchy of transportation modes, with "special avenues" for trains and cars; tree-lined public spaces and green parks.[5]

Urban design was becoming more than an eclectic intellectual field. It increasingly stood for a set of precepts followed by professionals. In Berlin, the competition registered a move away from compact Paris as a model, toward Greater London.[6] The goal was to centralize urban administration through annexations, while decentralizing the urban fabric. This movement was forward-looking, but it also represented what the urban historian Peter Hall called "a reaction to the evils of the nineteenth-century city."[7] Substantial reforms and public works, especially in sanitation, had already significantly improved urban life for many. Migrants chose cities to pursue social mobility, comforts, and freedoms, but also to escape more dire conditions in the countryside. A series of material advances made a massive difference, like running water, sewage, and electricity. Urbanites came to expect access to services including hospitals, schools, transportation, and policing. Any "civilized" city had a mayor and an administration that might be held accountable.

To the writers from one of Rio's illustrated magazines, the German exhibit's visions for the cities of tomorrow all sounded "beautiful and worthy of applause." How to get there remained an open question. In the German capital, amid conflicts between spheres of governance, the awarded projects did not come to fruition. The competition, however, created momentum for the establishment of a Greater Berlin in 1920. But regardless of specific roadblocks or pathways, the basic blueprint for modern cities was no longer primarily reserved for the North Atlantic. Jürgen Osterhammel refers to a process of "urban self-Westernization."[8] Haussmannian models had inspired reforms in cities such as Cairo, Istanbul, Tokyo, and Seoul, along with several others in Latin America. According to the historian, "it troubled no one that the model was of Western origin." He notes that "local circumstances imposed the most varied adaptations and omissions."[9] Infrastructural modernization swept over the planet, regardless of whether places were under official colonial rule. Toward the end of the 1800s, for example, Beijing finally developed a railway system. By then, the metropolitan area of an upstart city like Manchester surpassed the Chinese capital, which had begun the century as the world's largest. Meanwhile, Hankou, in present-day Wuhan, was brought into the capitalist fold. Although a major urban center in the 1850s, it had been relatively impervious to foreign financial interests.[10] Modern urbanization became a global process.

A surge in professional associations, conferences, and publications facilitated the circulation of ideas. Southern planners, designers, and urbanites could more easily find ways to engage with the latest debates about the future of cities in their own terms. Few places faced as many wide-open possibilities as Buenos Aires. Argentina's gross domestic product per capita was one of the ten highest in the world, closer to France and Canada than to neighboring countries. By 1914, the Argentine capital would pass Calcutta to become the largest metropolis outside the North Atlantic, reaching over 1.5 million inhabitants. Almost half of them had been born abroad. The city inaugurated its own iconic opera house in 1908, and Latin America's first subway system in 1913. The Teatro Colón's construction combined French-derived aesthetics, Italian laborers, and British financing, in a Spanish-speaking country on fertile lands taken from indigenous groups.[11] Anarchists bombed it in 1910.

Many transatlantic currents converged in Buenos Aires. It was called "the Athens of the Plata River, the Paris of South America, the Argentine New York."[12] Planners representing the main modern schools of thought vied to impress their views upon the city, including Le Corbusier. But Buenos Aires bent them to its image as much as the other way around, if not more. Well-connected local designers and engineers devised ingenious plans to negotiate the relationships between the urban core and suburbs. By 1947, nearly 3 million people lived in Buenos Aires; 5 million if we include the metropolitan area. A vast gridded fabric stood as a unique attempt to combine growth with order, and infrastructural cohesion with social diversity. Some developments lived up to progressive aspirations, others responded to conservative demands and unexpected changes. As in other Atlantic settings, the city was a springboard for new imaginations of the world of tomorrow.

───────

The fact that technical knowledge, shared expectations, and forward-looking stories more easily crossed boundaries does not imply symmetrical relations between or within cities, regions, and countries. If we take a step back, the dawn of the new century also coincided with the peak of North Atlantic confidence in its ability to shape urban futures. And if we understand *shape* as not just a metaphor, it can be useful to single out two tendencies: planning could privilege horizontal or vertical directions. The first extended the urban and/or suburban fabric, transforming the countryside. The second required remaking existing spaces by landfills, infill, razing, and/or building up. Both assumed growth, and they often coexisted. In the nineteenth century, transportation, communication, and construction technologies had allowed for more sprawling and denser urbanization to coexist. Technological advances continued to push and pull urban life further in new directions, well beyond the control of planners and the imaginative capacities of earlier generations. Besides airplanes and automobiles, other innovations became more reliable and prevalent: ever-taller skyscrapers, telephones, radio, cinema. Possibilities for the future exploded. In the 1800s, the term *futuristic* often referenced prophecies, mostly confined to theology. Now the adjective denoted "avant-garde, ultra-modern."[13]

In planning publications, the general tone of experts and officials showed restraint. They had learned lessons. We read of how plans should be both "comprehensive" and "tentative," drawing up scenarios for growth and changing requirements over the course of different time spans (twenty-five, fifty, one hundred years!). Rather than designing for posterity or trying to "judge the future," planners understood the importance of staying open to adaptation and "modification." To be effective, planning had to be more "sustained and continuous" than reactive or definitive.[14] Predicting the cities of tomorrow, however, became a widespread exercise not just among specialists, but also in news media,

FIGURE 5.1. Operagoers in Albert Robida's futuristic Paris: fashion, flight, bright lights! But more meets the eye: guards bear swords, women drive, gazes unsettle.

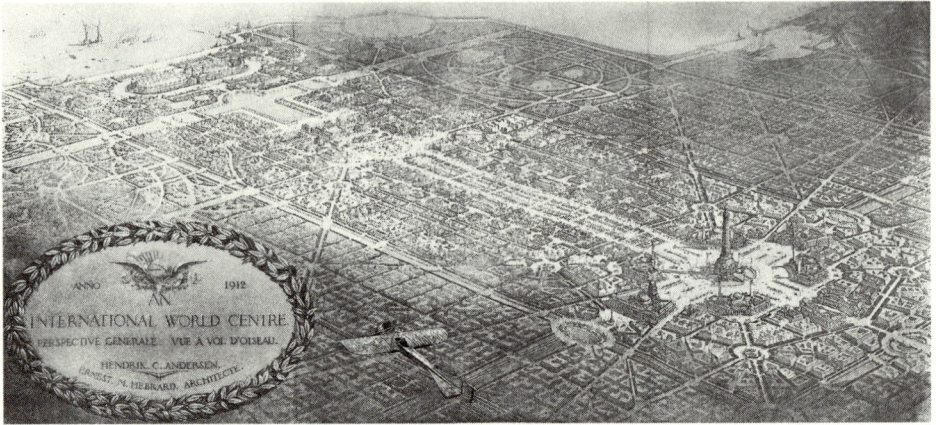

FIGURE 5.2. Sky-high ambitions of towering progress, with symmetry and low buildings, as an airplane flies.

fiction, and popular culture. And the limelight attracted more electrifying plans. In 1913, to great fanfare, a French Beaux-Arts architect and a Norwegian American sculptor presented "The Future City: An Artistic and Scientific World Center."[15] They looked for patrons and a site for the monumental city, designed to host initiatives devoted to international cooperation in communications, theology, law, and so on. World peace, harmony, and unity would blossom. Instead, the plans lingered, like dead branches trampled on by the march of nationalisms.

After World War I, some would look back with nostalgia. It was not for measured and grounded urban planning that they pined. The period between the 1870s and the 1910s became known as the Belle Époque. Other languages borrow the expression from the French, honoring Paris as a symbol of cultural dominance and urban modernity. Its Palais Garnier inspired operas as far afield as Manaus in the Brazilian Amazon (1896), Warsaw (1901), and Hanoi (1911). The great European metropolises experienced unprecedented power, while relative peace reigned among them. But there were winners and losers. Overseas, the experience of colonization was much more brutal than *belle*. Enlightenment dreams turned into nightmares. The 1889 World's Fair called itself *universal*. Successive exhibits often carried the billing of *colonial*, continuing to display those deemed as inferior in pens. People might have been hyper-aware of the French capital as a harbinger of what lay ahead, but they could not foresee some of the ways in which it was so. Scientific racism hardened, antisemitism resurfaced, ethnic invectives flared up. In retrospect, we can see where this is headed.

The 1889 event in Paris had featured one of the earliest automobiles. Haussmannian boulevards provided ideal playgrounds for the wealthy to practice the modern sport of car racing. France dominated the early years of the industry, which would do more to transform urban futures than any other. The story has many moving pieces, as we will see. Among them, tire manufacturing helped to fuel the Amazonian rubber boom, characterized not just by the construction of architectonic monuments to the Beaux-Arts, but also by coerced labor. The moneyed in Manaus might attend the opulent opera and afford modern fashions in the heart of the rainforest. They could feel like participants in a civilized future set in Paris. Yet, the tropical city's role remained largely peripheral, as suppliers of raw materials for industrialization.

At the beginning of the century, Europeans still maintained a grip on the evolution of modern planning well beyond the continent's shores. It would only begin to loosen up after the Great War and the Russian Revolution. Throughout the nineteenth century, European designers and engineers had pursued projects abroad, including Gustave Eiffel in Latin America. As planning professionalized and the figure of the urban expert emerged, French influence initially increased. A group of reformers, recognizing inequalities as a problem for social order, created the French Society of Urbanists in 1911. Positivism imbued them with faith in statistical methods. They thought planning professionals should combine science, art, and philosophy. Key practitioners associated with the organization crossed the Atlantic. The circulation of urban visions continued to reflect international relations. But any consensus about planning the cities of tomorrow started to break down almost as soon as it was formed. Competing visions grouped around individuals, organizations, or governments. In the capital of French Indochina, for example, reforms acted as an imperial tool. The colonial administration adopted the Haussmannian method of razing Hanoi's historic core to build a modern city. The process was authoritarian, but along with ample boulevards, street cultures flourished.[16] As new ideas and technologies came into vogue, strategies would change.

The rivaling and more formidable British empire chose to build New Delhi as an extension of the old city in the 1910s. Planners drew more from the US City Beautiful movement and Haussmannian Paris than London. Their more horizontal approach, however, reflected the English capital's own development. With over 7 million residents in the 1910s, London was still the world's largest city by over 2 million, ahead of New York, Paris, and Berlin. London "remained the ugly duckling of Europe's metropolises, always looking poorer than it really was."[17] Yet, the extensiveness of modern infrastructures set the city apart. By the early twentieth century, it had impressive sewage and street lighting coverage. Mass transit combined trams with pioneering uses of the motorbus and subways, allowing urbanization to sprawl through the construction of dwellings of lesser density, often semidetached. Great Britain lacked an urban model as imposing as the Haussmannian legacy. Scholars have speculated that this resulted from London's relative lack of centralized powers, parsimony, or an aversion to absolutist expressions. As Osterhammel sees it, "London did not need to lay the symbols on thick," since "the imperial nexus had its maximum impact away from the limelight."[18]

London's streets, commerce, and popular culture made visible the global reach of England, through the presence of foreigners, imported goods, and entertainment drawing on exotic lands. In New Delhi, imperial might would be expressed with pomp and monumentality in major government buildings. The massive dome of the palatial Viceroy's House (1929) recalled the early modern baroque as much as the Capitol in Washington (1800) or the Sacré Coeur basilica in Paris (1914). British colonial urbanization was also in line with a growing contemporary consensus around segregation. Planning increasingly sought to separate people along racial and ethnic lines. We can also interpret concentration camps in Africa as modern, foreshadowing Nazism. English visions of urban futures, at the same time, gained traction and vital potentials outside of state-sponsored initiatives. We might think of the science fiction of H. G. Wells or radical labor movements. And of Ebenezer Howard, probably the most influential urbanist to emerge from the turn-of-the-century. His work had roots in anarchist and socialist utopian traditions: more Cerdá than Haussmann.

Howard published *To-Morrow: A Peaceful Path to Real Reform* in 1898, revised in 1902 as *Garden Cities of Tomorrow*. In planning circles, references to garden cities became nearly ubiquitous in the following two decades. The book's scope was transnational. It described a shared consensus across Europe, America, and the British colonies: urban life was cramped and degrading, while rural areas lost population. In Howard's formulation, towns could provide "social opportunity" and "places of amusement," but also had "foul air" and "high rents." The country had "beauty of nature" and "bright sunshine," but faced "deserted villages" and "land lying idle." Howard wanted to develop them as a continuum: "Town and country *must be married*, and out of this joyous union will spring a new hope, a new life, a new civilization."[19] His prescription to bring together the advantages of both echoed aspects of earlier plans.

Garden cities allotted areas for leisure, manufacturing, agriculture, forests, and homes. They purported to organize land use, however, at a scale that extended beyond the existing metropolis. Intermunicipal railways, canals, and roads connected garden cities in a polycentric network that could be reproduced, with adaptations, anywhere. Indeed, the Garden City movement would reach many corners of the world. But the book's implied audience was primarily English. In the conclusion, it quotes from a plan that evoked the Parisian reforms to argue that London should also be reconstructed. Howard's own ambitions were far greater: he wanted to redistribute the population of the "unwieldy" capital, replacing its slums, where landlords exploited the poor, with lower-density greener spaces.

The plans envisioned continuing urban growth but sought to control it. Each garden city would have a population limited to around 32,000, taking up 1,000 acres surrounded by another 5,000 acres of rural land. They aimed to be self-sufficient, forming a cluster around a larger "central city" of 58,000 people on 12,000 acres. This would be around eight times less dense than London in 1900, but comparable to the current metropolitan area, and significantly denser than average exurban developments today. In later publications, Howard reinforced the importance of maintaining distances within "easy range" of a bicycle ride or walk, so that people could get where they wanted "economically" and "happily."[20]

Unlike other modern planners, Howard was not particularly attached to specific geometries or aesthetic forms. His illustrations can be deceptive—they are meant as diagrams rather than plans. Site conditions would dictate the actual layouts. But a representative garden city might be organized concentrically, with a tree-lined "Grand Avenue" forming a belt at a width of 420 feet—four times greater than the usual in Haussmannian Paris. These should host schools and churches. Roads with names like Boulevard Columbus radiate from a center, where a Crystal Palace was placed, along with a hospital, library, town hall, theater, museum gallery, and concert hall. The next rings contained houses and gardens. An outer ring was dedicated to factories for basic goods: clothing, furniture, boots, jam, etc. Beyond them, greenbelts served as buffers between towns, with reservoirs, waterfalls, large farms, cow pastures, agricultural colleges, and so on. In line with modern practices, these spaces also kept apart those considered unproductive, when not bothersome and dangerous. In the diagrams we find, for example, the insane asylum; homes for inebriates, convalescents, epileptics; blind and deaf asylums.

Howard was a religious man, conceiving of his garden cities of tomorrow as a kind of New Jerusalem. They would redeem the "unholy, unnatural separation of society and nature." His ethos was egalitarian, but neither Marxist nor anticapitalist. *To-morrow* can even read like a pitch to investors. It prized cooperation, however, rather than competition. Land would be held in a trust, with rents funding operations and interest paid out to investors. Both rent increases and profits were fixed. The historian Robert Fishman described the scheme as "philanthropic land speculation."[21] In Howard's utopian vision, everyone could win. Like many contemporary social reformers, he was a believer in progress. His plans united moral commitments and empirical approaches, which approximated him to positivists. Garden cities also embraced

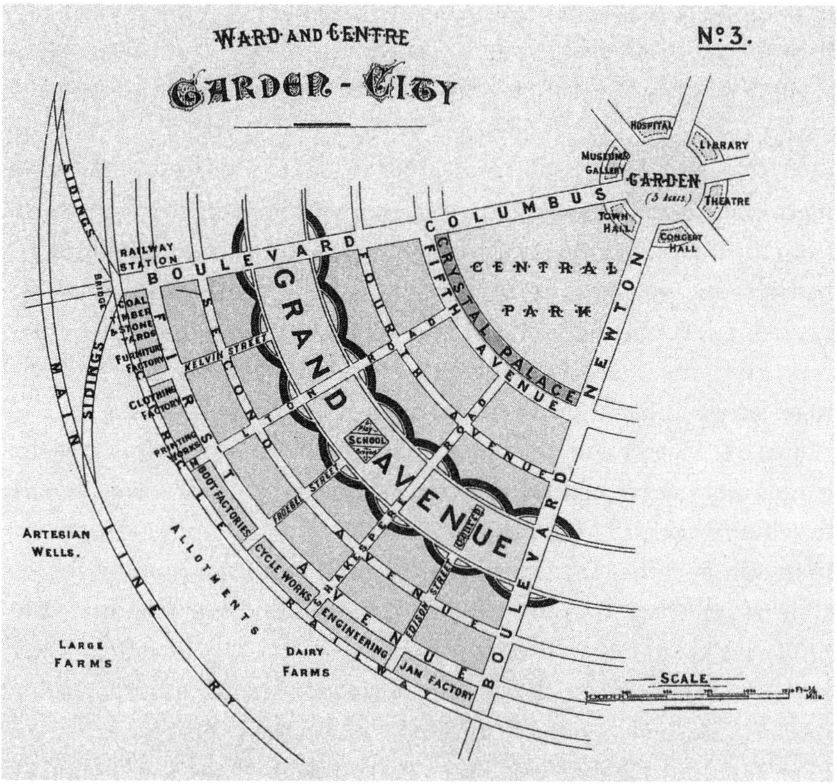

FIGURE 5.3. Howard was not attached to this geometry, but it became a trademark of his followers.

technologies, with railways playing an integral role and electricity serving as the energy source for smokeless industries. The book's rejection of contemporary urbanization, as the title suggests, was not about a return to an idyllic past. In fact, the very recognition of rural and urban spaces as interdependent made Howard a leading figure in forward-thinking urbanism, as planning expanded its perspectives and prospects.

Howard had no training in urban design. A London native and the son of a candy merchant, he worked as a stenographer before migrating to the United States in his early twenties. He tried his luck as a farmer in Nebraska and a reporter in Chicago in the aftermath of the Great Fire of 1871. This exposed him to two extremes of modern efforts to fixate flux: the state-led Homestead Act granting land to settlers in the countryside, and profit-seeking densification in the city. The United States suggested both potential pathways and cautionary tales. Bellamy's *Looking Backward* was a key influence.[22] Both championed collectivism. The novel, however, imagined the ideal Boston of the year 2000 as a dense metropolis, organized around a main core. Garden cities tried to break from the logic of compact city centers and commuter suburbs. Howard had left Chicago before the skyscraper era. His vision remained radically horizontal. As the Garden City movement evolved in the twentieth century, they resisted building up. Low density and dispersion proved to be very compatible with the car as an incentive for building out.

Just a few years after the publication of Howard's proposals, the first garden city was created in Letchworth. He was directly involved, but the development entailed compromises. More revenue went toward returns to investors, rather than staying within communities. Buildings in the style of the Arts and Crafts movement evoked a nostalgic return to premodern England. If aesthetically Letchworth was not exactly *of tomorrow*, it did unintentionally anticipate the dominance of cars in urban futures. The town had the first roundabout in the UK, in 1909. Its planners, Raymond Unwin and Barry Parker, devised the traffic solution with the Haussmannian Place de l'Étoile in mind. Garden cities became much more suitable for private cars than the crowded metropolis. A later garden city, Radburn in New Jersey, billed itself "a new town for the motor age" in the 1920s.[23]

Howard's concepts morphed in all sorts of unintended directions. Throughout the world, real estate developments paying homage to garden cities in their names became indistinguishable from other leafy suburbs and enclaves for the wealthy. Colonizers co-opted it. In Freetown, the capital of British West Africa, "garden city" settlements intended to separate Europeans from Africans.[24] In Dakar, the French attempted to impose the Parisian blueprint in a 1904 plan, with Beaux-Arts architecture and wide boulevards. As colonial strategies veered toward segregation rather than assimilation, the garden city became a tool to entrench racial and class divisions in French West Africa.[25] Something similar occurred with suburban-like extensions to Moroccan cities, geared

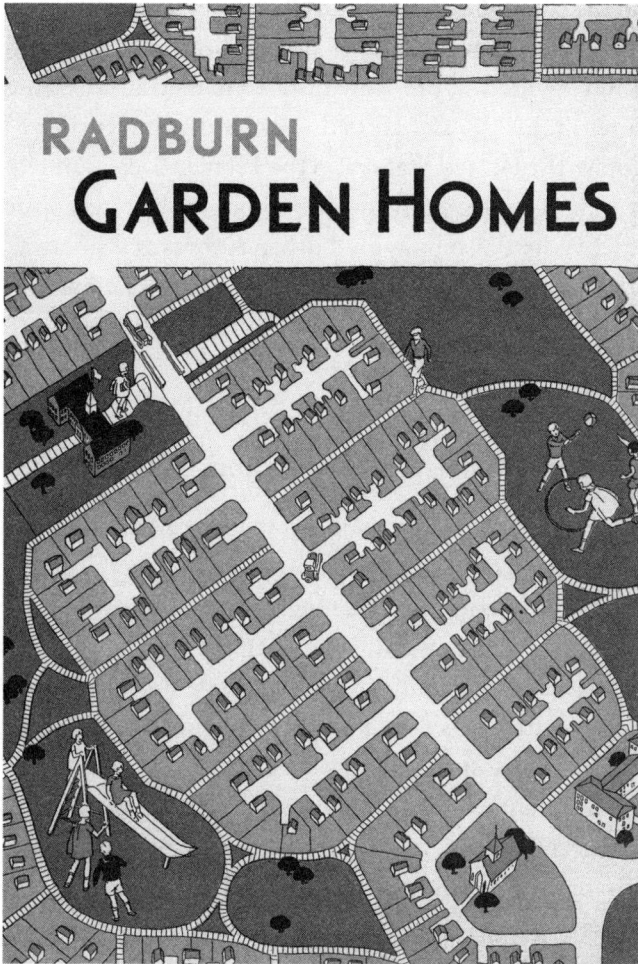

RADBURN
GARDEN HOMES

FIGURE 5.4. In New Jersey, promotional materials promise tomorrow's "town for the motor age," where children play safe from cars.

toward Europeans. As the historian Liora Bigon writes, colonial planners borrowed from Howard his protozoning system (separation of functions), a "preoccupation with the urban picturesque," and the use of greenbelts. They discarded the "communitarian ideas."[26]

In cities with decentralizing plans like Berlin and Buenos Aires, Garden City movements influenced low-rise and semihomogenous social housing or private suburbs rather than more autonomous or self-sufficient development. This included subsidized "cottage estates" for the working classes in London. Howard's focus on the fates of cities and the countryside as intertwined, at the same time, remained at the center of planning cultures in the UK and abroad—including the Regional Planning Association in the United States and the French Society of Urbanists.[27] As the twentieth century advanced, visionaries like Le Corbusier and Frank Lloyd Wright also imagined urban futures at scales well beyond the city. They embraced dispersion, privileging the car. But unlike Howard, modernist planners tended to incorporate verticalization, and they often did not share his egalitarian bent.

II. Destructive Torrents and Explosions

A century earlier, the Commissioners' Plan for Manhattan did not anticipate explosive vertical growth. It proved very adaptable to skyscrapers. Theorists like to comment that high-rise buildings function like the urban grid but turned upward. New York City needed all the space it could get. In 1898, the consolidation of the outer boroughs gave the city more room to expand. Its population passed London's, with the metropolitan region surpassing 10 million in the 1930s. Opened in 1931, the Empire State Building was the first occupied construction taller than the Eiffel Tower. By then, nearly all the major skyscrapers in the world were in the United States, most of them concentrated in Manhattan. Earlier in the century some had called for Haussmannization in Manhattan.[28] At the time, instead of state-led remodeling, profit-seeking developers drove much of the process of razing and rebuilding. This was also a representative pattern of urban growth: accumulative and haphazard. The high-rise Gillender Building on Wall Street, for example, was opened in 1897 and demolished in 1910, giving place to the even bigger Bankers Trust Building.[29]

We tend to pay more attention to futures foreclosed by displacement, when large-scale demolitions uproot people from their neighborhoods and homes. Forms of densification could be painful too, generating a sense of loss. Edith Wharton's "Mrs. Manstey's View" imagined what this experience might have been like.[30] The author came from wealth, and so did most of her characters. Mrs. Manstey was an exception. She lived alone in the third-floor backroom of a boarding house in Manhattan. The short story opened with a description: "The view from Mrs. Manstey's window was not a striking one, but to her at least it was full of interest and beauty." The narrator referred, we later learn, to a modest adjoining yard. This was on the same island where the Vanderbilts, the Carnegies, and the Guggenheims funded striking mansions. But Mrs. Manstey's view was not of the monumental city. She was in relative proximity to the poor tenements where the "other half" lived. Unlike many of them, at least she had a window.

Mrs. Manstey was the widow of a clerk, and the mother of a woman that had married in California. Visiting was too expensive. She had a dream as old as cities themselves: to live in the country with a garden. That desire "faded with age." Instead, Mrs. Manstey found meaning and tenderness in her view. It allowed for a relationship to time defined by the cycles of seasons: the future came every spring when the magnolia bloomed and in the "lilac waves." She found beauty not in City Beautiful, but in the rhythms of the urban landscape: a maid feeding the cats, and even "the trail of smoke from a far-off factory chimney." One day she became a victim of development. Her landlady informed her that the owner of the boarding house next door planned an extension. She was going to build up on the yard. A planner might see this as densification through infill. To Mrs. Manstey it was an existential threat. The view "surrounded and shaped her life as the sea does a lonely island." Now, she would lose it.

The landlady reminded Mrs. Manstey that there were no laws to prevent the new construction. The tenant explained her predicament and refused a room in the extension. She offered money, to no avail. The small-time developer misled her about when building would commence, dismissing her as "crazy." Capitalists could be merciless. Mrs. Manstey mustered a defense: setting the site on fire. In this more modern city, with better firefighting services, her plan failed. But the smoke from the blazes reached her. Mrs. Manstey contracted pneumonia. With the construction paused, she took in the sight of the flowering magnolia one more time, and died. The story concluded: "That day the building of the extension was resumed." Although Edith Wharton's narrator described without moralizing, we cannot help but empathize with Mrs. Manstey. Authoritarian capitalists and the state alike used violence to have their way against strikers or dissenters. Why couldn't she take matters into her own hands? After all, a livable future was at stake. We could see Mrs. Manstey as the original NIMBY.[31] At the same time, her actions could have killed people. Should we not think of her as a terrorist?

Mrs. Manstey resorted to destruction to keep her city from changing. Or in her view, to allow for ever-changing nature. In *Looking Backward*, Bellamy had predicted a "complete metamorphosis." But he referred to the present when he wrote: "A man may leave his native city in childhood, and return fifty years later, perhaps, to find it transformed in many features."[32] More than a century earlier, Rousseau's character Saint-Preux had described the recognition of urban modernity as *absurd*, but not *shocking*. Bellamy thought that urbanites would be "astonished, but [...] not bewildered" by transformations that rendered places unrecognizable within the lifetime of an inhabitant. Mrs. Manstey might have been more at home in European cities, which tended to maintain historic cores. Manhattan was an extreme version of a process that became characteristic of urbanization in the Americas. Writing about the first decades of the twentieth century, the literary critic Beatriz Sarlo drew attention to how Buenos Aires residents, at the age of thirty or forty, lived in a city completely different from the one where they were born, or migrated to.[33]

Some avant-gardes, like Mrs. Manstey, saw the potential of violence for seizing the future. In 1909, the Italian poet Filippo Marinetti published the Manifesto of Futurism, glorifying war as "the only true hygiene of the world."[34] Like Haussmann and other planners, Futurists embraced speed and technological innovation. But rather than safeguard the status quo, they wanted to blow up the past. The manifesto, published on the cover of a major Parisian newspaper, hailed disruptive cars, steamers, locomotives, and airplanes. It loudly called for upending liberal and bourgeois institutions, whether conservative or progressive: "We will destroy museums, libraries and fight against moralism,

feminism and all utilitarian cowardice." In 1913, French avant-garde artist
Francis Picabia called New York "the Futurist city."[35]

It is not surprising that the movement originated in Italy, where the
weight of the Renaissance and traditional culture could be stultifying.
Marinetti's attack on continuity in favor of rupture, nonetheless, inspired
hundreds of other Futurist manifestos throughout the world.[36] His com-
patriot Antonio Sant'Elia wrote a Manifesto of Futurist Architecture in
1914.[37] It rails against "modern" design, by which he meant neoclassicism
as well as the ornate styles of Haussmannian façades. He rejected the
academies and all historicism as a "grotesque anachronism." Rather than
"the monumental" or "the static," the architecture of the future should
have "a taste for the light, the practical, the ephemeral, and the fast." The
Futurist city should be like a machine, made of concrete, glass, and steel.
Sant'Elia indulged in the sorts of projects that would take off in the next
decade, renewing the meaning of modern in architecture. Fascinated by
new infrastructure like airplane hangars, he imagined buildings at massive scales, including train stations and power plants. His drawings
tended to lack people or trees. Mrs. Manstey would not be at home. The
manifesto celebrated impermanence, calling for a constant process of
destruction and rebuilding. It rejected the aspiration of planning for
posterity: "Every generation will have to build its own city."

None of Sant'Elia's designs were built. He died in the Great War.
Along with the Futurists, in earnest or as a provocation, others desired
warfare. Some saw it coming. Not many could envision the scale of consequences. On June 29, 1914, a headline announced: "Archduke's Death
Removes Danger of European Conflict."[38] The assassination of Franz
Ferdinand, the presumptive heir of the Austrian–Hungarian throne,
helped to set off a chain of events leading to around 40 million
casualties—the most of any military conflict until then. The illusions of
a common civilization in pursuit of progress, maintained in world's fairs,
gave way to carnage fueled by nationalism and technological advancements. World War I shattered the spectacle of continuous progress
toward a future brighter and better than the past. To those let into the
Belle Époque, the party was over. Those left out also suffered. Territorial
disputes between colonial European powers were key to the war. As a

FIGURE 5.5. Futurists like Sant'Elia rejected tradition and ushered the new through creative destruction.

result of warfare, famines, and the suppression of anticolonial rebellions, hundreds of thousands of Africans died.[39]

In Europe, many political figures promised a short conflict. H. G. Wells published *The War That Will End War* in 1914. War devastated Europe, and the expectation that crushing German militarism would lead to a lasting peace in fact helped create conditions for World War II. Veterans often spoke of doing as they were told. That too is a claim on the future. Young soldiers had to surrender their futures for something supposedly larger—the destiny of a nation, or civilization itself.

Though slight, there is something here analogous to the Pombaline or Haussmannian expectations of urban reforms for posterity: through concerted top-down actions, in a process of destruction and re-creation, master planners could solve problems once and for all. On the ground, British soldiers and German POWs talked openly about the war being "useless." This was more than the antiutilitarian ethos that Futurists had bargained for. One survivor concluded: "History will decide in the end that it was not worthwhile." In his certainty, there was still a faith in progress. Another summed up the sentiment of disenchantment: "Your nose is filled with fumes and death, the veneer of civilization has dropped away."[40]

Many World War I soldiers came from rural settings, and experienced a cruel form of modernization among strangers in the trenches. Railroads, the electric telegraph, and wireless radio gave unprecedented efficiency to destruction. Airplanes, an invention which would also play a role in planning, dropped bombs from above. The sky was no longer the limit. As the war ended, veterans wondered: "What was one gonna do next?"[41] Government services provided urban clothes, but young men arrived in cities and met with a lack of jobs, opportunities, and understanding about the intensity of what they had lived through.

III. Futures in Transit

The war was covered closely throughout the Americas, and it shook confidence in Europe as a model. In 1917, an article in a Brazilian illustrated magazine claimed predicting the future was the "supreme science." The author bemoaned the "long and uninterrupted" war as a denial of everything that "the most elevated spirits of the human elite" had foretold.[42] To him, only two visionaries retained their prestige: Jules Verne and H. G. Wells. A sense of disillusionment deepened. In 1919, a Brazilian writer described nineteenth-century Paris as "glorious," but saw the city as "sick," mired by a complete lack of organization in public services. Dirty streets were taken over by chaotic traffic. Sugar and butter were expensive. Compared to Brazil, he alleged, one found misery.[43] Most Latin American countries had stayed neutral in World

War I, including Argentina and Mexico. Despite close commercial ties to Germany, Brazil joined the Allies in October of 1917, six months after the United States. Nonetheless, the war's aftermath marked the acceleration of a shift of imagined urban futures away from Europe.

Futurist visions of constant renewal and Sant'Elia's vertical impetus had already been part of urbanization in the Americas, especially New York City and Chicago. After the war, the divergence widened. Major cities in the Americas built high-rises, including Rio de Janeiro, São Paulo, and Buenos Aires. In general, plans to rebuild European cities did not promote verticality.[44] Skyscrapers faced opposition in Europe, partly because they would compete with churches and public buildings for prominence.[45] Paris had to wait until the 1960s. Nowhere compared to the United States, where most states had buildings considered at the time to be skyscrapers. In 1928, Lewis Mumford wrote that they were the "one universal and accepted symbol of our period in America."[46] Skyscrapers became a fitting manifestation of might, as the country became the world's leading economic powerhouse.[47]

At the same time, urban growth in Europe slowed down after the rapid urbanization of the second half of the nineteenth century.[48] About 40 percent of Europeans lived in cities in 1910, but the continent only became urban-majority around 1950. Most Latin American countries followed suit in the 1960s and 1970s. In the United States, this occurred in the 1910s, as cities continued to boom. By 1950, less than one-fifth of its Northeast population resided in rural areas. In the first half of the century, the North Atlantic still had the highest rates of urbanization, while the rest of the world's population remained mostly in the countryside. In the Global South, Argentina stood out. Like the United States, the country became urban-majority early in the 1910s. Buenos Aires played an unusually central role, concentrating between a quarter to a third of the nation's population.

Popular magazines presented New York as the city of tomorrow in Latin America. In Argentina, Buenos Aires's oversized role as a political, cultural, and economic capital also loomed large in imaginations of the future. During the first half of the century, the city generated more ambitious fictional futures than counterparts in the Global South. As early as 1891, one novel had imagined Buenos Aires in the third millennium with automata-like vehicles, elevated railroads, electric trams, and streets lit up by "shining asphalt."[49]

Another author, Enrique Vera y González, located a positivist utopia in Buenos Aires, in the suggestively titled *La Estrella del Sur* (The Star of the South). His novel projected the city in 2010 with 40 million people and skyscrapers of nearly 500 feet. It overestimated population growth, but the first buildings to reach that height in Buenos Aires were completed around then. In this vision, scientific progress led to synthetic food, domestic robots, and flying vehicles—all staples of twentieth-century science fiction. In 1908, the writer Julio Dittrich envisioned Buenos Aires in 1950 as a socialist utopia.[50] Electric cars replaced horse-powered vehicles. They were available through municipal concessions and obeyed strict speed limits. Steam-fueled electric trains traveled to New York City in around three days. In illustrated magazines, drawings of Buenos Aires crisscrossed by elevated rail and flying vehicles proliferated.[51] By 1927, a local newspaper predicted Buenos Aires in 2177 as the city that Jules Verne could not fathom—even denser with skyscrapers and aircrafts.[52]

Argentina was much wealthier than elsewhere in the South Atlantic, with GDP per capita between 4 to 6 times larger than Brazil's. Popular media in Buenos Aires measured the city against Northern competitors. Periodicals might cover the poor conditions of the "other side" in New York, or celebrate their growth as only comparable to Chicago's.[53] By 1910, incomes in Chicago were still around 70 percent higher than in the Argentine capital, but this was significantly less than in the 1890s or in the 2010s.[54] The idea of a Buenos Aires made up of skyscrapers reflected increasingly common expectations in dominant cities of the North Atlantic. High-rise, "antiseptically clean" buildings became pervasive in futuristic fiction.[55] During the nineteenth century, engineering opened up the underground for the construction of crucial infrastructure. In the twentieth, the sky became the next urban frontier.

In the novel *The Sleeper Awakes* (1910), H. G. Wells took on a plotline familiar from Mercier's and Bellamy's stories. The protagonist wakes up in London two hundred years into the future. Unlike his predecessors,

FIGURE 5.6. In 1910, Buenos Aires is imagined in 2010: the star of the south rises.

however, he finds a dystopian society. The city had grown vertically. If in Haussmannian buildings the poor often lived in attics above the rich, now the working classes inhabited labyrinthine subterranean dwellings, invisible to the ruling classes living high up above them. The skyline was dotted with "Titanic buildings" connected by suspension bridges.[56] The following year, an article in Buenos Aires on New York as "the city of tomorrow" described the view from atop the Singer building, predicting that class segregation would reserve such sunny spaces to the rich, relegating the poor to the shadows below.[57] This of course also reflects commercial ocean liners with first-class passengers above and migrants in steerage below. In English, the very use of *upper class* grew steadily beginning in the early 1900s, declining after midcentury.[58]

A vertical imagination often assumed that flight would be ubiquitous in urban settings. In the nineteenth century, railways and steamers revolutionized transportation between cities. Within them, advances were not quite as dramatic. In the early twentieth century, however, automobile and airplane technologies opened new possibilities. This coincided with a broad change: machines, so often associated with the dangers of factories in the previous century, became increasingly perceived for quality-of-life improvements. After an inflection point, people tended to expect innovations ascending in a steep line, rather than plateauing.[59] After balloons, Zeppelins, and early airplanes, it seemed logical to assume all sorts of other flying vehicles in the immediate horizon. Flying around the city became a constant feature of imagined vertical densification in the 1910s and 1920s. At the same time, it was nearly impossible to conceive of leaps in transportation technologies without mass transit remaining central. Collective vehicles had an edge over automobiles.

Reimagining mobility became integral to most futuristic exercises. Many followed the template on the cover of *King's Dream of New York*, named after the guidebook publisher Moses King. These bold images of New York's future circulated widely in the 1910s, including as postcards. They showed "the city of skyscrapers" connected horizontally though bridges and railways on top floors, as well as airships and small planes. The trains high above partially reflected a reality. A Greek migrant, who worked as a peddler, would reminisce about his first impressions of the big city: "New York astonished me by its size and magnificence, the buildings shooting up like mountain peaks, the bridge hanging in the sky, the crowds of ships and the elevated railways." Yet, he added, "I think that the elevated railways astonished me more than anything else."[60] Why not imagine that mass transit would follow buildings into the sky?

Magazines like *The Sphere* in the UK covered the "air car," which looked like a double-decker bus with wings.[61] They also offered "a glimpse of future locomotion" with even larger double-deckers crossing a gorge on an elevated monorail—an image that also circulated across

FIGURE. 5.7. The sky is not the limit; images of Manhattan's future served as a template for publications in booming cities like Buenos Aires.

the Atlantic in Argentina.[62] In a later issue, readers learned about an amphibian, Zeppelin-like airship with wings, presented as an "artist's dream of the future."[63] Over time, especially after World War I, high-tech fantasies increasingly originated in the United States. There were a wild range of promising novelties. In 1920, the *Electrical Experimenter* showcased the "Sea Going Ferris Wheel" running on underwater train tracks.[64] Other even more sensational inventions pervaded popular media: city-skyscrapers half a mile high, cities along railroad tracks, cities on boats for 800,000 people. Several of these stories, originally published in the United States, reverberated throughout the Atlantic.

Scientific magazines brandished transformative inventions as an inevitability. In 1919, for example, a cover image of the *Electrical Experimenter* showed rail hovering above the city, with a confident headline: "Wheel-less Trains Glide on Water-Film."[65] The innovation promised to be cheaper and less disruptive to build than subways. And it would be superior to airships, due to higher carrying capacity. Automobiles were not seen as direct competitors. Other articles covered now prosaic solutions, like "shafts of light" to regulate street traffic.[66] In 1920, an issue depicted "Chicago's New Monorail" running amid the skyscrapers. Inspired by a precedent in Germany, this was presented as a quiet and low-maintenance alternative.[67]

Typically, these futuristic illustrations showed an urban landscape in the background. Skylines were invariably dense and dotted with high-rise buildings. Chicago's sleek monorail represented what was to come. Behind it, we see buildings of the present. Down below, there are streets choked in traffic. This was part of a pattern. The implication seems to be that private cars do not belong in the future. Even the language of "horsepower" placed them in the lineage of obsolete predecessors. Cars were just too inefficient to meet the demands of modern cities. Unlike the suspended monorail, capable of moving more people while taking up far less space, they could not be reconciled with the dense, vibrant streetscapes of tomorrow. It really could be easier to imagine flight as a realistic alternative. In the imagined Buenos Aires of 2177 that would blow away Jules Verne, mass transit was widespread while cars had fallen into disuse.

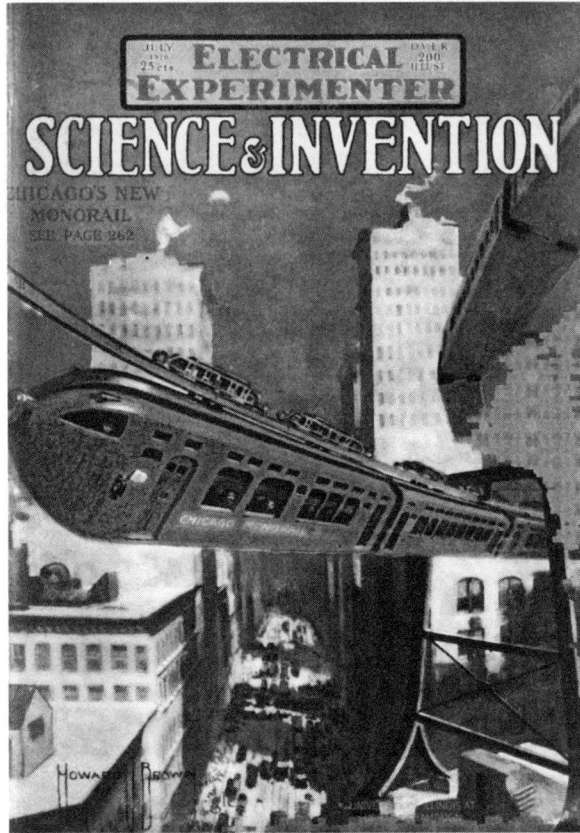

FIGURE. 5.8. A monorail takes to the sky, leaving behind streetcars, automobiles, and subways.

Though some of these ideas might have been far-fetched, most major metropolitan areas had ambitious plans to extend mass transit in the 1910s. Even in smaller towns in the United States, people assumed that in the future transportation would be moved to the skies or underground.[68] An article on New York "a century hence" claimed that each avenue in Manhattan would "undoubtedly" have a subway running beneath.[69] Certainties aside, several projects to build new subway and rail lines were postponed during World War I, shelved after the Great Depression hit, and abandoned once highways took over. Due to the early rise of car ownership, urbanization in the United States had already begun to deviate from other places. The number of passenger vehicles in the country grew at an astonishing rate, from 5 per 1,000 people in 1910 to 187 in 1930. This meant that around half of families owned a car. Most major European countries would only reach comparable numbers in the 1960s and 1970s; Argentina, Mexico, and Brazil, in the 2000s; China, India, and South Africa, in the 2010s.[70]

The victory of the car in the United States and later much of the world was by no means inevitable, or even predictable. In the beginning of the century, cities still relied heavily on horse-led streetcars. This ended in New York City by the late 1890s, and in Paris by World War I. Electric streetcars moved about twice as fast, but also needed track systems. In the late nineteenth century, bicycles represented a rupture: they allied freedom of movement with efficiency. The New Woman feminists embraced their ability to confer independence. As the scholar Paul Smethurst put it, bicycles at the time embodied "the cult of speed" and a "celebration of the future."[71] An article in *Scientific American* predicted that along with electric railroads and cars, they would "relegate the horse-drawn vehicle to the past."[72] Many remained skeptical that anyone would "prefer the inanimate road machine driven by petroleum to the noble steed whose graceful action is among the most beautiful things in life."[73] In the motor versus horse debates, few seemed to question that bicycles had a place in the future. One publication dismissed the argument that the "ill-smelling automobile" would supersede the bicycle as "rank nonsense." As we saw in postcards of urban futures, bikes easily coexisted with flying vehicles.

At first, bikes represented the American future more than cars. A *New York Times* article on "the horseless carriage" drew a contrast between Europe and the United States. The automobile clubs of London and Paris were as popular among their wealthy classes as the bicycle clubs in the United States were "among all classes."[74] This would age within a generation. Unintentionally, by advocating for paved roads, well-connected organizations like the League of American Wheelmen laid the groundwork for the roles to reverse. Infrastructure initially meant for bikes ended up allowing for the massive expansion of car ridership. In the United States in 1899, there were 1.2 million bikes sold. In 1908,

the number dropped to 860,000. That year, the Ford Model T was released. Electric vehicles were viable contenders, often advertised as "ad-
mirably adapted to city needs" due to their relative quietness and lower
speeds.[75] Oil-fueled cars, capable of running for longer distances, would
prove more suitable for suburbanization. In 1926, the first Uniform Vehicle Code was created. Laws privileged automobiles, driving the bicycle off the roads that connected cities to their surroundings.

Streetcars still prevailed in urban transportation, even in the United
States. In Detroit, which headquartered the Ford Motor Company,
streetcar lines expanded from 187 miles in 1902 to around 544 in 1920,
when it was the fourth largest city in the country. This extensive network connected the city and surrounding towns. Relying on mass transit for workers, Ford initially built cars in the city, progressively moving
operations to more spacious suburbs. In nearby Highland Park, the
company inaugurated the largest manufacturing plant in the world in
1910. It was the first car factory to use a moving assembly line. Production peaked at one Model T every ten seconds. The complex ran on a
cutting-edge power station. Fueled by coal and gasoline, it generated
electricity equivalent to half of what all of Detroit required.[76] Buildings
featured elements that would later be associated with avant-garde architectural modernism. Instead of load-bearing walls and divisions, it had
open floor plans and horizontal windows, relying on reinforced concrete columns and ample use of glass. It was nicknamed Crystal Palace.
We again have rupture and continuity.

Henry Ford declared in 1922 that "we shall solve the problem of the
city by leaving the city."[77] He overlooked the problems that the car solution would cause. But it was a prophetic statement, anticipating suburbanization in later decades. The innovator also played an active role in
making it so. The Ford company relocated operations to the even larger
River Rouge Plant in suburban Dearborn in the early 1920s. Its founder
had even more ambitious designs for the future. As the historian Jonathan Levy explains, "Ford's vision was total."[78] He wanted to rebuild
civilization based on the "Ford Man," with the logic of an assembly line:
predictable, efficient, regimented. The company fought labor unions
and sought to dictate how employers should behave even at home: no

"drinking," "riotous living," "indebtedness," "lack of thrift," or "domestic trouble."[79] Ford managed to drastically reduce labor turnover with higher pay and shorter hours. There was more to it. Levy notes that many of the company's workers had been European peasants, and experienced "the rupture of the industrial revolution." Now, he speculates, workers could perceive that "economic life was at last settling down into a long-term structure." The company promised them continuity. As millions of cars rolled off assembly lines, they would eventually rupture urban fabrics and transform our futures.

Ford had ambitions beyond the United States. By the mid-1920s, the company had built assembly plants on every continent except Antarctica. The first one in a non-anglophone country was in Buenos Aires. Ford meddled in foreign affairs. A leading antisemite, he would support Hitler's rise in Germany.[80] In 1934, the philosopher Antonio Gramsci argued that "American Fordism [. . .] was as totalizing as Italian Fascism, or German Nazism, or Soviet Communism."[81] Mussolini's regime had imprisoned him in 1926. We might ask: if Gramsci's comparison does not seem apt, is it only because cars ultimately won? The other three isms, we might add, all embraced investment in automobility as an "industrial investment multiplier."[82] Ford's plans, at any rate, suffered setbacks. After the transition from steam- to electric-powered manufacturing, he worked with Thomas Edison to go further. They tried to create the "Detroit of the South": an "Electric City" dispersed across a 75-mile highway, following a river. Energy from hydro-electric dams would spare the sprawling car-centric utopia from smoke pollution. This did not pan out.[83] Ford did build a company town in the middle of the rubber-rich Brazilian Amazon. Started in 1928, it was abandoned in 1934.

Ultimately, jungles and urban life remained too unwieldy to conform to any single man's fantasies of control. Ford, however, pointed to a new future, mobilizing technologies to escape the city. Car culture turbocharged the old Jeffersonian ethos of the United States as an antiurban society. As Princeton's president, Woodrow Wilson accused cars of "encouraging the spread of socialism" in 1906.[84] As the nation's president (1913–1921), he championed them. In the 1928 national election, one of Herbert Hoover's campaign ads touted how "Republican prosperity" had brought not just "the proverbial 'chicken in every pot'" but "a car in every backyard, to boot."[85] Ford supported Hoover. His Democratic rival Al Smith personified an urban America. Raised in Manhattan's Lower East Side, he made a name in reformist municipal politics and was elected New York governor for four terms. Smith suffered vicious anti-Catholic attacks. He overperformed in cities but lost in a landslide. Since then, few mayors have moved on to higher office in the United States, unlike in other countries. And gas prices have stayed a hot topic in national elections.

By 1929, around 80 percent of the cars on the planet could be found in the United States, almost one per household.[86] The Great Depression hit car companies hard. Trains and streetcars still proved crucial to intermunicipal mobility, but trends continued to diverge in comparison to Europe and elsewhere. Rail passenger miles in the United States peaked in 1920, and then quickly began to decline. Because rail expansion did not keep up with population growth, mileage per capita decreased over 50 percent in the 1920s. This did not occur in France, for example. Passenger rail miles continued to grow, matching the United States on a per capita basis around 1940. Passenger rail in other parts of the world kept expanding during the period. Nonetheless, especially when we account for freight trains, the rail network in the United States was so much more extensive by 1920 that few countries ever caught up on a per capita basis.[87]

———

Urban designers generally endorsed private cars as a mechanism for decentralization or "deconcentration."[88] The incipient culture of professional planning hewed a bit closer to statistical tables than to fanciful flights. Le Corbusier's designs helped to fuse science with a bit of science fiction. His pseudonym, adopted in 1920, evoked the oracular mystique of the *corbeau*, crow or raven in French. He began to articulate a bolder vision of a car-centric future. Both Le Corbusier and Henry Ford had a special relationship to the inner workings of clocks in their formative years. One grew up in the heart of Switzerland's watch-making industry, the other learned from disassembling and reassembling a pocket watch.[89] Both became drawn to mechanics. We could say they shared an obsession with molding time. In Detroit, the architect declared car manufacturers could best "undertake the production of the homes of tomorrow."[90] After visiting the River Rouge complex, he expressed admiration for the "totality of thought and action."[91] Like Ford, he would also develop Nazi sympathies. But Le Corbusier preferred to highlight the poetic qualities of his upbringing in a mountain region. He pursued a more creative pathway: not leaving cities, but radically reinventing them for a new era.

Akin to the Futurists, Le Corbusier thought that "the conquest of speed has always been the dream of mankind."[92] Europe had the chance of jumpstarting the urbanism of tomorrow. This meant reorganizing spaces to ensure efficient circulation. In 1922, in his thirties, he devised a Contemporary City for 3 million inhabitants. *Contemporary* implied that with this plan the future had arrived. It consisted of a business center with twenty-four identical skyscrapers spaced out in a vast gridded park, encircled by low-rise public buildings and luxury residences, a green belt, and beyond them, "garden cities" housing two-thirds of the population. To allow for the separation of speeds and constant movement, the transportation system was layered. A landing platform for flying taxis stood at the center of a network of railroads and raised highways. Le Corbusier oriented his plans around vehicular traffic and the needs of the wealthy. To him, congestion in New York was a problem because businessmen had to leave their automobiles and ride the subway.[93] His ideal city had clearly established hierarchies, and transit reflecting them: cars moved around in constant flux, at the service of socioeconomic fixity.

Le Corbusier sought motor companies as sponsors, and he succeeded for his next iteration. For the 1925 World's Fair on Modern Decorative and Industrial Arts in Paris, he codesigned a pavilion for the magazine *L'Esprit Nouveau* (The New Spirit), which opposed tradition and embraced mass-produced objects. In the exhibit, they mounted a model of Le Corbusier's Plan Voisin, named after an automobile and aircraft manufacturer. His vision glorified machine production: steel,

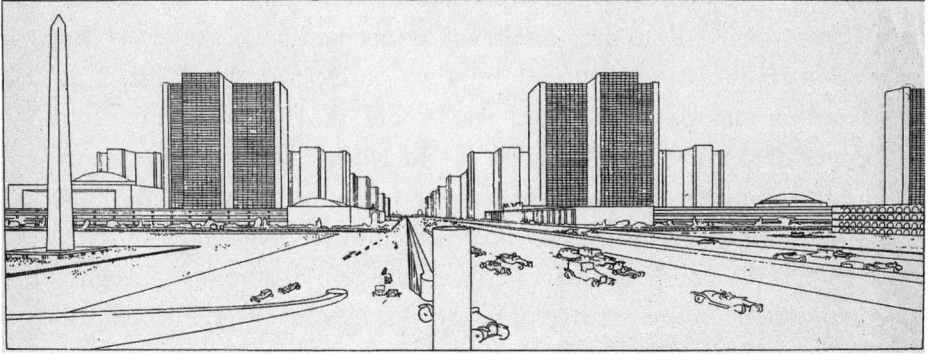

FIGURE 5.9. "Contemporary city of three million inhabitants." With modernist garden cities for airplanes and cars, Le Corbusier's future arrives.

concrete, and glass replaced brick and stone. Seeking rupture with the past, the design invited sunlight and fresh air. The plan went further than the architecture. Owing nothing to fictional utopias, Le Corbusier proposed to update the French capital for the motor age.

His Contemporary City was reconceived as a renewal project. The "new Paris" required razing 2 square miles of the existing city— especially the Marais, which had mostly survived reforms. Le Corbusier saw himself outdoing Haussmann, with scales inconceivable to a nineteenth-century planner. He described "widely spaced crystal towers which soar higher than any pinnacle on earth."[94] Yet, this vertical future was the antithesis of New York. Le Corbusier called its downtown streets "appalling nightmares." Instead of sidewalks where "human life pullulates," a rational city would have pedestrians surrounded by vast lawns and cars moving freely without traffic. The Plan Voisin combined density and sprawl, while promising lucrative deals for investors. Le Corbusier's radical ideas did not gain traction, but he was just beginning.

If the extent to which cars would foreclose other futures remained unclear, this was partly because many city dwellers did not find them appealing. Flattening sales in the early 1920s reflected that. In *Fighting Traffic*, the historian Peter Norton argues that before US cities could be destroyed and reconstructed for cars, a violent process of "social

FIGURE 5.10. Le Corbusier and the Plan Voisin: the Olympian master planner dictates.

reconstruction" had to take place. At first, cars were perceived as "unruly intruders," incompatible with traditional uses of streets, like merchantry, hanging out, and playing.[95] People nicknamed them the "devil wagon." By 1925, sheet music warned children: "Don't play on the street;" "the street is for autos."[96] Urbanites, including safety advocates, downtown businesses, and pedestrians, organized against cities that prioritized easing congestion over other social needs.

Car interests, represented by automobile clubs, dealers, and companies like Ford and General Motors, proved to be more powerful. This "motordom," Norton shows, recast mobility "in terms of political freedom and market freedom," sidestepping "difficult questions of justice."[97] Cars routinely injured and killed pedestrians. Yet, speed limits became seen as an "oppressive" threat to both efficiency and liberty. The main competitive advantage of cars was being able to use public spaces for free, unlike the strictly regulated and taxed mass transit. There was no mechanism to charge for the high cost that parking and driving imposed on shared infrastructure, nor for the space they occupied. One study in 1927 referred to them as a "parasite on the street."[98] In a vicious cycle, the more private cars took over public thoroughfares, the harder it became for buses or streetcars to circulate. By the 1930s, it was difficult to envision the streets of tomorrow without a dominant role for the automobile.

Yet, even in the United States, cities remained dense, and sidewalks stayed vibrant for at least another generation. In 1930, a greater proportion of the US population lived in the ten largest cities than at any other point. That share, around 15 percent, has steadily declined. The populations of major cities in the US Northeast and the Midwest, however, continued to grow, peaking in the 1950 census.[99] They dispersed significantly in the following decades, as people moved to the suburbs, or to the more car-centric cities of the West and the Sun Belt. Los Angeles, which had boomed as an oil town, would host the first Olympic Games in the Pacific in 1932. Yet, although the conditions for suburban sprawl and a shifting balance of power had begun to set in, New York City did not relinquish its hold on the imagination of urban futures—especially when perceived from outside the United States. And that meant vertical rather than horizontal growth.

———

World War I generated dystopian narratives. In the 1920s, science fiction novels and comics showed high-tech and gargantuan cities as fertile ground for evils and repression. People sometimes equated the towers of New York to Babel or Babylon. With similarly pessimistic views, Oswald Spengler's *The Decline of the West* engaged more earnestly in futurology. The German philosopher thought Western vitality would only last for another 50 years, and urbanization was part of the problem. The influential treatise described the peasant as "soil-bound" and eternal, "propagating himself from generation to generation."[100] The urbanite was an "intellectual nomad," rootless and cosmopolitan.[101] Cities, associated with money, threatened rural tradition. Spengler's ideas were an inspiration to Nazis. Though not couched in explicit antisemitism, the book's antiurban discourse resonated in some of their talking points. Adolf Hitler, for example, expressed "revulsion for the big city" in *Mein Kampf* (1925). But whereas the Nazi project would point toward the future, Spengler diagnosed the contemporary "Megalopolis" as a sign of the impending downfall of Western civilization.

The Decline of the West predicted "cities laid out for ten to twenty million inhabitants," with "buildings that will dwarf the biggest of today and notions of traffic and communication that we should regard as fantastic to the point of madness."[102] In the present, Spengler found "suburbs and garden cities invading the wide countryside." He realized that escaping the city could also be part of urbanization. Neither Ebenezer Howard's visions nor other decentralizing plans could rescue people from the Megalopolis, which "denies all Nature." Nature in this worldview was subordinate to humans, serving to instill life. In contrast, "the giant city [. . .] sucks the country dry, insatiably and incessantly demanding and devouring fresh streams of men."[103] This language could easily be in *Mein Kampf*.[104] To Spengler, the future was urban, but there was no vital future in the city.

The image of this dehumanizing future could be projected onto New York City more easily than anywhere else: it had become the world's largest and most vertical metropolis, as well as a global symbol of capitalism. Perhaps the most iconic science fiction representation of urban futures from the 1920s, Fritz Lang's *Metropolis* (1927), was shaped both by Spengler's philosophies and by the director's perception of the American city. During a trip to New York in 1924, Lang saw it as "the crossroads of multiple and confused human forces (irresistibly driven) to exploit each other and thus living in perpetual anxiety."[105] He compared the skyline to "a vertical veil," meant to "dazzle, distract and hypnotize" with a set of illusions. *Metropolis* recycled the trope of a future with the rich atop high-rise buildings, while workers toiled in mechanic factories deep underground. The cityscape looked a bit like Moses King's "Dream of New York," with flying vehicles and elevated rails running along horizontally, amid skyscrapers. But rather than streetcars on the ground level, Lang's future city had cars moving slowly, stuck in traffic, while airplanes and monorails sped above. And instead of ornate

FIGURE 5.11. Overshadowed by the Tower of Babel (a steam punk precursor), Lang's film imagines modernist buildings and overlapping transit.

Beaux-Arts façades, we find design closer to the modern Art Deco and Bauhaus styles, with more streamlined forms and rigid geometries. The film got the trends right in terms of architecture, but wrong in terms of transportation.

Narratives of Western decline might be in vogue again in the twenty-first century, but the specific contours of Spengler's prediction have become irrevocably dated. He never quite considered that modern urbanization would eventually become a distinctly non-Western phenomenon. Nor that right-wing nativists and left-leaning environmentalists alike might share some of his antipathies. Though Spengler intended it as further evidence of the corrupting reach of cities, he did presciently identify how the urban fold extended beyond cities not just through horizontal expansion, but also with new media technologies: "for the country-dweller," he wrote, "radio reception means intimate touch with the news, the thought, and the entertainment of the great city."[106] Integrated markets and capital flows had already allowed for connections. There was a cultural dimension too. The refrain of a samba hit in Brazil sings: "I live in the countryside / I have never lived in the city / I buy the newspaper / to learn what's new."[107] It played for both rural and urban audiences. Whether in print or radio, communications media helped people to see themselves sharing a future with strangers, and thus forming part of a nation.[108]

Spengler also gets at something even more "intimate" and not necessarily bounded within the nation-state. Urban stories emanating from the radio reached people outside of cities, impacting their worldviews and aspirations. With film, this cultural fold cut across spatial and linguistic barriers even more. Movies became the paramount mode for the dissemination of narratives about cities and the prospects that they opened for individuals. Throughout the century, migrants would arrive in cities that they had been exposed to as places of excitement and possibility on the screen. During the heyday of cinema as mass entertainment, plots set in New York City tended to have happy endings.[109] The cinematic city did not reflect actual demographic diversity, seldom including migrant characters. But many told stories of self-reinvention, including petty thieves learning how to act like nobles, social workers reforming gangsters, and working-class women marrying wealthy men.[110]

Films began to represent futures in transit, broadly aligning with changes in how people used and perceived transportation. In early movies, characters often took trains to and from the city. A chance encounter with a stranger in the subway could lead to marriage—and economic mobility.[111] In *Speedy* (1928), a greedy magnate targeted a horsecar operator, with sights on a streetcar monopoly. The comic hero, a horsecar taxi driver played by Harold Lloyd, made sure the villain paid fair price. In other movies, characters become rich from inventing automobiles, or are splashed by them. Trucks kill children. Road accidents cause serious injuries.[112] Cars make for slapstick humor with explosions or malfunction. They are sites of romance, pick-up scenes, and male predation. In 1933, King Kong wrecked elevated rails. By 1942, Orson Welles's *The Magnificent Ambersons*, set in the Midwest, already looks back on the period before automobiles as a gentler time. Like the 1918 novel on which it was based, it saw the cult of speed and the rush toward ideal futures as a fool's errand: "the faster we're carried, the less time we have to spare."[113]

Often more attuned to bird's-eye views, planners tried to reconcile the appeals and perils of metropolitan life. Just two years after *Metropolis*, Hugh Ferriss published his *The Metropolis of Tomorrow*. The influential designer had predicted that, "when the evolution of the city is accomplished," then "the people of New York will actually live in the sky."[114] His book compared the view of New York not to a veil, but to a curtain "not yet risen." A visitor from another time or place might ask: "What apocalypse is about to be revealed? What is its setting? And what will be the purport of this modern metropolitan drama?"[115] Ferriss was ambivalent toward "the lure of the city" and vertical urbanization, but assumed New York anticipated trends that would take place elsewhere. In the question of how to build the metropolis of tomorrow, therefore, a broader future was at stake.

The book collects his drawings of existing towering buildings in US cities, and projections about what was to come. These included airplanes, traffic congestion, and ever-taller skyscrapers made of glass, steel, and concrete. To each he offered a solution: setbacks for more sunlight; hangars atop skyscrapers; more ground floor dedicated to cars. Like Le Corbusier, Ferris proposed a vertical separation for transit and a horizontal separation of functions, dividing the city into zones for Business, Art, and Science. The third part of the book contains visualizations of an imaginary metropolis. Though the author's atmospheric charcoal drawings of Ziggurat-like buildings proved to be more lasting than his planning theories, he was ultimately building an argument in favor of "conscious design." Ferriss wished for cities to be more serene and cohesive, centering the needs of humans rather than "the financial appetites of property owners."[116] And yet, his metropolis of tomorrow looked imposing and menacing. Over the years, these images would invite associations to Gotham City.

Mrs. Manstey had lived in a world with more modest and prosaic futures. She could not bear seeing garden views destroyed by "financial

FIGURE 5.12. Ferriss attempted to maximize building area after New York adopted zoning in 1916. Form follows the law.

appetites." Would she have found solace in Ferriss's metropolis, over-looking one of the hanging gardens that he placed amid spaced-out sky-scrapers? Both agreed that frenzied development needed to be curbed. Mrs. Manstey thought that she could personally alter the fate of her neighborhood but realized that the law was not on her side. That had begun to change. By now, for starters, she would have been able to vote. The Nineteenth Amendment was ratified in 1920. And in 1916, New York City had passed the first comprehensive modern zoning codes. Zoning was an instrument to manage development and shape the future, both citywide and in specific sites. One goal of Ferriss's book, in fact, was to draft building volumes that reflected the new restrictions—setbacks, for example, responded to regulations on how much area could be built above a given lot. One of the motivations was to ensure that sunlight made it all the way down to ground level.

Even with the newly established limits, a fully built-up New York City would still be able to accommodate tens of millions of residents (1960s zoning laws reduced that). Debates around zoning ensued in nearly every city. Many adopted New York–style setbacks, sometimes for aesthetic rather than functional reasons. By 1929, more than 650 municipalities actively regulated land use with planning commissions.[117] Incumbents argued that height limits would curb congestion, ignoring how sprawl incentivizes car use. People disagreed vehemently about what the future would (or should) look like. A whole set of futurist thinkers and designers, including in science fiction, vastly underestimated the long-term consequences of automobiles and zoning for horizontal development. The idea of vertical segregation never quite panned out like they thought.

Metropolis envisioned the wealthy in secluded Edenic gardens on top of high-rises. Instead, in societies that adopted cars at a massive scale, many of those that could afford them moved to detached homes with backyards beyond the inner ring of streetcar suburbs. Zoning regulations became a tool for all sorts of political projects, including those seeking to keep undesired racial or ethnic groups from moving to new car-centric suburban neighborhoods. In most places outside the United States, where car ownership only boomed later, the poor often resided in peripheries, commuting by rail or bus. That could make them, from the perspective of power centers, even less present and visible than the underclasses of Fritz Lang's dystopian city.

The plot of *Metropolis* also revolved around the changing boundaries of relationships.[118] It showed familiar tensions of forbidden love: after a chance encounter, Freden, the son of the city's ruthless magnate, fell for Maria, a woman from the working classes. He was aghast at their conditions. She roused workers by prophesying the arrival of a "mediator." A mad scientist then kidnapped Maria, replacing her with a robot

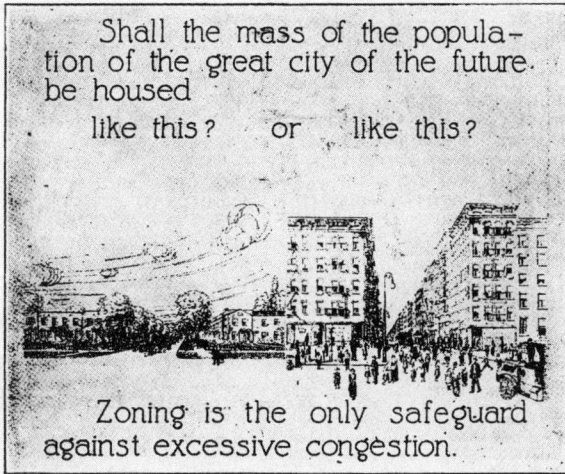

FIGURE 5.13. In the 1920s, these Philadelphia homeowners asked some questions but overlooked others. Where are the cars? How will people get places?

double who sowed discord. Freden rescued Maria from the inventor, who died. He turned out to be the irredeemable villain. In the happy ending, the capitalist father and a labor leader shake hands. Maria and Freden are together. Unlike in *New Heloise*, class differences did not pose insurmountable obstacles.

The idea of a future where reconciliation might be possible played itself against the background of explosive conflicts. The emergence of the Soviet Union opened possibilities that enticed some and terrified others. When the Brazilian magazine confronted the crisis of prognostication, it offered as a self-evident example: "Who predicted the Russian Revolution?" and "who [. . .] was capable of predicting its consequences?"[119] Assessing those consequences was difficult enough, let alone foreseeing them. In Rio de Janeiro, a short-lived anarchist rebellion took over the streets in 1918, motivated by events in Russia and local factors that synthesized transatlantic forces: war-related inflation, precarious labor conditions, violence against strikers, and the collapse of a skyscraper under construction. Throughout the world, the Russian Revolution became a beacon of hope for a more just world.

The USSR created another basis for generating political futures. It challenged the centrality of North Atlantic models in Latin America and West Africa. Especially early on, Soviet designers mobilized a variety of daring urban visions. The architect Lazar Khidekel introduced a new vertical scale with his Aero-cities (1925–1930). He shared some of the concerns that had motivated the Garden City movement. He approached them, however, by imagining urbanization elevated above earth's surface, organized along horizontal layers, nonhierarchically and without separation of functions. The idea was to free up cities from the geography below, as a way of preserving nature. It emerged from an intellectual environment that expected urbanization to keep up a frenzied pace: "the culture of the city will sooner or later embrace all the provinces and subject them to its technology."[120] Khidekel imagined "garden cities" with mobility, housing, and cultivation raised on structural frames. This radical departure from the emerging planning consensus understood that sprawling development could not coexist with healthy ecosystems.

Others went even further. In Georgii Krutikov's "City of the Future" (1928), humanity would inhabit outer space. Circulation between structures propelled by atomic power took place through "universal vehicles."[121] These capsules were capable of navigating space, terrain, and water, while also serving as temporary homes. This was a moment when the boundaries between practicality and possibility loosened up, partly because of unpredictable developments like the Russian Revolution. Krutikov attempted to ground his transportation designs on the work of a rocket scientist. Avant-garde projects kept expanding the scales of vertical space and mobility as a solution to chaotic and individualistic capitalism. They attempted to reconcile technology, growth, and ecological balance with an eye toward planetary futures rather than nation-bounded progress.

Several Soviet contemporaries criticized such projects as unrealistic and not grounded in material conditions.[122] Instead, under Stalin's rule, in 1928 the USSR began to implement the Five-Year Plan to usher in industrialization and centralized collective agriculture. One of the motivations was the prospect of warfare with the West. Productivity and urban

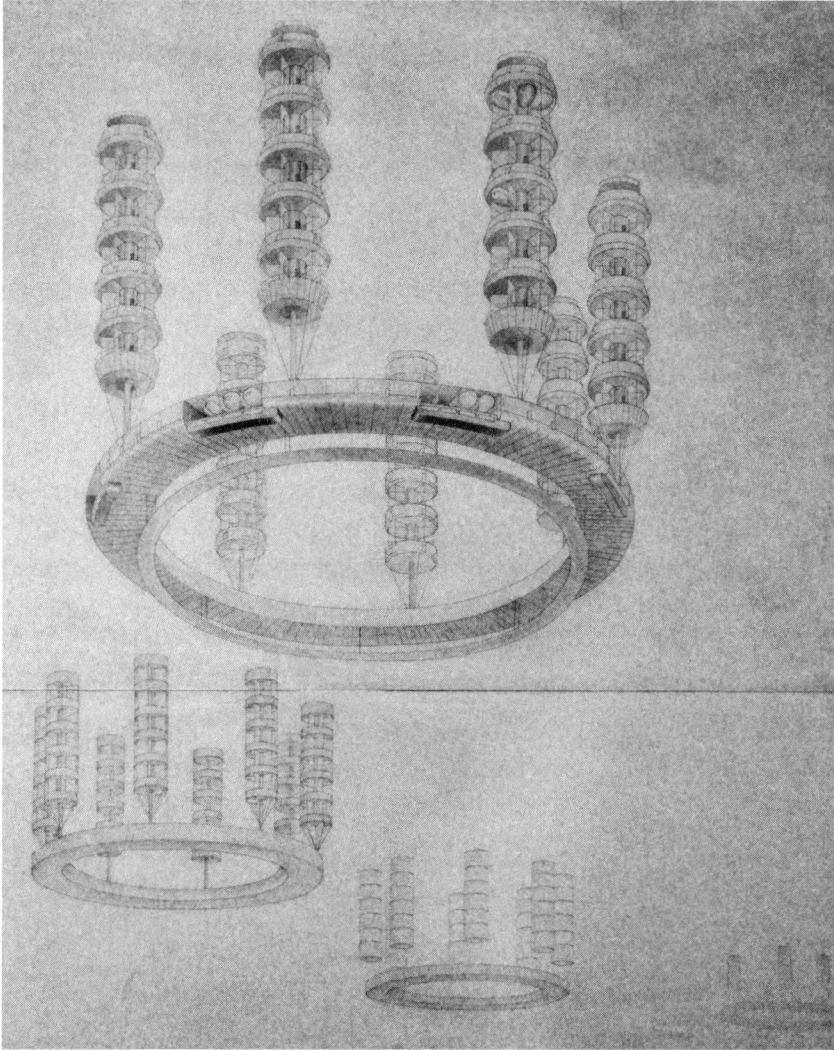

FIGURE 5.14. Propelled by atomic power and "universal vehicles," Soviet dreams of humanity in outer space.

infrastructure rapidly improved. Unlike capitalist-oriented economies, the Soviet Union experienced massive industrial growth during the Great Depression.[123] More than 20 million peasants moved to cities.[124] In practice, however, top-down technocratic approaches could also be detached from material conditions. The plan placed enormous stress on people and ecosystems. It led to ecological devastation, labor camps, and massive famines. In the early 1930s, no country was shielded from crises and instability. Modernizers on the political right and left would look to Detroit as an inspiration for economic dirigisme and social engineering.[125] In the immediate aftermath of the Five-Year Plan, Stalin insisted on directing the "backward" country toward "new and modern technology," to liberate it from "the whims of world capitalism."[126]

Even before Stalinism's heavy hand, Yevgeny Zamyatin wrote perhaps the first urban dystopia set in the future. It was also the first work of fiction censored in the Soviet Union, in 1921. The novel *We* was eventually published in the West in 1929, causing a stir.[127] Around one thousand years into the future, the One State ruled. After defeating the countryside in warfare, it concentrated the surviving population in an authoritarian city-state surrounded by a glass wall. The novel presents human history as a "transition from nomadic forms to more sedentary ones."[128] Zamyatin's future city denied nature, keeping off the "irrational" and "ugly" outside—including birds. Petroleum-based foods helped to eradicate hunger. The first-person plural of the title hinted at the imposition of a regimented collective life. Melville's Bartleby would have suffered under the scientific management of workplaces. All time was accounted for with mathematical precision, leaving no room for imagination. Zamyatin clearly feared that industrialization and production-oriented urban life would make humans machine-like. Capitalist and Communist dystopias are not that far apart.

The future city of *We* had a clock tower at the center, and "impeccably straight streets."[129] People were assigned numbers instead of proper names, and clothing was standardized based on class. Flying vehicles coexisted with trains. The city was contained rather than sprawling. Vertical buildings dominated the skyline, all made of glass. Zamyatin, like many of his contemporaries, was living in the timeline of the Crystal Palace. But in *We*, progress did not usher in happy endings. The plot involved dissidence, and the authoritarian state wins out. Glass transparency allowed for oppressive surveillance.

The implication was still that glass would be the material of the future. This was a pervasive expectation across the Atlantic too. Hugh

FIGURE 5.15. As the Art Deco Empire State Building tops up, a prescient street scene in 1931.

Ferriss even tried to write a prophetic poem: "Buildings like crystal. / Walls of translucent glass. / Sheer glass blocks sheathing a steel grill."[130] As in the nineteenth century, the spectacle of glass could represent threatening or alluring futures. It also concealed changes hiding in plain sight. In 1931, *Everyday Science and Mechanics* featured "The Glass Skyscraper." That year, the Art Deco Empire State Building was inaugurated. It might have seemed like the era of steel and glass high-rises was just beginning. Instead, the Great Depression dampened expectations and made such ambitious projects harder to pull off. The Empire State was not surpassed until the World Trade Center.

On the magazine's cover, the depiction of the ground level was probably an afterthought but proved prescient: cars took over the streets. They relied on glass, but even more on another material that underpinned modernity in the twentieth century: aluminum. Alcoa ads in the 1930s promised as much, inviting readers to "peer into the future." As Mimi Sheller argues, aluminum was key to "mobile modernity," and "opened whole new vistas in the quest for speed and lightness." Its practical uses coexisted with "massive powers of destruction," beginning in the mining process.[131] Aluminum transformed the everyday life of the modern consumer, as well as warfare. Now, as the car era began, two new materials vied with steel and glass as the building blocks of urbanization: aluminum and oil. They helped to pull growth in horizontal directions.

Throughout the 1930s, nonetheless, images of landing strips on rooftops and monorail transit zipping through vertical skylines continued to circulate widely. But the winds were shifting. In 1937, Shell Motor Oil created an advertisement campaign that seemed as speculative as any other. One ad announced with confidence: "This Is the City of TOMORROW." High-rise towers stood spaced apart, with a network of highways below. Another promised to drivers the ability to move through a city without interruptions, in a "continuous flow." It recalled visions by Ferriss and Le Corbusier. The company hired Norman Bel Geddes for the job. He had worked as a set designer in theater and film, including on the futuristic city of *Things to Come* (1936), a science fiction film based on a novel by H. G. Wells. Neither Shell's nor Wells's cityscapes seemed to reserve a place for greenery. And they were firmly grounded on architectural paradigms that now counted as modern, privileging cleaner lines and surfaces instead of ornate details.

Wells had imagined a utopian world where the airplane reigned, in the distant 2100s. Shell promised a new reality to drivers by 1960. One variation of the ad summed it up in bold letters: "Through the City of

FIGURE 5.16. An ad campaign for Shell Motor Oil, setting the stage for the wildly popular Futurama at the New York World's Fair in 1939–1940.

Tomorrow without a STOP." The Corbusian dream had gone main-stream. Some ads printed a profile picture of Norman Bel Geddes, de-scribed as an "authority on future trends"—white, male, expert-looking. They quoted him: "When traffic delays and confusion seem hopeless, remember that men of vision are working on the problem." The solutions were express highways "free from stop and go," unencumbered by sidewalks, pedestrians, stop lights, or intersections. Expectations created by such campaigns both anticipated and forged futures in transit. The actual future would be less compact and vertical than the images suggested. And all those cars needed to be parked somewhere. Even more than tall buildings, surface lots turned out to occupy the space of the future.

General Motors hired Bel Geddes to design their exhibit at the New York World's Fair in 1939–1940. It was the event's biggest draw: 5 million people visited the pavilion, called Futurama. Now, corporations rather than nations took the lead. Spectacle gained another dimension. As a sales strategy, designers reimagined existing products with fresh looks. Gone were the clunky cars of previous generations, replaced by streamlined machines for a new age. The prosperous city of Futurama followed the blueprint laid out in the Shell campaign. It was built on the separation of speeds, with sidewalks raised above highways. Perhaps optimistically, dioramas included a fair number of buses and pedestrians. Visitors were introduced to the idea of a nationwide network of expressways for cars: speedy, efficient, and seamless. This was not just about the car as a transportation device, but about the possibility of partaking in a forward-looking lifestyle. The pavilion sought to put the Great Depression in the rear-view mirror. Visitors left with a button reading "I Have Seen the Future."[132]

IV. The Star of the South

Socialistic urban utopias in the mold of *Looking Backward* became harder to pull off after World War I and the Russian Revolution. We might attribute this to more disenchanted and sectarian political environments. Increasingly, progress had to be measured up against the United States or the USSR. And gradually, car culture narrowed the range of potential urban futures. At the beginning of the century, however, the sky was not the limit—neither for urbanization, nor for Argentina. When Enrique Vera y González wrote *The Star of the South*, he imagined a weakened Europe and a powerful Africa in the early 2000s.

New York City and Buenos Aires were the world's largest and most prominent cities. In this future world order, as in the past, key urban spaces functioned as metonymic of national status. New York stood at the center of a continuous metropolis running from Lynn in Massachusetts to Mt. Vernon in Virginia. The United States was presented as militaristic: it had invaded Latin American countries and conquered Canada. Argentina equaled the northern rival in technology and geopolitical might, while besting it in quality of life. No one went hungry, and no one worked excessively. Buenos Aires, with 80 million residents, was the capital of a Latin American Confederation presided over by its mayor.[133]

The novel conceived of interurban mobility with abundant flying vehicles of various sizes. Rail was best suited for long-distance travel: the train between New York and Buenos Aires only took thirty hours. The US metropolis was a constant reference point. Its skyscrapers pointed toward the modern future, but the layout seemed stuck in an earlier era. Manhattan's dimensions became quaint. In Buenos Aires, a district with narrower streets followed the "North American taste."[134] Because it had not been as built up, the author could imagine the metropolitan area accommodating vast cultivation fields. Compared to other capitals, Argentina's had purer air and powerful vistas. Great diagonals traversed the city, forming a "colossal X" with a "gorgeous plaza."[135] This was not the scale of the Iberian colonial grid, nor of Haussmannization. Avenues had around 2,000 feet in width, twenty times wider than Fifth Avenue in New York. They provided both awe-inspiring scales and a sense of "unity."[136] Religion had a diminished role. The central square contained grand gardens and a statue of the nineteenth-century statesman Bartolomé Mitre, as well as City Hall and other towering buildings. The Commissioners' Plan just could not keep up.

Vera y González anticipated a fixation with New York as ground zero for vertical growth. In Argentina, the US city was sometimes a cautionary tale, either from the angle of religious piousness or anticapitalist critique. It became common, however, for popular magazines to reproduce images of modern futures inspired by Manhattan.[137] One even reprinted the futuristic depiction from Moses King's New York, changing the title to "Buenos Aires in the Future."[138] Mass media in the

Argentine capital appeared to embrace verticality more emphatically than Southern counterparts. There was a recurring imagination of air travel, underground transportation systems, and of course, the construction of Latin America's tallest buildings.[139] Skyscrapers, rather than signifying a universal standard, set urbanization in the Americas apart from Europe. The architectural scholar Margarita Gutman observes that one Argentine magazine grouped together images of New York, Rio, and Buenos Aires in order "to invoke a future of [. . .] shared progress."[140] It became common for designers to identify a tension between Old World horizontality and New World verticality.[141]

The Mexican architect Francisco Mujica envisioned an urban modernity rooted in a distinctly indigenous past. He associated the pyramidal forms in Manhattan's skyscrapers to temples in Mexico and Central America. His combination of horizontal (car-centric) mobility and vertical building proposed a "Neo-American style" as a reaction against European precedents. Mujica had studied urbanism in Paris, where he first published the *History of the Skyscraper* (1929). The idea of creating modern cities in opposition to the Old World found fertile ground among transatlantic avant-gardes, many of them drawing on the attitudes of Futurists and Oswald Spengler.[142] Latin American artists, architects, and policymakers attempted to refashion national identities based on miscegenation, instead of Anglo-American segregation or European supremacy. Some, like Mujica, imagined the Americas taking charge of urban futures. His proposals, in the meantime, were not greeted as practical in New York City.[143] Perhaps they were still too ahead of their time, or Mujica was not the right messenger for key constituencies. Ten years later, with a whole other ideological baggage, Futurama would not look all that different.

Throughout Latin America, we can observe both a growing sense of New York City as the capital of modernity and an emerging discourse of appreciation for native traditions. Yet, the rupture with the colonial past was often more symbolic than material. Urban wealth continued to implicate the dispossession of indigenous groups in the hinterlands, and multiracial urban cultures coexisted with socioeconomic subordination for Afro-descendants. A mismatch between representation and

FIGURE 5.17. A "Neo-American style" blending pre-Hispanic pyramids, Manhattan skyscrapers, and freeways.

material conditions widened. Throughout Latin America, marginalized groups became cultural protagonists. Yet, urban planning remained by and large a top-down affair dominated by lettered elites. To them, North Atlantic cities continued to act as models and sources of new debates in urbanism. At the same time, the region produced its own expectations for the future. Urbanization in Buenos Aires opened pathways that reflected these intersections between transatlantic and local dynamics.

People in Buenos Aires had more pressing concerns than flying vehicles, skyscrapers, or technical planning debates. And sometimes they had more exciting perspectives. Most had moved from the European countryside or the Argentine pampas. They worked demanding jobs, around 10 percent of them in manufacturing.[144] Progress seemed tangible and tenable. In 1912, the country achieved universal male suffrage. Access to public schooling was about two times lower than in France or the United States, but three times greater than in Brazil. The city had comparably high coverage of water, sewage, and electricity. On the surface, the early twentieth-century Argentine capital looked European. The population was much whiter than in other major Latin American cities. Boulevards lined by neoclassical and Beaux-Arts façades recalled Haussmannian Paris. Until a coup in 1930, there was relative political stability. Oligarchic circles concentrated power, and gender inequalities cut deep. Women only obtained the right to vote in 1947. But especially for men, working-class neighborhoods engendered enticing forms of belonging in the big city. Social life often revolved around soccer and tango clubs.

As Beatriz Sarlo has written, Buenos Aires is not Paris.[145] The city came together kaleidoscopically. Italian artisans built unique and distinct small houses. Suburban train stations and warehouses had English styles. New York was the image of the future. Indigenous faces walked the streets. Radio soap operas and movies competed with Hollywood fare, often showing the Buenos Aires working classes as dignified, unlike the greedy and pretentious wealthy.[146] And on weekends, locals danced to their own tunes. At the same time, however, political elites had a penchant for French urban designers. Charles Thays, a protégé of Adolphe Alphand, moved to Buenos Aires. He worked as director of public parks and promenades between 1891 and 1920, creating multiple green spaces. Joseph-Antoine Bouvard, another collaborator of Alphand, played a prominent role in the Parisian Universal Exhibition of 1889. He was invited to make plans for the Argentine capital, ahead of a 1910 Centennial Exhibit to commemorate the anniversary of national independence. Jean-Claude Nicolas Forestier, an admirer of Olmsted, had also trained under Alphand in Paris before collaborating with the Buenos Aires government in the 1920s.

Familiar concerns with hygiene, aesthetics, and circulation guided the proposals of these European planners. They invariably included diagonals to add direct transportation routes, while also making layouts more picturesque. But rather than mimic, locals asserted their views and adapted Eurocentric ideas to Argentine realities. Planning visions for the future often followed a universal blueprint. Buenos Aires had particular starting points. Compared to other major capitals, fast-paced expansion was not as encumbered by an existing urban fabric. Growth could take advantage of surrounding open fields. As early as the 1870s, debates about public space shaped development. President Domingo Faustino Sarmiento argued that landscaped parks could help "our people be a people," manifesting a civilized future in opposition to the countryside and the past.[147] Yet, instead of focusing investment on a central park, planners distributed them throughout working-class suburban neighborhoods. Most of them had a gridded layout. Rectilinear thoroughfares did not necessarily lead to and from the historic center. Planners used the grid as a forward-looking tool rather than a link to the Spanish colonial legacy. The historian Adrián Gorelik posits the park and the grid as keys to the city's evolution. He notes that their relationship had been antagonistic in modern urbanization: whereas parks embodied the public sphere, the grid was an instrument of private speculation. In Buenos Aires, planners deployed both in sync, as part of a reformist approach.

As the city expanded, whether to concentrate or sprawl was a dilemma. Gorelik highlights Carlos Maria Morales, the director of public works, for realizing the growing importance of suburbs for the future of Buenos Aires.[148] During his two decades heading that office, the civil engineer did not assume that the wealthy should escape a crowded center, nor that the poor had to deal with precarious conditions at the margins. Rather, the provision of public parks, services, and transit to gridded working-class neighborhoods at a metropolitan scale became a way of integrating the peripheries into the capital and the nation— both materially and symbolically. On the one hand, grids and diagonals leading to public buildings, parks, or plazas created some sense of union. On the other, neighborhoods generated identities and enabled micro-futures grounded on local cultures and politics. Soccer and tango set individual *barrios* apart, at the same time as they became elevated to national symbols. This went against the wishes of some lettered elites. A polycentric but cohesive metropolitan region, with strong working-class suburbs, became a threat to the dominance of the traditional and bourgeois city. Opponents attempted to redirect the focus of planning back toward the historic center.

In Argentina, deconcentration was most often part of a progressive vision. As in Ebenezer Howard's proposals, reformists preferred an extended city with resources distributed more equitably. For that reason, despite having very different motivations from Henry Ford or Le Corbusier, many Latin American socialists embraced the motor age. Buses and cars allowed for greater flexibility from set routes, while also avoiding the consolidation of power among streetcar companies. Buses seemed more modern, offering greater comfort and cheaper operations. Streetcars often involved foreign investors, in a business that engaged in rampant real estate manipulation. Gaining early knowledge about future line concessions allowed insiders to profit from flipping land. A monopolistic streetcar system reinforced hierarchies between parts of the city, privileging the center. Bus and taxi *colectivos* could cater to neglected peripheries, bolstering local control, cooperation, and vivacity.[149]

A comprehensive 1925 plan for Buenos Aires embodied tensions and compromises between progressive reformers and conservatives. Created by a commission of mostly architects, it became known after mayor Carlos Noel. He had studied in Paris, like his brother Martin Noel, another member of the group. They tried to find a balance between competing aims, and drew from a range of sources, including plans by Hobrecht, Cerdá, and garden cities. Throughout the document, there are references to how solutions are subject to evolving conditions. The planned subway additions followed a layout both radial and grid-like, adding lateral connections. A reformed Plaza de Mayo would "maintain in the future its character of main plaza" and fulfill the role of "true exponent of national greatness."[150] This monumental center grouped administrative buildings, recalling the visions of City Beautiful. But interventions also centered the peripheries. Generous green parks would be added to *barrios*, forming several nodes.[151] Boulevards intended to better integrate new neighborhoods to the old city. The commission suggested that the city acquire land, to secure an ability to shape the future. They also focused on zoning, and contemplated the entire territory of the Buenos Aires Federal District, which had been established in 1880. The plan covered a vast area with gridded layouts: dozens of times larger than Lisbon's Baixa; about

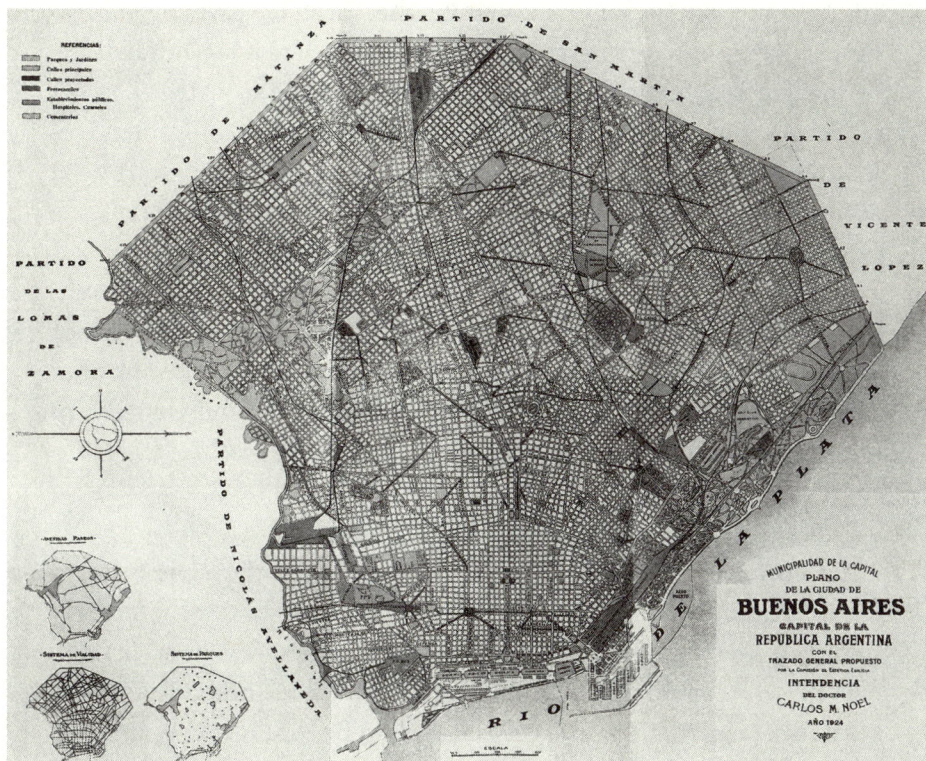

FIGURE 5.18. A more polycentric plan for Buenos Aires, with gridded and radial layouts, adding lateral connections.

3.5 times greater than Manhattan; nearly twice all of Paris; and several times what the Passos reforms targeted in Rio.

The Noel Plan was not approved but became a touchstone. Parts of its vision were enacted. Planned parks and grids throughout the *pampas* acted not just as instruments of hygiene and rational order, but as forms of cohesion, producing common denominators and a perception of shared futures. Against this backdrop, Le Corbusier arrived in Argentina in 1929. He delivered lectures to audiences including university affiliates and well-connected groups like the Friends of the Art. The designer spoke of Buenos Aires as the "Southern capital of the New World," gigantic and energetic, but with "an old spirit." Due to an accumulation of planning mistakes, he claimed, it was a city "without hope."[152] Like the artistic avant-gardes, Le Corbusier was theatrical. He gave the impression of having a sweeping sense of history and where it was headed. His performances, bridging poetry and science, could be seductive. Le Corbusier drew up plans in ways at once idiosyncratic and objective-sounding, as if they constituted an edict from above. He abided by the notion that "the plan must rule"—one of his doctrines. Therefore, the planner, Le Corbusier himself, must rule above it, both a technician and a messiah. The future arrived through him. Le Corbusier was not enticed by modern cities as platforms for chance encounters. He was not fond of parties and could be humorless. The efficiency-minded planner would be turned off by Bartleby. Totalitarian dispositions suited him more than carefree attitudes or ambivalence. To the wealthy and influential women that received him in Argentina, he came across as an arrogant European.[153]

Le Corbusier's vision for Buenos Aires turned to the River Plate, as the 1925 Plan had already done. But his pitch was to concentrate resources in wealthier areas. Its centerpiece was a new Business City, rising vertically over the river, just to the south of the historic core.[154] With New York in mind, Le Corbusier asked: "Can Buenos Aires become one of the great cities of the world?" Skyscrapers and freeways were part of the formula for "space, light, and order." He argued that Buenos Aires had grown with its back to the river and should rectify that. This gesture was more disruptive than nostalgic: the city would look unrecognizable. Yet, although formally radical, the grand solution was also politically conservative. The rhetoric of seizing the future catered to elitist desires to redirect investments toward the center, away from the socialistic peripheries. Bourgeois classes viewed suburban expansion as threatening to their economic interests, and inscrutable to their cultural sensibilities. Le Corbusier's appeal to the establishment did not stop some from accusing his plan of Communism—the "purist aesthetics" came across as egalitarian.[155]

Le Corbusier had grand ambitions for South America. He did not foresee how much the trip would impact him. Until then, his visions privileged rigid geometric patterns. In his youth he had penned a poem in homage to the right angle. In *Urbanisme* (1924), Le Corbusier called curved lines "the way of donkeys," and straight lines the "way of men."[156] By then, gridded patterns had already begun to fall out of favor.[157] But like any good modernist, Le Corbusier could not miss an opportunity to create a myth of rupture. In Buenos Aires, he boarded his first flight and saw the sinuous waterscapes of the River Plate region. He often claimed that from the airplane everything became clear. From the experience he devised, as usual, a doctrine—the Law of the Meander. In the Renaissance, Alberti had already theorized about beautiful cities meandering like rivers. To Le Corbusier, the revelation allowed him to operate at a larger territorial scale. The river was not just an analogy. It was a part of the environment that planners must contend with, as urbanization expanded like never before.

After Buenos Aires, Le Corbusier flew to Montevideo, São Paulo, and Rio de Janeiro. In Brazil's capital, he boldly conceived of housing on top of stilts, rising around 100 yards from the ground. The architecture competed with Rio's mountains. But the meandering lines also conformed to the mountains—the topography informed and prevailed. This is a watershed in Le Corbusier's thinking. The design diverged from his earlier rectilinear proposals, as well as from competing plans for Rio. He now proposed to solve congestion by elevating freeways to new heights. They would be on top of the buildings, reserving glorious views for drivers.

Le Corbusier's plans for South American cities did not amount to much at first. The 1929 financial crash tempered any futuristic impetus. But more suitable conditions would soon emerge for a Corbusian turn. In Buenos Aires, the economic crisis hit tram companies hard, speeding up the transition to car-oriented mobility. Back in Europe, Le Corbusier continued to develop and promote his designs. He became a leading figure in the International Congresses of Modern Architecture (CIAM), founded in 1928. His activities with the group culminated in the Athens Charter in 1933, a document that oriented modern planning for decades. Later that year he published the first edition of *The Radiant City: Elements of a Doctrine of Urbanism for the Equipment of the Machine-Age Civilization* in France, collecting many of his sketches and writings. The book outlined principles at the heart of CIAM.

FIGURE 5.19. Le Corbusier sketches an unbuilt future. Rio's sinuous landscapes prevailed over the straight line.

The *Radiant City* contained proposals for thirteen cities on four continents. Le Corbusier sought no less than "the rebirth of the human body," and expressed "a belief in the future of a new civilization."[158] The book opened praising Ernest Mercier, a key figure in France's oil industry. In the name of improving circulation, Le Corbusier called for the "death of the street." Sidewalks, pedestrians, and mixed uses in open spaces cluttered up "the pregnant present." Street corridors had to disappear and be replaced with freeways. Like garden cities, town and countryside were to be planned in conjunction. But unlike Howard, Le Corbusier appealed to the state, at a moment when public services were expanding. Recalling nineteenth-century modern planning, the new

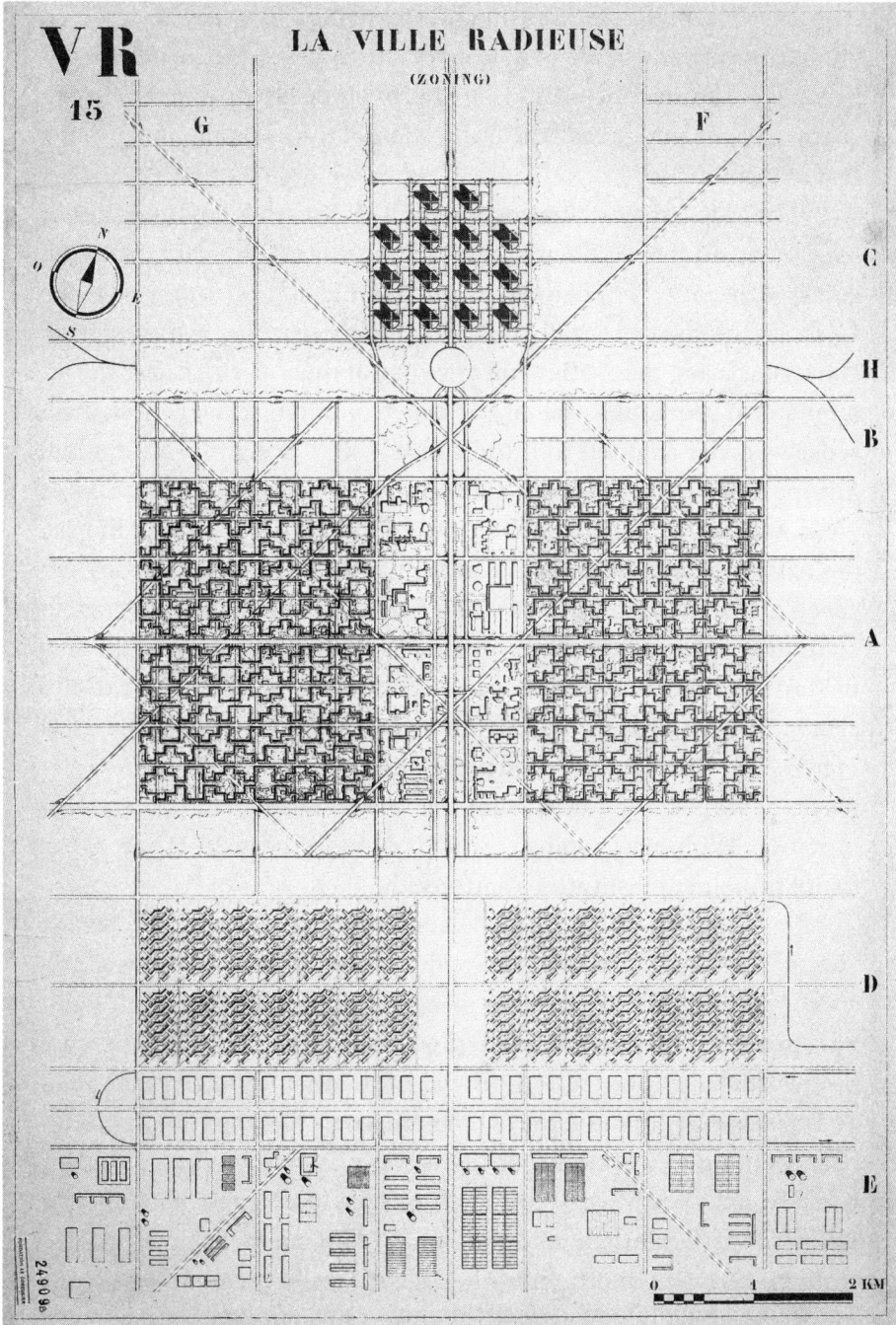

FIGURE 5.20. Zoning for the Radiant City. All buildings have an assigned place and function in this orderly "civilization of the automobile."

doctrines prized functionalism and rationality. But they rejected an urban composition made of rigid symmetries and street corridors with sidewalks. The ideal city would have tall buildings set apart in vast green spaces, strict zoning, and "the civilization of the automobile replacing that of the railroad."[159]

By the 1930s, major cities no longer had discernible boundaries or self-contained shapes. Their metropolitan areas extended into junction cities, with pockets of density around rail hubs. In *Aircraft* (1935), Le Corbusier reaffirmed the planning possibilities enabled by seeing from above, declaring that "cities will arise out of their [own] ashes." He attempted to reorganize the city at a metropolitan scale, conferring a sense of order adapted to futures in transit. Though he always had European cities in sight, the dynamic and explosive urbanization of Latin America provided more fertile ground for his doctrines. In 1937, the Argentine architects Juan Kurchan and Jorge Ferrari Hardoy engaged Le Corbusier to devise a new master plan for Buenos Aires. In contrast to the 1925 plan, they sought to subordinate *barrios* in the spatial order, so that they functioned as peripheral "satellites" to the city center. This required razing dense neighborhoods for the construction of freeways. The plan proposed more than tripling the extension of city blocks to around 400 yards, a dimension seen as adequate for car transportation. With strict zoning, it would reinforce the historic core as the site of prominent institutions and wealth.

Introducing the plan, Le Corbusier crowed that "a formidable destiny awaits" the city that he had deemed hopeless. Buenos Aires was still "sicker than any other city," after many errors during a period of "lightning growth."[160] His modern methods would save it. The plans were never officially adopted but proved influential. In later years, Juan Perón's regime adopted some of their proposals for social housing. Kurchan went on to work on another master plan in 1971, under military rule. The locations of a new university campus, the airport, and freeways followed the Corbusian blueprint. They often cut through traditional working-class neighborhoods. And after redevelopment projects in the 1990s, a version of the Business City sprung up in the skyscrapers lining the River Plate in Puerto Madero. In 2022, the documentary *A Plan for*

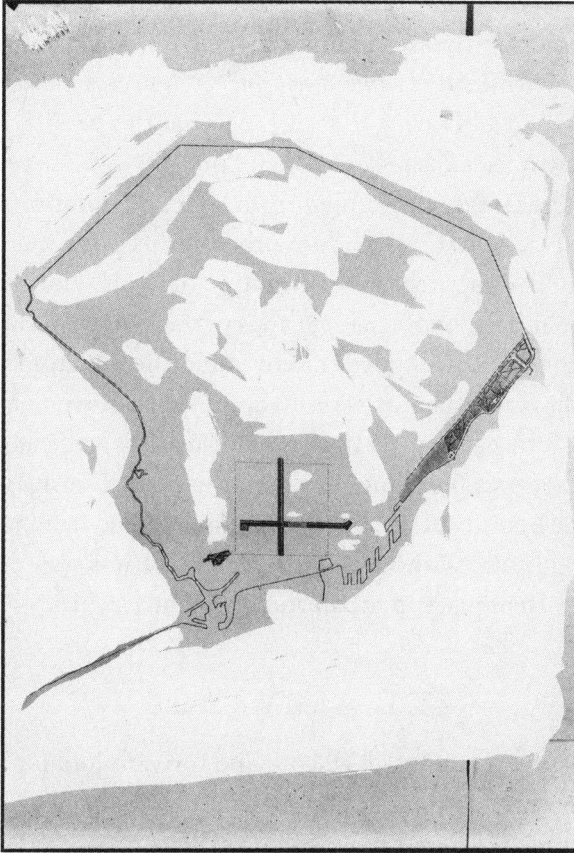

FIGURE 5.21. Hardoy and Le Corbusier's vision reasserts the city center, with intersecting roads: again, a cross to propel futures.

Buenos Aires looked back on the twists and turns of Le Corbusier's relationship to the Argentine capital. The film, featuring prominent designers and scholar, testifies to how we cannot dismiss the enduring poetic appeal of Corbusian dreams. Unlike Ford, he understood that humans are more mysterious than assembly lines.

The period prior to the 1930s plans, to the historian Adrián Gorelik, could be characterized by the emergence of a "metropolitan public space" in Buenos Aires. He identifies "peculiar modes of territorial organization, cultural transformation, popular sociability, and urban policies" with collective horizons.[161] This possibility of a more egalitarian development process, centering the *barrios*, was disrupted by "the triumph of *modernization without reform*."[162] In 1930, a military coup had installed a dictator. During that decade, shanties proliferated—they became known as *villas miseria*. Social progressives lost ground and planning increasingly decoupled from shared aspirations of a more egalitarian society. Rather, modern urban forms provided a patina for development that privileged concentration of wealth and the reproduction of inequalities. An official 1981 atlas of the history of Buenos Aires, funded by the municipal government under the dictatorship, referred to the city's historic plans as part of a continuous movement toward an "irrevocable future seen from the eye of the planet's artificial satellite."[163] The motor age was blending into the space age. The sky was not the limit, but the bounds of what could be planned had flattened. For one, there was no future without the car. And the ethos was clear: people should know their place in urban and global hierarchies.

V. Divided We Stand

Italian fascists emulated the bellicose and forward-looking attitudes of Futurists, but also co-opted classical symbols. Rome, the Eternal City, had experienced ups and downs like perhaps no other Western metropolis. In the sixteenth century, the reforms of Pope Sixtus V already showed some lack of sentimentality toward the traditional urban fabric. They opened straight avenues through compact neighborhoods, to connect major churches. After becoming the capital of the United Kingdom of Italy in 1871, Rome underwent relatively modest renovations. In the new century, like Marinetti before him, Mussolini sought to seize the future. Italy's resurgence required bold reforms. Across the Atlantic, magazines published glowing reviews: plans for Rome recalled Haussmann, they claimed, and would "transmit to posterity a legacy that lived up to the past."[164] In the late 1920s, Mussolini's Forum and avenues leading to monuments could be hailed as the "most audacious project of the future."[165] Demolitions were inevitable. As Rome's fascist governor stated, the reforms embodied the "ideals of a modern era."[166] Wide avenues would act as backdrops to military processions instead of religious pilgrimages. And they would serve cars, while coexisting with the ruins of a glorious ancient empire.

Europe largely lagged the Americas in building architectural modernity. The pull of the past weighed heavy. It exerted enough pressure to keep skyscrapers from competing with historic domes and towers. Some Italian fascists sought to remedy that. In 1932, to a boisterous crowd, Mussolini inaugurated the Piazza della Vittoria in Brescia, showcasing one of Europe's tallest modern skyscrapers at the time, which he celebrated as a feat of "contemporary history."[167] Built in reinforced concrete, it could have belonged in any number of American downtowns. The architect was Marcello Piacentini, a Fascist favorite. He went on to design a tower for a São Paulo oligarch in the 1930s and directed plans for the 1942 World's Fair in Rome, following an orthogonal layout and modernist principles. World War II derailed them.

Berlin had one of the most significant concentrations of modern high-rises in the Old World. Even its skyline could not compare with American cities. The German capital was ahead of the curve in building a highway system, a project that Hitler particularly favored but that drew support from other corners. In Germany, both left-leaning Bauhaus-affiliated modernist designers and their Nazi detractors sought urban renewal. The desire to catch up, however, was by no means a consensus. Rather, as nativism and the scapegoating of minorities surged, leaders and planners on both sides of the Atlantic aligned around the goal of curating *who* belonged in the future. Urban policies for segregating ethnic groups undergirded nationalist politics. Rendering the right to the city as exclusive was a growing facet of modernization. Mussolini's regime, following Nazi Germany, began to institute "racial laws" in 1938, restricting the rights of Africans and Jews. The latter were banned from prestigious positions and had their properties taken away.

Many opposed biological racism, sometimes as an intrusion of "Nordicism." Fascist focus had been on persecuting socialists. Now, restricting access to spaces based on race and ethnicity became a growing component of rigid compartmentalization, and a feature of the modern order. After World War I, nation-states ramped up the implementation of mechanisms to regulate movement, requiring passports and policing borders.[168] A period of extraordinary migration began to end—between the 1840s and the 1930s, as much as 10 percent of the global population moved to a different country, over 55 million of them across the Atlantic.[169] Xenophobia always simmered, sometimes boiling over into anti-immigrant outbursts, and several states tried to curtail movement, often targeting nonwhite diasporas.[170] In the 1920s, as the prestige of racist science increased, especially eugenics, so did the legal barriers on the ability of poorer people to seek a new life abroad. In the United States, the 1924 Immigration Act instituted quotas based on national origins, and the inflow of migrants plunged.

Likewise, more cities adopted segregationist policies. In the US South, Jim Crow continued to shape social life. The country experienced the first wave of the Great Migration between 1910 and 1940. Around 1.6 million African Americans moved from the countryside to Northern cities. In industrial Chicago, they approached 10 percent of the population by World War II. The Midwestern metropolis had spaced-out skyscrapers, elevated rail, and car-oriented plans. This role as a pioneering modern city extended to serving as a laboratory for segregation. African Americans fled the Ku Klux Klan and fear of lynching. In the North, they still faced rampant discrimination. Segregation was never just about spatial separation. It was also about exclusion from labor markets and resources. Segregationist laws could subordinate and humiliate people, effectively denying them a right to the future.

The long history of ethnic and racial prejudice in the Atlantic world inspired visions for the future among Nazi–fascists and some modern planners. Hitler looked toward the United States as a precedent for a multitiered society that subjugated minorities.[171] Nativist, classist, and antiurban politics had been enmeshed for decades. A couple generations earlier, a prominent US ambassador had associated universal suffrage for men with "dangerous classes" and Communism, locating the origin of the threat in "the slums of European cities."[172] By the 1930s, a modern city informed by eugenics science could hope to segregate races and ethnic groups as "rationally" as it separated industrial and residential uses, or speeding cars and pedestrians.[173] Precise contours differed.

Latin Americans and French planners veered toward a more old-fashioned Lamarckian understanding of evolution, based on the possibility of improvement. Under the right environmental circumstances, through heavy-handed and top-down methods, inferior groups could be bettered. This either kept racial hierarchies intact or reinforced them. In the United States, an understanding of race rooted in Mendelian genetics maintained that putatively superior blood stock had to be protected.

Modern planning tapped into reactionary aspirations, but on the ground, realities were often messier and more contingent. The boundaries of who should have a place in the future remained contested, and conservative pushback often came in response to progressive change. The Nazi–fascist investment in masculinity and male control of public spaces occurred as the rights of women expanded, for example. Decades of concerted feminist efforts accelerated in the 1920s and 1930s, with women able to vote in Canada, Germany, Uruguay, the United States, the UK, and Brazil. Other countries followed suit (in France and Argentina, only after World War II). Urban planning remained a male-dominated field.

Similar struggles over citizenship and belonging also shaped debates on migration. Growing restrictions could coincide with openness toward political inclusion. In the years leading up to the 1924 Immigration Act in the United States, a series in the *Ladies' Home Journal* captured some of the interplay between foreignness, assimilation, and urbanization. Assuming growth to be limitless, the magazine preferred towns to industrial cities. They advocated for planning as an instrument to turn immigrants into "future Americans." Dirty alleyways and maze-like streets hindered "the spiritual process of Americanization," which required "souls that look out of windows that open onto American streets."[174] The dream of a wide and leafy street echoed the garden cities of tomorrow and anticipated Corbusian modernism. Here, integration implied a set of social services: English classes, garbage removal, sanitation, and relatable religious leaders. The magazine's writers wanted immigrant women to have "*less work*" and "a chance to live." Their vision did not require extracting fun from functionalism. Parties mattered: "an

hour's rollicking fun" was presented as a far more effective Americanization program than civics lessons.

In the United States, these optimistic narratives contained seeds of
the idea of a nation of immigrants. They also hinted at the backlash
against cities as foreign, and the expectation that spatial dispersion was
compatible with an American ethos. The *Ladies' Home Journal* authors,
at the same time, could not imagine the amount of space that cars and
government-backed mortgages would open for sprawl. Redlining
deemed dense urban areas as riskier for investment. Suburbanization
became a tool for segregation and for a more inclusive whiteness, incorporating groups that had been discriminated against like the Irish. The
future offered homeownership as the basis of wealth, family, and community. But suburbanization mostly barred non-Eurocentric groups,
especially African Americans, from the dreams of a white-picket-fenced
house. The plan was to keep them from joining in the fun.

Housing policies and real estate practices helped to reproduce inequalities during the 1920s and 1930s.[175] Residents of white suburbs
received more favorable terms for mortgages. The prospect of racial integration generated fears of decline in property values, creating a self-
fulfilling prophecy. Whites had financial incentives to leave the city and
to exclude others from their new neighborhoods. Lenders discriminated against the urban neighborhoods accessible to colored people.
Poverty and racialized minorities became segregated in central areas,
while homeownership in subsidized suburbs served as a basis for wealth
creation. This helped to set the terms of political disputes and future-
making in the United States well into the twenty-first century.

Just as in the rest of the Americas, however, Afro-descendants carved
out places for themselves in US cities. Isabel Wilkerson's *The Warmth of
Other Suns* (2010) tells the "epic story" of the Great Migration, full of
wounds, survival, and reinvention. African American relationships to
the future had qualities all their own. A gas station owner could put a
shotgun to your head, to make sure you waited until all the white patrons got served first. Being a parent might mean having to explain to
your child why they were barred from a playground. Wilkerson shows
how pathways were not linear, but people found ways of making better

lives in urban environments. One of the book's subjects, Ida Mae Gladney, left rural Mississippi, where a family member was almost killed after
being accused of stealing a turkey. She migrated to Chicago, working
domestic jobs before settling into a career as a hospital aide. Even with
the added obstacles, Gladney managed to buy a home in the city's South
Side.

In interviews during the Great Depression, formerly enslaved people
could show some sense of optimism. One woman said, "I think the
future looks bright," despite the "pretty bad" ways of youngsters. Another person with a positive outlook on the future of race relations did
not see "much dark days ahead." A third praised F.D.R., who "lets every-
body git somethin'," including the poor.[176] Paul Laurence Dunbar,
whose parents had been enslaved, described the national capital with
ambivalence: "taking it all in all and after all, negro life in Washington
is a promise rather than a fulfillment." He continued: "But it is worthy
of note for the really excellent things which are promised."[177] Even
when promises remained out of reach, Dunbar suggests, they could
open possibilities. But he also dispelled illusions. Early in the century
he wrote *The Sport of the Gods* (1902), a novel where black migrants
from the South sought to make it in New York. They largely met with
tragedy in the big city.

A generation later, sites for the projection of urban dreams shifted
from the stage to the screen, increasing their reach. In 1920, Jessie Redmon Fauset wrote a story called "The Sleeper Wakes" (1920), where a
young African American woman moved to New York.[178] Influenced by
the movies, she knew the city was "the place for her," and had "no fear
of her future." At first, city life fulfilled its promise as a platform for
chance encounters. Among strangers, the character could pass as white.
She networked and thrived, until it became clear that racism was not
confined to the South. Though fictional stories by African American
authors are seldom about happy endings in urban settings, they nonetheless suggest a widening range of possibilities in an urbanizing world.

During this period, even aesthetic reactionaries chose to present
themselves as forward-looking. In architecture, some detractors of modernism upheld tradition for posterity's sake. They feared that there

would not be any of the past left in the future. Unadorned and generic towers in the International Style posed a threat to authentic national communities. In this view, modern technologies should be part of design, but not modernist architecture.[179] Such critiques became footnotes in the history of design but held sway in groups as divergent as white supremacists, Soviets, and Nazi–fascists. Other times, to safeguard a perceived past, visions for the future converged around the violent reshaping of built environments with little regard for what or who stood in the way.

In Latin America, technocrats and political leaders also articulated ideal futures that assigned people to a place in a global order, even if notions of racial purity generally had less appeal in "miscegenated" societies. José Vasconcelos, a prominent intellectual and influential education minister in Mexico during the 1920s, envisioned Iberian–American societies as "the final race, the cosmic race."[180] The world's dominant metropolis, Universópolis, would be in the Amazon. Vasconcelos imagined the evolutionary selection of the best racial traits culminating in a high-tech and aesthetically superior city. It would rise in contrast with Anglotown, which symbolized decline, following Spengler's predictions. In office, Vasconcelos supported literacy programs and cultural nationalism. He rejected positivism, in favor of modernization based on racial development, fusing practical knowledge with spirituality. Latin American *mestizaje* ideologies celebrated mixture, while sometimes incorporating eugenics and maintaining racist hierarchies. Those with more forward-looking projects, like Vasconcelos, tended to admire the Nazi–fascist capacity for mobilization.

Nazi Germans embraced the idea of blood purity and racial hierarchy with uncommon zeal, and dreamed of a new Berlin that might reflect aspirations for the future. Their vision took the idea of capitals as metonymic of nations to extremes. Earlier German planning had prioritized expansion over remodeling. The Nazis broke from that. Berlin would be rebuilt as Germania, designed by Albert Speer under Hitler's direction. They scoffed at contemporary cities, instead inviting comparisons to Ancient Egypt and Rome. But the scales seemed out of science fiction. A 3-mile central axis would culminate in the Volkshalle, the People's Hall.

FIGURE 5.22. Model for "Germania," with a monumental hall for huge crowds.

Inspired by the Roman Pantheon, the oculus of the dome itself would be larger than the St. Peter's Basilica in the Vatican. Its height rivaled Manhattan's Chrysler building. Inside, around 180,000 people would be able to attend speeches by the Third Reich leader. Bigger was better, but only for those entitled to the future. Germania was never built.

In 1940, the Nazi sympathizer Anne Morrow Lindbergh published *The Wave of the Future* in the United States. She was married to the popular aviator Charles Lindbergh, a vocal supporter of the anti-interventionist America First movement. Referring to Communism, Fascism, and Nazism, she asked: "what will the historian, looking back on us from the distant future, think of these movements?"[181] Lindbergh suggested that future scholars might understand Hitler in the same way that her contemporaries glazed over the "atrocities" of the leaders of the French Revolution. As "a nation who pinned its faith on dreams rather than on memories," the United States should understand Nazi victory as inevitable.[182] She predicted: "the wave of the future is coming and there is no way of fighting it."[183] The first part was right, but the second was wrong.

6

After the Future?
(1940s Onward)

LAGOS + BRASÍLIA, SUBURBIA,
ALGIERS, DAKAR, THE PACIFIC RIM,
AND MORE.

I. We Were Never Modernist

World War II caused some 80 million deaths. After the Holocaust, two atomic bombs, and the most widespread military conflict in history, where could the future go? In 1951, Hannah Arendt wrote that "never has our future been more unpredictable." The defeat of the Axis powers was followed by "the anticipation of a third World War." She decried the "reckless optimism" and the "reckless despair" of contemporaries. Five years later, Theodor Adorno claimed that "the horror is that for the first time we live in a world in which we can no longer imagine a better one." Both had Jewish backgrounds and moved from Germany to the United States. In coming years, they would witness bombarded cities rebuilt, booming economic prosperity, and roaring countercultures. The Space Race launched a Soviet satellite into orbit in 1957 and American men to the moon in 1969. Back on earth, as politics polarized, urbanization proceeded with automobility as a north star. New computing technologies led to an era of predictive sciences, creating sophisticated models to analyze and influence traffic flows, consumer behaviors, electoral strategies, and riot prevention. To "data diviners" and "electronic prophets," never had the future been so malleable.[1]

In the North Atlantic, the aftermath of the war sped up the trajectory toward decentralization, regearing industrial capacity to build infrastructures for suburban "total living," especially in the United States (see figure 6.1).[2] As professional specializations consolidated, modernist architects and designers gained prominence in academia and media, but lost power to engineers and social scientists. The imagination of the cities of tomorrow remained as wide-ranging and wild as it had been in the interwar period, but economic and cultural forces overdetermined the victory of cars. Nonetheless, history continued to elude anyone's anticipations. A series of shocks and crises frayed any possibility of a lasting consensus. Visions for the future fractured and multiplied in developments from decolonization movements in the Global South to deindustrialization in the North, or from the fall of the Soviet Union to the War on Terror; in evolving communications from television to smart phones; and more narrowly in urban settings, from the oil shortages of the 1970s to the reclaiming of spaces from cars and energy transitions. The overarching story of ever-growing cities, in the meantime, moved out of the North Atlantic. You could find the future riding the metropolitan subway in Seoul, an SUV in Dubai, or an e-bike in Bogotá.

Urbanization in the Global South has surpassed expectations and precedents. Like Lisbon, New York, Paris, Rio de Janeiro, and Buenos Aires before it, Lagos stands at the crossroads of invented futures. Between 1950 and 2020, its population increased more than 40-fold. Within a lifetime, the Nigerian hub evolved from a small town into a sprawling megalopolis of over 21 million. The official boundaries cover about 450 square miles, an area around 20 times larger than Manhattan's. In any given year during the twenty-first century, as many people moved to Lagos as the entire population of Lisbon in 1755. Several of the challenges faced in Lagos and counterparts are familiar from the history of planning, including pressures on ecosystems, housing, congestion, and socioeconomic inequities. But their scale is new: the management of sewage, transportation, health, security, and education involve populations greater than those of large countries from the nineteenth century, or small countries today.

Africa concentrates the future of urbanization. There are some continuities in the micro-futures of migrants pursuing better lives, from London in the 1800s to Lagos, Luanda, or London in the 2000s. For the poorest, the best-case scenario for urbanization often relies on self-built constructions, improvised mobility in minibuses, vans, or motorcycles, and infrastructures yet to be built. The dynamics of planning macrofutures changed, but large-scale projects continue to matter. Our planet's welfare hinges on how megalopolises develop, perhaps particularly in sub-Saharan Africa. To be more specific: how will they achieve higher living standards? Can the pressures of local elites for investments oriented toward car-centric gated communities be overcome? Will the most ecologically predatory legacies of transatlantic modernist planning prevail?

We will return to contemporary Lagos as a fitting anchor to the latest chapter in the history of urban futures. It may already be the largest metropolitan area in transatlantic history. Back in 1947, New York City had the dubious honor. There, some modernists sought to position themselves for whatever new order might emerge after the war. That year, Le Corbusier wrote a letter to his mother announcing "total Victory."[3] Harry Truman had used the same phrase to declare the end of World War II. To the US president, it was a time of celebration, but the future remained precarious: "Civilization cannot survive another total war."[4] When Truman announced the defeat of Germany, he explained that their forces "surrendered to the United Nations."[5] The victorious organization went on to build its headquarters in Manhattan. That was the subject of Le Corbusier's gloating: "The World City is being built in New York on my ideas."[6] Privately, he had written to his mother early in the war that Hitler could lead to the better organization of Europe, with "each nation in its place."[7] Now, the design of the UN building seemed to offer even higher stakes. He predicted that once this news became public, everyone would see "the Corbu explosion everywhere."[8]

Le Corbusier turned out to be mostly wrong about the particulars. The UN building was designed instead by a committee coordinated by

Wallace Harrison, a US architect with strong ties to powerful stakeholders like Nelson Rockefeller. A younger designer emerged in the process:
the Brazilian Communist Oscar Niemeyer. Le Corbusier, who clearly
wanted sole authorship of the project, experienced this as a personal
defeat.[9] His prediction of a Corbu explosion, however, proved to be
prescient. In the postwar decades, planners throughout the world
adopted modernist Corbusian principles. They privileged not just cars
but also detached towers, rejecting traditional street corridors in favor
of freeways. Le Corbusier's urban visions remained a dominant influence until at least the 1960s.

After his collaborations in Argentina, Le Corbusier devised new
plans for Algiers in 1942. As in Rio, he had proposed curvilinear highways on top of residential buildings during the early 1930s. The descriptions paid lip service to the "unforeseeable in life," but the planner still
ruled. Like more conventional competing proposals, it contained strict
zoning. The local council unanimously rejected the Corbu explosion.
His vision of Algiers as a "meeting point of Western and indigenous
civilizations" would fall out of favor.[10] Throughout the Atlantic world,
the language of urbanization as an expression of *civilization* gave place
to discourse around *development*.[11] Increasingly, instead of aspiring for
fixed ideal models, progress consisted of a dynamic process of incremental improvements. Algerians achieved independence from France
in 1962, after almost eight years of war. Few looked back on Le Corbusier's plans for the capital, but modernist templates held sway, from
the design of public housing to the layout of highways. Urbanization in
Algiers, as elsewhere in the Global South, largely consisted of collec-
tively self-built neighborhoods inhabited by poor migrants from the
countryside. Such *informal* or *organic* growth had been common
throughout urban history. It now occurred, however, at a faster pace,
larger scale, and coeval with modernist planning.

Expanding metropolitan areas increasingly exceeded municipal
boundaries, leaving city authorities with weakened hands. In earlier
decades, national or imperial leaders had empowered planners to transform city centers. Now, focus turned more toward urbanization as an
engine of development, instead of capital cities showcasing civilized

"After total war can come total living"

FIGURE 6.1. After the war, which dreams are over? For who?

ideals. Postwar governments tended to subordinate planning to broader national interests. Meanwhile, the near-total victories of the nation-state and the car narrowed the range of possibilities for organizing societies spatially. Corbusian modernist forms became useful tools to plan cities for those outside them: freeways privileged those leaving to the suburbs. In concert, profits from vertical growth and motor vehicles often flowed there too.

Paradigms of modernity shifted from Europe to the United States, and from New York to Los Angeles. In Europe, governments rebuilt cities after the war.[12] Across the Atlantic, they razed buildings to make space for cars to move (and park) more freely. North American suburbanization proceeded with fewer constraints as growth moved toward the Pacific. During the 1950s, the United States produced around three-quarters of the cars in the world. Numbers doubled during that decade.[13] The future had arrived, leaving the Old World in the dust. From São Paulo to Lagos, migrants continued to chase aspirations in crowded sidewalks. Yet to be modern meant not just being in a city but driving a car. Walking the streets of New York for the first time in 1952, Drita Ivanaj's family, Albanian–Italian migrants, was not awed by the skyscrapers. Maybe they had become familiar from movie screens. Rather, she recalled: "What impressed my mother mostly was the fact that there were more cars than people practically."[14]

———

Europe's reduction in global affairs reflected in transatlantic urbanization. In his history of postwar Europe, Tony Judt describes "the withering away of [. . .] 'master narratives'" with "models of progress and change or revolution and transformation."[15] Master narratives and master plans could still endure, and so did the influence of many European planners. Yet the planning profession no longer looked readily to Europe for models. "Old" Europe, Judt writes, had been "an intricate, interwoven tapestry of overlapping languages, religions, communities and nations."[16] Between the wars, that was destroyed. The historian quotes the Hungarian-born Arthur Koestler, who lived through the disillusionment with Soviet Communism: "what an enormous longing for a new human order there was in the era between the world wars, and what a miserable failure to live up to it." Of course, authoritarian movements and total wars had also found nourishment in the period's longings. In contrast, the welfare programs and cooperative institutions built in postwar Europe did not result from a future-oriented impetus. Rather than fueled by optimism, Judt argues, social reforms responded to insecurity and anxiety, "as a prophylactic to keep the past at bay."

The futured had moved. After visiting Petrograd and Moscow in 1919, a US journalist critical of municipal corruption described his impressions: "I have seen the future, and it works." He later became

disenchanted with the Soviet Union. In the 1950s, a newspaper columnist used the same famous quip to praise suburban shopping malls in
the United States.[17] Metropolitan areas throughout Europe tried to
catch up, adding arteries and ringways. Postwar dueling plans opted for
a more "compact city" in East Berlin, versus the "international style"
with vertical slabs and sprawling freeways in the West.[18] In the late
1950s, the petrochemical company town of Mourenx in France also
followed the modernist blueprint, styling itself as "Tomorrow Paris."
Ambitious motorways planned for Paris and London would face roadblocks, including protests, and remained largely on paper.

Throughout Africa and Asia, in the meantime, forward-looking
independence movements sought ruptures with the Eurocentric past.
The revolutionary Frantz Fanon, for example, highlighted the importance of hope and "opening up new horizons" to liberation struggles.[19]
But when he and others referred to *shaping* the future, they rarely considered the actual forms of cities. In practice, postcolonial urban development would prove captive to path-dependence, saddled by limited
economic resources and leverage. The design scholar Ijlal Muzaffar,
focusing on case studies in the Third World, describes this as "development without capital."[20] He shows how, in the decades after World
War II, architecture and urban planning served to project an image of
modernity and progress while concealing structural inequities, colonial
legacies, and a lack of funds.

In many of the fastest-growing cities, inadequate housing and transit
infrastructures led to self-built neighborhoods. A shack closer to jobs
could be preferable to an arduous commute from distant peripheries,
usually by bus. Settling on the outskirts of a city was often the only alternative for newcomers. Even in 1950s Paris, migrants from the French
countryside and North Africa moved to shanties far off from the city
center. Spatial segregation went beyond Haussmannian dreams. Mass-
built modernist public housing helped to address shortages, but rarely
kept up.

During the 1960s, modernist solutions began to lose favor among
urban planners. So did the profession's authority to drive and implement
visions. Whatever fantasies Corbusian modernists entertained about the

future, the planner never really ruled anyhow. In much of the world, ideological opponents converged around automobiles as both a symbol of progress and a vehicle for states to pursue growth. Suburban dispersion followed jobs in new industrial plants. Stark differences aside, Cold War rivals promoted development. Economic productivity relied on the vast chains of motor and oil industries, at the same time as the spatial imagination of the future continued to become less compact and more extended. Modernist ideals gave cover to these transformations but did not necessarily propel them. The Corbusian victory had more to do with structural conditions than with seductive powers.

II. Which Dreams Are Over?

In 1956, *Time* magazine published a cover with an image of the recently inaugurated Brazilian president Juscelino Kubitschek.[21] He had campaigned on "Fifty Years' Progress in Five," with a plan to transition from an agrarian to an industrial economy. In the background, a map of Brazil juxtaposing urban skylines in the south to the forested north foreshadowed the utopian capital of Brasília. Located near the country's geographic center, the new city was part of a project to build a network of roads to develop the hinterlands. Lúcio Costa led the planning, with Oscar Niemeyer as the architect of striking modern buildings blending glass, white façades, and curved forms. They largely followed a Corbusian blueprint. With wide freeways, the city would be a paradise for drivers. It lacked corridor streets or enclosed squares. Based on a cross, the plan bent the North–South axis, evoking an airplane. The main thoroughfares converged in an interstate bus station at the heart of the city. Planners organized functions along CIAM lines, with separated zones for housing, work, transportation, and recreation. Brasília brought together two key facets of contemporary planning: a capital symbolically ushering in the modern future, and national development centering the car.

Brazil's new capital could be understood as the culmination of a dream dating back to the early days of the urban boom in Europe: an efficient, rational, and beautiful city planned for posterity. In 1960, the

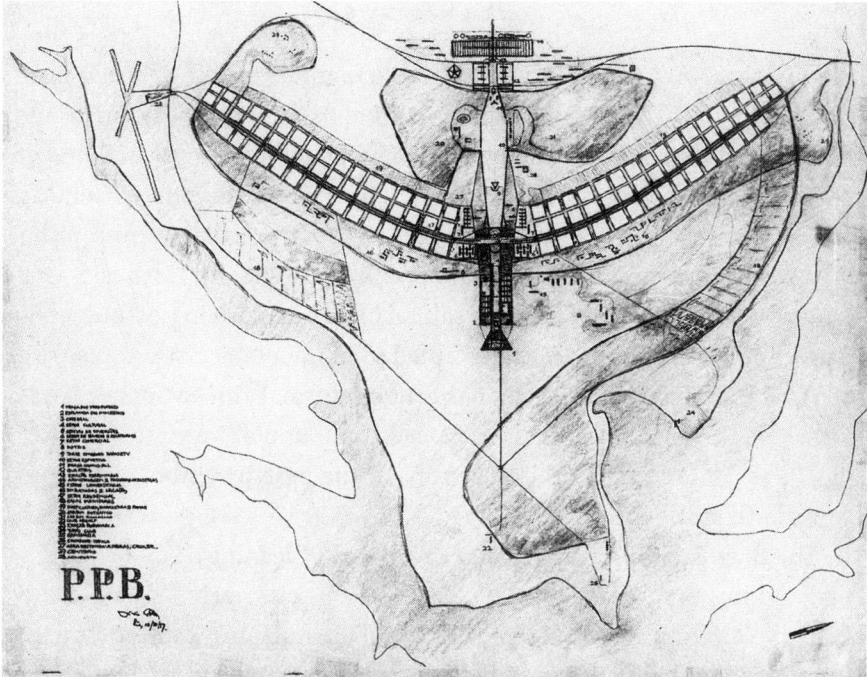

FIGURE 6.2. Brasília's Plan, with strict zoning. An airplane? Another cross.

FIGURE 6.3. The future arrived, with glorious architecture and a lot of asphalted surfaces.

glossy magazine *O Cruzeiro* hailed the inauguration: "The Future now has its capital." This recalled a famous title from 1941 by the Austrian-born Stefan Zweig. After fleeing the Nazis, he published *Brazil, Land of the Future*. Now, the tropical country could "leave behind time itself," as "Brasília jumps over the twentieth century."[22] The article went on: the city was "the encounter with the future." In the 1950s, Le Corbusier had collaborated on the new Punjabi capital of Chandigarh in postindependence India. The project also attempted to fulfill modernist promises by starting from scratch rather than through reform. Prime Minister Jawaharlal Nehru, an anticolonial icon, used comparable language: Chandigarh was "unfettered by the traditions of the past, a symbol of the nation's faith in the future."[23]

The Brazilian capital had been a dream of left-leaning utopian designers, and it was supposed to be a city without class privileges. Yet the history of planning is once again a story about unintended consequences. Population grew faster than projected, and national inequalities quickly asserted themselves. Poor migrants from the countryside settled in makeshift "satellite cities," while well-connected and mostly white transplants from urban areas took over modern apartment blocks meant to be egalitarian. A military coup in 1964 led to more than two decades of dictatorship. The city's dispersion proved resistant to popular dissent. With the new capital as a node, the right-wing regime developed roads connecting coastal cities and the Amazon. These have served as vectors for deforestation and the decimation of Amerindian societies.

In 1960, as upscale magazines celebrated Brasília's inauguration, others already saw it as a failure. In design, a field as rife with rivalries as any, Corbusian visions were losing cachet. A younger set of CIAM participants challenged modernist orthodoxies. Le Corbusier left the organization in the mid-1950s, and it dissolved in 1959. The tide in planning was turning. Cars had never ceased having skeptics even as they became dominant.[24] Victor Gruen, the pioneering architect of shopping malls, championed walkability and repudiated car-oriented suburbanization.[25] In Brazil, a self-taught modern urban designer, Lota Macedo Soares, saw cars as "the greatest enemy of beauty and comfort in a great city."[26] In 1961, Jane Jacobs opened *The Death and Life of Great American Cities* in a fighting spirit: "This book is an attack on current city planning and rebuilding." It became a seminal defense of walkable and compact cities with diverse uses. And in 1962, Lewis Mumford wrote that "Le Corbusier's image of the city is still often regarded as the last word in modern design."[27] He did not mean that as praise. Mumford criticized excessively spaced-out buildings, standardized design, and mechanization. Soon enough, Joni Mitchell would sing about how "they paved paradise to put up a parking lot."

Several planners came to understand that an urban future without pedestrian life would represent a major loss. That included Josep Lluís Sert, who worked with Le Corbusier, served as CIAM president (1947–1956), and became dean of the Harvard Graduate School of Design (1953–1969). CIAM alums and dissidents promoted debates drawing lessons from past mistakes, experimenting with new methods, and incorporating knowledge from non-Western cultures as well as fields like botany, mathematics, literature, and anthropology. Team Ten in Europe and the Metabolism movement in Japan embraced cities as ever-changing and streets as sites of vitality. They favored flexibility and connections over finality and separations. Further afield from CIAM, with ties to London's Architectural Association and avant-garde art scenes, the Archigram collective envisioned high-tech modular structures, pitting colorful pop aesthetics and indeterminacy against functionalism. Like them, the revolutionary Situationist International valued chance encounters in urban spaces, but to counter the alienation of capitalist consumer society. These groups left a rich legacy of unbuilt plans or bold site-specific projects, influencing design education and exciting theorists in much of the world. In practice, state bureaucrats and private investors held more sway.

Critics and advocates of modernist planning tend to overestimate the impact of designers. Policies encouraging urban growth and industrialization had been a key component of broader political projects aiming to free poorer nations from underdevelopment, in postwar parlance. In Latin America, that too came under scrutiny during the 1960s. Dependency theory, influential in the social sciences, posited that resources from the economic peripheries further enriched the developed core, locking them in relationships of exploitation. Among intellectuals, urban discourse began to focus less on modernization, and more on how cities reproduced structural inequities. By the 1980s, the countryside would be increasingly imagined as the setting for revolutionary processes capable of toppling the unjust Latin American social order.[28] Urban planning and design became less-relevant channels for utopian longings and egalitarian ideals. Comparable disillusionment happened throughout the Atlantic. In 1979, the demolition of Pruitt-Igoe, a set of CIAM-aligned public housing towers built during the 1950s in St. Louis, marked a symbolic ending. In the UK, the Margaret Thatcher era (1979–1990) represented a turn away from modernist architecture and its commitments to public housing.[29] Large-scale government-funded modernist projects were deemed to have failed. Architects and planners often got the blame, even when the shortcomings involved mismanagement or dynamics beyond their control.

———

Other aspects of modernist dreams lived on. In Futurama, General Motors had envisioned a car utopia, or what the architecture theorist Reyner Banham would call an *autopia*.[30] The 1939–1940 exhibit framed the "wonder world of 1960" as the culmination of an ongoing transformation. Scientists and engineers, based on "modern" and "pioneering" research, opened the way to "new horizons." Futurama displayed geometric and vertical cities, "replanned around a highly developed modern traffic system," surrounded by pastoral landscapes.[31] It was an interplay of fixity and flux. As one scholar puts it, "to drive [. . .] was to live motion without change."[32] For viewers, this modern future could be located anywhere familiar to them. The world of tomorrow still had "trees, hills and valleys, flowers and flowing streams." Futurama assured the audience that "these eternal things wrought by God are lovely and unchanging." By 1960, car-centric sprawl had obliterated many such ecosystems. Futurama II, held in the 1964–1965 New York World's Fair, touted "a future not of dreams, but of reality." It was set even further in time, in

2064. General Motors advertised images of the next frontiers: space exploration, submarine trains, and "forest highways" cutting through tropical jungles. For viewers, these were located in a remote place. The future could be even more dispersed, yet still under control.

Futurama II's "Tomorrow-land" heralded "abundance and a greater dignity for us all." On the one hand, hierarchies between nations might have been less explicit than in London's 1851 Great Exhibition, but they remained more-or-less intact. On the other, corporations could now also act as imagined communities. Here, the *us all* implied the universe of General Motors consumers. Although their utopias never quite materialized, GM's vehicles were already greatly impacting cities, social life, and economies. At the time, there was no larger company in the world. Like General Motors, between the 1950s and the 1990s the most valuable corporations in the United States had direct ties to the car industry.[33] This resulted from what we might call a suburbanization plan, at a scale that extended far beyond any single city: the US Federal-Aid Highway Act in 1956. Congress approved funding for 41,000 miles of highway networks. Partly inspired by the first Futurama and the German Autobahn, the Interstate Highway System set in motion perhaps the century's most significant public investment in infrastructure. Other nations took notice. The project proved more consequential to urban history than the spectacular modernist capitals of Chandigarh and Brasília.

Proponents of the Highway Act presented dispersal as a defense against the threat of Soviet bombings. In practice, the right to flee was nearly exclusive to white urbanites. Not all lives mattered. Jane Jacobs held "decentrist" planners as the main culprits in the "death" of great American cities. But the spatial reorganization of metropolitan regions had multiple political and economic causes.[34] Urban cores could not fulfill the needs of manufacturing plants, and housing followed jobs. Opponents of unionization and racial integration preferred suburbs because they made it harder to advance those efforts. Several corporate interests lined up. Adlai Stevenson, the Democratic nominee who lost national elections to war hero Dwight Eisenhower in 1952 and 1956, quipped that "the New Dealers have all left Washington to make way for the car dealers." Tax codes incentivized sprawling developments.[35]

FIGURE 6.4. Postwar, industries redirected efforts toward car infrastructure. Here the vision was still more Moses King than Robert Moses (1946).

Along with fossil fuel and motor industries, multiple companies found in postwar suburbanization an opportunity to create domestic markets, with government agencies as major customers. Cement and concrete associations lobbied for the construction of elevated freeways to allow for evacuation "in a time of emergency."[36] The Bohn Aluminum and

Brass Corporation proposed to solve traffic congestion in advertisements imagining futuristic cities. They showed highways stacked on top of each other, full of cars, all dependent on their products.

Mass media, in popular entertainment or advertisements, reflected and generated suburban desires. Firestone's "champion tires" campaign suggested a future where radical separation of functions and compartmentalization made life smoother and happier. The ads portrayed flying vehicles and highways leading to a vertical downtown (the urban workplace); highways in the countryside (the commute); a modernist house (the suburban home); a sports car on a beach (leisure in nature). A campaign by America's Independent Electric Light and Power Companies tapped into similar dreams. Two women and their dog ride on a personal flying vehicle to a detached house where ultrasonic waves wash dishes without soap or water: "the time isn't too far off, the experts say." Another depicted a family playing board games in a self-driving car on a highway. In a third, a man enjoys "future electric living" on a reclining chair, while a machine mows the lawn and gives the unruly hedges a rectilinear shape.[37] In the United States, this was not exclusive to mainstream or conformist cultures. Though written prior to the Highway Act, the publication of Jack Kerouac's On the Road (1957) would inspire readers to get behind the wheels in pursuit of freedom, meaning, or kicks.[38]

Individual vehicles replaced collective transportation. In the 1910s and 1920s, mass media had offered tantalizing visions of high-tech mass transit in compact cities. In the 1950s and 1960s, magazines and advertisements imagined flying saucers in suburbia. As cars became more of a common denominator, imagined futures tended to value private over public spaces. This anticipated shifts that helped define the rest of the century. Egalitarianism lost stock with modernist disappointments and anti-Communism. It also had to compete with shinier prospects. Futurama pitched "trees under individual glass houses." Mechanix Illustrated now depicted the suburban detached homes of tomorrow encased in glass domes. Nineteenth-century Crystal Palaces had been designed as popular attractions for the masses. Now, each nuclear family or consumer could aspire to their own. The future had changed, and could still sell well. Market segmentation became a feature of capitalism

FIGURE 6.5. Corporations absorb and accelerate modernist plans, with separation of functions and fewer "traffic hazards" (1945).

YOUR PERSONAL "FLYING CARPET" Step into it, press a button, and off you go to market, to a friend's home, or to your job. Take off and land anywhere; no parking problems. Plug in to any electric outlet for recharging. They're working on it!

MORE POWER TO YOU!

America's independent light and power companies build for your new electric living

Tomorrow's higher standard of living will put electricity to work for you in ways still unheard of!

The time isn't too far off, the experts say, when you'll wash your dishes without soap or water—ultrasonic waves will do the job. Your beds will be made at the touch of a button. The kids' homework will be made interesting and even exciting when they are able to dial a library book, a lecture or a classroom demonstration right into your home—with sound. (Some of this is happening already.)

To enjoy all this, you'll want a lot more electric power, and the independent electric companies of America are already building new plants and facilities to provide it. Right now these companies are building at the rate of $5,000,000,000 a year, and planning to double the nation's supply of electricity in less than 10 years.

America has always had the best electric power service in the world. The electric companies are resolved to keep it that way.

AMERICA'S INDEPENDENT ELECTRIC LIGHT AND POWER COMPANIES

Company names on request through this magazine

FIGURE 6.6. The Jetsons held a mirror to fantasies of high-tech appliances: personal "flying carpets" would pose "no parking problems" (1958).

FIGURE 6.7. Consumers could now aspire to their own Crystal Palace (1957).

beginning in the late 1950s. In these images, everyone is white. The American Dream knew no limits, for those that could afford it.

These affluent futures were not to be shared. The Interstate Highway System redistributed resources from cities to suburbs, reproducing social and racial hierarchies. Richard Nixon's first presidential campaign, in 1960, distributed a brochure with the heading "For the Future," pleading: "this is a time to think straight and make the right choice."[39] It showed a white family with the father surrounded by a doting wife and daughter. *Straight* now operated mostly as a metaphor. Shunning rectilinear grids, developers adopted curves for suburban roads to slow down cars without requiring them to stop, and layouts that discouraged drivers from passing through.[40] Critics of postwar suburbia see this as a story about complacency, conformity, and rampant individualism. Mass consumption, however, could also provide venues for people to exercise their citizenship and push for expanded rights.[41] In the United States, they often equated driving and freedom. To African Americans, cars could promise "an escape from the racialized structures of American society."[42] This was not necessarily a story of good versus evil. But it certainly had winners and losers.

Building the Interstate Highway System often entailed the destruction of compact urban communities, even if that was not the purpose of the 1956 Act. Funding provided by the 1949 Housing Act led to "slum clearance" and modernist housing projects. One of the first attempts at "urban renewal" was conducted in the US capital, evicting around 22,000 residents from black-majority neighborhoods in southwest Washington, DC. In most of these plans, engineers prevailed over planners and communities with a "traffic first" approach that neglected concerns and existing conditions.[43] Similar to how the Passos reforms in Rio de Janeiro destroyed sites connected to the fight for abolition, several new highways in the United States shattered places at the heart of Civil Rights struggles. This war on cities, a process that has been called *urbicide*, foreclosed possibilities opened by legal victories.[44] While the boundaries of civic inclusion expanded, new barriers went up. In several cities, white opposition to mass transit increased after racial segregation was outlawed.[45] Nominally race-blind investments in car infrastructure helped white suburbanites find ways to legally exclude minorities and benefit from rising home prices, as inner cities declined. The color line evolved into a color belt, at the metropolitan scale.

In the 1950s, the growth rate in the United States was ten times greater in suburbs than in cities. Between 1940 and 1960, homeownership rose from 42 percent to 62 percent.[46] The underwriting practices of the Federal Housing Administration privileged white Americans and discriminated against dense neighborhoods. The nation was on course toward growing racial wealth gaps and spatial segregation. Suburbanites became a majority in the 1970s. Cities, instead of serving as spaces onto which modernity was projected, became increasingly framed as doomed by intractable problems. In the suburban age, they were often places to be saved. The historian Lizabeth Cohen uses those terms in her book on the planner Edward Logue, active in redevelopment projects in the United States from the 1950s to the 1980s. The futurist and provocateur Buckminster Fuller had also accepted the premise. In the late 1950s, he proposed a geodesic dome over Midtown Manhattan. Rather than signal a glittering future, the glass membrane intended to control climate, helping to save the city by lowering the costs of heating, cooling, and snow removal. An urban crisis served as the backdrop, with cities losing wealthier residents and resources to the suburbs.

Robert Moses, the most emblematic US planner of the period, sought to relegate multiethnic and mixed-use Manhattan to the past. He saw himself as an heir of Haussmann and Le Corbusier. His griping made it clear who was not worthy of the right to urban futures: "They expect me to build playgrounds for that scum floating up from Puerto Rico."[47] Moses sought to reorient metropolitan New York around the car and social hierarchies. Eventually, he would be cast as the villain against the sidewalk champion Jane Jacobs. In 2021, a musical called *Straight Line Crazy* told the Robert Moses story to sold-out audiences at an upscale stage in New York. The title implied that, by the twenty-first century, the rectilinear biases of Pombaline plans and Nixon's campaign had definitely lost their hegemony in lettered cultures. It is worth noting that while Moses desired linear highways cutting through the jumbled streetscapes of Lower Manhattan, he implemented sinuous landscapes in picturesque roads and parks for prosperous white sub-urbs. Robert Moses took from his predecessors not an attachment to particular forms, but an understanding of urbanization at metropolitan scales—and he used it to further segregation.

Public urban spaces ceased being key denominators for the sanc-tioned futures of powerful stakeholders. During the Cold War, the lan-guage of a "city on a hill" made a comeback, elevating the United States as a beacon of hope while actual cities declined. Intellectuals of the Chicago School of Sociology had predicted a downtrend of urban cen-ters, influencing government funding decisions in a self-fulfilling proph-ecy.[48] And gone were the days of robber barons supporting municipal library systems. The social infrastructure of cities crumbled; crime in-creased. Fuller had imagined a viable future Manhattan in a bubble. In fact, however, US cities continued to host diverse populations and to burst through any fantasies of homogeneity. They helped to nurture the countercultures and student movements of the 1960s, expanding the limits of the thinkable in clothing, music, and behavior. Feminism thrived. More liberal immigration policies and the second Great Migra-tion of African Americans transformed the demographics and social fabric of US cities. As the historian A. K. Sandoval-Strausz shows in Barrio America, Latin American migrants "saved" cities like Chicago from a tailspin of population loss and disinvestment.[49]

In many cities, diverse coalitions organized to protect their urban communities from being demolished for highways or new develop-ments, with some success.[50] African Americans understood that "urban renewal" often meant "negro removal." In the late 1960s, a pamphlet protested: "White Man's Road . . . thru Black Man's Home!"[51] Govern-ment was a driving force but could also curb excesses. President Eisen-hower, for example, signed a law that prevented turning a monumental Greek Revival building in Washington, DC, into a parking lot—and it went on to house the National Portrait Gallery and American Art Mu-seum. Under Lyndon Johnson's administration, funding for mass transit increased, but it was too late. Decades of pent-up frustrations with bad service did not help: the business model of streetcars, for example, had relied on profits from real estate and utilities rather than transportation.

FIGURE 6.8. Jokinen's Amsterdam would not have become a biking city.

With reduced demand, dozens of transit companies stopped operating. Across the Atlantic, Corbusian and Moses-style proposals proliferated, like the 1967 Jokinen Plan for Amsterdam. Funded by the car lobby and created by a US planner, it purported to "give the city a chance." Fierce opposition derailed the project. Some European countries retained a compact urban fabric at least partly because they lacked capital for car-centric modernization. In Lisbon, the iconic Commerce Square became a parking lot, but Pombaline buildings survived.

Speculative visions for cities also blossomed outside the realm of professional planning. Design avant-gardes harmonized with the cultural effervescence of the 1960s. The poet June Jordan teamed up with Buckminster Fuller to imagine a futuristic Skyrise for Harlem, a massive housing project for the neighborhood's mostly African American residents.[52] There were countless arresting and ambitious ideas throughout the world. The vast majority remained on drawing boards. Path dependencies, above all in the form of car dominance, proved too intractable. Other factors stalled the cycles of undoing and outdoing that had been characteristic of modern urbanization, especially in the North Atlantic. This too is not simply a story with heroes and villains, but one that speaks to narrowing futures. Antidevelopment motivations varied widely, and animated liberals, socialists, preservationists, and environmentalists, as well as conservatives, xenophobes, and racists. Zoning, initially an instrument to give shape to booming cities, increasingly became a pretext to set built environments in amber.[53] It became a tool to not make room for undesirable newcomers.

We might see *The Jetsons* as an expression of this continuity and inertia. The cartoon sitcom became a hit in much of the world. On the surface it was about revolutionary innovation and technological leapfrogging. But the all-white characters transposed a very particular present onto the future. They lived in an outer-space version of sprawling suburbia, with Googie architecture, private vehicles, gender conformity, and wonky gadgets at the service of middle-class comfort. Their built environment did not prioritize social infrastructure. People still lived mostly in apartments rather than single-family buildings. But dramas unfolded in domestic spaces. The detached home fulfilled the promise of a detachment from the social body. This was a closed future, seemingly freed from the thorny politics of the past and present. Average viewers of *The Jetsons* lived in a changing society. But contemporary transformations to the built environment now seemed to be a matter of degree rather than a fundamental reordering. In the 1920s, about one-fifth of households in the United States had flush toilets; one-third had telephones and electricity. By the 1970s, a vast majority of people had access to these infrastructures. *The Jetsons* represented a society where change happened more predictably.

————

Grandiose modern projects had been in vogue in Latin American cities since at least the 1930s. A monumental avenue tore through Rio's fabric in the 1940s. Some rejected top-down visions, preferring sidewalks and urban mixtures as sources of vitality. In a famous couplet, the Brazilian poet Manuel Bandeira shunned Rio's panoramic vistas, or "the line in the horizon." He was more interested in oblique alleyways. When Brasília was inaugurated, the author Clarice Lispector refused to take sides. She visited the new capital in 1962, and authored a text that opened with ambivalence: "Brasília is constructed on the line of the horizon."[54] The image evoked a city rising amid the flat landscapes of Brazil's central plains. Horizons are fitting metaphors for the future. They are always, by definition, just beyond reach.

Lispector's descriptions sometimes evade logic, and that is the point. Her enigmatic prose, like urban planning, often produces expectations that are frustrated. Brasília was conceived with strict separation of functions. Without invective, she exposed rational compartmentalization as a pipe dream: "a construction with space factored in for the clouds." Urbanites, like aerosol formations in the sky, refuse fixity. The city lacked alleyways; it was "built with no place for rats." A city without rats would have no place for a "whole part of us, precisely the one horrified by rats." This absence appears to mock any technocratic aspiration to reform humanity: "They wished to deny that we are worthless." Lispector preferred not to be saved: "Hell understands me better." She understood that wayward desires and anxieties govern human behavior as much as enlightened self-interest or cost-benefit analyses. Humans could simply never conform to preconceived notions of order and progress.

Lispector rejected the triumphant embrace of Brasília, but she did not engage in nostalgic critiques. Both modern planning and the seedy sociability of alleyways had been rooted in masculinity. She grasped how public health, aligned with social ideals and vying for antiseptic spaces, might leave little room for deviations from the norm. Brasília's unusual forms, however, could also evoke a sense of the present manifesting the future's unpredictability. They defied any assigned meaning. The lived-in city, Lispector surmised, would frustrate utopian longings and become a place of unforeseen qualities. She saw Brasília as "a final simplification of ruins: the ivy is yet to grow." Over time, ivies grew, and rats found their way, along with all sorts of other messy modes of unanticipated urbanization. Residents and shopkeepers used street-facing façades intended for loading, for example, instead of the assigned store entrances facing the lawns of residential blocks. Skaters took over smooth surfaces not meant for them. Brasília became a hub of counterculture and punk scenes.

At less local scales, developments followed known patterns. Under Kubitschek's government, Brazil more than doubled its system of paved interstate roads.[55] This made it easier for migrants to move from the countryside to cities, including Brasília. The rich drove cars, the poor rode buses. In the metropolitan area, precarious self-built peripheries looked like any other in the region, while wealthy enclaves resembled suburbia. No city can be an island. In 1964, a US-backed military coup exemplified how the Cold War heated up in the Global South, with proxy conflicts and brutal anticommunist dictatorships. Some dreams were indeed over. In 1967, a documentary crew interviewed migrants that had relocated to Brasília from the drought-stricken northeast.[56] The laborers hinted at wage theft, union busting, and police violence. They showed disappointment with broken promises. The filmmakers boarded a bus arriving from a state around 1,200 miles away. A young woman held a baby. Another child cried in the background. What kinds of futures animated her? What did she expect from the modern city? The migrant was posed a question: "How's it gonna be, good or bad?" Her response should inspire all futurologists: "I don't know."

III. Endings and Beginnings

In rapidly growing cities, especially in the Global South, postwar fantasies of stability failed to gain ground. Guillermo Meza's midcentury paintings, for example, suggested an urban future of ecological apocalypse. He was of indigenous descent and had been raised in a low-income *colonia* in Mexico City. Other contemporaries followed suit, expressing anxieties about hydraulic infrastructures drying out ecosystems to serve urbanization.[57] At the time, the atomic age had made it possible to imagine the end of the world without religion. And in some corners of the world, it was already becoming easier to envision environmental catastrophes than progress.

Illusions of history as predictable came under greater stress after the 1968 uprisings and the 1970s oil crises. The events of 1968, like those of 1848, had a transatlantic dimension: demonstrators took to the streets in Paris, Chicago, Rio de Janeiro, and many other cities, for myriad reasons. In Mexico City, they converged on a modernist public square that aimed to symbolize a future of order and harmony between the country's "three cultures": the indigenous and Hispanic legacies, alongside the modern nation.[58] Military forces brutally attacked the student-led protestors, in what became known as the Tlatelolco Massacre. In France, in the 1970s, rising oil prices helped bring an end to "the glorious thirty [years]" period of postwar economic growth, car-centric urbanization, and rising living standards. Throughout the Atlantic, fantasies of stability did not survive contact with reality.

In the 1970s, the future came under attack. Alvin Toffler's *Future Shock* became a transatlantic best-seller. The book and subsequent film expressed concern with "the premature arrival of the future," and the "sickness" that came from too much change.[59] The Club of Rome sponsored *The Limits to Growth* (1972), a report concerned with development in a planet of finite resources. The Algerian-born economist Georges Elgozy criticized the pretenses of technocrats: the future was a bluff, and "tomorrow would not take place."[60] A harsh critic of centralized planning won the Nobel Prize in Economics.[61] The Sex Pistols in London voiced the punk distrust of institutional promises with the slogan *No Future* (1977). Clarice Lispector updated her views of the modernist capital: "Brasília is a future that happened in the past."[62] A local rock band would sing of how "the future is no longer what it was before."[63]

At the same time, for every expression of disillusionment, many more future-peddlers arose. The future became a big business. Toffler turned his concern with technologies into a pitch for a kind of futurology consultancy. Forecasting discourses and techniques permeated both the public and private sectors. Some futures from the past returned to circulation. George Orwell's dystopian *Nineteen Eighty-Four* (1949) became a popular source of insights about the present. The British author, after all, had imagined urban life in the 1980s as marked by pro-paganda, inequality, and high-tech surveillance. His novel's protagonist had a job to rewrite articles that missed forecasts about production, and to destroy the overly optimistic originals. Orwell's future city brought together the ruins of Victorian London and a modern "world of steel and concrete," with "monstrous machines and terrifying weapons."[64] In a departure from earlier futures, standardization and uniformity were no longer represented as desirable. The writer was of course engaging in the convention of setting a story in the future to criticize authoritarian-ism in his own time. In retrospect, Orwell's fiction grasped the political power of prognostication, but overestimated accountability. The very job assigned to the protagonist assumed that wrong predictions would face scrutiny. In reality, companies, governments, and researchers did not have a routine of studying the record of earlier predictions. Like fortune-tellers and prophets before them, futurologists carried on.

Nineteen Eighty-Four assumed forecasters would overestimate pro-duction. Sometimes they missed the mark in the opposite direction. The alarmist *The Population Bomb* (1968), authored by prominent Stan-ford researchers, predicted imminent global famines that did not mate-rialize. And in 1976, the influential environmentalist Lester R. Brown predicted that most humans would not live in cities due to "additional energy costs."[65] Instead, capacities for food and energy production and storage surged, along with urban populations. Those that expressed fear about overpopulation did not seem to pay much heed to the stresses that cars place on the planet's resources and ecosystems. In George Or-well's future, meanwhile, people mostly moved around by air or subway. His novel associated cars to the excesses of the rich in the past. Their actual adoption surpassed expectations among novelists and industry experts alike.[66] The production of automobiles doubled between the 1940s to the 1960s, and then again in the next two decades.

George Orwell was reasonable to assume car adoption would not accelerate as it did. Automobility, after all, required destroying huge swaths of cities because they were incompatible with existing spaces. In urban settings, cars as a mass product are such an affront to the common good that their victory strained credulity. It is a matter of physical volume more than morality. Generally, transit systems benefit from ridership demands. Each new car, however, becomes a problem to an existing one, because driving and parking required a lot more space than the modes they replaced. In other words, the advantages of driving decrease as the number of cars increases. The more cars in urban areas, the more people get stuck in traffic and in search of parking. This scenario was perhaps too dystopian for *Nineteen Eighty-Four.*

Since flying vehicles did not arrive, several governments and companies realized that they had to invest in other transportation modes. Canadian cities saw the United States as a cautionary tale. Toronto built a subway system in the 1950s. Montreal, in the 1960s. Vancouver, in the 1980s. East Asian cities have been particularly successful at building mass transit. The comparable lack of fossil fuels made it crucial to develop mobility around rail. In Northern Europe, the oil shortages of the 1970s empowered urban residents to make way for bicycles as a more affordable, safer, and healthier alternative. Car industries became enmeshed in conflicts around unionization and strikes. During the 1980s and 1990s, nonetheless, car production and usage rose more rapidly than ever before. Driving became central to globalization and to the upper-class experience of cities across the world. A worldwide growth in car production coincided with the heyday of what became known as a neoliberal agenda.

In the 1980s, Margaret Thatcher and her conservative allies used the slogan "There Is No Alternative" to argue for the superiority and inevitability of capitalist market economies. In 1989, the Berlin Wall fell. It had been built to stop people from fleeing to the West. That same year, the term *Washington Consensus* entered in circulation. It referred to business-friendly measures like deregulation, privatization, and transnational trade. In practice, power shifted from labor to capital. Two years later, the formal end of the Soviet Union inspired a belief in "the end of history." Urban designers had largely lost political relevance, but other lettered elites cultivated some of the expectations of finality underlying modern planning at its peak. In the United States, the political scientist Francis Fukuyama entertained the idea of a plausible consensus around liberal democracy as "the end point of mankind's ideological evolution," and "the final form of human government."[67]

Fukuyama assumed modern industrial societies would be mostly urban but gave little thought to how actual urban spaces might evolve. Where would all those automobiles fit? Where would migrants live? Would vast and unequal cities engender a sense of belonging or hostility? He thought democracies would be well-equipped to address ecological challenges. The same year his book *The End of History and the Last Man* came out, the Eco '92 Earth Summit in Rio de Janeiro brought together more heads of state than any single event in history. The UN-sponsored conference sought to set frameworks for sustainable development. It was a spectacle of confidence in the ability of governments, businesses, and "the international community" to solve global problems.[68]

In the meantime, globalization and capitalism maintained symbiotic relationships to oil-based production and car-centric urbanization. The latter would outlast any illusions of linear progress in politics or economics. Across the globe, the wealthier residents of even the poorest cities gained greater access to expressions of global belonging like cable television, telephone services, international travel, and imported goods. Many moved to gated condos. New technologies mediated their relationship to globalization, while the car mediated their relationships to immediate surroundings. Rather than the creation of new collective futures, the emergent dream was to afford being part of a modern world of material prosperity that already existed. Yet futures remained contested, and history proved to be as unwieldy as ever. The 9/11 terrorist attacks in 2001 and the invasion of Iraq put a dent in US hegemony. With the global financial crisis in 2007–2008, the sensation that the free market or liberal democracies held a monopoly on global futures further dissipated. Fantasies of stability became less tenable even among the most sheltered elites. Climate change entered the lexicon. In the meantime, car production continued to grow worldwide, nearly a third of it in China by 2023.

———

In the twenty-first century, urban change continued to accelerate outside the Global North. In the Atlantic world, it has concentrated in West Africa. Since early modernity, Lagos has been at the crossroads of transatlantic history. The Portuguese arrived in the 1470s, naming it after their word for lagoon. Nnedi Okorafor, a Nigerian American novelist, notes that they did not think "to ask one of the natives for suggestions."[69] Lagos is also the name of a city in southern Portugal. It had perhaps the first slave market in early modern Europe and was devastated by the 1755 earthquake. The namesake came into the fold of the Benin Kingdom and then the Yoruban Oyo Empire. The latter sent embassies to Rio. Both engaged in the transatlantic slave trade. Foreigners left behind language, metals, and muskets, and took cloths, spices, and humans. Lagos became a key port. The British invaded in 1851, officially banned slavery, and made it a colonial possession supplying palm oil. Lagos was elevated to capital of the newly created Colony and Protectorate of Nigeria in 1914, and retained that status until 1991. Growth took off after the discovery of oil wells in the Niger Delta during the 1950s and Nigerian independence in 1960.

Despite the creation of a Town Improvement Ordinance in 1863, British colonization subjected Lagos to comparatively little comprehensive planning. There are familiar patterns, nonetheless. The city was connected to the interior by railway, and to London via telecommunications cables in the late nineteenth century. And sanitary preoccupations undergirded spatial segregation: rulers created white residential areas, putatively to avoid diseases like yellow fever. Liora Bigon notes that "the only installations intended there for Africans were the cemetery and prison."[70] After independence, Nigerian upper classes took over some of the spaces that had been inhabited by colonial elites, like Ikoyi and Victoria Island. Lagos became central to statecraft, but the national government often neglected its infrastructure.[71] The city's administrative structure remains fragmented across several Local Government Areas. Created in 1967, the more extensive Lagos State handles most issues at the metropolitan scale, including transportation, health, and housing. Economic growth has been largely fueled by oil production, though emissions and vehicles per capita remain considerably lower than in major cities in other regions.

The Dutch architect Rem Koolhaas visited Lagos from 2001 to 2004 and concluded: "Lagos is not a kind of backward situation but an announcement of the future."[72] He wanted to celebrate the vital ingenuity of the city's dwellers, in contrast to the perceived blandness of developed centers. Koolhaas, however, projected fantasies. His work was criticized for essentializing the African city, romanticizing everyday struggles, and overlooking how Nigerian history and partisan politics shaped urban processes.[73] A few years earlier, the Martinican writer Édouard Glissant had contrasted New York as representative of "cultures of intervention" to Lagos as "emerging," because it lacked the "means of speaking up in the planetary flow of Communication."[74] He criticized a contemporary "obsession" with futurologies: "any possible laws of such a science would be stamped by the same principle of uncertainty that governs the métissage of cultures."[75] Koolhaas, the theorist of *Delirious New York*, might have wanted to be the seer of the next big thing. But Lagos was already big—it had more residents in the early 2000s than the entire population of the United States at the time of the 1811 Commissioners' Plan. The city was a site of mixtures and possibilities. And it was as saddled by given conditions and legacies from the past as anywhere else in the twenty-first century.

Several urban plans in Lagos have focused on flood prevention and coastline control, often through landfill projects. One of the most ambitious of these projects, Eko Atlantic, began to take shape in the early 2000s, adjacent to Victoria Island and a couple miles from Lagos Island, which concentrate wealth and major businesses. The plan aims to accommodate at least 250,000 prosperous residents in an area about one-sixth of Manhattan's. The name came from a Yoruban word for Lagos, but the forms follow a familiar modernist vision: car-centric rectilinear layouts, glassy towers, and separation of functions. The private development seeks less to remake an existing city than to create a "modern and efficient" enclave.[76] It advertises a "gateway to emerging markets of the continent." One of the earliest flagship commercial tenants was a British-based international oil company. Some refer to Eko Atlantic as "the Manhattan of West Africa," others prefer to look toward the Pacific, seeing it as the "future Hong Kong of Africa."[77]

Urbanization in West Africa picked up after North Atlantic narratives of progress became discredited. Yet certain tropes persisted. In 2013, Bill

Clinton joined Nigerian president Goodluck Jonathan in a ground-breaking ceremony for Eko Atlantic. The former US president hailed it as a triumph of the human spirit in line with the Egyptian pyramids, the Panama Canal, and the airplane. Clinton spoke about the development as part of a future where "Nigerians will be able to choose where they wish to live."[78] In practice, such statements carry the implication that some should enjoy a right to the future while others will be left behind. A decade after this event, streets and pipes had been laid out but most of the site remained vacant. As many as two-thirds of Lagos residents inhabit precarious and poor neighborhoods, mostly in peripheral areas. They are expected to make do in a city with barely any public housing programs. We can expect Eko Atlantic as a choice only for those that can afford it.

One local publication praised how "this futuristic city will be everything that Lagos is not."[79] The rhetoric of a modern plan as the antithesis of a chaotic city has precedents throughout the Atlantic, including Nigeria. It helped justify the construction of the new national capital of Abuja in the 1980s. Like Brasília, Abuja has a more central location in the country. Its master plan, created by prestigious North American design firms, also privileged rectilinear layouts and efficient motor vehicle traffic. Like Brasília, Abuja did not evolve according to plans. Self-built housing quickly became the solution to shortages.[80] In Eko Atlantic, in contrast, the *futuristic* ethos does not even pretend to contemplate the fate of the poor. The project promises an exclusive escape from urban problems not in pastoral outskirts but within the city. Its high-tech image aims to project a new modern Lagos. In the 2010s, one scholar notes, the city went "from being a symbol of urban disorder to a widely cited example of effective African governance."[81] This mode of urban planning creates opportunities to attract capital, often from abroad. Bill Clinton was probably not invited only to deliver a speech.

Planning experts Oluwafemi Olajide and Taibat Lawanson situate Eko Atlantic among other projects leading to displacement and further socioeconomic segregation in Lagos. They describe a growing "disconnect between the developmental priorities of the state government and the livelihood aspirations and needs of local communities."[82] They view this as part of "the rise of the neoliberal city," but the label might mislead. In these urban developments, after all, the state retains a leading role, even if the goal is to serve the interests of well-connected stakeholders rather than the public good.

In central Lagos, low-income settlements had long occupied an area called East Badia. The head of a chieftaincy claimed his family had hereditary ownership of the lands. Nigerian courts granted them those rights in 2013. Demolitions and forced evictions ensued, leaving at least 10,000 people in a state of destitution.[83] Locals blamed the traditional ruler. Government denied a role, but according to eyewitnesses, officials and police oversaw the bulldozers, or "caterpillars" as Lagosians call them. Real estate developers then bought up the land. In processes like these, the state does not take the back seat. Across the water from the Eko Atlantic peninsula in Tarkwa Bay, evictions enabled property development controlled by the military.[84] In such instances, governments create essential infrastructures at the behest of investors. Is it a coincidence that Eko Atlantic involves a financial conglomerate with links to one of Nigeria's 1990s military dictators?[85]

Real estate investors can also come in the form of other governments. This is the case with Chinese funding in the planned city of Quilamba, outside the Angolan capital of Luanda. Paid by oil exports to China, the new city for around 200,000 residents benefited from subsidies when private buyers failed to materialize.[86] Capital flows from the North Atlantic become less commanding as economic might grows in the Pacific. Urban anthropologist Wangui Kimari identifies everyday associations among Kenyans between "the Chinese" and "wished-for" actions.[87] The Chinese state refers to China–Africa relations as "future-oriented," marked by "aspiring young people."[88] This is, however, not a geopolitical update of Haussmannization. Planning scholars Tom Goodfellow and Zhengli Huang propose the expression *contractor cities* to convey how contingencies govern contemporary developments more than any deliberate top-down approach. Funders and firms involved in Chinese investment in Africa "create opportunities for themselves and others, and ultimately set in motion infrastructures beyond their control that

are subsumed into the local context."[89] Whether or not anyone moves
to Quilamba could be beside the point.

Despite major variations within Lagos and across the Atlantic, we can
discern patterns. The weakening of centralized and large-scale urban
planning has given place not to more democratic governance but to
different forms of elite capture. This does not necessarily favor private
real estate developers. In many metropolitan areas in the United States,
for example, a de facto partnership between local governments and
homeowners uses regulations to increase property values by suppress-
ing housing supply. The losers in these processes have their futures foreclosed by housing insecurity. Whether in the United States or Nigeria,
they are burdened by high rents, displacement, or homelessness.

Many newcomers to Lagos are forced to live in informal settlements,
like more than a billion urban dwellers in the world, according to UN
estimates. *Informal* refers to self-built housing as well as a lack of basic
infrastructures, land titles, or state-sanctioned planning. It is a useful
umbrella term and substitute for derogatory language. At the same time,
the prefix *in* implies an absence of *formal* qualities. In effect, all built
environments have forms, even if they skirt official standards. *Informal*
too often serves as a proxy for poverty, unregulated, precarious, shape-
shifting, impermanent, or improvised.[90] The descriptor might harken
back to the expectation that spatial order needs to possess rigid geometries. It can evoke backwardness and a negation of modernist or futuristic desires. Yet, what we call *informal* has more of an assured place in
foreseeable urban futures than any given *smart city* program or high-
tech trend.

The Eurocentric early modern invention of the future, manifested in
a straight line cutting through a maze-like urban fabric, still resonates.
Planners have certainly expanded their repertoires: Alphand, Olmsted,
Le Corbusier, Moses, and others found appeal in meandering lines. In
the twenty-first century, we can discern less from planned layouts. Grids
are more common in Lagos than in Kinshasa, reflecting francophone
colonial legacies. But such formal variations can have little bearing in
the present. Amid cities of the Global South, the greater visual contrast
is between formal and informal settlements, or between rich and poor

neighborhoods. Appearing to be worlds apart might obscure how they are knit together through interdependence. Centrally located shanty towns are solutions for inadequate mass transit, bringing jobs and workers into proximity. They are *the other side*, the complement and consequence of exclusive enclaves like Eko Atlantic. While the latter can act as havens for transnational financial interests to operate with minimal regulations, the former can function as enclaves excluded from basic rights and living standards. Designers rightfully value the ingenuity of self-built solutions. But they too are signs of relaxed oversight and inadequate infrastructures. Historically, informal settlements belong less in the nineteenth-century lineage of collective self-governance and should be understood more as an integral offshoot of modern urbanization.

Contemporary self-built neighborhoods tend to be places with many of the same problems that afflicted early modern cities: sanitation, violence, poverty. In the Global South, however, they often invert the progression of "slums" in North Atlantic cities. Instead of being places that have deteriorated due to public negligence, they tend to move from makeshift solutions and bottom-up resourcefulness "toward a more rationalized environment."[91] In Lagos, the coastal informal settlement of Makoko was largely built on stilts by residents. As many as 300,000 inhabit the community, forming a cosmopolitan milieu where people routinely speak French, English, Egun, and Yoruba. Some dredge clay from the lagoon's bottom and sell it to building sites across the city. Others peddle goods in canoes, build boats, or smoke fish. Children play in the water. They once could have attended a floating school, designed by Kunlé Adeyemi, which collapsed. For them, imagined futures might be a matter of survival or salvation, dreams of making it, or something only accessible to people elsewhere—in foreign countries, in the stories of Nollywood movies, or in glittering nearby developments. The fates of Makoko and Eko Atlantic are both in tension and intertwined.

Places of worship abound in Makoko, especially Christian churches. An *Ultra Modern* shopping center is within walking distance. Several modernist buildings are nearby, including the National Stadium, highrises of the University of Lagos, and the National Theater of Nigeria, a sculptural landmark in concrete. This monumental structure was built

FIGURE 6.9. In Makoko, many temporalities converge.

for the Second World Black and African Festival of Arts and Culture in 1977, after the Nigerian Civil War (1967–1970), as a harbinger of Pan-African progress. In the 2010s, rumors circulated that Dubai-based investors sought to turn the space into a shopping mall. Most of these spaces are integrated into car-centric infrastructures. Reaching them does not make for an easy stroll. They stand apart from a place like Makoko, where mobility centers on canals, canoes, walking, motorcycles, and collective transportation.

From one of the main highway bridges leading to the Lagos airport, the agglomeration of tin-roofed houses on wooden stilts is highly visible. For some, this makes Makoko an embarrassing sight of backwardness, and a promising site for real estate development. Compared to nineteenth-century experiments in self-governance, it is easier for a community like Makoko to take the nation-state and global capitalism for

FIGURE 6.10. The National Theater stands as a memory of modernist futures.

granted. This might mean living with the possibility of forced evictions, as well as seeing formal rights as a key to individual enfranchisement and collective agency. In 2012, state officials began to violently demolish homes in Makoko. One resident died. Pushback against the authoritarian process led to a collaboration between community members, scholars, NGOs, and government agencies to create a "people-centered" plan instead.[92] It seeks to keep Makoko's place in the future of Lagos, and to improve living conditions for residents. Echoing some of the very beginnings of modern urban planning, a major initial focus was on health.

———

Africa concentrates the future of urbanization, to a great degree, as a demographic fact.[93] The 600-mile coastal stretch between Abidjan in the Ivory Coast and Lagos, including Accra in Ghana, Lomé in Togo, and Cotonou in Benin, likely experienced the world's most rapid urbanization during the 2010s and early 2020s. Physical infrastructures cannot meet the basic needs of growing populations. Doing so requires massive capital investments. Daunting tasks, including tackling extreme poverty and pollution, require urgency, but forward-looking attention also raises interconnected questions: Can these cities improve mobility systems without entrenching car dependency? Can they upgrade the living standards of overcrowded settlements while avoiding the inefficient dispersion of the US model, with its much larger ecological footprints and high costs?

Throughout West Africa, colonial railroads prioritized connections between cities and the hinterlands. After independence, highways linked urban hubs, and roads allowed cities to grow outward through sprawling settlements. Scholars have interpreted a preference for driving as a response to colonial oppression. It expresses a desire for freedom, entrepreneurship, and (male) autonomy.[94] In contemporary Dar es Salaam, people associate car usage to *maendeleo*, or progress.[95] The popular "Lagos Anthem" equates automobiles with success: "My friend drives an Aston Martin / I drive a Bugatti / It's Friday night and we're going to have fun / Yet they say 'there's no money in Lagos.'"[96] Mozambican rapper Azagaia, in contrast, sang that foreign aid goes to "rich and arrogant" leaders who buy BMW and Mercedes sports cars, amid "selfish dreams" and the "daily brainwashing" of Africans.[97] The battle over futures continues, with urban spaces as the arena.

Car ownership remains a lot less prevalent in sub-Saharan Africa than in other regions of the world. Traffic, however, is already a major problem. As elsewhere in the Global South, motorbikes, vans, rickshaws, buses, cars, and pedestrians vie for road space. Modernist paradigms for the separation of speeds and the smooth-flowing freeways of Futurama generally apply only in wealthier areas. The reliance on oil in Corbusian urbanization, however, is visible in ever-present gas stations, a key node of modern landscapes and unwitting examples of the modernist setback. Cars might still tap into an aspiration to belong in the future, but they are also about convenience and survival. Who prefers to ride in a slow-moving and packed minibus, or to venture through dangerous roads with few protections for pedestrians?

Scholars show that representations of driving in West African culture and media are ambivalent. In a chapter of her novel *Lagoon* (2014),

Nnedi Okorafor imagined characters trying to flee turmoil in Lagos by car. The city had been invaded by aliens. The expressway then becomes a sentient monster that swallows the gridlock, people and all. Much of "Africanfuturist" work and contemporary science fiction does not bother to set stories in a precise future date, as if such confident predictions could no longer be taken seriously. Or perhaps it is because, as science fiction author William Gibson famously claimed in the late 1990s, "the future is already here, it's just not very evenly distributed."[98] These remarks work as much for technological advancements as for environmental catastrophes. Both cell phones and floods unleashed new possibilities in Lagos. But Okorafor's city is not just a place in crisis. It is living through transformations and brimming with energy. We can interpret her expressway as an overdetermined car-centered future devouring the past, just as we might think of pastoral nostalgia in suburbia as the past devouring the future.

Gridlocks denote both immobility and volatility—a sense that things can turn on a whim. In her study of Dakar, Senegal, the anthropologist Caroline Melly theorizes about the uses of the term *embouteillage*, or bottleneck. It describes traffic, as well as roadblocks for dreams of migrating, working through bureaucracies, or living amid crammed and deficient infrastructures. The book shows how people associate flux, or being mobile, with social status and the "critical means of securing the future." The flow of money, products, ideas, and bodies are crucial "to stake claim to urban permanence."[99] At the macro-level, this happens outside the control of urban dwellers. Their micro-futures are at once predicated on mobility and hindered by experiences of regulatory logjams, interruptions, and impossibilities. As a metaphor, bottlenecks capture those dynamics: the frustration as well as "the promise of future movement."[100]

Teleological narratives about collective progress seem to resonate less in the twenty-first century, and not just among those that feel excluded from official institutions or global flows. Theories of modernization, so influential in earlier planning, had imagined development as a predictable set of stages that different nations could undergo in similar ways. Those expectations have largely vanished. This represents a fragmentation of futures. Still, standards of desirability remain transnational. Visitors from smaller cities might perceive Lagos as "Europe within Nigeria."[101] Drivers and passengers compare traffic in Dakar with New York or Paris. West African politicians appeal to a future inspired by Dubai rather than by the postcolonial potentials of *négritude*. Real estate projects catering to the wealthy highlight sustainability and pedestrian-friendly streetscapes. An urban planet paradoxically intensifies both global connections and local divisions.

Climate change also unites and divides. It encompasses the entire planet and cuts across lettered discourse even if it more directly impacts the poorer. Lagos officials have responded with initiatives like Operation Green Lagos Project and the Lagos State Climate Change Summit. Eko Atlantic, in the meantime, has been criticized as "climate apartheid," with upgrading Makoko praised as a better alternative.[102] From an ecological perspective, both have density preferable to detached single-family homes in car-reliant settings. There are of course brilliant urbanists pursuing multiple pathways in Africa.[103] And as elsewhere, climate as a framing, however well-intentioned, can flatten local dynamics. The historian and theorist Achile Mbembe, for example, points to more salient repertoires replacing the roles that religions of salvation once occupied. To him, an "imaginary surplus" of media and images is "increasingly delegated to capital and to all kinds of objects and technologies."[104] Throughout cities of the Global South, people are surrounded by images of change but often feel stuck. The anthropologist Jane Guyer calls this a combination of "fantasy futurism and enforced presentism."[105] A similar perception exists among some in the North that see themselves as left behind. Prospects of transformation can arouse fear or resentment.

Given the unprecedented urban scales, environmental pressures, and current mass media economies, it is possible that the histories of other cities might not be particularly useful for us to make sense of what will unfold. African urbanization has already leap-frogged in telecommunications technologies. Within a matter of a few years, mobile phones became widespread, connecting urbanites to social media networks and extending the urban fold into the countryside through financial transactions, chat groups, or Nollywood movies. What might leapfrog-ging mean in transportation and energy systems? Lagos is building an elevated and surface light rail system that vows to be extensive enough to cater to half of the population. In the past, streetcar systems and cities grew in tandem, before they failed to compete with cars. The US-based artist Olalekan Jeyifous imagines a futuristic Lagos with multimodal mobilities and mixed building stocks. His photomontages display open-ness to change, but no wide-eyed faith in linear progress.[106] On the ground, countless Lagosians and newcomers keep seeking better lives in the city. If in some settings the phrase *after the future* denotes exhaus-tion, in others it can still evoke pursuit.

Epilogue

I. Pedestrian Futures

We might do well to focus less on past versus future, left versus right, or even capitalism versus socialism, and more on walking versus driving. In the eighteenth century, Louis-Sébastien Mercier imagined the Paris of 2440 as a place where rich and poor got around on foot. The narrator's guide in the utopian future explained: "The nobles of our days use their own legs, and therefore have more money and less of the gout."[1] Mercier assumed that if the "original inhabitants of the earth" saw the Paris of the 1770s, with the dangers of carriages running over people, they would have been incredulous and indignant.[2] Who knows how they would have reacted to cars? In *The City in History*, Lewis Mumford offered a truism: "the rich ride, the poor walk."[3] Mercier, however, could still be right about the Paris of 2440. The French capital has been trending in that direction, with added subway lines, safe bicycle lanes, and economic incentives leading to major reductions in car usage. Authoritarian roots should not forbid us from all the fruits of Haussmannian reforms, like a compact fabric, integrated transit systems, and generous public spaces.

A contemporary reader could make another association: pedestrian-friendly neighborhoods are sites of gentrification, especially in the Global North. Displacement is often blamed on newcomers. It would be much more productive to focus on building walkable places for anyone that desires to live in them. And of course, Mumford's dictum requires a follow-up: the rich ride *what*, exactly? A carriage, car, train, bike, or bus? After his tenure as the mayor of Bogotá, Enrique Peñalosa was fond of saying: "an advanced city is not one where the poor get around in a car, but rather one where even the rich use public transportation."[4] His first administration (1998–2001) transformed a car-choked downtown thoroughfare into a pedestrian avenue, and created a bus rapid transit system, the TransMilenio, which expanded in later years. Walkable cities and mass transit at a metropolitan scale respond to the connected challenges of maintaining vibrant urban cores while ensuring access and mobility across them.

Mercier was onto something. Walking around, for those that are able, has significant financial, social, and health benefits.[5] Unbeknownst to him, there are many environmental advantages too. Cities alone will obviously not solve all or even most planetary problems. But pedestrian-friendly urbanization should be an easy priority in the pursuit of viable and better futures for our planet. We need alternatives to car culture, a leading driver of emissions, pollution, energy use, and resource extraction. Vehicles alone consume about 12 percent of steel production on the planet. Highways and bridges also demand massive amounts of steel; in the United States, they take up around 45 percent of cement production.[6] Car-enabled housing sprawl, in the form of single-family homes, requires significantly more resources and energy per capita even if we exclude driving. Generally, these costs are indirectly subsidized by residents of apartments, rowhouses, or multifamily buildings.[7] And of course, roads and parking lots wreak havoc on natural habitats. From the perspective of fauna and flora, impervious surfaces matter more than population density.[8] A migrant bird returning to a swamp and finding a big box store has met a death sentence. If highway construction through neighborhoods is *urbicide*, we should think of car-centric sprawl as *ecocide*.

Nonetheless, cars are often downplayed in the environmental imagination. They are a little bit like the purloined letter in a famous detective story by Edgar Allan Poe. Investigators looked in "every nook and corner" of a hotel apartment for a stolen letter, failing to find it. In fact, the letter was hidden in plain sight.[9] Similarly, the obvious impacts of driving are often overlooked.[10] Rachel Carson published her *Silent Spring* in 1962, just a few months after Jane Jacobs's *The Death and Life of Great American Cities*. Carson's title evoked a desolate future where "no birds sing." Pesticides like DDT killed them.[11] Her seminal book helped to avert worst-case scenarios, ushering in a push for regulations. In at least one sense, however, that spring was loud. Cars and trucks roared through a rapidly changing American landscape. Neither of these great books paid much heed to the role of driving in the destruction of cities and ecosystems. In their defense, this only became clearer in retrospect. Later thinkers have fewer excuses. Focus on car-centric development is nearly absent or muted in books by Al Gore and Greta Thunberg, as well as in climate initiatives in universities, philanthropies, and the private sector.[12]

Jane Jacobs and Rachel Carson fought powerful groups and interests. Yet, they also articulated visions for the future and worked to achieve change through institutional channels. Since then, as the political theorist Wendy Brown and others observe, liberal or left-leaning progressives became disenchanted with progress, and nihilism surged in right-wing politics.[13] Dating back to the Romantics, lettered cultures, especially in anglophone settings, have told apocalyptic stories of a "last man" roaming a devastated earth. Versions of this trope permeate doomster fantasies. We can speculate that catastrophism is able to generate self-fulfilling prophecies as well as antibodies. We know that it holds appeal in online social media, which seem to reward oppositional stances more than proposals. There is, to be fair, a lot to stand against. Scholars of urbanization, however, should submit predispositions against new developments to greater pressure. It is important to ask both about the consequences of building something as well as not building it. We should also keep counterfactuals in mind. What might have happened to the poor in Paris or Rio without modernizing reforms?

New ideas or projects that break out from circles of experts can gain a life of their own. The "15-minute city" urges mixed-use planning, with amenities and services within short reach of every resident. In anglophone countries, it fueled online conspiracies about "prison camps" to restrict circulation, and became a target of conservative politicians.[14] In hyper-digital cultures, are all progressive ploys destined to become lighting rods in culture battles, with at best fifteen minutes of fame? Cities as varied as Singapore and Stockholm are building on legacies of transit-oriented development while advancing more multifunctional, human-scaled neighborhoods. We do not need to assume that urban spaces lose appeal to social media in any kind of zero-sum or linear way. In the past, the experience of anonymity could be about alienation, fear, or freedom. It was highly gendered. Smart phones change the equation: they track, match, record, facilitate, etc.

Cities historically sped us up. Now, compared to digital spheres, they can slow us down. Experiences grounded in physical places have renewed potentials: more prone to serendipity, but also sometimes gaining from orchestration online. With algorithms determining information flows, that can mean learning about fun gatherings around shared interests, memes inciting paranoid policies, or race riots provoked by fake news. We should also not lose sight of how new media engenders ruptures as well as continuities. Social movements use online tools on behalf of familiar and emerging causes. Communities mobilize for squatter's rights and sanitation. Radicals cultivate utopian horizons and self-organizing principles. Reactionaries organize to stop housing projects, bike lanes, or migration. Reformists seeking more flexible zoning aim for legislative victories.[15] Amid fractured mediascapes, however, can urban visions reignite a sense of large-scale possibility? Where will the future go?

II. Where Can the Future Go?

In the first two decades of the twenty-first century, the fast-moving tech sector might have been the world's most influential economic and cultural force. The disruption-loving future-makers, however, proved to possess an atrophied urban imagination. Electric cars are excellent for reducing fossil fuel consumption, but not the embedded emissions in vehicle production. And they do nothing to improve traffic or land use. That largely also applies to autonomous cars, which appear to be *just around the corner* (a metaphor that also captures potential threats for pedestrians). Elon Musk's Hyperloop combined the limitations of cars (carrying capacity) and subways (challenging to build). Ride-hailing apps might offer marginal advantages, but likely set back public investment in mass transit, and do not appear to be viable as a business model. Carbon capture technologies remain a distant proposition, and cannot compete with swamps as carbon sinks—bayous are higher tech.[16] Digital landscapes are littered with vestiges of the next-big-thing, like cemeteries of dead-end innovations (Yik Yak? NFTs?). E-bikes, with less hype or support, can be more meaningfully disruptive—they provide pathways to less car-centric lifestyles, and their popularity has surpassed expectations.

Silicon Valley's built environment reflects the US tech industry's failure to reinvent urban futures. Aside from new corporate headquarters surrounded by parking, it had relatively little to show after a period of extraordinary wealth production. Previous economic and cultural booms left indelible marks in the urban fabric. In those terms, the San Francisco Bay Area's brand of progressive politics has been unusually conservative. Homeowners putting up signs welcoming refugees do not always ask—*where?* Apartment construction or wind turbines tend to invite more environmental consternation than golf courses or highways. To be sure, Silicon Valley's imagined futures do play out partly in cyberspaces. And in the twenty-first century, major movements moved between streets and screens (in the United States alone, the Tea Party, Occupy, Black Lives Matter, and MAGA). Meanwhile, the Bay Area's most dramatic urban transformation was probably in equity gains for homeowners, and reduced accessibility for mostly everyone else. A combination of high incomes and low housing inventories priced people out, increasing rent burdens and homelessness. From that perspective, anywhere that has not foreclosed mobility through mass adoption of cars or ultra-strict zoning might be considered more future-oriented.

Deeply ingrained NIMBY-ism in California politics, however, can hardly be attributed to tech industries, and often thrives in groups with anti-tech sensibilities. Skepticism toward cities, after all, runs deep in the United States. But even in a country where bashing cities does not raise many eyebrows, there has been a growing strand of urban triumphalism. In the 1970s and 1980s, Hollywood portrayed crime-ridden cities, dotted by dystopian skyscrapers, as hopeless. Since the 1990s, there has been a flurry of representations of dense cities as more desirable in mainstream media, from Seinfeld's New York to Black Panther's Wakanda—and memes of skyscraper utopias.[17] This tracks with other changes: fictional fortunes rose along with real estate prices and luxury towers, as those that could afford it moved to walkable, transit-rich, and compact neighborhoods. Pushing back on the "bad rap" of cities, the economist Edward Glaeser made use of mounting evidence to argue for them in his *Triumph of the City: How Our Greatest Invention Makes Us Richer, Smarter, Greener, Healthier, and Happier* (2012). A host of other works have celebrated the social and environmental virtues of cities.

Images of urban futures, at the same time, migrated to East Asia. In *Blade Runner*, released in 1982 and set in a dystopian 2019, a cyberpunk Los Angeles evoked contemporary Tokyo or Hong Kong. In another science fiction movie, *Her*, from 2013, a man in a futuristic Los Angeles falls in love with his AI virtual assistant. The outdoor scenes with vertical skylines and pedestrian plazas are shot in Shanghai. Since then, the Chinese city added the population equivalent of more than four LAs. Today, we might be closer to the fictional technologies than to building actual skyscrapers in California. East Asian urban hubs, meanwhile, followed a trajectory of protagonism comparable to the North Atlantic cities featured in this book. They hosted the heirs of World's Fairs with tens of millions of attendees, from the Expo '70 in Osaka to the Expo 2010 in Shanghai, as well as the Olympics (Tokyo in 1964, Seoul in 1988, Beijing in 2008, Tokyo again in 2020). Asian settings often showcase the latest technologies, from the Shinkansen bullet trains in Japan to driverless robotaxis in Wuhan. Cultural phenomena like anime and K-pop became global.

Asian urbanization has also become more of a source of planning paradigms. In the early 2000s, Seoul removed an elevated freeway that ran through its downtown, restoring the Cheonggyecheon stream, creating public spaces, and spurring development. Economic growth accompanied the rise of megacities like Shenzhen and Hangzhou. More recently, urbanists from throughout the world have looked to the "sponge city," a concept that the Chinese landscape architect Yu

Kongjian developed. It employs nature-based infrastructures, with permeable surfaces for water management and flood mitigation. This can depend on freeing up land with vertical buildings, as many East Asian cities currently do. In the region, according to survey data, people report being satisfied with "good affordable housing" at rates nearly twice higher than in North America.[18] Generally, surveys capture greater optimism with the future and more positive outlooks on globalization outside the North Atlantic. At the same time, residents of Western Europe report some of the highest overall satisfaction with their cities in the world. There are too many contradictions, fractured patterns, and simultaneous storylines for distinctions like East–West or Atlantic–Pacific–Indian Worlds to still hold much water.

If we return to urban scales, we can find different pathways to positive outcomes. Vienna has drawn on legacies of socialist governance and modernist design to create new public housing complexes. Tokyo has streamlined and centralized zoning laws that allow for market-oriented developments. They rely on very different financing models, political framings, and architectonic forms. In both, instead of car infrastructure, planning privileges mass transit, walking, and access to jobs, services, and amenities. Yet, even in wealthy nations, achieving a combination of high living standards with relatively low carbon footprints requires state capacity and coordination across spheres of governance. Regardless of how any local efforts fare, we cannot expect bottom-up approaches to meet metropolitan and planetary challenges. Some level of centralization is required to streamline approvals and construction processes. Too many overlapping jurisdictions and interest groups render infrastructure projects unworkable, or lead to delays and inflated costs.

It might not be a coincidence that in a less imperialist Europe, several cities manage to tap into large-scale ambitions not so much to flex a national or ethnic superiority, but to improve mobility systems. Amsterdam, Barcelona, Copenhagen, and Paris have shown how a return to technologies of the past, like the bicycle, can be part of a transition away from the car's chokehold on the future. These scenarios are only viable, however, if metropolitan areas have functioning mass transit. Cities throughout the world have significantly expanded their subway networks in the twenty-first century, including Cairo, Istanbul, Madrid, Moscow, and São Paulo. Several Chinese cities built entire metro systems from scratch. On that count, major anglophone cities lag behind. In the United States, federal, state-level, or hyper-local governance make it challenging to address metropolitan scales.

In the future, building housing for climate refugees or to compensate for retreating from flood-prone areas will likely introduce additional strains on cities and infrastructures. Urbanization that appropriately responds to climate change depends as much on innovation and breakthroughs as on maintenance and coordination. The right to the future can be about change or permanence, flux or fixity, rupture or continuity. It depends on people's ability to make a home, as well as the flexibility to stay or leave. Undoing transportation bottlenecks calls for multiple modes and fewer vehicles moving more people. Undoing housing bottlenecks calls for more units where people can move to and from. Not all changes require reinventing the wheel. Overly prescriptive plans often backfire. There are as many potential answers in e-bike sales in suburbs as in the enduring pedestrian cultures of our oldest cities. We should not, however, place the burden of adaptation on those with fewer economic resources. In practice, well-meaning and well-connected opponents of visible changes to places they cherish risk doing precisely that.

———

What will the cities of tomorrow be like? Until early in 2025, the artificially intelligent ChatGPT expressed optimism. Answering like an upbeat consultant, the chatbot predicted that they will be smart, sustainable, and walkable, with more mixed-use developments, affordable housing, green spaces, diversity, verticality, and inclusiveness. Not a bad recipe. Even the most enthusiastic urbanist, however, understands that cities are not a panacea, and that roadblocks cannot be wished away. And no one that has witnessed community review processes in the United States would ever minimize the hurdles that humans, markets, and institutions face to overcome inherited conditions. These framings can be irrelevant for countries and cities mired in poverty, or with less robust civil societies. And in booming metropolises, planning and fiscal policies involve unprecedented trade-offs between priorities: decarbonization versus climate adaptation, for example. But in housing, the North Atlantic provides cautionary tales about the perils of overreacting to historical lessons. In much of the United States, for instance, excesses of top-down and developer-dominated approaches gave place to too much deference to incumbents and labyrinthine regulations.

The Jetsons reproduced suburbia, but still had apartment buildings. Today, it can be easier to travel to outer space than to build multifamily housing in US suburbs. In most places, zoning laws forbid any building that is not a single-family detached house.[19] Obtaining variances kick in protracted and multilayered processes. Loosening the grip of zoning is instrumental to any plans for retrofitting suburbs into more transit-rich and sustainable places, while also relieving pressures on urban communities to accommodate or spur growth. In practice, community review often acts as a lever for naysayers to veto even modest changes to the built environment. In hearings, homeowners and landlords might call for *all* voices to be heard, for *more data*, or for *holistic* plans as tactics to kill new projects through delays. In response to proposals with just a handful of floors, they might fearmonger about becoming Manhattan, or a loss of *neighborhood character*. The planning profession, in the meantime, has become largely "reactive rather than proactive, corrective instead of preemptive, rule bound and hamstrung and anything but visionary."[20]

Officials with power over planning decisions can have a knack for only listening to voices that confirm politically palatable positions. Obstructionism creates counterproductive distortions. Inclusionary zoning, mandating affordable units in market-rate developments, has become a popular planning mechanism. It can make financing unfeasible and often passes on the costs of subsidies to newcomers. For those reasons, it finds support among housing foes. And if new buildings are only allowed next to car-centric traffic corridors, they expose newcomers to noise and air pollution, as well as unsafe streets. Carefully structured participatory planning, with plural perspectives, can enrich projects. Design benefits from public feedback. Yet, patients are better positioned to know symptoms than to diagnose. Cities relinquish expertise at their own peril.

An enterprising scholar could study correlations between housing abundance, affordable rents, and cultural effervescence (the Harlem Renaissance and the Cidade Nova in early twentieth-century Rio come to mind). Today, those with overly possessive attitudes to urban fabrics tend to be oblivious to downstream consequences of blocking housing supply in growing areas. Living costs rise, while the tax base remains constrained. Aging populations are unable to downsize, while families without access to intergenerational wealth are priced out. Real estate appreciation for a homeowner means inflation for a renter. Renters get squeezed, landlords cash in. From a progressive standpoint, a reflex to judge any deregulation as *neoliberal* or right-wing tends to be short-sighted. Well-crafted regulations protect marginalized communities from rapacious development or slum clearance. Stringent or arbitrary codes hinder efforts to build and meet demand. When construction is cumbersome and litigious, it privileges larger, corrupt, or monopolistic companies. Resistance to aesthetic or regulatory changes has social and environmental consequences. Alternatives to cars and clean energy can be subjected to more scrutiny than perpetuating a status quo. In recent years, policymakers, pundits, and activists aware of these dynamics or willing to update their priors have changed tack.[21]

Urban governance presents well-known problems. In general, municipal boundaries only capture a portion of a metropolitan area. City Halls have limited tools. Planning poses a more specific impasse. How can we weigh the interests of people that stand to benefit in a future scenario? Children and outsiders that have not yet arrived at a place do not get a vote or a voice. They need places to live too. Let it be clear that the point here is not to pit development against conservation. Preserving historic quarters and architecture is itself a form of securing urban futures, furthering cultural belonging, aesthetic continuities, tourist industries, and so on. (Historic preservation can also be invoked for banal sites though, to derail housing developments.) The key argument, rather, is that planning decisions should start from the premise that people need to live somewhere. If we do not build, people do not disappear. Instead, when newcomers have enough income, they will find housing and displace an existing resident with less income. Sprawl, overcrowding, or homelessness follow. Housing shortages and transit scarcity have cascading effects. Ultimately, they foreclose the ability of the most vulnerable to pursue futures. We should not just dwell in abstract hypotheticals: someone trying to leave an abusive relationship is trapped without access to mobility. How can they move on without available transit or the means to buy a car? How can they move out if rents are unaffordable? Who will speak for them at a community meeting?

Cities can render amorphous yearnings into a material set of possibilities or limits. There are basic needs: water, sewage, health, safety, jobs, energy, schools. The extent to which urban life is stifling or freeing, however, largely hinges on ease of access to diverse options in transit, housing, and what sociologists call third spaces or social infrastructure (libraries, playgrounds, music venues, places of worship, etc.).[22] Great cities create conditions for the widest range of possible futures while also adapting to changing aspirations. Some things we control, others are up in the air. In terms of forms, the cities of tomorrow do not have to be all that different from yesterday's compact urban cores. At the same time, we can only know so much about the impacts of climate change, social crises, and evolving technologies in engineering, medicine, artificial intelligence, drones, and so on. We can try, however, to outline an arc within the period covered in this book. First, *people as infrastructure*: the enslaved carry elites on litters and dispose of their bodily fluids; street performers entertain, peddlers deliver goods, etc. Then, at the height of planning powers, *infrastructure before people*: a public concession connects a vacant area to sewage or transit lines, enriching landowners and developers. Next, *people before infrastructures*: migrants arrive in overwhelmed cities and create self-built settlements. Last, *infrastructures without people*: automated systems, the internet of things, algorithms, etc. In the North Atlantic, this was somewhat of a progression. In many booming megalopolises today, these realities coexist in proximity.

It is not always easy to draw a line between where the past ends and the present begins. Michael Bloomberg, shortly after taking office as

New York's mayor in 2002, declared that "to look to the past [. . .] doesn't do anything for the future."[23] During the 2010s, it became more commonplace to reference how historical legacies shape injustices in the present. In the United States, for example, oft-quoted phrases from William Faulkner came to evoke the lines connecting slavery, Jim Crow, redlining, and police violence: "The past is never dead. It's not even past."[24] A robust Marxist scholarly tradition looks back to find complicities between urban planning and capitalist exploitation.[25] Conversely, there are designers and billionaires with exuberant confidence in the irrelevance of history and their abilities to control the future. They continue to embark on vanity projects to plan cities from scratch, as if there is only tomorrow.[26] The scientist and author Vaclav Smil, in the meantime, debunks "the myth of ever-faster innovations."[27] In a way, we are still navigating the ripple effects of the explosive technological transformations of the latter part of the nineteenth century.

Dante's *Inferno* imagined prophets that tried to see too far into the future undergoing a grotesque punishment. They had to live forever with their heads twisted backward. Given the proliferation of modern soothsayers, the medieval Italian poet could very well confuse our world with hell. But predicting can be an invaluable exercise to sharpen our understanding of the present. Envisioning a range of scenarios expands our ability to adapt. Planning remains indispensable, and should draw on multiple tools and perspectives. History can inform our models and heuristics. This should not imply just keeping tabs of who was right or wrong. In the past, we find evidence to bolster arguments from competing camps. Winston Churchill, in 1931, predicted that "fifty years hence," with new wireless communications, "the congregation of men in cities would become superfluous."[28] Post-Covid discourses around work-from-home and less-desirable downtowns stuck in a "doom loop" revive that line of thought. They could age poorly, or yet be right. Regardless, technical forecasts and art alike, across time, help us better perceive the boundaries of possibilities.

One constant in the history of urbanization is a degree of indeterminacy. Another is that the appeal of cities has continued to endure. Some attribute the urban pull to agglomeration effects, others to our nature as social beings. Whatever lies ahead, our changing cities and uncertain futures are intertwined. In Italo Calvino's enigmatic *Invisible Cities*, we read poetic fragments of fictional conversations between Kublai Khan and Marco Polo. The explorer shares impressions from his travels. Like a modern city, the book has structures, but no beginning or end. Marco Polo sees a man in a square and imagines that if he had taken another path at a crossroads in the past, he could have been in that place. Other possible futures await, and he moves on.

Calvino's narrator chimes in: "futures not achieved are only branches of the past: dead branches."[29] But what is a dead branch? As it falls to the ground and decays, microorganisms recycle nutrients and new habitats form. The future can be a thing of the past, but it is never dead. Yet, who can be where and imagine or achieve what is never a given. Being a Venetian merchant or a Mongol emperor provides affordances. Futures close for some and open for others. The shapes of urbanization can limit or maximize possibilities. They can tap into our worst, our best, and anything in between. The past might not offer clear lessons. But it can be a source of forms, modes, and dreams to keep nurturing life.

ACKNOWLEDGMENTS

WHILE WORKING on this book, I learned from so many projects, places, and people. Thank you to all my friends, colleagues, acquaintances. Trying to make sense of cities in classrooms, lecture halls, and office hours has been a joy. I am grateful for the hundreds of students who joined this adventure in courses such as "Environmental Problems, Urban Solutions," "Urban Studies Research Seminar," "Cities and Nature," and "Urban Modernism and Its Discontents" at Princeton. At Harvard: "Imagined Futures," "Latin American Cities and Visual Cultures," "Living in an Urban Planet," "Literature and Urban History," "The Nature of Cities," "Writing and Urban Life," "Design and Ecology," "Back to the Future: Cities of Tomorrow throughout History." I was lucky to work with many wonderful teaching fellows, and to co-teach with Mario Gandelsonas, Aaron Shkuda, Lilia Schwarcz, Beatriz Jaguaribe, Diane Davis, Sidney Chalhoub, Tiya Miles, and Laura Frahm.

Several students helped me with key research assistance, and even reading drafts. In alphabetical order by first name: Alice Chang, Amelia Roth-Dishy, Claire Wigglesworth, Daniel Pinckney, Diekara Oloruntoba-Oju, Emma Fang, Eva Gildea, Hewson Duffy, Junnan Mu, Zeynep Bromberg. More specific acknowledgments can be found in endnotes. Amelia coined "futures in transit." Emma and Alice were exceptional in the Summer Arts and Humanities Research Program. Hewson went above and beyond with his editorial work.

Thank you, *in memoriam*, to dear thinkers who continuously inspire: Svetlana Boym, Nicolau Sevcenko, Joaquim-Francisco Coelho, and Michael Sorkin.

Institutions play major roles in urbanization (a fact perhaps too latent in this book). They keep me busier than anyone should be, and created conditions that made this book possible. I am grateful for my time at Princeton, in the Department of Spanish and Portuguese, co-directing the Princeton-Mellon Initiative in Architecture, Urbanism, and the Humanities, and elsewhere. I have also been so lucky to work with Robert Devins on a book series devoted to architecture and urbanism at the University of Texas Press. At Harvard, I am thankful for my departments (Romance Languages and Literatures, and African and African American Studies) as well as the program in History and Literature, the GSD, the Mahindra Humanities Center, DRCLAS, the Bloomberg Center for Cities, the Harvard University Center for the Environment, which offered support for research assistants, and every other program I've been active in. This book benefited from conversations with many people, among them: Brodwyn Fischer, Duncan White, Gareth Doherty, Germán Labrador Méndez, Gyan Prakash, Henry Grabar, João Moreira Salles, Joe Blackmore, José Marcelo Zacchi, Lauren Kaminsky, Lucia Allais, Magda Maaoui, Marcia Castro, Mariana Cavalcanti, Mariano Siskind, Mark Elliott, Michael Pollan, Paul Marino, Pedro Meira Monteiro, Rachel Price, Rosario Hubert, Sarah Whiting, Stan Allen, Steve Biel, Sunil Amrith, Thaïsa Way, Tommie Shelby, Washington Fajardo, and Yosvany Terry.

I was hosted for talks in the final stretch at the University of Rochester and UMass Amherst, and I am grateful to Peter Christensen and Pari Riahi for those invitations. Early on, Kirsten Weld helped me with the book proposal. Alex Csiszar and Emily Dolan also provided feedback (e amizade). Andrew K. Sandoval-Strausz made this book much stronger with generous and rigorous comments. Anonymous readers at Princeton University Press helped tremendously. Kenneth Maxwell read two chapters, and influenced my scholarship and life in so many positive ways. I am deeply thankful to Miguel Lago and Daniel Agbiboa for help with key passages, as well as Jonathan Levy, Murat Cokol, and Alison Isenberg (one of my role models) for reading. I also learned so much working on anchor institutions with Karen Brooks Hopkins. And I want to highlight the intellectual environment and resources of the Harvard-Mellon Urban Initiative in the years when this book came to fruition. I am grateful for the support of the Mellon Foundation, including Justin Garrett Moore, Mariët Westermann, and especially Dianne Harris. At Harvard, Robin Kelsey, as dean, offered crucial encouragement, and I was so fortunate to collaborate with him on a number of projects. I had the honor of working with Johanna Delahunty and Andrea Davies, and of co-directing with Eve Blau and Liz Cohen, who also offered valuable notes on my book proposal. If you ever helped me but do not find your name here, please forgive me. I should have kept better notes for this acknowledgments section.

My pathways have been as improbable as any, and I deeply appreciate what higher education in the United States makes possible. As we find ourselves back on the cusp of unimaginable changes, I want to acknowledge relationships that ground my sense of being. My immediate family has filled my life with meaning and love. To my daughter Lola Rozas Carvalho and to my wife Michael Elizabeth Rozas: may we keep inventing futures together.

There are several communities I would like to thank: the Olá Program at King Open School, the Radcliffe Child Care Center, Danehy Park soccer, special shout-out to Pinstagram. Agradeço minha irmã, Roberta, sua coragem e fé na vida. Minha mãe querida, Lilian. Meu pai. The Rozas family. And many friends, for hosting me while this book was being written, and all else (including reading!): Marcelo Mendes, Daniela Machado, Darina Zlateva, Takuma Ono, Renata Bertol, Gabriel Duarte, Paulinha Alves, Pedro Jaguaribe, Christopher O'Connell, John Harlow, Sian Tom, Noah Eaker, Jessica Sindler, Michael Martinez, Katie Putnam Martinez, Katie Pawlik, Julian Kelly, Beau Sacoccia, Claire Bangser, Jesse Nisselson, Allison Mooney, Ayres Neto, Andreia Santos, Dudu Zobaran, Karin Goodfellow, Peter Tsapatsaris, Lucas Carvalho, Shefali Oza, Aram Harrow, Karen Harris, and Paulo Carvalho. If you know I love you and your name is not here, consider hosting me before the next book.

Much appreciation for everyone who kindly helped with images and at archives. Nicole DiMella provided patient and expert assistance. Thank you as well to Idurre Alonso, Rachel Anderson, Sara Rogers, Isabelle Godineau, Margarita Gutman, Lucio Branco, Fred Kameny, and Sinai Sganzerla. I had the privilege of working with an extraordinary team at Princeton University Press, including Natalie Baan, Jennifer Harris, and Emma Wagh. Priya Nelson was the best editor I could have imagined. And finally, to whoever is reading, thank you, obrigado.

NOTES

Preface

1. The event with David Graeber and Peter Thiel took place at the General Society of Mechanics and Tradesmen of the City of New York on September 9, 2014. It was widely covered in the press and can be easily found online.

2. In the original Chevrolet ad, in Spanish: *el futuro llegó.*

3. Agatha is the "precog" based on Philip K. Dick's "The Minority Report" (1956) and says the line in the movie adaptation directed by Steven Spielberg (2002).

4. In the original, in Italian: *voi ci rubate il futuro noi ci riprendiamo le città.*

Introduction

1. Seligman et al., *Homo Prospectus.* Gilbert, "Prospection," *Stumbling on Happiness.*

2. Published in *Der Humorist* on March 15, 1848, quoted in Clark, *Revolutionary Spring,* 305.

3. The graphs, meant to show basic patterns, were created with the help of Zeynep Bromberg. They use data compiled by the University of Toronto (http://www.globalcitiesinstitute.org). We shift from municipal to metropolitan population starting around 1950.

4. The descriptors Global North/Global South largely correspond to developed/developing countries. This book will prefer the geographic differentiation to the latter, even if it is also imperfect. Graphs of total urban populations by continent would show a sequence of ascending curves, staggered over time. Opting to highlight the share of largest urban hubs across the world, instead, conveys global demographic shifts, while also aiming to recognize the symbolic, cultural, and political importance of major cities.

5. Chakrabarty alludes to that construct in *Provincializing Europe,* an influential critique of diffusionism.

6. Levy, *Ages of American Capitalism,* xv.

7. See, for example: Beckert, *Imagined Futures*; Appadurai, *The Future as Cultural Fact*; Andersson, *The Future of the World*; Urry, *What Is the Future?*; Attali, *A Brief History of the Future.*

8. Jauss, "Literary History," 33.

9. Núñez and Sweetser, "With the Future behind Them."

10. Benjamin, *Illuminations,* 11, 12, 249.

11. Grabar, *Paved Paradise,* xiv.

12. In response to the Sputnik launch in 1957. Quoted in Lepore, *If Then,* 76.

13. Coronil, *The Magical State,* 10.

14. Carvalho, *Occupy All Streets*, 84–86.

15. My translation. Lispector, *Um sopro de vida*, 160.

16. "Le Dessus et le dessous de Paris," quoted in Rice, *Parisian Views*, 178.

17. My translation. Émile Zola, "Les Squares," *Le Figaro*, June 18, 1867.

18. My translation. Alphand, *Les promenades de Paris*, 182–183.

19. Arrhenius received the Nobel Prize for Chemistry in 1903. Quoted in Christianson, *Greenhouse*, 115. At current rates, the doubling of CO_2 will occur in the twenty-first century.

20. Arrhenius, *Worlds in the Making*, 55.

21. "Experience and Poverty," *Selected Writings*, 731.

22. Rawson, *The Nature of Tomorrow*, ix, 5 et passim.

23. Nixon, *Slow Violence*.

24. See Meyer, *The Environmental Advantages of Cities*. A growing literature keeps adding evidence to the argument. See, for example, Subin et al., "U.S. Urban Land-Use Reform."

25. Data for Europe and the United States can be easily accessed (https://coolclimate.berkeley.edu/maps; https://openghgmap.net). Differences can range from 5× to 30×.

26. Phillips, *Austerity Ecology*.

27. One study estimates that 78 percent of microplastics in oceans derive from tire rubber. Jim Robbins, "Road Hazard: Evidence Mounts on Toxic Pollution from Tires," *Yale Environment 360*, September 19, 2023.

28. This borrows from a formulation by William James quoted in Matthew Karp, "History as End," *Harper's Magazine*, July 2021.

1. In Pursuit of the Future (1750s–1790s)

1. For testimonies of survivors, see Tavares, *O Pequeno Livro do Grande Terramoto*, 71–89.

2. Neiman, *Evil in Modern Thought*, 245.

3. My translation. Voltaire, "Poème sur desastre de Lisbonne."

4. Neiman, *Evil*, 246. On philosophical debates following the earthquake, also see Marques, "The Paths of Providence."

5. Koselleck, *Futures Past*, 280.

6. Nelson, *The Time of Enlightenment*.

7. My translation. See the original in *Oeuvres de Maximilien Robespierre*, 495. For the first part of the quote, I rely on the translation in Koselleck, *Futures Past*, 13.

8. See the Abbé de Saint-Pierre, in *Observations on the Continuous Progress of Universal Reason* (1737). We can also think of the US declaration of independence in 1776, or the philosophies of Benjamin Franklin.

9. Bercé, *History of Peasant Revolts*, 276.

10. See Minois, *L'âge d'or*. Google Books Ngram Viewer searches show usage of the word "civilization" growing sharply from the 1760s to the 1850s in both English and French. This growth happens later in Italian (1810s), and in Spanish and German (1870s). The tool is unavailable in Portuguese. The word "progress" spikes up in the early 1700s in French, and in the 1740s in English. Its usage begins to drop sharply in these languages starting in the 1960s, when the term "development" surges.

11. Koselleck, *Futures Past*, 277.

12. Koselleck, *Futures Past*, 13.

13. On the opposition to the calendar, see Shaw, *Time*, 83–121.

14. Robespierre advocated for abolition. Under Haitian pressure, in February 1794 the French National Convention abolished slavery. Napoleon reinstated it in 1802. In 1804, Haitians declared independence. Their first constitution banned slavery "forever."

15. For the impact of gold from Brazil on the nascent global economy, benefiting in particular Great Britain, see Paquette, *Imperial Portugal*, 25 et passim, and Pinto, *O Ouro Brasileiro*, 238–334.

16. V. S. Pritchett in 1955, quoted in Tavares, *O pequeno livro*, 207, and Mike Davis, *Dark Raptures*, 9. Both compared the bombing of Hiroshima to the Lisbon earthquake.

17. Leibniz, *Theodicy* (1706), 228.

18. Nelson, *The Time*, 72.

19. Maxwell, *Pombal*, 17.

20. A working paper by economic historians Davis Kedrosky and Nuno Palma stipulates that in 1750 Portugal had an "output per head higher than France or Spain." See "The Cross of Gold" (2021). Russell-Wood calls gold the "lubricant" of the Portuguese Empire in *The Portuguese Empire*, 144.

21. See the "Alvará de licença para fundação de um Convento dedicado ao dito Santo na Vila de Mafra" (1711), housed in Lisbon's Arquivo Nacional da Torre do Tombo, Chancelaria de D. João V, Livro 35, fl. 355v.

22. *The Global City*, 57, 114.

23. The convent had been inaugurated in 1730. See *Gazeta de Lisboa* (March 18, 1756) and Alberto da Fonseca Rebello, *Catalysis Ou Assolação da Cidade de Lisboa Pelo Terramoto do Primeiro de Novembra de 1755* [. . .] (Palácio Nacional de Mafra, Biblioteca Volante 2-9-6-13).

24. My translation. Quoted in Figueiredo, *Boa Ventura!*, 228. Popular discontentment also reflected the fact that over 1,300 people died during construction.

25. He was Secretary of War and Foreign Affairs (1750–1755), and then Secretary of the State (1756–1777). I rely on Maxwell, *Pombal*, and will use the historiographic convention of referring to him as Pombal, although he only acquired the title in 1769.

26. Quoted in Maxwell, "Lisbon: The Earthquake of 1755 and Urban Recovery under the Marquês de Pombal," *Out of Ground Zero*, 22.

27. França, *Lisboa pombalina e o Iluminismo*, 10.

28. França, *Lisboa pombalina e o Iluminismo*, 10.

29. The comment is widely attributed to him, but some argue it originated in anti-Pombal literature. See Kendrick, *Lisbon Earthquake*, 75.

30. Tavares, *O pequeno livro*, 122.

31. Maia's *Dissertação* is transcribed in Ayres, *Manuel da Maya*, 25–50.

32. My translation. Maia, in Ayres, *Manuel da Maya*, 45.

33. See Tallon, "The Portuguese Precedent for Pierre Patte's Street Section."

34. Maxwell, "Lisbon," and Maria Helena Barreiros, "Urban Landscapes: Houses, Streets, and Squares of 18th Century Lisbon," in *Cultural History of Early Modern European Streets*, 20.

35. My translation. Laugier, *Essai sur l'architecture*, 234.

36. My translation. Voltaire, "Des embellissemens de Paris," 76–90.

37. See, for example, França, *Lisboa pombalina.*

38. *The Historical Charters and Constitutional Documents of the City of London,* edited by Walter de Gray Birch, 226.

39. Maia ultimately dismisses sidewalks for pedestrians, inspired by English streets. On transatlantic influences, see Wilson, *The Ashley Cooper Plan,* 100. The rejected plans for London feature prominently in urban histories.

40. See Riitta Laitinen and Dag Lindstrom, "Urban Order and Street Regulation in Seventeenth-Century Sweden," *Cultural History,* edited by Laitinen. Other cases include Catania in Sicily, and parts of Copenhagen, Oslo, Berlin, and Vienna. Also see Bruce, *Sunlight at Midnight,* 1–104.

41. Some historians of science refer to a "geometrical spirit." Edgerton, *Art and Cartography,* 10–50.

42. Mumford, *The City in History,* 172.

43. My translation. Rama, *La ciudad letrada,* 17.

44. Jean-François Lejeune attributes the phrase to Siegfried Giedion, citing *Space, Time, and Architecture.* I was unable to locate it. Lejeune nonetheless makes the case, arguing "the Laws envisaged a constant and open extension," in contrast to a premodern "strong concept of fortification." *Cruelty and Utopia,* 39. For my own analyses I consulted the reprinted *Recopilación de leyes de los reynos de las Indias.*

45. Lejeune, *Cruelty and Utopia,* 39.

46. Horta Correia, "Pragmatismo e utopismo," 109.

47. I am indebted to the historian Kenneth Maxwell for sharing insights based on unpublished archival research, showing how Pombal "made huge fortunes for [. . .] largely British Lisbon-based enterpreneurs" providing materials like glass stone lintels, and cement (quoted from personal correspondence on January 7, 2022).

48. My translation. "Alvará de 12 de maio de 1758," *Collecção da legislação Portugueza,* 605.

49. See "Carta régia de 3 de Março de 1755," cod. 11393 fl. 106, National Library of Portugal; "Instruções passadas ao Governador D. António Rolim de Moura em 19 de Janeiro de 1749," quoted in Araújo, "A Urbanização da Amazônia e do Mato Grosso no século XVIII," 51.

50. My translation. *Collecção da legislação Portugueza,* 605.

51. My translation. "Ordenanzas de descubrimiento, nuevo población y pacificación de las Indias dadas por Felipe II," July 13, 1573. In *Recopilación de leyes,* ordinance 36.

52. He died in 1760. França, *Lisboa pombalina,* 107.

53. Walker, "Enlightened Absolutism and the Lisbon Earthquake."

54. Tavares, *O pequeno livro,* 128.

55. Barreiros, "Urban landscapes," in Laitinen, *Cultural History,* 36.

56. My translation. Malagrida, *Juizo da verdadeira causa do terremoto,* 11.

57. Clergyman of Gloucestershire, *An Exhortation* [. . .].

58. This and the next quote are from *Histories of the Future,* edited by Susan Harding and Daniel Rosenberg, 4.

59. My translation. Quoted in Tavares, *O pequeno livro,* 129.

60. Tavares, *O pequeno livro,* 137.

61. Harding and Rosenberg, *Histories of the Future*, 4–5. Also Koselleck, *Futures Past*, 13, 16.

62. Mumford, *City in History*, 387–389.

63. Giedion identifies in this work by Domenico Fontana the beginnings of the layout of a modern city in *Space, Time, and Architecture*, 123.

64. Mumford, *City in History*, 393.

65. See Patte, *Monuments erigés en France* and *Mémoires sur les objets les plus importants de l'architecture*.

66. França, *Lisboa pombalina*, 28–29. Also see Rossa, *Além da Baixa*, 1998.

67. França, *Lisboa pombalina*, 93.

68. The painting had a height of 290 cm and a width of 354 cm, or about 9.5 by 11.6 ft. It is sometimes called "The Expulsion of the Jesuits"; they can be seen lined up to board ships in front of Belém Palace.

69. The building represented looks like the Jerónimos monastery.

70. Quoted in Maxwell, "Lisbon: the earthquake of 1755," 37, from Pombal's "Most Secret Observations," written on June 6, 1775. Though inspired by French models, the sculptor was from Portugal, unusual for major commissions until then.

71. My translation. The entry is widely attributed to Jaucourt. *Encyclopédie*, vol. 13, 157.

72. Following the latest scientific thought, he proposed in the *Tratado da conservação da saúde dos povos* (1756) that air circulation and sunlight prevented illness, likely influencing Lisbon's plans. I am gratetul to Kenneth Maxwell for sharing extracts from his diary (at the archives of the Bibliothèque de la Faculté de Médecine in Paris).

73. Tavares, *O pequeno livro*, 27.

74. My translation. *Encyclopédie* (1758–1771), vol. 9, 573.

75. See Maxwell, "Lisbon," 37.

76. My translation. See "Réponse de José Corrêa da Serra [. . .]," annotated by Petit, "Notice inédite."

77. See, for example, Longchamps, *Malagrida*, and *The Proceedings and Sentence of the Spiritual Court of Inquisition of Portugal, against Gabriel Malagrida*.

78. *Histories of the Future*, 5.

79. Alkon, *Origins of Futuristic Fiction*. Mercier's book is also a starting point for Clarke, *The Pattern of Expectation*.

80. The Holy See and Spain censored it in 1773. See Wilkie Jr., "Mercier's *L'An 2440*," and Forsström, *Possible Worlds*.

81. My translation. Mercier, *L'An 2440*, iii.

82. Quoting Freeman's translation, *Astraea's Return*, 7. Earlier quotes are from Hooper's translation, *Memoirs of the year two thousand five hundred*, 39, 17, 12.

83. My translation. Mercier, *L'An 2440*, 15.

84. Mercier, *Memoirs*, 46, 86, 98, 38.

85. In the original, "peutit people," Mercier, *L'An 2440*, 38. Earlier quotes from pages 32, 124, 37.

86. Ribeiro Sanches made a similar argument: slavery was an affront to human dignity, and an impediment to Portugal's development because it stupefies slaveholders. Mercier, *Memoirs*, 170. Earlier references from pages. 212, 208, 233.

87. *Memoirs*, 190.

88. Nègre was capitalized in French. Mercier *L'An 2440*, 385. Quoted from Mercier, *Memoirs*, 190, 214.

89. In the original, "Les villes sont le gouffre de l'espèce humaine." Rousseau, *Emile*, 41.

90. Rousseau, *Emile*, translated by Foxley, 63.

91. Darnton, *The Great Cat Massacre*, 242.

92. Rousseau, *Julie*, 190, 192, 193.

93. Mercier, *L'An 2440*, vol. 2, 72.

94. Blanning, *The Pursuit of Glory*, 46.

95. Koselleck, *Futures Past*, 17–18.

96. Israel, *Democratic Enlightenment*, 41, 50–56.

97. Figueiredo, *Boa Ventura!*, 270, 274.

98. França, *Lisboa pombalina*, 55.

99. Maria Helena Barreiros, "Urban Landscapes," 19.

100. Guillaume Raynal was a rare intellectual who, before the Haitian revolution, predicted that slavery would lead to massive revolts. But the events ahead overwhelmed everyone's forecasting capacities.

101. Rosenberg, "An Eighteenth-Century Time Machine," 242.

102. Rosenberg, "An Eighteenth-Century Time Machine," 233.

103. Mercier, *L'An 2440*, vol. 2, 51.

104. Mercier, *L'An 2440*, vol. 2, 55.

105. Rosenberg, "An Eighteenth-Century Time Machine," 247.

106. França, *Lisboa pombalina*, 90.

107. França, *Lisboa pombalina*, 90.

108. My translation. *Elogio ao illustrissimo e excellentissimo senhor marquez do Pombal*, 4.

109. My translation. The poem was modeled after Luís de Camões's *Os Lusíadas*. Ramalho, *Lisboa Reedificada*, 85.

110. My translation. By no less that Carvalho e Melo, the future Pombal. *Elogio de D. Luiz Carlos Ignacio Xavier de Menezes*, 33.

111. Oliveira, *Lisboa Restaurada*, 66.

112. Almeida, *Lisboa Destruída*.

113. See quoted passages in Tavares, *O pequeno*, 115–116.

114. Giedion, *Space, Time, and Architecture*, 197.

115. See Tinhorão, *Domingos Caldas Barbosa*.

116. See "Lundum de cantigas vagas," published in the second volume of *Viola de Lereno*.

117. Scott, *Seeing Like a State*.

2. New Worlds Emerge (1790s–1840s)

1. Improved agricultural methods, government response, and more disciplined armies led to declines in mortality rates. See Blanning, *Pursuit of Glory*, 3–194.

2. The exception was Western Africa, where populations declined in the eighteenth and nineteenth centuries. See Manning, "African Population." For estimates of global populations

throughout history, see the Maddison Project at the University of Groningen: https://www.rug
.nl/ggdc/historicaldevelopment/maddison/.

3. Utopian communities, even when conceived as enclaves at a remove from cities, still
considered seriously the importance of the built environment. See Hayden, *Seven American
Utopias*.

4. Boya Zheng, in unpublished research, shows that their philosophies proved to be widely
influential beyond the Atlantic, impacting developments in China.

5. In France alone, we can think of Raynal, Diderot, Condorcet, and the Baron d'Holbach.

6. We might interpret enclosure laws as an alternative to the Laws of the Indies as an origin
story for modernity. Sevilla-Buitrago inserts them within a history of "capitalist urbanization"
and erosion of collective spaces in *Against the Commons*. In *Waters of Liberation*, Fontanilla
demonstrates that after the abolition of slavery in Jamaica in 1838, colonial jurists systematically
resorted to legalities to expropriate lands from black freeholders.

7. Safier argues that efforts to chart indigenous populations in the Amazon served "for
graphically demonstrating" a "population-based justification for territorial rights," *The Imperial
Map*, 156.

8. Duffy, *Nomad's Land*. Scholars like José Carlos Salas are working on how postcolonial
states in the Spanish Americas also attempted to enforce fixed property regimes on more fluid
indigenous customs based on collective tenure.

9. Blanning addresses how European courts were no longer peripatetic by the end of the
seventeenth century, writing that "the characteristic urban economy of the period 1660–1815
was not a port but a court." *The Pursuit of Glory*, 112.

10. In 1600, around 5 percent of the English population resided in London. By 1800, it had
grown to over 13 percent, compared to the Parisian share of about 2 percent of France, Lisbon's
6 percent of Portugal, and slightly lower shares for Naples in the Kingdom of the Two Sicilies.
These percentages tended to be even lower outside Europe. The contiguous populations of Qing
and Maratha, concentrating nearly half of the world's population, had much smaller shares living
in their capitals and urban centers. Across the Atlantic, the largest cities hovered around 100,000
inhabitants. Mexico City and Rio de Janeiro, the two most populous in the Americas, had around
2–3 percent of the inhabitants of Mexico and Brazil. The third, New York City, had about 1.3 percent
of the US total in 1810. In Western Africa, only Sokoto seemed to have over 100,000 inhabitants,
barely more than 1 percent of the Sokoto Caliphate's total. These shares generally increased over
time. London's stays about the same. Calculations based on censuses or estimates by scholars
(Chandler, *Four Thousand Years of Urban Growth*; Bairoch, *Cities and Economic Development*).

11. Banning, *The Pursuit of Glory*, 76.

12. Bender, *Toward an Urban Vision*, 4.

13. White, *The Intellectual versus the City*.

14. Rousseau, *Emile*, 418.

15. GDP estimates show this happening during the nineteenth century. Maddison, *Contours
of the World Economy*.

16. Brown, *Tacky's Revolt*, 8.

17. Koselleck, *Futures Past*, 19.

18. Carvalho et al., *O Livro de Tiradentes*.

19. Letter from September 6, 1816, *The Papers of Thomas Jefferson*, 36.

20. These letters can be found in Davis, "The Abbé Correa in America, 1812–1820." In the 1790s, Jefferson passed on the opportunity to aid South American revolutionaries who reached out for assistance.

21. *The Writings of Thomas Jefferson*, vol. 10, 244.

22. Koselleck, *Futures Past*, 19.

23. See Dudley, *Building Antebellum New Orleans*.

24. *The Writings of Thomas Jefferson*, vol. 7, 27.

25. Feller, *The Jacksonian Promise*, 14.

26. Grund, *The Americans*, 151.

27. Grund, *The Americans*, vol. 2, 317.

28. Grund, *The Americans*, vol. 2, 317, 316, 318.

29. See Stovall, *White Freedom*, and Carvalho, "Writing Race in Two Americas."

30. *The Papers of Thomas Jefferson*, vol. 32, 167.

31. *The Writings of Benjamin Franklin*, vol. 8, 567.

32. Kostof, *The City Shaped*, 133–135.

33. Herzog, *Frontiers of Possession*, and Furtado, *Oráculos da Geografia Iluminista*.

34. Krieger, *City on a Hill*, 15, 33.

35. Kostof, *The City Shaped*, 100.

36. Rybczynski, *City Life*, 62, 67–70.

37. Upton, *Another City*, 123, 137, 135.

38. Quoted in Krieger, *City on a Hill*, 191.

39. Quoted in Krieger, *City on a Hill*, 198.

40. Krieger, *City on a Hill*, 197.

41. L'Enfant's plan is available digitized on the website of the US Library of Congress.

42. Mercier's book circulated widely in the United States. Jefferson had a copy and exchanged letters with the author.

43. The description is from Upton, *Another City*, 118. There's persuasive evidence that Washington's plan was also inspired by a Spanish precedent. See San-Antonio-Gómez, "Similarities between L'Enfant's Urban Plan for Washington, DC, and the Royal Site of Aranjuez, Spain."

44. Mumford, *City in History*, 407.

45. *The Works of Charles Dickens*, 98. Krieger titles his chapter on Washington after Dickens's moniker.

46. Rybczynski, *City Life*, 97.

47. Their remarks are transcribed in Ballon, *The Greatest Grid*, 34–42.

48. Quoted in Page, *The City's End*, 18.

49. Page, *The City's End*, 20.

50. Bandarra, a sixteenth-century Portuguese prophet whose popularity had a resurgence in the Lusophone world during the early 1800s, was also known as a shoemaker.

51. Information here largely draws on Koeppel, *City on a Grid*, and Ballon, *The Greatest Grid*.

52. Quoted in Koeppel, *City on a Grid*, 83.

53. Tafuri, *Architecture and Utopia*, 38.

54. Tafuri, *Architecture and Utopia*, 38.

55. Koolhaas, *Delirious New York*, 18.

56. Koeppel, *City on a Grid*, 94.

57. This relies on Glaeser, "Urban Colossus."

58. Glaeser, "Urban Colossus," 7.

59. He was a Hamilton protégé. Quoted in Koeppel, *City on a Grid*, 30.

60. Quoted in Koeppel, *City on a Grid*, xxi.

61. That phrase is quoted in Koeppel, *City on a Grid*, xx. Subsequent quotes are from Schuyler, "The Art of City Making."

62. From De Witt, *The Elements of Perspective*, iii, quoted in Reuben Rose-Redwood, "Mythologies of the Grid in the Empire City," 235.

63. Quoted in Rose-Redwood, "Mythologies of the Grid," 237. Rose-Redwood departs from a historiographic tendency of interpreting the grid in terms of utilitarian aims.

64. Kostof, *City Shaped*, 121.

65. Marcuse, "The Grid as City Plan," 290–291.

66. Tafuri, *Architecture and Utopia*, 40.

67. Sennett, "American Cities," 208.

68. Sennett, "American Cities," 208. My italics.

69. Mumford, *City in History*, 387.

70. Koeppel, *City on a Grid*, 142.

71. Koeppel, *City on a Grid*, 142.

72. Letter from March 7, 1819. Gratz, *Letters of Rebecca Gratz*, 49.

73. Letter from May 4, 1828. Gratz, *Letters*, 154.

74. Letter from February 23, 1840. Gratz, *Letters*, 435.

75. Letter to Benjamin Gratz, from April 15, 1863. Gratz, *Letters*, 699. She was being critical of people ignoring the Civil War. The charge of urban idleness, nonetheless, was recurrent in the United States. Beecher, for example, writes: "there are large establishments of idle and wicked persons, in most of our cities, who associate together, to support themselves by every species of imposition." *A Treatise on Domestic Economy*, 217.

76. Rosenbaum, *A Voyage to America Ninety Years Ago*, 61–62.

77. Tafuri, *Architecture and Utopia*, 1.

78. Rosenbaum, *A Voyage to America*, 62.

79. Sackersdorff Farm, in *Maps of Farms Commonly Called the Blue Book* (New York Public Library Digital Gallery). Also see Freeland, *American Hotel*.

80. Mumford, *City in History*, 409. Lagging construction methods and cultural resistance to high-rises would be significant factors in Europe.

81. Lecrouver, *From East Prussia to the Golden Gate*, 278.

82. The novel was published in serial form between 1837 and 1843. The town was Angoulême, and the original reads "la plus funeste immobilité." This translation is quoted from Rothschild, *An Infinite History*, 1.

83. Quoted from the translation by Ellen Marriage. The later developments happen in the sequel, *The Splendors and Miseries of Courtesans* (1838–1847).

84. Balzac had written in the novel's preface that "chance is the greatest novelist in the world; to be fruitful you only have to study it."

85. The formula of chance encounters playing a role in a character's changing fortunes is also found in Horatio Alger's stories, for example.

86. See Slater, *Charles Dickens*.

87. On how Sue's fiction was informed by letters from readers inhabiting the Parisian milieu he wrote about, see Prendergast, *For the People by the People?*

88. This happens in the sequel, *The Mysteries of the Court of London*, inspired by Chartist principles.

89. Grau-Lleveria, "La ficción política," 14.

90. Buntline, *The Mysteries and Miseries of New York*, 58.

91. Letter to James Madison from 1787, while he was in Paris. *The Papers of Thomas Jefferson*, Vol. 12, 438.

92. Streeby, *American Sensations*.

93. Reynolds, *The Mysteries of London*, 4.

94. See Hindes, *Revealing Bodies*.

95. My translation. Balzac, *Oeuvres Illustrées*, 85.

96. That was about 40 percent of the total population in the 1840s. See Bergad, "Slavery in Cuba and Puerto Rico," 98–128.

97. According to 1872 census. Brazil likely became the world's largest coffee producer in the 1840s.

98. See Hogendorm and Lovejoy, *Slow Death for Slavery*.

99. His name was George Frederick Cooke. Quoted in Williams, *Capitalism and Slavery*, 49.

100. *Anais do Senado*, 1843, vol. IV, p. 346.

101. About 15 percent of the Brazilian population was enslaved (1872 census), compared to 12.7 percent in the United States (1860 census). In Brazil, most Afro-descendants were freed-persons, compared to around 11 percent in the United States.

102. Douglass, *Narrative of the Life of Frederick Douglass*, 8, 41, 46.

103. Douglass, *Narrative*, 101.

104. Douglass, *Narrative*, 105.

105. See for instance his letter from Belfast, in 1846, to William Lloyd Garrison, in *Life and Writings of Frederick Douglass*, vol. I, 125.

106. Interview with Delia Garlic in 1936, *Federal Writers' Project: Slave Narrative Project* (Alabama, vol. 1), 137.

107. See Reis, *Rebelião Escrava no Brasil*. He estimates that 42 percent of the city was enslaved, of which around 64 percent were African. This is comparable to Rio de Janeiro.

108. Cowling, *Conceiving Freedom*.

109. Grimké, *The Grimké Sisters*, 98.

110. Quoted from Owen, "Letter to His Royal Highness the Prince Regent of the British Empire," *A New View of Society*.

111. He was an important advocate of the 8-hour workday, for example. Wilson, *The Angel and the Serpent*, 125–135.

112. My translation. Fourier, *Théorie des quatre mouvemens*, 425.

113. See Guarnieri, *The Utopian Alternative*. His influence extends to the anarchism of Proudhon and thinkers like David Harvey.

114. Picon, *Les Saint-Simoniens*.

115. See the University of Cambridge's *Atlas of Victorian and Edwardian Population*, available online.

116. Engels was the son of a German textile industrialist and experienced the realities of Manchester firsthand. *The Condition of the Working Class in England* (1845) was published in Germany, and in English translation in the 1880s. Several publications attribute to this book a prediction about the "grim future of capitalism and the industrial age," but I was unable to locate that phrase.

117. Sennett, *Building and Dwelling*. Bazalgette led London's Metropolitan Board of Works, created in the 1850s.

118. Walker, *Victorian Visions*, 224.

119. Etzler, *The Paradise within Reach*, 79.

120. Etzler, *The Paradise within Reach*, 163.

121. Walker, *Victorian Visions*, 231. On crystal palaces, see the next chapter.

122. Walker makes this connection. *Victorian Visions*, 234.

123. This might recall the boom in the turnpike system in the United States at the time. Griffith's narrator refers to these vehicles by different names, and it is hard to have a precise sense of what she meant.

124. "From the N.Y. Observer. Dr. Humphrey's Tour," *Biblical Recorder* (April 20, 1836), 4.

125. Tocqueville, *Democracy in America*, 289.

126. The speech is transcribed in *The Recollections of Alexis de Tocqueville*, 11, 14.

127. In German, *nüchternen* for sober. It is a literal translation. For connections between temperance, abolitionism, and suffrage, see Schrad, *Smashing the Liquor Machine*.

128. Clark, *Revolutionary*, 345–350.

129. Metternich wrote on March 1st that "Europe is facing the year 1793 again [...], we are headed toward horrible events!" Quoted in Murray-Miller, *Revolutionary Europe*, 165.

130. For a second time, since Napoleon had reinstituted it.

131. "Speech at the Anniversary of the *People's Paper*," quoted in *The Marx-Engels Reader*, 577–578.

132. My translation. "Se vogliamo che tutto rimanga com'è bisogna che tutto cambi." *Il Gattopardo* was published posthumously in 1958.

133. Bury, *The Idea of Progress*, 318.

134. The formulation alludes to Anderson's seminal *Imagined Communities*.

135. Clark, *Revolutionary*, 729.

136. See Weyland, "The Diffusion of Revolution."

137. Carvalho, "Os Nomes da Revolução."

138. See Boyer, *Urban Masses*.

139. *Account of the Terrific and Fatal Riot*, 6.

140. Available at NYU's Folger Digital Image Collection.

3. Everything Seems Possible (1850s–1880s)

1. Clark, *Revolutionary*, 729.

2. In France, the Polytechnic School founded in 1794 instilled a culture of calculations, engineering futures, in contrast to the Fine Arts tradition's investment in the past. Quotes are from Alphand, *Les Promenades*, volume I, lix. My translations.

3. Alphand, *Les Promenades*, 59.

4. Mumford, *Designing the Modern City*, 26.

5. Ogle, *The Global Transformation of Time*, 2.

6. Williams, *The Country and the City*, 16.

7. Foley, "From Wall Street to Astor Place."

8. In the "Camden & Amboy Rail Road and Transportation Company's First Annual Report," printed in *The Register of Pennsylvania*, vol. VII, no. 23 (1831), 362.

9. "The Pacific Railroad and How It Is to Be Built," *Putnam's Monthly* 2.11 (1853): 505.

10. Karuka, *Empire's Tracks*, 45, 75, 132, et passim. In the eighteenth century, Jeremy Bentham had already wanted glass in the Panopticon.

11. Schley, *Steam City*, 6.

12. Attributed to Ah-nen-la-de-ni (Daniel La France). Holt, *The Life Stories of Undistinguished Americans*, 207–208.

13. See Armstrong, "Languages of Glass." Benjamin noted the use of glass and iron in "buildings that served transitory purposes," *Reflections*, 159.

14. "The Great Exhibition and Its Visitors," *Putnam's Monthly*, 2.12 (1853): 582. The magazine owners had an interest in promoting the event. They also published its catalogue. The building was in present-day Bryant Park.

15. "Our Crystal Palace," *Putnam's Monthly* 2.8 (1853): 121.

16. Others had also proposed the combination of iron and steel as the future of architecture. See Jobard, "L'Architecture de l'avenir," 27.

17. *Official descriptive and illustrated catalogue of the Great Exhibition* [. . .].

18. "Our Crystal Palace," *Putnam's Monthly* 2.8 (1853): 127. Subsequent quotes are from the same page. The October issue opened with the question: "What impression do we, and should we, make abroad?" 345.

19. Dostoevsky, *Notes from Underground*, 15.

20. Mayhew, *London Labour and the London Poor*.

21. June 7, 1855. "Minutes of Evidence Taken before Select Committee," *Report from the Select Committee on Metropolitan Communications*, 90. In 1857 an unnamed French engineer published *Les Cités de Chemins de Fer*, with a proposal sharing some of the same elements, like a railway encircling Paris and glass-domed buildings.

22. Hobsbawm and Ranger, *The Invention of Tradition*.

23. Harvey writes that "one of the myths of modernity is that it constitutes a radical break with the past." *Paris: Capital of Modernity*, 1. He argued that proponents of the Parisian reforms built that myth.

24. "Sketches in a Paris Café," *Putnam's Monthly* 2.12 (1853): 627–632.

25. My translation for "Il n'y est que le provisoire qui dure en France." "Sketches," *Putnam's Monthly* 2.12 (1853): 627.

26. Baudelaire, *Selected Writings*, 403.

27. Quoted in McAuliffe, *Paris, City of Dreams*, 29.

28. Jordan, *Transforming Paris*, 159.

29. Jordan, *Transforming Paris*, 220.

30. This ambition had precedents as early as the 1300s. Jordan, *Transforming Paris*, 187. As Gaillard has shown in *Paris, la ville*, many elements of the reforms drew on earlier plans, including from a committee headed by Saint Simon.

31. Moncan and Herteux, *La Paris d'Haussmann*, 64–65.

32. Moncan and Herteux, *La Paris d'Haussmann*, 58–61. Jordan, *Transforming*, 355.

33. Jordan, *Transforming*, 358.

34. Nilsen, "Paris: Haussmann, the Railways, and the New Gates to the City."

35. McAuliffe, *Paris*, 59. Queen Victoria attended. The official name was Exposition Universelle des Produits de l'Agriculture, de l'Industrie et des Beaux-Arts.

36. Mumford, *Designing*, 26.

37. Nelson, "Defining the Urban," 229.

38. Giuntini, "2 ITU, Submarine Cables," 37.

39. Çelik, *Empire, Architecture, and the City*, 73.

40. Çelik, *Empire*, 12.

41. Quoted from Carroll, "Imperial Ideologies," 67–68. Napoleon III himself did not like the term "colony," as he thought that the French should not substitute Arabs as the majority. As a child, the chief architect of the Boulevard de l'Impératrice had fled the Haitian Revolution. Part of it today is named after Che Guevara.

42. My translation. *L'Exposition universelle de 1867*, 31. The publication makes reference to how other several countries can look forward to a brighter future.

43. Jordan, *Transforming*, 9.

44. Quoted in Jordan, *Transforming*, 287.

45. Quoted in Bresler, *Napoleon III*, 304–305.

46. Jordan, *Transforming*, 85.

47. Jordan, *Transforming*, 304. Loyer, *Paris XIXe Siècle*, 332.

48. See Frégier, *Des classes dangereuses*; Chevalier, *Laboring Classes*; Kalifa, *Vice, Crime, and Poverty*.

49. Delaroy, *Des moyens de contenir les classes dangereuses*.

50. Jordan, *Transforming*, 198.

51. Jordan, *Transforming*, 198.

52. Shapiro, *Housing the Poor of Paris*, 48 et passim.

53. McAuliffe, *Paris, City of Dreams*, 77.

54. The debt was not paid down until 1929. Jordan, *Transforming*, 224, 305.

55. McAuliffe, *Paris, City of Dreams*, 143, 195.

56. Hopkins, *Planning the Greenspaces*, 127.

57. It was called Service des Promenades et Plantations. Alphand remained in that role beyond the Second Empire and became an important influence throughout the Atlantic, as we will see.

58. Jordan, *Transforming*, 264.

59. Zola, *La Curée*, 94. Published in 1872.

60. McAuliffe, *Paris*, 60–61.

61. Robert Sherard quoted in Jordan *Transforming*, 348.

62. In 1860. Quoted in Jordan *Transforming*, 348,

63. McAuliffe, *Paris*, 142.

64. Léon Halévy in 1867, quoted in Maneglier, *Paris Impérial*, 263.

65. César Daly, *Conférence internationale* (1867), 78, quoted in Sadighian, *The World Is a Composition*, 77.

66. My translation for "Bramo assai, poco spero." Nuitter, *La Nouvel Opéra*, 19. The often misquoted original, from *Gerusalemme liberata* (1581), reads "brama assai, poco spera, e nulla chiede," which is in the second person and adds "asks for nothing."

67. Sand, "Rêverie à Paris," translated by Shapiro.

68. Baudelaire, "The Swan," translated by Huneker.

69. Quoted in Gluckstein, *The Paris Commune*, 41.

70. My translation for "aux travailleurs nouveautes / bon marché exceptionnel."

71. Milza, *L'année terrible*, 77 et passim.

72. There is much debate about the numbers, with estimates ranging from 10,000 to 25,000. Merriman, *Massacre*, 253 et passim. Also Eichner, *The Paris Commune*.

73. Meyer, *Dividing Paris*, 8 et passim.

74. Jordan, *Transforming*, 326.

75. Karl Marx's pamphlet *The Civil War in France*, published in 1871, included the text.

76. Goncourt, *Pages from the Goncourt Journal*, 194.

77. Letter from March 31, 1871; Sand, *Correspondance*.

78. Beaumont, "Cacotopianism."

79. Meyer, *Dividing Paris*, 6.

80. Walker, "Lost in the City of Light," 34–35.

81. O'Shea, *Future Histories*, 115.

82. And that, of course, military asymmetries cannot be underestimated. Anarchists and revolutionaries continued to be inspired by the Commune, for example, in postrevolutionary Mexico.

83. Oliveira, "Imagining an Old City in Nineteenth-Century France."

84. Bentlin, "Understanding the Hobrecht Plan."

85. Examples include Milan, Brussels, and Budapest. Mumford, *Designing*, 26.

86. Schorske, *Fin-de-Siecle Vienna*.

87. The surveys had been commissioned in 1854. The 1860 plan was a variation of an 1855 version. Grupo 2C, *La Barcelona de Cerdà*.

88. They had precedents in Argentina. "La razón en la ciudad: el Plan Cerdà," 51, 82, et passim.

89. Bohigas, "En el centenerio del Plan Cerdà," 7–13.

90. Cirici-Pellicer, "Significación del Plan Cerdá," 45–47.

91. My translation. Cerdá, *Teoría*, 7.

92. Cerdá, *Teoría*, 7.

93. Cerdá, *Teoría*, 8, 14, 18.

94. Cerdá, *Teoría*, 14–15.

95. Cerdá articulated his doctrines as "medicine" for the "profound malaise that afflicts modern societies." *Teoría*, 12.

96. Cerdá, *Teoría*, 50 et passim. We are, once again, not too far from Baudelaire's description of modernity.

97. Sutton, *Les Icariens*. Cerdá's plans also drew from the worker cooperatives in Barcelona. One biographer highlights the influence of Saint-Simonianism. Estapé, *Vida y Obra de Ildefonso Cerdá*.

98. My translation. Cabet, *Voyage en Icarie*, 39.

99. Cabet, *Voyage en Icarie*, 39.

100. The word is also recurrent in Cerdá's writing. In *Les Saint-Simoniens*, Picon shows that for Saint-Simonian engineers, modern science and technology coexisted with religion and a sense of wonder.

101. Paccoud, *A Politics of Regulation*. Major investors in Haussmannization, the Pereire brothers were also Saint-Simonianists, with ideas that entangled material progress and Jewish-inflected messianism.

102. Cerdá, *Teoría*, 565–566.

103. Newman and Holton, *Boston's Back Bay*.

104. About 250 acres, in Barcelona's case. Aibar and Bijker, "Constructing a City."

105. Krieger, *City*, 110.

106. On the *New-York Tribune*, Greeley followed up: "But on a farm in the West [. . .] dissatisfied young men could not only make money, and live decently, but also be of some use to the country" (December 13, 1867). The famous phrase, however, does not appear to originate with him. See Fuller, "Go West, Young Man—an Elusive Slogan."

107. In *Crabgrass Frontier*, Jackson details the material and ideological factors behind suburban expansion, including federal subsidies.

108. In a matter of a few decades, abundant passenger pigeons went extinct, and bisons nearly so.

109. Fein, *Frederick Law Olmsted and the American Environmental Tradition*.

110. Koeppel, *City*, 124.

111. Olmsted, *The Papers of Frederick Law Olmsted*, vol. III, 192.

112. Rosenberg, "An Eighteenth-Century Time Machine," 248. In contrast, he attributed to Diderot and D'Alembert an "open and activist vision of the future of human knowledge," 249.

113. Olmsted, *Frederick Law Olmsted*, 98.

114. *New York Daily Herald*, June 5, 1870, 12.

115. "The Completion of the Central Park—the Future of New York," *New York Times*, June 28, 1860, 4.

116. Olmsted, *Frederick Law Olmsted*, 45.

117. Olmsted, *Frederick Law Olmsted*, 172.

118. Olmsted, *Frederick Law Olmsted*, 189.

119. Olmsted, *Frederick Law Olmsted*, 169. Olmsted quoted an "astute editor" who wrote that it was "folly to expect in this country to have parks like those in old aristocratic countries," since American habits are more licentious and less refined, only to praise the behavior of ordinary people in the park, in contrast to the rich in carriages.

120. It was titled "Public Parks and the Enlargement of Towns." Olmsted, *Frederick Law Olmsted: Essential Texts*, 201 et passim.

121. Theodora Kimball, the first librarian of landscape architecture at Harvard, wrote that passage with Olmsted's "advice and criticism." Olmsted, *Frederick Law Olmsted*, 17. They maintain elsewhere that "five hundred acres is the smallest area that should be reserved for the future wants of such a city, now, while it may be obtained," 27.

122. In 1858. Olmsted, *Frederick Law Olmsted*, 239.

123. Miller, *Before Central Park*.

124. Brent Staples, "In Search of the Black Utopia," *New York Times*, January 8, 2022.

125. Alexander, *African or American?*

126. Staples cites the historian Alexander Manevitz, author of *The Rise and Fall of Seneca Village* (forthcoming), who "estimates that by 1855, the village contained only 1 percent of the city's black population—but had 20 percent of its black property owners and 15 percent of its black voters." The New York state legislature had made property ownership of a certain value a condition for black men to vote.

127. Rosenzweig and Blackmar, *The Park and the People*.

128. *Putnam's Monthly* 2.10 (1853): 347–348.

129. *Frederick Law Olmsted: Essential Texts*, 208.

130. Rosenzweig and Blackmar, *The Park and the People*, 173–175.

131. This is a common slogan in Spanish planning literature, often attributed to Cerdá.

132. Busquets, *Barcelona*, 190.

133. Wynn, "Barcelona: Planning and Change 1854–1977." Since the 1990s, the basic blueprint has been adaptable enough for taller high-tech constructions in El Poblenou.

134. See www.barcelona2159.org.

135. Quoted in Koeppel, *City*, xx.

136. "The Future of Central Park," *New York Times*, April 12, 1909, 6.

137. Judy Sternlight and Carl Sherman, "Future Shock in Central Park," *New York Times*, February 6, 2000, 17.

138. Jordan, *Transforming*, 358.

139. "Rachida Dati, a member of the right-wing Republican Party who ran for Paris mayor in 2014 and 2020, noted, 'we need a good architectural integration of new buildings, like during Haussmann's era.'" Quoted in Freemark et al., "Housing Haussmann's Paris," 311.

140. Mumford, *City in History*, 349.

141. Van Zanten, *Building Paris*, 46. Paccoud, in "Planning Law, Power, and Practice," more recently provided further evidence of bureaucratic tensions and competing priorities among various government actors.

142. Yates, *Selling Paris*, 4.

143. For example, contemporary Horace Say noted a higher prevalence of cholera in prereform Paris. In the twentieth century we might think of Sigfried Giedion (1941), David Pinkney (1957), and Jeanne Gaillard (1997). See Freemark et al., "Housing Haussmann's Paris."

144. See Meyer, *Dividing*, versus Freemark et al., "Housing." The latter shows "that projects often were constructed on greenfield land, or in a manner that reaffirmed pre-existing demographic distributions," 294.

145. David Harvey, *Limits to Capital*, and *Paris, Capital of Modernity*. Applications of Harvey's critical framework to contemporary settings tend to underestimate how much power homeowners amassed in the twentieth century relative to developers. In contrast, Yates estimates that in Paris at the end of the 1900s "less than 2 percent of households were owner-occupants," *Selling Paris*, 18.

146. See, for example, Sutcliffe, *The Autumn of Central Paris*.

147. See, for example, Merrifield, *The New Urban Question*.

148. See Shapiro, *Housing*.

149. Freemark et al., "Housing," 11.

150. Freemark et al., "Housing," 11, 15.

151. See for example Higonnet, *Paris, Capitale du Monde des Lumières au Surréalisme*.

152. Meyer described Haussmann as the "epitome of visionary boldness" to planners from "Daniel Burnham to Robert Moses"—among them, Le Corbusier. *Dividing*, 18.

153. We can think of Aldo Rossi in the 1970s and the work of François Loyer, for example.

154. Giedion, *Space*, 215.

155. My translation. The plot is set between 1815 and the rebellions in June of 1832, though the book is full of digressions about other periods. Hugo's own experiences in the 1848 barricades served as a source.

156. My translation. Murger, *Scènes de la vie de Bohème*, xi.

157. Théophile Gautier, "Future Paris" (1851), and Arsène Houssaye, "Future Paris," (1856); versus Joseph Méry, "The Ruins of Paris" (ca. 1856), and Alfred Bonnardot, "Archeopolis" (1857). See Walker, "Lost in the City of Light."

158. Verne, *Paris in the Twentieth Century*, 73.

159. Verne, *Paris*, 204.

160. Verne, *Paris*, 3.

161. Verne, *Paris*, 119.

162. Verne, *Paris*, 211.

4. Possibilities and Limits (1870s–1910s)

1. Friedman, *Fortune Tellers: The Story of America's First Economic Forecasters*.

2. Smiles, *Self-Help*, 216. This book was a Victorian favorite.

3. Twain and Warner, *The Gilded Age*, 543.

4. The drawings attributed to Jean-Marc Côté were published in Asimov, *Futuredays*. The flurry of inventions recalls popular novels of the "scientific marvelous" genre, like Albert Robida's futuristic *Le Vingtième siècle* (1890) translated as *Electric Life*.

5. My translation. Nabuco, *Minha Formação*, 183.

6. Data available at www.slavevoyages.org shows 4.8 million enslaved people arrived in the Portuguese Americas between 1530 and 1856.

7. My translation. Nabuco, *Essencial*, 137–138.

8. My translation. Nabuco, *Minha*, 183.

9. Nabuco, *Minha*, 188.

10. My translation. Nabuco, *O Abolicionismo*, 179.

11. Reis, "African Nations in Nineteenth-Century Salvador, Bahia," 73.

12. Nagô denoted Yoruba speakers in Brazil. Quoted from an autobiographical letter from 1880. My translations. Gama, *Obras Completas: Liberdade (1880–1882)*, 60–68. This edition is the most complete and reliable source on Gama.

13. Reis, "African Nations," 70.

14. My translation. Letter from November 6, 1877, to *A Provincia de São Paulo*, published in *Lições de Resistência*.

15. Gama, *Obras Completas: Liberdade*, 60–68.

16. The phrase was a subtitle in Washington's *The Future of the American Negro*, x.

17. Estimates from Tarcísio Rodrigues Botelho, "A População Brasileira em 1850."

18. Washington, *The Future*, 224.

19. Washington, *The Future*, 189.

20. See Sarmiento, *Civilización y Barbarie*.

21. Pavony, "The Emergence of Capital Cities in Nineteenth-Century Latin America," in Alonso and Casciato, *Metropolis*, 35.

22. Pavony, "The Emergence," 35.

23. Reis, "African Nations," 64; Carvalho, *Porous City*.

24. Reis, "African Nations," 69.

25. Childs, "Re-Creating African Ethnic Identities in Cuba," 85–86.

26. Carvalho, *Cidade Porosa*, 51–53.

27. According to scholars this is by coincidence rather than direct influence. Crosas Armengol, "Reticulas Verdes, Nuevas Ciudades Decimonónicas."

28. My translation. Quoted in Crosas Armengol, "Reticulas," 28.

29. Almandoz, "From Postcolonial Cities to the First Metropolises," in Alonso and Casciato, *Metropolis*, 84.

30. Main sources for this paragraph are Fernández Christlieb, *Europa y el Urbanismo Neoclásico en la Ciudad de México*, and Reese, "The Urban Development of Mexico City, 1850–1930," 139–144.

31. Tenorio-Trillo, *I Speak of the City*, 13.

32. Osterhammel, *The Transformation of the World*, 261.

33. Lomnitz, *Deep Mexico, Silent Mexico*, 51. Díaz ruled Mexico in 1876, 1877–1880, 1884–1911.

34. Tenorio-Trillo, *I Speak of the City*, 18.

35. Reese, "Urban Development," 139.

36. The main sources for this section were the *Crónica Oficial de las Fiestas* [. . .], 158, 171, 173, et passim. And Alatorre, *Recuerdo del Primer Centenario de la Independencia Nacional*. We can associate this Nike to Walter Benjamin's "angel of history."

37. My translation. *Crónica oficial*, appendix, 74.

38. *Crónica oficial*, 76–77.

39. *Crónica oficial*, 76.

40. Alexander, "The Fever of War."

41. For example, in tomes 4 and 6 of *Cours de Philosophie Positive*, Comte implies that cities are the sites of future civilized life.

42. Comte, *Discurso*, 32.

43. My translations. *Minha Formação*, 99–101.

44. *Minha Formação*, 59.

45. *Minha Formação*, 133.

46. "Ahead" is in English in the original. *Minha Formação*, 135.

47. *Minha Formação*, 146.

48. *Minha Formação*, 158.

49. *Minha Formação*, 190.

50. *Minha Formação,*189.

51. *Crónica oficial,* 76.

52. Jackson, *Crabgrass,* 111.

53. My translations. Published in *A Semana* on October 16, 1892.

54. Quoted in Hohne, *Riding the New York Subway,* 58.

55. Riis, *How the Other Half Lives,* 2.

56. Alland, *Jacob A. Riis,* 34.

57. Riis, *How the Other Half Lives,* 83–84.

58. Riis, *How the Other Half Lives,* 3.

59. Riis wrote a book about Roosevelt. Hacker, *The Gilded Age,* 148.

60. Riis, *How the Other Half Lives,* 33.

61. Riis, *How the Other Half Lives,* 83, 25.

62. This was amply covered in the press, where the descriptor "dark continent" was recurrent. Precedents to these had been restricted to aristocratic audiences. This practice lasted until the 1930s. The press suggested to readers that Somaliland peoples were there of their own volition. Auerbach, "Empire under Glass," 140.

63. My translations. Azevedo, *O Cortiço,* 11.

64. Valle, *The Beehive,* 26, 146. After abolition, between a quarter and a fifth of city residents lived in tenements.

65. Azevedo, 39.

66. Sklar, *Florence Kelley,* 236.

67. Kelley, *Autobiography,* 73.

68. Kelley, *Autobiography,* 103.

69. Kelley, *Autobiography,* 103. She corresponded with Engels and translated his *The Condition of the Working Class in England in 1844.*

70. Kelley, *Autobiography,* 97.

71. Quoted from the revised second edition. Crane, *Maggie,* 2.

72. Crane, *Maggie,* 62.

73. Crane, *Maggie,* 69.

74. Crane, *Maggie,* 103.

75. US real wage increased by 60 percent; wheat by 256 percent; corn by 222 percent; coal by 800 percent; rail track by 567 percent; and steel surpassed British, German, and French production combined. Kennedy, *The Rise and Fall of the Great Powers,* 242–244.

76. Roemer, "Contexts and Texts," 207–208. He estimates that 20 percent of utopists could be deemed socialist, 10 percent capitalist, and 10 percent totalitarian.

77. Bellamy, *Looking Backward,* 22.

78. Bellamy, *Looking Backward,* 189.

79. The Detroit Bicentennial in 1901 echoed this with the last float in a parade titled "Future of Detroit, 2001," which "pointed to how elite white men wanted to see the future of the city," representing "a beautiful triumphal arch, illustrative of the industrial progress of the city." Mays, *City of Dispossessions,* 62.

80. Rydell, *The Reason Why the Colored American Is Not in the World's Columbian Exposition,* 9. Three years later, the US Supreme Court ruled in Plessy v. Ferguson, a case over train cars, that racial segregation was legal.

81. Frederick Jackson Turner presented his "frontier thesis" in Chicago that year, positing the Midwest as "the future of the Republic." Turner, *The Frontier in American History*, 155.

82. Kelley, *The Autobiography*, 87.

83. Burnham, *Plan of Chicago*, 4, 25.

84. Burnham, *Plan*, 18, 33.

85. From a speech, printed in "Stirred by Burnham, Democracy Champion," *Chicago Record-Herald*, October 15, 1910.

86. Carvalho, *Cidade Porosa*, 89.

87. Lamarão, *Dos Trapiches ao Porto*, 143.

88. Osterhammel, *Transformation*, 282, 278.

89. Osterhammel, *Transformation*, 250.

90. Osterhammel, *Transformation*, 275. Also Scobie, *Buenos Aires*.

91. My translation. *A Semana*, July 22, 1894.

92. My translation. *A Semana*, February 14, 1897.

93. Chalhoub, *Visões da Liberdade*.

94. Vaz, *Contribuição*, 160. Benchimol gives lower numbers.

95. Chalhoub, *Visões*, 186.

96. Canudos veterans were among the first to build shanties on hillsides, adopting "favela" from the name of a plant common in the northeast.

97. Berjman, "The Domination of Nature," in Alonso and Casciato, *Metropolis*, 101.

98. My translation. *Gazeta de Notícias*, October 10, 1902. Alvear had been mayor; Prado was still in office.

99. Benchimol, *Pereira Passos*.

100. Benchimol, *Pereira Passos*, 192–194.

101. *Jornal do Brasil*, June 17, 1903.

102. My translation. *Jornal do Brasil*, March 29, 1904. *Alinhar* was a keyword in the press.

103. Hall, *Cities in Civilization*, 737, and Chapman, *The Life and Times of Baron Haussmann*, 217.

104. Azevedo, *A Grande Reforma Urbana*.

105. Osterhammel, *Transformation*, 282.

106. Benchimol, *Pereira Passos*, 52.

107. Benchimol, *Pereira Passos*, 211–212.

108. Needell, *A Tropical Belle Epoque*, 40.

109. *A Renascença*, June 1905, 274.

110. My translation. Speech by Augusto Liberalli in the *Revista do Clube de Engenharia*, February 1901, 176.

111. The letters are found in Lenzi, "Francisco Pereira Passos—Possibilidade de um outro olhar."

112. My translation. *A Renascença*, July 1904, 131.

113. *A Renascença*, July 1904, 32. Text by Souza Rangel.

114. My translation. *Gazeta de Notícias*, February 16, 1902. Miasma theories generated anti-densification measures or building up on natural environments, perceived as a solution to breeding grounds for foul air.

115. In the early 1860s. Benchimol, *Pereira Passos*, 73.

116. Almandoz, "From Postcolonial Cities," in Alonso and Casciato, *Metropolis*, 90.

117. Sevcenko, *A Revolta da Vacina*, 46.

118. Valle, *Beehive*, 214.

119. My translation. Quoted in Benchimol, *Pereira Passos*, 234.

120. *A Renascença*, July 1904, 34.

121. *Gazeta de Notícias*, December 13, 1903.

122. *Gazeta de Notícias*, August 29, 1909.

123. My translation. Sevcenko, *Revolta*, 48.

124. Sevcenko, *Revolta*, 36.

125. Meade, "Civilizing Rio," 10.

126. Sevcenko, *Revolta*, 50.

127. Sevcenko, *Revolta*, 56, 59.

128. This included praise in the *Times* (London) and *Le Figaro* (Paris) as well as in Sanitary Conferences in Copenhagen and Berlin. Sevcenko, *Revolta*, 59.

129. My translation. From *Jornal do Commercio*, quoted in Sevcenko, *Revolta*, 60–61.

130. It is worth remembering that the Plessy v. Ferguson Supreme Court case upholding "separate but equal" facilities was about racially segregated car trains.

131. Meade, "Civilizing Rio," 7.

132. In terms of both income and health indicators. Meade, *"Civilizing Rio,"* 50–51.

133. I am indebted to Orlando Calheiros for these insights on this instrument and Afro-Brazilian religions.

134. My translations. The song was recorded in 1933.

5. The Sky Is Not the Limit (1900s–1940s)

1. My translations. Rio, *Vida Vertiginosa*, 3–11.

2. Rio, *Vida*, 333–341.

3. *Proceedings*, 65–70.

4. Borsi, "Drawing the Region." In the anglophone world, the Scottish polymath Patrick Geddes was also pioneering regional planning in Scotland and India.

5. Quotes are from the coverage of the exhibit in Charlottenburg in the Rio de Janeiro illustrated magazine *Fon-Fon!*, October 1910. The event was also covered in *The American City*, where George Ford described it as "a development in modern civic endeavor that means a great deal for the future," as cities began to realize that "radical steps must be taken to prevent the cities strangling themselves," vol. 3, 1910, 538.

6. Bernhardt, *Bauplatz Groß-Berlin*, 277.

7. Hall, *Cities of Tomorrow*, 9–10.

8. Osterhammel, *Transformation*, 291–292.

9. Osterhammel, *Transformation*, 291–292.

10. Osterhammel, *Transformation*, 294.

11. Carranza and Lara, *Modern Architecture in Latin America*, 10–16.

12. My translation. Gutman, *Buenos Aires*, 407.

13. Weekley, *Etymological Dictionary*.

14. I am grateful to Emma Fang's extensive research in the archives of *The American City* and *The City Plan*, identifying representative trends and themes. Quotes here are from Robert Whitten, "The Constitution and Powers of a City Planning Authority," *The City Plan*, 1915, 33–37.

15. Andersen and Hébrard, *Creation of a World Centre of Communication.*

16. Wright, *The Politics of Design in French Colonial Urbanism.*

17. Osterhammel, *Transformation,* 296.

18. Osterhammel, *Transformation,* 315.

19. Howard, *Garden Cities,* 18.

20. Howard, "The Transit Problem," 127–132.

21. Fishman, *Urban Utopias,* 46, 78, 85.

22. Fishman, *Urban,* 34–35 et passim.

23. Schaffer, *Garden Cities for America.*

24. Lynch et al., "'Transforming Freetown.'"

25. Dakar became capital of French West Africa in 1902. It had been called a "distant suburb of Paris" in 1889. See Bigon, *Garden Cities,* 51 et passim, and Bigon and Hart, "Beneath the city's grid."

26. Bigon, *Garden Cities,* 36, 46.

27. Georges Benoit-Lévy, the inaugural secretary of this French organization, had founded the Association of Garden Cities in 1903 and authored *Cités Jardin d'Amerique* (1905).

28. Schuyler, "The Art of City-Making," 25 et passim.

29. Friedman, *The Structure of Skyscrapers,* 126.

30. The story was first published in *Scribner's Magazine,* July 1891. Its basic plot would have been plausible through the 1910s and in other cities.

31. The acronym for Not in My Back Yard, currently used to describe opponents of development or change, in opposition to YIMBYs (Yes in My Back Yard).

32. Bellamy, *Looking,* 47.

33. Sarlo, "Los Debates," 190.

34. "Le Futurisme," *Le Figaro,* February 20, 1909, 1.

35. Quoted in Bender, *The Unfinished City,* 117.

36. Puchner, *Poetry of the Revolution,* 73.

37. My translations. "L'Architettura Futurista, Manifesto," published in *Lacerba* (Florence), August 1, 1914.

38. *Vancouver Sun,* June 29, 1914.

39. Strachan, *The First World War,* 95–101 et passim.

40. Quoted from oral history recordings played in the documentary *They Shall Not Grow Old* (2018), directed by Peter Jackson.

41. *They Shall Not Grow Old.* On the anticipation of violence as itself wounding or traumatic, see Paul Saint-Amour, *Tense Future.*

42. My translation. *Eu Sei Tudo: Magazine Mensal Illustrado,* February 1917, 20–21.

43. "Aspectos de Paris," *Gazeta de Noticias,* June 6, 1919. It was signed by João do Norte, pseudonym of Gustavo Barroso, a prominent antisemitic and ultranationalist intellectual.

44. Agache, *Comment Reconstruire.* He was a key figure in the French Society of Urbanists.

45. Vance, *The Continuing City,* 374–376.

46. Mumford, "American Architecture Today," 189.

47. Levy writes that "U.S. manufacturing productivity increased at an annual rate in excess of 5 percent—the fastest rate of growth of any decade on record," *Ages,* 348.

48. Based on data from censuses and Bairoch, *Cities*, 216.

49. Ezcurra, *Buenos Aires en el Siglo XXX*.

50. Dittrich, *Buenos Aires en el 1950*.

51. Drawing by Arturo Eusevi for an article by Enrique Vera y González, "Buenos Aires en el año 2010," in *PBT*, May 25, 1910. I am grateful to Margarita Gutman for allowing me to reproduce this image.

52. This included a drawing by US illustrator Louis Biedermann, whose "pictorial forecasts" of New York circulated as stand-ins for a future Buenos Aires. Published in *Crítica*, n. 5118, on October 23, 1927, reproduced in Gutman, *Buenos Aires*, 245.

53. Gutman, *Buenos Aires*, 106 et passim.

54. Campante and Glaeser, "Yet Another Tale of Two Cities."

55. Gold, "Under Darkened Skies," 338.

56. Wells, *The Sleeper Awakes*, 44. The book was rewritten based on an earlier serialized story.

57. *PBT*, n. 344, July 1, 1911, quoted in Gutman, *Buenos Aires*, 396.

58. According to Google Books Ngram Viewer, this is a clear trend.

59. Henry Litchfield West, for example, asked: "But what are to be the miracles of the 20th century? What is there left to discover?" The answer, he predicted, "will be in the navigation of the air." *Washington Post*, December 31, 1900.

60. Holt, *The Life Stories*, 71.

61. Designed by a Mr. Davidson, published on August 25, 1909.

62. *The Sphere*, November 20, 1909.

63. *The Sphere*, August 24, 1912.

64. On the cover of the June 1920 issue. The magazine succeeded *Modern Electrics* and was renamed *Science and Invention* later that year. It was founded by Hugo Gernsback, who started his career in the electronics industry and became a pioneer of science fiction.

65. *Electrical Experimenter*, August 1919.

66. *Electrical Experimenter*, July 1920, 256.

67. *Electrical Experimenter*, July 1920, 262–263.

68. See for example, Ernest Poole, "A City's Dream of a City," *Richmond Palladium and Sun-Telegram*, June 20, 1910.

69. *Electrical Experimenter*, August 1920, 1071.

70. Based on statistics compiled from national databases by Claire Wigglesworth.

71. Smethurst, *The Bicycle*, 5.

72. "The Bicycle," *Scientific American*, July 25, 1896, 68.

73. Oliver McKee, "The Horse or the Motor," *Lippincott's Monthly Magazine*, March 1896.

74. *New York Times*, October 2, 1898.

75. Quoted from 1913 ads for Detroit Electric and Woods Electric car companies.

76. Levy, *Ages*, 356–357.

77. Quoted in Krieger, *City on a Hill*, 6.

78. Levy, *Ages*, 327, 350.

79. Quoted from Ford's "sociology department," which inspected worker's homes and was shut down in 1919 due to pushback. Levy, *Ages*, 340.

80. Wallace, *The American Axis*.

81. Gramsci's "Americanismo e Fordismo," quoted in Levy, *Ages*, 328.

82. Levy uses the phrase in *Ages*, 168, 190, 235, 327.

83. Hager, *Electric City*.

84. He called them arrogant and elitist. Angry responses countered that cars bolster "commercial" advantages, *New York Times*, March 4, 1906.

85. *New York Times*, October 30, 1928.

86. Levy, *Ages*, 349.

87. The UK led in rail extension per square mile. Calculations based on statistics compiled from national databases by Claire Wigglesworth.

88. We might think of Frank Lloyd Wright's "Broadacre City" (1932) or the work of Ludwig Hilberseimer. Disputes over transportation were also of course about power and control. See Foster, *From Streetcar to Superhighway*.

89. Levy, *Ages*, 329.

90. Interview to Florence Davies of the *Detroit News*, November 22, 1935.

91. Quoted in Levy, *Ages*, 346.

92. Writing from 1924. Le Corbusier, *City of Tomorrow*, 190.

93. Le Corbusier, *City of Tomorrow*, 118.

94. Le Corbusier, *Oeuvre*, 111–116.

95. Norton, *Fighting Traffic*, 1.

96. "Beware Little Children," sheet music, 1925. National Museum of American History, Archives Center.

97. Norton, *Fighting Traffic*, 6 et passim. Conglomerates including oil, bus, and tire companies also sometimes bought streetcar lines to destroy them. Urry, *What Is the Future?*, 128–129.

98. Buttenheim, quoting a bus consultant in "The Problem of the Standing Vehicle," 144. The study presciently stated: "the most active and determined opposition to restricted parking is apt to come from the merchants who in the long run would be most benefited by it," 148.

99. Of the ten largest US cities in 1950, eight recorded their largest population ever in that year: Chicago (2), Philadelphia (3), Detroit (5), Baltimore (6), Cleveland (7), St. Louis (8), Washington, DC (9), and Boston (10). The exceptions are New York, which surpassed its 1950 population in 1970 and since 2000, and Los Angeles, which has grown continuously.

100. Spengler, *The Decline of the West*, vol. 2, 96.

101. Spengler, *Decline*, 110.

102. Spengler, *Decline*, 101.

103. Spengler, *Decline*, 94, 101.

104. Hitler wrote that the "big city" "avidly sucked men in and then so cruelly crushed them." *Mein Kampf*, 27.

105. Quoted in John Gold and George Revill, *Representing the Environment* (2004), 229.

106. Spengler, *Decline*, 95.

107. "Moro na Roça," by Arnaldo Passos and José Batista, was first recorded by Flora Matos in 1951.

108. See Anderson's *Imagined Communities*, highlighting the importance of nineteenth-century newspapers to the construction of nationhood.

109. I am grateful to Alice Chang and Hewson Duffy who helped me catalogue fifty-one films set in New York between 1901 and 1940.

110. *Lights of New York* (1916); *Regeneration* (1915); *The Delicious Little Devil* (1919).

111. *Subway Sadie* (1926).

112. *Manhandled* (1924); *The Crowd* (1928).

113. This was one of the opening lines in the movie.

114. In a 1925 interview with the *New York Evening Post*, quoted in Mansfield, *Cosmopolis*, 13.

115. Ferriss, *The Metropolis of Tomorrow*, 15.

116. Ferriss, *Metropolis*, 16.

117. Mumford, *Designing*, 113.

118. The movie was based on a novel by Thea von Harbou, who also wrote the screenplay. Fritz Lang was her second husband (1922–1933). She went on to collaborate on Nazi films. He declined an invitation by Joseph Goebbels to head a studio, eventually settling in Hollywood.

119. My translation. *Eu Sei Tudo*, February 1917, 21.

120. Quoted in Sarkis et al., *The World as an Architectural Project*, 60–63.

121. Sarkis et al., *World*, 124.

122. Sarkis et al., *World*, 131.

123. Gregory and Sailors, "The Soviet Union during the Great Depression."

124. Hoffmann, "Moving to Moscow."

125. Link, *Forging Global Fordism*, 2 et passim.

126. Link, *Forging*, 11.

127. It came out in English in 1924 and French in 1929, influencing works like George Orwell's *1984* (1949). The original in Russian was published in New York in 1952, and finally in the USSR in 1988.

128. Zamyatin, *We*, 12.

129. Zamyatin, *We*, 7.

130. Ferriss, *Metropolis*, 124. More prosaically, for example, a Brazilian magazine in 1922 swooned over future cities enveloped in glass, with temperature control. *Eu Sei Tudo: Magazine Mensal Illustrado*, July 1922, 57.

131. Sheller, *Aluminum Dreams*, 3–4.

132. This and other items can be found in the 1939–1940 New York World's Fair Collection at the Museum of the City of New York.

133. Vera y González, *Estrella*, 79. The idea of a continental union centered in Argentina's capital was recurrent in the period (Gutman, *Buenos Aires*, 173).

134. My translations. Vera y González, *Estrella*, 80.

135. Vera y González, *Estrella*, 22.

136. Vera y González, *Estrella*, 80.

137. Gutman, *Buenos Aires*, 86, 109, 405 et passim.

138. This was in a 1929 issue of *El Hogar*, reproduced in Gutman, *Buenos Aires*, 107–109.

139. Singh, "City of Tomorrow," 67–81. Also Gutman, *Buenos Aires*, 89 et passim. The tallest buildings in Latin America during the 1920s and 1930s were in Buenos Aires (Palacio Barolo and Edificio Kavanagh).

140. Gutman, *Buenos Aires*, 99.

141. See, for example, *El Rascacielos* (1934) by the Cuban architect Joaquín Weiss.

142. On Mexico's "estridentistas," see Pappe, *Estridentópolis*.

143. Jean Pelletier, "City of the Future," *Brooklyn Daily Eagle*, September 14, 1930.

144. Campante and Glaeser, "Yet Another Tale," 16. Around 30 percent of Argentina's inhabitants during the period were born abroad.

145. Sarlo, "Buenos Aires: el exilio de Europa," *Letra internacional* (2018), 5–22.

146. Karush, *Culture of Class.*

147. My translations. Gorelik, *La Grilla y el Parque*, 70.

148. Born in Uruguay, Morales took that position in the mid-1890s. He was also a member of the Society of Architects and president of the Argentinean Scientific Society. Gorelik, *Grilla*, 137–45, 255, et passim.

149. Páramo, *Un Fracaso Hecho Historia.* Gorelik refers to transit *colectivos* as emblematic of "viveza criolla" (Creole sharpness or *savoir faire*), *Grilla*, 401.

150. Comisión de Estética, *Proyecto Orgánico* (1925). My translation.

151. Green spaces more than doubled to 14 percent. "La Ciudad Pensada," *Modelo Territorial de la Ciudad de Buenos Aires*, 7.

152. Le Corbusier, *Précisions*, 14, 87, 181.

153. Nicolini, "Le Corbusier," 106–113.

154. Liernur, *Red Austral.*

155. Casciato, "Architects and Urban Planners," in Alonso and Casciato, *Metropolis*, 264.

156. This was the title of the book's first chapter. My translation. It was in part a response to Camillo Sitte's praise of picturesque urbanism.

157. It received criticism from theorists and designers, including Camillo Sitte, Patrick Geddes, and Georg Simmel.

158. Le Corbusier, *La Ville Radieuse*, 7.

159. Le Corbusier, *La Ville Radieuse*, 149.

160. The "Plan Director para Buenos Aires" with Le Corbusier's introduction was published in *La Arquitectura de Hoy*, April 1947.

161. Gorelik, *Grilla*, 16.

162. Gorelik, *Grilla*, 16.

163. My translation. Difrieri, *Atlas de Buenos Aires*, 13.

164. My translation.

165. *O Malho*, June 7, 1929.

166. *O Malho*, June 7, 1929, quoting Prince Potenziani. The Via dell'Impero, for example, ran for a mile from the Coliseum to the Piazza Venezia. The fascist urban designer Armando Brasini saw himself as the heir of Sixtus V. After the war he worked for the government of Saudi Arabia. Nicoloso, *Mussolini.*

167. A recording of the speech can be found in the Archivio Luce Cinecittà. The design recalled an unbuilt project by the same architect for the Chicago Tribune, a decade earlier.

168. Torpey, *Invention*, 122–157.

169. Hoerder, *Migrations.*

170. Nineteenth-century immigration controls for Asians and Africans had existed throughout the Atlantic. The English Aliens Act of 1905 was an early turning point toward more restrictive policies.

171. Whitman, *Hitler's American Model*, and for a global history, Nightingale, *Segregation.*

172. Scruggs, "Restriction," 493–494.

173. López-Durán, *Eugenics in the Garden*.

174. Esther Everett Lape, "Putting America into Your Town," *Ladies' Home Journal* 36, September 1919.

175. In 1924, the National Association of Real Estate Boards "promised punishment and revocation of membership to any broker who disrupted patterns of racial homogeneity on a given block or neighborhood." Taylor, *Race*, 10. See Rothstein, *Color*, on the role of government.

176. Transcribed interview from *Slave Narrative Project Federal Writers' Project: Slave Narrative Project*.

177. Washington, DC, was one of the first cities with significant African American presence outside the South. Dunbar, *Sport*, 278.

178. Fauset's story was first published in *The Crisis*, the magazine of the National Association for the Advancement of Colored People (NAACP), which had a circulation of around 100,000 issues at the time.

179. Perhaps the most prominent example was Bloomfield, *Modernismus* (1934).

180. My translation. Vasconcelos, *Raza*, 54. Published in 1925.

181. Lindbergh, *Wave*, 16.

182. Lindbergh, *Wave*, 39.

183. Lindbergh, *Wave*, 37.

6. After the Future? (1940s Onward)

1. Quoted descriptors from Lepore, *If Then*, 3.

2. In the Revere Copper and Brass Inc. ad (see figure 6.1), from 1943, "total living" entailed the promise of "a community building within walking distance" of suburban homes, with a hobby shop, play spaces, gym, and theater.

3. My translation. Letter from February 20, 1947, reproduced in Jenger, *Le Corbusier*, 291.

4. Broadcast from September 2, 1945. These are transcribed in *The American Presidency Project* (online) at the University of California, Santa Barbara.

5. Broadcast from May 8, 1945.

6. He was alluding to the earlier "La Cité mondiale" project for the League of Nations.

7. My translation. In the original: "l'aménagement de l'Europe," with "chaque nation dans son rôle." Letter to his mother from October 31, 1940, in Jenger, *Le Corbusier*, 140.

8. My translation for "l'explosion Corbu partout." Jenger, *Le Corbusier*, 291.

9. Cohen and Benton, *Le Corbusier*, 363.

10. Le Corbusier, *Oeuvre Vol. 4*, 44.

11. Google Books Ngram Viewer shows "civilization" plummeting from the 1930s to the 1980s, with "development" growing sharply and "urban development" surging until the 1970s.

12. Diefendorf, "Urban Reconstruction" 128–143. This was often under the sway of modernist planning. Sometimes reconstruction combined functionalist concerns like road widening and decentralization with conservative aesthetics, affirming tradition.

13. The International Organization of Motor Vehicle Manufacturers provides production statistics on their website.

14. Interview of Drita Ivanaj by Margo Nash on February 20, 1974. *Ellis Island Oral History Project*, Series NPS, no. 0050, 9.

15. Judt, *Postwar*, 7.

16. Judt, *Postwar*, 89.

17. Quoted in Levy, *Ages*, 488.

18. About a third of Berlin had been destroyed by bombing. Wagner-Conzelmann, *Die Interbau*, 30, 40.

19. Fanon, *Wretched*, 231 et passim.

20. Muzaffar, *Modernism's Magic Hat*. We might also think back to Gorelik's critique of "modernization without reform" in Argentina.

21. The issue was published on February 13, 1956.

22. My translation. "O futuro já tem capital," *O Cruzeiro*, May 7, 1960.

23. Mumford, *Designing*, 249.

24. John Bond, "Transit Program Launched: Planners Favor an Essential Rapid Transit Project," *Christian Science Monitor*, May 29, 1945.

25. Born in Austria, he fled the Nazis to the United States, and eventually returned to Vienna, where he worked on pedestrianization projects.

26. My translation. Quoted in Oliveira, *Flores*, 113.

27. Mumford, *Mumford*, 182.

28. Gorelik, *La Ciudad*. This change was of course also inspired by the Cuban Revolution.

29. Mumford, *Designing*, 227.

30. Banham, *Los Angeles*, 213 et passim.

31. Archival images of Futurama are easily available online.

32. Seiler, *Republic*, 104.

33. Based on the *Fortune* magazine database of largest companies.

34. See, for example, Sugrue's now classic *The Origins of the Urban Crisis*.

35. Malls, for example, benefited from "accelerated depreciation schedules for commercial real estate" and "tax breaks on new construction." Levy, *Ages*, 522.

36. Also in the UK, where the Cement and Concrete Association sponsored ads pitching freeways for Air Raid Precautions: "Evacuation! The most effective A.R.P."

37. I am grateful to Alice Chang for helping me research magazine archives for these materials.

38. In the novel, the characters also ride the bus quite a bit. The *Route 66* television series (1960–1964) showcased life on the road, but already with some measure of nostalgia.

39. This can be found in the Ralph E. Becker Collection of Political Americana, National Museum of American History (Washington, DC).

40. By 1938, the FHA "pressured developers to adopt non-gridded layouts." Mumford, *Designing*, 189.

41. We might think of restaurant service regardless of skin color, or regulations to ensure product safety. Cohen, *A Consumers' Republic*.

42. Seiler, *Republic*, 101, 114, et passim.

43. Mumford, *Designing*, 206–207.

44. Marshall Berman uses the expression, including in "Emerging from the Ruins."

45. See, for example, the chapter on Atlanta in Berman, *Lost Subways*.

46. Levy, *Ages*, 515.

47. According to Caro, *The Power Broker*, 1168.

48. Mumford, *Designing*, 211.

49. Sandoval-Strausz, *Barrio America*.

50. As early as 1949, a Chicago businessman sent the US president a telegram protesting evictions for the construction of "super highways." Harry Robbins, President of Bakers Drug Company, in National Archives and Records Administration, September 19, 1949.

51. By Sammie Abbott, in the Community Archives, ECTC Collection, Washingtoniana Division.

52. June Meyer, "Instant Slum Clearance," *Esquire* 63.4 (April 1965).

53. The phrase borrows from Anbinder, *Cities of Amber*.

54. Lispector, *Complete Stories*, 581.

55. It expanded to around 6,200 miles, with the goal of stimulating the automotive industry and consumption. Schwarcz and Starling, *Brasil*.

56. *Brasília, Contradições de uma Cidade Nova*, directed by Joaquim Pedro de Andrade.

57. Vitz, *A City*, 2 et passim.

58. The "plaza of the three cultures," completed in 1966, was designed by Mario Pani, a prominent Mexican architect.

59. Toffler, *Future*, 11.

60. Elgozy, *Le Bluff*.

61. Hayek, in 1974. In the 1940s, General Motors had produced a cartoon and booklet of his *The Road to Serfdom*, where "planners" (in scare quotes) and utopian promises lead to the forfeiture of freedoms.

62. The text is from 1974. Lispector, *Complete*, 582.

63. Legião Urbana, "Índios" (Renato Russo), released in 1986.

64. Orwell, *Nineteen Eighty-Four*, 74.

65. Quoted in Meyer, *Environmental*, 38.

66. Macoun, "Effects."

67. Fukuyama's "The End of History?" was first published in the *National Interest* in 1989. Fukuyama, *End*, 3.

68. *Agenda 21*.

69. Historians of Lagos have also noted the invisibilization of locals. Colonizers did the same in Rio de Janeiro (January River). Okorafor, *Lagoon*, 1.

70. Bigon, *History*, 152.

71. Bekker and Fourchard, *Governing Cities in Africa*.

72. Koolhas, *Lagos*.

73. Fourchard, "Lagos," 40–56.

74. Glissant, *Poetics*, 141.

75. Glissant, *Poetics*, 161–162.

76. Quoted from the website of the development: https://www.ekoatlantic.com/.

77. Quoting publicity materials and Onno Ruhl, former World Bank Director for Nigeria, in the *Nation*, Lagos, January 22, 2014.

78. Quoted in an Eko Atlantic press release, dated February 28, 2013.

79. Editorial in *Hope for Nigeria*, "The Lagos Atlantic City Progress," January 17, 2016.

80. Obiadi and Onochie, "Abuja," 23–43.

81. Gramont, *Governing*, 1.

82. Olajide and Lawanson, "Urban Paradox," 1763–1781.

83. Emmanuel Akinwotu, "The Forced Evictions of Badia East, Lagos: 'This Is Not Right,'" *Guardian*, October 16, 2015.

84. Emmanuel Akinwotu, "Class Divide: Mass Demolitions Drive Poor from Valuable Land in Lagos," *Guardian*, March 12, 2021.

85. The Lebanese investor Gilbert Chagoury of the Chagoury Group served as an advisor to Sani Abacha, accused of corruption and violently targeting environmentalists on behalf of multinational oil interests.

86. Fernandes, *Os Acordos*, 62 et passim.

87. Kimari, "'Under Construction,'" 135–152.

88. I am grateful to Junnan Mu for conducting research in Chinese official literature and translating from "China Africa Collaboration in the New Era," released November 21, 2021.

89. Goodfellow and Huang, "Contingent Infrastructure," 655–674.

90. These have been widespread conditions throughout history. The term is used in the social sciences since at least the 1950s. Informal as illegal means it should apply to a host of upper-class private condos in Latin America that skirt regulations, for example.

91. Sorkin, *What Goes Up*, 201–202.

92. The Makoko/Iwaya Waterfront Regeneration Plan was a finalist in the Buckminster Fuller Institute challenge in 2014, and can be found in a link on their website, for example.

93. Paice, *Youthquake*.

94. Tsey, *From Head-Loading to the Iron Horse*; Green-Simms, *Postcolonial Automobility*.

95. The word in Kiswahili is key to Joshua Grace's *African Motors*.

96. I am grateful to Diekara Oloruntoba-Oju for the reference and translation. The song by Nigerian rapper Omoniyi Temidayo Raphael, known as Zlatan, was released in 2020.

97. My translation of the song "Revolução Já" (Revolution Now), first released in 2013. Azagaia is the stage name of Edson da Luz, whose death in 2013 set off massive street demonstrations in Maputo.

98. Gibson, "The Science of Science Fiction."

99. Melly, *Bottleneck*, 88.

100. Melly, *Bottleneck*, 15. She found that citizenship contains limited possibilities of "belonging and presence," 16.

101. Chigozie Obioma in the *Guardian*, February 22, 2016.

102. Martin Lukacs, "New, Privatized African City Heralds Climate Apartheid," *Guardian*, January 21, 2014; Tuana, "Climate Apartheid."

103. See, for example, Pieterse, *City Futures*; Simone and Pieterse, *New Urban Worlds*.

104. Mbembe, "Society," 29.

105. Guyer, "Prophecy," 410. At first, she associates that to "the lived implications of the economic policies of structural adjustment under military rule in Africa," but later finds it "far more generalized."

106. We could not obtain permission to reprint, but images of his "Falomo Roundabout," from 2015, can be found online.

Epilogue

1. Mercier, *Memoirs*, 27.

2. Mercier, *Memoirs*, 9. Car accidents injure as many as 50 million people annually, killing around 1.3 million. Urry, *What Is the Future?*, 131.

3. Mumford, *City*, 370.

4. My translation. Quoted from interview in the Bogotá-based Colombian magazine *Semana* on December 12, 2010.

5. For a review of health-related studies, see Westenhöfer, "Walkability."

6. Data compiled in Hasanbeigi, "Federal."

7. See Blais, *Perverse Cities*, and Berrill, "Linking."

8. Del Tredici, "Flora of the Future."

9. The story was first published in Poe's *The Gift* in the 1840s.

10. Daniel Burnham predicted that once cars replaced foul-smelling horse-powered transportation, the air and streets of cities would be "clean and pure." Burnham, "City of the Future," 373.

11. The line "And no birds sing" is from a Keats poem, quoted in the epigraph. It serves as the title of chapter 8.

12. I am grateful to Eva Gildea and Amelia Roth-Dishy for comprehensive research on the relative lack of attention to cars and the advantages of compact cities.

13. Brown, *In the Ruins of Neoliberalism*. She theorizes antidemocratic politics as downstream from neoliberalism.

14. On responses to Carlos Moreno's planning concept, see Tiffany Hsu, "He Wanted to Unclog Cities. Now He's 'Public Enemy No. 1,'" *New York Times*, March 8, 2023.

15. Data for the United States can be found in Stacy et al., "Land-Use Reforms."

16. I am grateful to Daniel Pinckney for research assistance. In a narrow sense carbon storage and capture are not comparable. The latter remains energy intensive. Even in the rosiest predictions new technologies will remove a small fraction of what we release by destroying ecosystems.

17. The *Society if . . .* meme shows a dense futuristic city with greenery, glassy towers, and flying vehicles as a consequence of some desirable change, usually with an ironic twist.

18. I consulted years of surveys from Gallup Analytics and Ipsos Global Trends databases.

19. See http://zoningatlas.org/atlas. On the role of participatory politics in exacerbating housing shortages in the United States, see Einstein, *Neighborhood Defenders*.

20. Campanella, "Jane Jacobs and the Death and Life of American Planning." In *Future Cities*, Dobraszczyk makes a case for more imagination in architecture.

21. See, for example, Bill McKibben, "Yes in Our Backyards: It's Time Progressives Like Me Learned to Love the Green Building Boom," *Mother Jones*, May/June 2023.

22. Klinenberg, *Palaces for the People*.

23. Quoted in Koeppel, *City*, xix.

24. From his novel *Requiem for a Nun* (1951).

25. See Sevilla-Buitrago, *Against the Commons*, or Lefebvre, *Production*.

26. Examples include Marc Lore's Telosa, Saudi Arabia's Neom, Bill Gates's Belmont, or the Peter Thiel–funded Praxis.

27. Smil, *Invention and Innovation*, 160.

28. Reprinted in Churchill, *Amid These Storms*, 275.

29. The book was published in Italy in 1972. Calvino, *Invisible Cities*, 29.

BIBLIOGRAPHY

Press Cited

A Avenida

American City

A Província de São Paulo

Architectural Record

A Renascença

A Semana

Biblical Recorder

Brooklyn Daily Eagle

Chicago Record-Herald

Christian Science Monitor

City Plan

Crisis

Diario Crítica

Der Humorist

Detroit News

Diario Critica

Electrical Experimenter

El Hogar

Esquire

Eu Sei Tudo: Magazine Mensal Illustrado

Everyday Science and Mechanics

Fon-Fon!

Fortune

Gazeta de Lisboa

Gazeta de Notícias

Guardian

Jornal do Brasil

L'Architecture d'Aujourd'hui

La Caricature

Lacerba

Ladies' Home Journal

Le Figaro

L'Esprit Nouveau

Lippincott's Monthly Magazine

Mechanix Illustrated

Nation (Lagos)

New York Daily Herald

New York Times

New York Tribune

O Cruzeiro

O Malho

PBT: Semanario Ilustrado

Putnam's Monthly: A Magazine of
American Literature, Science and Art

Revista do Clube de Engenharia

Science and Invention

Scientific American

Scribner's Magazine

Sphere

Time

Times (London)

Washington Post

Works Cited

Account of the Terrific and Fatal Riot at the New-York Astor Place Opera House, on the Night of May 10th, 1849 [. . .]. New York: H. M. Ranney, 1849.

Agache, Alfred. *Comment Reconstruire Nos Cités Détruites: notions d'urbanisme s'applicant aux villes, bourgs et villages*. Paris: A. Colin, 1915.

Agenda 21: Programme of Action for Sustainable Development; Rio Declaration on Environment and Development. New York: United Nations, 1993.

Aibar, Eduardo, and Wiebe E. Bijker, "Constructing a City: The Cerdà Plan for the Extension Barcelona." *Science, Technology, and Human Values* 22.1 (1997): 2–30.

Alatorre, Manuel Díaz Flores. *Recuerdo del Primer Centenario de la Independencia Nacional*. Mexico City: Rondero y Treppiedi, 1910.

Alberti, Leon Battista. *On the Art of Building in Ten Books*. Translated by Joseph Rykwert, Neil Leach, and Robert Tavernor. Cambridge, MA: MIT Press, 1988.

Alexander, Leslie M. *African or American?: Black Identity and Political Activism in New York City, 1784–1861*. Urbana: University of Illinois Press, 2012.

Alexander, Ryan M. "The Fever of War: Epidemic Typhus and Public Health in Revolutionary Mexico City, 1915–1917." *Hispanic American Historical Review* 100.1 (2020): 63–92.

Alkon, Paul. *Origins of Futuristic Fiction*. Athens: University of Georgia Press, 1987.

Alland, Alexander. *Jacob A. Riis, Photographer and Citizen*. New York: Aperture, 1974.

Almeida, Theodoro de. *Lisboa Destruída*. Lisbon: A. Rodrigues Galhardo, 1803.

Alonso, Idurre, and Maristella Casciato, eds. *The Metropolis in Latin America 1830–1930: Cityscapes, Photographs, Debates*. Los Angeles: Getty Research Institute, 2021.

Alphand, Adolphe. *Les Promenades de Paris: Histoire, Description des Embellissements* [...]. Paris: J. Rotschild, 1867–1873.

Anais do Senado do Império do Brasil. Brasília: Senado Federal, Subsecretaria de Anais, 1978.

Anbinder, Jacob. *Cities of Amber: Antigrowth Politics and the Making of Modern Liberalism, 1950–2008*. PhD diss., Harvard University, 2023.

Andersen, Hendrik Christian, Ernest M. Hébrard, et al. 1913. *Creation of a World Centre of Communication*. Paris; Rome: s.n., 1913.

Anderson, Benedict. *Imagined Communities: Reflections on the Origin and Spread of Nationalism*. London: Verso, 1983.

Andersson, Jenny. *The Future of the World: Futurology, Futurists, and the Struggle for the Post Cold War Imagination*. Oxford: Oxford University Press, 2018.

Appadurai, Arjun. *The Future as Cultural Fact: Essays on the Global Condition*. London: Verso, 2013.

Araújo, Renata Malcher de. "A Urbanização da Amazônia e do Mato Grosso no século XVIII: povoações civis, decorosas e úteis para o bem comum da coroa e dos povos." *Anais do Museu Paulista: História e Cultura Material* 20.1 (2012): 41–76.

Armstrong, Isobel. "Languages of Glass." In *Victorian Prism: Refractions of the Crystal Palace*. Edited by James Buzard, Joseph W. Childers, and Eileen Gillooly. Charlottesville: University of Virginia Press, 2007.

Arrhenius, Svante. *Worlds in the Making: The Evolution of the Universe*. New York, London: Haper, 1908.

Asimov, Isaac. *Futuredays: A Nineteenth Century Vision of the Year 2000*. New York City: Henry Holt & Co, 1986.

Attali, Jacques. *Une Brève Histoire de l'Avenir*. Paris: Fayard, 2006.

Auerbach, Jeffrey. "Empire under Glass: The British Empire and the Crystal Palace, 1851–1911." In *Exhibiting the Empire: Cultures of Display and the British Empire.* Edited by John M. MacKenzie and John McAleer. Manchester: Manchester University Press, 2015.

Ayres, Christovam. *Manuel da Maya e os engenheiros militares portugueses no terremoto de 1755.* Lisboa: Imprensa Nacional, 1910.

Azevedo, Aluísio. *O Cortiço.* Rio de Janeiro: Ediouro, 1990.

Azevedo, André Nunes de. *A Grande Reforma Urbana: Pereira Passos, Rodrigues Alves e as ideias de civilização e progresso.* Rio de Janeiro: Editora PUC-Rio, 2016.

Bairoch, Paul. *Cities and Economic Development: From the Dawn of History to the Present.* Chicago: University of Chicago Press, 1988.

Ballon, Hillary, ed. *The Greatest Grid: The Master Plan of Manhattan.* New York: Columbia University Press, 2012.

Balzac, Honoré de. *Illusions Perdues.* Paris: Librairie Nouvelle, 1857.

Balzac, Honoré de. *Oeuvres illustrées de Balzac.* Paris: Maresoq et compagnie, 1851.

Balzac, Honoré de. *Splendeurs et Misères des Courtisanes: texte intégral.* Paris: Garnier, 1975.

Banham, Reyner. *Los Angeles: The Architecture of Four Ecologies.* New York: Harper & Row, 1971.

Barbosa, Domingos Caldas. *Viola de Lereno: collecção das suas cantigas, offerecidas aos seus amigos.* Lisboa: Na officina nunesiana, 1798.

Baudelaire, Charles. *The Poems and Prose Poems of Charles Baudelaire.* Translated and edited by James Huneker. New York: Brentano's, 1919.

Baudelaire, Charles. *Selected Writings on Art and Artists.* Translated and edited by P. E. Charvet. New York: Penguin, 1972.

Beaumont, Matthew. "Cacotopianism, the Paris Commune, and England's Anti-Communist Imaginary, 1870–1900." *ELH: English Literary History* 73.2 (2006): 465–487.

Beckert, Jens. *Imagined Futures: Fictional Expectations and Capitalist Dynamics.* Cambridge, MA: Harvard University Press, 2017.

Beecher, Catherine. *A Treatise on Domestic Economy for the Use of Young Ladies at Home and at School.* Boston: Thomas H. Webb and Co., 1843.

Bekker, S. B., and Laurent Fourchard. *Governing Cities in Africa: Politics and Policies.* Cape Town: HSRC Press, 2013.

Bellamy, Edward. *Looking Backward, 2000–1887.* Edited by Matthew Beaumont. Oxford: Oxford University Press, 2007.

Benchimol, Jaime L. *Pereira Passos: Um Haussmann Tropical.* Rio de Janeiro: Departamento Geral de Documentação e Informação Cultural, Divisão de Editoração, 1990.

Bender, Thomas. *Toward an Urban Vision: Ideas and Institutions in Nineteenth Century America.* Lexington: University of Kentucky Press, 1982.

Bender, Thomas. *The Unfinished City: New York and the Metropolitan Idea.* New York: New Press, 2002.

Benjamin, Walter. *Illuminations: Essays and Reflections.* Translated by Harry Zohn. New York: Schocken Books, 1986.

Benjamin, Walter. *Reflections: Essays, Aphorisms, Autobiographical Writings.* Translated by Edmund Jephcott. New York: Schocken Books, 1986.

Benjamin, Walter. *Selected Writings, Volume 2: 1927–1934*. Translated by Rodney Livingston. Edited by Michael W. Jennings, Howard Eiland, and Gary Smith. Cambridge, MA: Harvard University Press, 1996.

Benoît-Lévy, Georges. *Cités-jardins d'Amerique*. Paris: Henri Jouve, 1905.

Bentlin, Felix. "Understanding the Hobrecht Plan: Origin, Composition, and Implementation of Urban Design Elements in the Berlin Expansion Plan from 1862." *Planning Perspectives* 33.4 (2018): 633–655.

Berardi, Franco. *After the Future*. Translated by Arianna Bove. Edited by Gary Genosko and Nicholas Thoburn. Edinburgh; Oakland, CA; Baltimore, MD: AK Press, 2011.

Bercé, Yves-Marie. *History of Peasant Revolts: The Social Origins of Rebellion in Early Modern France*. Ithaca, NY: Cornell University Press, 1990.

Bergad, Laird. "Slavery in Cuba and Puerto Rico, 1804 to Abolition." In *The Cambridge World History of Slavery*. Edited by David Eltis and Stanley L. Engerman. Cambridge: Cambridge University Press.

Berman, Jake. *Lost Subways of North America: A Cartographic Guide to the Past, Present, and What Might Have Been*. Chicago: University of Chicago Press, 2023.

Berman, Marshall. "Emerging from the Ruins." *Dissent* 61.1 (2014): 59–66.

Bernhardt, Christoph. *Bauplatz Gross-Berlin: Wohnungsmärkte, Terraingewerbe und Kommunal-politik im Stätdtwachstum der Hochindustrialisierung (1871–1918)*. Berlin: W. de Gruyter, 1998.

Berrill, Peter, Kenneth T. Gillingham, and Edgar G. Hertwich. "Linking Housing Policy, Housing Typology, and Residential Energy Demand in the United States." *Environmental Science and Technology* 55.4 (2021): 2224–2233.

Bigon, Liora. *A History of Urban Planning in Two West African Colonial Capitals: Residential Segregation in British Lagos and French Dakar (1850–1930)*. Lewiston, NY: Edwin Mellen Press, 2009.

Bigon, Liora, and Thomas Hart. "Beneath the City's Grid: Vernacular and (Post-)Colonial Planning Interactions in Dakar, Senegal." *Journal of Historical Geography* 59 (2018): 52–67.

Bigon, Liora, and Yossi Katz, eds. *Garden Cities and Colonial Planning*. Manchester: Manchester University Press, 2016.

Birch, Walter de Gray, ed. *The Historical Charters and Constitutional Documents of the City of London*. London: Whiting, 1887.

Blais, Pamela. *Perverse Cities: Hidden Subsidies, Wonky Policy, and Urban Sprawl*. Vancouver: University of British Columbia Press, 2010.

Blanning, Tim. *The Pursuit of Glory: Europe 1648–1815*. London: Penguin Books, 2008.

Blomfield, Reginald. *Modernismus*. London: Macmillan and Co., 1934.

Bohigas, Oriol. "En el centenerio del Plan Cerdà." *Cuadernos de Arquitectura* 34 (1958): 7–13.

Borsi, Katharina. "Drawing the Region: Hermann Jansen's Vision of Greater Berlin in 1910." *Journal of Architecture* 20.1 (2015): 47–72.

Botelho, Tarcísio Rodrigues. "A População Brasileira em 1850: uma estimativa." *Economia e Políticas Públicas* 7.2 (2019): 135–166.

Boyer, Paul. *Urban Masses and Moral Order in America, 1820–1920*. Cambridge, MA: Harvard University Press, 1978.

Bresler, Fenton. *Napoleon III: A Life*. New York: Carroll & Graf, 1999.

Brown, Vincent. *Tacky's Revolt: The Story of an Atlantic Slave War.* Cambridge, MA: Harvard University Press, 2020.

Brown, Wendy. *In the Ruins of Neoliberalism: The Rise of Antidemocratic Politics in the West.* New York: Columbia University Press, 2019.

Bruce, Lincoln W. *Sunlight at Midnight: St. Petersburg and the Rise of Modern Russia.* Boulder, CO: Basic Books, 2000.

Buntline, Ned. *The Mysteries and Miseries of New York: A Story of Real Life.* New York: Berford & Co., 1848.

Burnham, Daniel H. "A City of the Future under a Democratic Government." *Town Planning Conference, Transactions.* London: Royal Institute of British Architects, 1911.

Burnham, Daniel H., and Edward H. Bennett. *Plan of Chicago: Prepared under the Direction of the Commercial Club during the Years MCMVI, MCMVII, and MCMVIII.* Chicago: Commercial Club, 1909.

Bury, J. B. *The Idea of Progress.* London: MacMillan, 1921.

Busquets, Joan. *Barcelona: The Urban Evolution of a Compact City.* Rovereto: Nicolodi, Harvard University Graduate School of Design, 2005.

Buttenheim, Harold S. "The Problem of the Standing Vehicle." *Annals of the American Academy of Political and Social Science* 133.1 (1927): 144–155.

Cabet, Étienne. *Voyage en Icarie.* Paris: Au Bureau du Populaire, 1845.

Calvino, Italo. *Invisible Cities.* Translated by William Weaver. New York: Harcourt, 1974.

Campanella, Thomas. "Jane Jacobs and the Death and Life of American Planning." *Places Journal,* April 2011.

Campante, Filipe, and Edward Glaeser. "Yet Another Tale of Two Cities: Buenos Aires and Chicago." *Latin American Economic Review* 27.2 (2018).

Caro, Robert. *The Power Broker: Robert Moses and the Fall of New York.* New York: Alfred A. Knopf, 1974.

Carranza, Luis E., and Fernando Luiz Lara. *Modern Architecture in Latin America: Art, Technology, and Utopia.* Austin: University of Texas Press, 2014.

Carroll, Christina. "Imperial Ideologies in the Second Empire: The Mexican Expedition and the Royaume Arabe." *French Historical Studies* 42.1 (2019): 67–100.

Carvalho, Bruno. *Cidade Porosa: dois séculos de história cultural do Rio de Janeiro.* Translation by Daniel Estill. Rio de Janeiro: Objetiva, 2019.

Carvalho, Bruno. "Occupy All Streets: Protesting a Right to the Future." In *Occupy All Streets: Olympic Urbanism and Contested Futures in Rio de Janeiro.* Edited by Bruno Carvalho, Mariana Cavalcanti, and Vyjayanthi Rao Venuturupalli. New York: Terreform, 2016.

Carvalho, Bruno. *Porous City: A Cultural History of Rio de Janeiro (from the 1810s Onward).* Liverpool: Liverpool University Press, 2013.

Carvalho, Bruno. "Writing Race in Two Americas: Blackness, Science, and Circulation of Knowledge in the Eighteenth-Century Luso-Brazilian World and the U.S." *Eighteenth Century* 57.3 (2016): 303–324.

Carvalho, Bruno, John Huffman, and Gabriel Rocha, eds. *O Livro de Tiradentes: Transmissão Atlântica de Ideias Políticas no Século XVIII.* São Paulo: Penguin/Companhia das Letras, 2013.

Carvalho, Marcus, J. M. de. "Os nomes da revolução: lideranças populares na Insurreição Praie-ira, Recife, 1848–1849." *Revista Brasileira de História* 23.45 (2003): 209–238.

Carvalho e Melo, Sebastião José de. *Elogio de D. Luiz Carlos Ignacio Xavier de Menezes.* Lisbon [?]: 1742.

Çelik, Zeynep. *Empire, Architecture, and the City: French-Ottoman Encounters, 1830–1914.* Seattle: University of Washington Press, 2008.

Cerdá, Ildefonso. *Teoría General de la Urbanización.* Madrid: Imprenta Española, 1867.

Chakrabarty, Dipesh. *Provincializing Europe: Postcolonial Thought and Historical Difference.* Princeton, NJ: Princeton University Press, 2000.

Chalhoub, Sidney. *Visões da liberdade: uma história das últimas décadas da escravidão na corte.* São Paulo: Companhia das Letras, 1990.

Chandler, Tertius. *Four Thousand Years of Urban Growth: An Historical Census.* Lewiston, NY: St. David's University Press, 1987.

Chapman, Joan Margaret, and Brian Chapman. *The Life and Times of Baron Haussmann.* London: Weidenfeld and Nicolson, 1957.

Chevalier, Louis. *Laboring Classes and Dangerous Classes in Paris during the First Half of the Nineteenth Century.* New York: Howard Fertig, 1973.

Childs, Matt D. "Re-Creating African Ethnic Identities in Cuba." In *The Black Urban Atlantic in the Age of the Slave Trade.* Edited by Jorge Canizares-Esguerra, Matt D. Childs, and James Sidbury. Philadelphia: University of Pennsylvania Press, 2013.

Christianson, Gale. *Greenhouse: The 200-Year Story of Global Warming.* New York: Penguin Books, 2000.

Churchill, Winston. *Amid These Storms: Thoughts and Adventures.* New York: Charles Scribner's Sons, 1932.

Cirici-Pellicer, Alexandre. "Significación del Plan Cerdá." *Cuadernos de Arquitectura* 35 (1959): 45–47.

Clark, Christopher. *Revolutionary Spring: Europe Aflame and the Fight for a New World, 1848–1849.* New York: Crown, 2023.

Clarke, I. F. *The Pattern of Expectation, 1644–2001.* New York: Basic Books, 1979.

Clergyman of Gloucestershire. *An Exhortation Address'd Particularly Unto the People of London* [. . .]. London: Printed for Thomas Trye, near Grays-Inn Gate in Holbourn, 1756.

Cohen, Jean-Louis, and Tim Benton. *Le Corbusier Le Grand.* London: Phaidon Press, 2008.

Cohen, Lizabeth. *A Consumers' Republic: The Politics of Mass Consumption in Postwar America.* New York: Knopf, 2003.

Collecção da legislação Portugueza desde a ultima compilação das ordenações, Vol. 1. Lisboa: Typ. Maigrense, 1830.

Comisión de Estética Edilicia. *Proyecto orgánico para la urbanización del municipio, El plano regulador y de reforma de la Capital Federal.* Buenos Aires: Talleres Peuser, 1925.

Comte, Auguste. *Cours de Philosophie Positive.* Paris: Bachelier, 1830–1842.

Comte, Auguste. *Discurso Sobre el Espíritu Positivo.* Translated by Julián Marías. Madrid: Alianza Editoria, 1980.

Coronil, Fernando. *The Magical State: Nature, Money, and Modernity in Venezuela.* Chicago: University of Chicago Press, 1997.

Cowling, Camilla. *Conceiving Freedom: Women of Color, Gender, and the Abolition of Slavery in Havana and Rio de Janeiro*. Chapel Hill: University of North Carolina Press, 2013.

Crane, Stephen. *Maggie, a Girl of the Streets: A Story of New York*. New York: D. Appleton, 1896.

Crónica oficial de las fiestas del primer centenario de la Independencia de México. Mexico: Talleres del Museo Nacional, 1911.

Crosas Armengol, Carles. "Reticulas Verdes, Nuevas Ciudades Decimonónicas. El paradigma del Vedado." *Revista Iberoamericana de Urbanismo* 2 (2009): 27–40.

Danowski, Déborah, and Eduardo Viveiros de Castro. *The Ends of the World*. Translated by Rodrigo Nunes. Cambridge, UK: Polity Press, 2017.

Darnton, Robert. *The Great Cat Massacre and Other Episodes in French Cultural History*. New York: Viking, 1984.

Davis, Mike. *Dark Raptures*. Berkeley, CA: Doreen B. Townsend Center for the Humanities, 1998.

Davis, Richard Beale. "The Abbé Correa in America, 1812–1820." *Transactions of the American Philosophical Society* 45.2 (1955): 87–197.

Delaroy, Eduard de Rautlin. *Des moyens de contenir les classes dangereuses*. Paris: Imprimerie Centrale des Chemins de Fer, 1854.

Del Tredici, Peter. "The Flora of the Future." *Places Journal*, April 2014.

De Witt, Simeon. *The Elements of Perspective*. Albany: H. C. Southwick, 1813.

Dickens, Charles. *Oliver Twist: Or, the Parish Boy's Progress*. London: Richard Bentley, 1838.

Diefendorf, J. M. "Urban Reconstruction in Europe after World War II." *Urban Studies* 26.1 (1989): 128–143.

Difrieri, Horacio. *Atlas de Buenos Aires*. Buenos Aires: Municipalidad de la Ciudad, Secretaría de Cultura, 1976.

Dittrich, Julio. *Buenos Aires en el 1950: Bajo el regimen socialista*. Buenos Aires: Ventas por Mayor, 1908.

Dobraszczyk, Paul. *Future Cities: Architecture and the Imagination*. London: Reaktion Books, 2019.

Dostoevsky, Fyodor. *Notes from Underground*. Translated by Constance Garnett. New York: Heritage Press, 1967.

Douglass, Frederick. *Life and Writings of Frederick Douglass*. Edited by Philip Foner. New York: International Publishers, 1950.

Douglass, Frederick. *Narrative of the Life of Frederick Douglass, an American Slave and Incidents in the Life of a Slave Girl*. New York: Random House, 2011.

Dudley, Tara. *Building Antebellum New Orleans: Free People of Color and Their Influence*. Austin: University of Texas Press, 2021.

Duffy, Andrea E. *Nomad's Land: Pastoralism and French Environmental Policy in the Nineteenth-Century Mediterranean World*. Lincoln: University of Nebraska Press, 2019.

Dunbar, Paul Laurence. *The Sport of the Gods*. New York: Dodd, Mead and Company, 1902.

Edgerton, Samuel Y. "From Mental Matrix to Mappamundi to Christian Empire." In *Art and Cartography: Six Historical Essays*. Edited by David Woodward. Chicago: University of Chicago Press, 1987.

Ehrlich, Paul R. *The Population Bomb*. New York: Ballantine Books, 1968.

Eichner, Carolyn J. *The Paris Commune: A Brief History.* New Brunswick, NJ: Rutgers University Press, 2022.

Einstein, Katherine Levine, David M. Glick, and Maxwell Palmer. *Neighborhood Defenders: Participatory Politics and America's Housing Crisis.* New York: Cambridge University Press, 2020.

Elgozy, Georges. *Le Bluff du Futur: Demain N'Aura Pas Lieu.* Paris: Calmann-Lévy, 1974.

Elogio ao illustrissimo e excellentissimo senhor marquez do Pombal. Lisbon: Officina de Filippe da Silva e Azevedo, 1786.

Encyclopédie, ou dictionnaire raisonné des sciences, des arts et des métiers [. . .]. Edited by Denis Diderot and Jean d'Alembert. Paris: Briasson, 1751–1765.

Encyclopédie, ou, Dictionnaire raisonné des sciences des arts et des métiers par une société de gens de lettres [. . .]. Edited by Denis Diderot and Jean d'Alembert. Lucca: chez Vincent Giuntini imprimeur, 1758–1771.

Engels, Friedrich. *The Condition of the Working Class in England.* London: G. Allen & Unwin, 1892.

Estapé, Fabián. *Vida y Obra de Ildefonso Cerdá.* Barcelona: Ediciones Península, 2001.

Etzler, John. *The Paradise within Reach of All Men, without Labor, by Powers of Nature and Machinery.* London: John Brooks, 1836.

Ezcurra, Eduardo de. *Buenos Aires en el Siglo XXX.* Buenos Aires: J. A. Alsina, 1891.

Fanon, Frantz. *The Wretched of the Earth.* New York: Grove Press, 1968.

Federal Writers' Project: Slave Narrative Project. Administrative Files. Manuscript/Mixed Material. Washington, DC: Library of Congress, 1936.

Fein, Albert. *Frederick Law Olmsted and the American Environmental Tradition.* New York: George Braziller, 1972.

Feller, Daniel. *The Jacksonian Promise: America, 1815–1840.* Baltimore, MD: Johns Hopkins University Press, 1995.

Fernandes, Sofia da Graça Cordeiro. *Os acordos de financiamento entre a China e Angola.* PhD diss., Instituto Universitário de Lisboa, 2015.

Fernández Christlieb, Federico. *Europa y el Urbanismo Neoclásico en la Ciudad de México: Antecendente y Esplendores.* México, D.F.: Plaza y Valdés, Instituto de Geografía, UNAM, 2000.

Ferriss, Hugh. *The Metropolis of Tomorrow.* New York: I. Washburn, 1929.

Figueiredo, Lucas. *Boa Ventura! A Corrida do Ouro No Brasil (1697–1810).* Rio de Janeiro: Editora Record, 2011.

Fishman, Robert. *Urban Utopias in the Twentieth Century: Ebenezer Howard, Frank Lloyd Wright, and Le Corbusier.* Cambridge, MA: MIT Press, 1982.

Foley, Barbara. "From Wall Street to Astor Place: Historicizing Melville's 'Bartleby.'" *American Literature* 72.1 (2000): 87–116.

Fontanilla, Ryan Joel. *Waters of Liberation: An Environmental History of Nineteenth-Century Jamaica.* PhD diss., Harvard University, 2023.

Forsström, Riikka. *Possible Worlds: The Idea of Happiness in the Utopian Vision of Louis-Sébastien Mercier.* Helsinki: Finnish Literature Society, 2002.

Foster, Mark S. *From Streetcar to Superhighway: American City Planners and Urban Transportation, 1900–1940.* Philadelphia: Temple University Press, 1981.

Fourchard, Laurent. "Lagos, Koolhaas and Partisan Politics in Nigeria." *International Journal of Urban and Regional Research* 35 (2011): 40–56.

Fourier, Charles. *Théorie des quatre mouvemens et des destinées générales.* Leipzig: s.n., 1808.

França, José Augusto. *Lisboa pombalina e o Iluminismo.* Lisbon: Bertrand Editora, 1987.

Franklin, Benjamin. *The Writings of Benjamin Franklin.* New York: Macmillan, 1906.

Freeland, David. *American Hotel: The Waldorf-Astoria and the Making of a Century.* New Brunswick: Rutgers University Press, 2021.

Freemark, Yonah, A. Bliss, Lawrence J. Vale. "Housing Haussmann's Paris: The Politics and Legacy of Second Empire Redevelopment." *Planning Perspectives* 37.2 (2022): 1–25.

Frégier, Honoré. *Des classes dangereuses de la population dans les grandes villes.* Paris: J.-B. Baillière, 1840.

Friedman, Donald. *The Structure of Skyscrapers in America, 1871–1900: Their History and Preservation.* Springfield, IL: Association for Preservation Technology, 2020.

Friedman, Walter. *Fortune Tellers: The Story of America's First Economic Forecasters.* Princeton, NJ: Princeton University Press, 2013.

Fukuyama, Francis. *The End of History and the Last Man.* New York: Free Press, 1992.

Fuller, Thomas. "Go West, Young Man—an Elusive Slogan." *Indiana Magazine of History* 9 (2004): 231–243.

Furtado, Júnia Ferreira. *Oráculos da geografia iluminista: Dom Luís da Cunha e Jean-Baptiste Bourguignon d'Anville na construção da cartografia do Brasil.* Belo Horizonte: Editora UFMG, 2012.

Gaillard, Jeanne. *Paris, la ville (1852–1870).* Paris: Harmattan, 1997.

Gama, Luiz. *Lições de Resistência: artigos de Luiz Gama na imprensa de São Paulo.* Edited by Lígia Fonseca Ferreira. São Paulo: Edições Sesc, 2020.

Gama, Luiz. *Obras Completas: Liberdade (1880–1882).* Edited by Bruno Rodrigues de Lima. São Paulo: Editora Hedra, 2021.

Geddes, Norman Bel. *Magic Motorways.* New York: Random House, 1940.

Gibson, William. "The Science of Science Fiction." *Talk of the Nation.* NPR, November 30, 1999.

Giedion, Sigfried. *Space, Time, and Architecture: The Growth of a New Tradition.* Cambridge, MA: Harvard University Press, 1941.

Gilbert, Daniel. *Stumbling on Happiness.* New York: Knopf, 2006.

Giuntini, Andrea. "2 ITU, Submarine Cables and African Colonies, 1850s–1900s." In *History of the International Telecommunication Union (ITU): Transnational Techno-Diplomacy from the Telegraph to the Internet.* Edited by Gabriele Balbi and Andreas Fickers. Berlin: De Gruyter, 2020.

Glaeser, Edward. *Triumph of the City: How Our Greatest Invention Makes Us Richer, Smarter, Greener, Healthier, and Happier.* New York: Penguin, 2011.

Glaeser, Edward. "Urban Colossus: Why Is New York America's Largest City?" *FRBNY Economic Policy Review* 11.2 (2005): 7–24.

Glissant, Édouard. *Poetics of Relation.* Translated by Betsy Wing. Ann Arbor: University of Michigan Press, 1997.

Gluckstein, Donny. *The Paris Commune: A Revolution in Democracy.* London: Haymarket Books, 2011.

Gold, John. "Under Darkened Skies: The City in Science-Fiction Film." *Geography* 86.4 (2001): 337–345.

Goncourt, Edmond de, and Jules de Goncourt. *Pages from the Goncourt Journal.* Edited by Robert Baldick. Oxford: Oxford University Press, 1962.

Goodfellow, Tom, and Zhengli Huang. "Contingent Infrastructure and the Dilution of 'Chineseness': Reframing Roads and Rail in Kampala and Addis Ababa." *Environment and Planning* 53.4 (2021): 655–674.

Gorelik, Adrián. *La Ciudad Latinoamericana: Una Figura de la Imaginación Social del Siglo XX.* Buenos Aires: Siglo Veintiuno Editores, 2022.

Gorelik, Adrián. *La Grilla y el Parque: Espacio Publico y Cultura Urbana en Buenos Aires, 1887–1936.* Buenos Aires: Universidad Nacional de Quilmes, 1998.

Grabar, Henry. *Paved Paradise: How Parking Explains the World.* New York: Penguin Press, 2023.

Grace, Joshua. *African Motors: Technology, Gender, and the History of Development.* Durham, NC: Duke University Press, 2021.

Gramont, Diane de. *Governing Lagos: Unlocking the Politics of Reform, Carnegie Endowment for International Peace.* Washington, DC: Carnegie Endowment for International Peace, 2015.

Gramsci, Antonio. *Americanismo e Fordismo.* Milan: Riuniti, 1991.

Gratz, Rebecca. *Letters of Rebecca Gratz.* Edited by David Philipson. Philadelphia: Jewish Publication Society, 1929.

Grau-Lleveria, Elena. "La ficción política romántica en Los misterios del Plata." *Decimonónica* 7.1 (2010): 1–20.

Green-Simms, Lindsey. *Postcolonial Automobility: Car Culture in West Africa.* Minneapolis: University of Minnesota Press, 2017.

Gregory, Paul, and Joel Sailors. "The Soviet Union during the Great Depression: The Autarky Model." In *The World Economy and National Economies in the Interwar Slump.* Edited by Theo Balderston. London: Palgrave Macmillan, 2003.

Griffith, Mary. *Three Hundred Years Hence.* Philadelphia: Carey, Lea & Blanchard, 1836.

Grimké, Angelina, Emily Grimké, and Sarah Moore Grimké. *The Grimké Sisters: Sarah and Angelina Grimké, The First American Women Advocates of Abolition and Woman's Rights.* Boston: Lee & Shepard Publishers, 1885.

Grund, Francis Joseph. *The Americans, in Their Moral, Social and Political Relations.* Boston: Marsh, Capen and Lyon, 1837.

Grupo 2C. *La Barcelona de Cerdá.* Barcelona: Flor del Viento, 2009.

Gschwend, Annemarie Jordan, and Kate J. P. Lowe, eds. *The Global City: On the Streets of Renaissance Lisbon.* London: Paul Holberton Publishing, 2015.

Guarnieri, Carl. *The Utopian Alternative: Fourierism in Nineteenth-Century America.* Ithaca, NY: Cornell University Press, 1991.

Gutman, Margarita. *Buenos Aires, El Poder de la Anticipación: imágenes itinerantes del futuro metropolitano en el primer Centenario.* Buenos Aires: Ediciones Infinito, 2011.

Guyer, Jane I. "Prophecy and the Near Future: Thoughts on Macroeconomic, Evangelical, and Punctuated Time." *American Ethnologist* 34.3 (2007): 409–421.

Hacker, Jeffrey H. *The Gilded Age and Dawn of the Modern 1877–1919.* New York: Routledge, 2013.

Hager, Thomas. *Electric City: The Lost History of Ford and Edison's American Utopia*. New York: Abrams Press, 2021.

Hall, Peter. *Cities in Civilization*. New York: Pantheon Books, 1998.

Hall, Peter. *Cities of Tomorrow: An Intellectual History of Urban Planning and Design in the Twentieth Century*. Oxford: Blackwell Publishers, 1996.

Harding, Susan, and Daniel Rosenberg, eds. *Histories of the Future*. Durham: Duke University Press, 2005.

Harvey, David. *Limits to Capital*. Chicago: University of Chicago Press, 1982.

Harvey, David. *Paris, Capital of Modernity*. New York: Routledge, 2006.

Hasanbeigi, Ali, Dinah Shi, and Harshvardhan Khutal. "Federal Buy Clean for Cement and Steel: Policy Design and Impact on Industrial Emissions and Competiteveness." *Global Efficiency Intelligence* (2021): 1–51.

Haussmann, Georges-Eugène. *Mémoires du Baron Haussmann*. Paris: Victor-Havard, 1890.

Hayden, Dolores. *Seven American Utopias: The Architecture of Communitarian Socialism, 1790–1975*. Cambridge, MA: MIT Press, 1979.

Hayek, Friedrich. *The Road to Serfdom*. London: G. Routledge & Sons, 1944.

Herzog, Tamar. *Frontiers of Possession: Spain and Portugal in Europe and the Americas*. Cambridge, MA: Harvard University Press, 2015.

Higonnet, Patrice. *Paris, Capitale du Monde des Lumières au Surréalisme*. Paris: Tallandier, 2005.

Hindes, Jessica. *Revealing Bodies: Knowledge, Power and Mass Market Fictions in G.W.M. Reynolds's Mysteries of London*. PhD diss., Royal Holloway, University of London, 2015.

Hobsbawm, Eric, and Terence Ranger, eds. *The Invention of Tradition*. Cambridge: Cambridge University Press, 1983.

Hoerder, Dirk. *Migrations and Belongings: 1870–1945*. Cambridge, MA: Harvard University Press, 2014.

Hoffmann, David. "Moving to Moscow: Patterns of Peasant In-Migration during the First Five-Year Plan." *Slavic Review* 50.4 (1991): 847–857.

Hogendorn, Jan, and Paul Lovejoy. *Slow Death for Slavery: The Course of Abolition in Northern Nigeria 1897–1936*. Cambridge: Cambridge University Press, 2011.

Hohne, Stefan. *Riding the New York Subway: The Invention of the Modern Passenger*. Cambridge, MA: MIT Press, 2021.

Holt, Hamilton, ed. *The Life Stories of Undistinguished Americans as Told by Themselves*. New York: J. Pott & Co., 1906.

Hopkins, Richard S. *Planning the Greenspaces of Nineteenth-Century Paris*. Baton Rouge: Louisiana State University Press, 2015.

Horta Correia, José Eduardo. "Pragmatismo e utopismo na criação urbanística de raíz portuguesa no século XVIII." *Revista da Faculdade de Ciências Sociais e Humanas da Universidade Nova de Lisboa* 2.8 (1995): 103–112.

Howard, Ebenezer. *Garden Cities of To-Morrow*. England: S. Sonnenschein & Co., 1902.

Howard, Ebenezer. "The Transit Problem and the Working Man." *Town Planning Review* 4.2 (1913): 127–132.

Hugo, Victor. *Les Misérables*. Brussels: A. Lacroix, Verboeckhoven, 1862.

Israel, Jonathan. *Democratic Enlightenment*. New York: Oxford University Press, 2011.

Jackson, Kenneth T. *Crabgrass Frontier: The Suburbanization of the United States*. Oxford: Oxford University Press, 1985.

Jacobs, Jane. *The Death and Life of Great American Cities*. New York: Random House, 1961.

Jauss, Hans Robert. "Literary History as a Challenge to Literary Theory." *New Literary History* 2.1 (1970): 7–37.

Jefferson, Thomas. *The Papers of Thomas Jefferson: Digital Edition*. Edited by Barbara B. Oberg and J. Jefferson Looney. Charlottesville: University of Virginia Press, 2009.

Jefferson, Thomas. *The Writings of Thomas Jefferson*. Edited by Paul Leicester Ford. New York: G. P. Putnam and Sons, 1899.

Jenger, Jean, ed. *Le Corbusier: Choix de Lettres*. Berlin: Birkhäuser, 2002.

Jobard, Jean Baptiste. "L'architecture de l'avenir." *Revue Gènèrale de l'Architecture et des Travaux Publics* 26.2 (1849): 27.

Jordan, David P. *Transforming Paris: The Life and Labors of Baron Haussmann*. New York: Free Press, 1995.

Judt, Tony. *Postwar: A History of Europe since 1945*. New York: Penguin Press, 2005.

Kalifa, Dominique. *Vice, Crime, and Poverty: How the Western Imagination Invented the Underworld*. New York: Columbia University Press, 2019.

Karuka, Manu. *Empire's Tracks: Indigenous Nations, Chinese Workers, and the Transcontinental Railroad*. Berkeley: University of California Press, 2019.

Karush, Matthew B. *Culture of Class: Radio and Cinema in the Making of a Divided Argentina, 1920–1946*. Durham, NC: Duke University Press, 2012.

Kedrosky, Davis, and Nuno Palma. "The Cross of Gold: Brazilian Treasure and the Decline of Portugal." *CAGE Online Working Paper Series* 574 [Competitive Advantage in the Global Economy], 2021.

Kelly, Florence. *The Autobiography of Florence Kelley*. Edited by Kathryn Kish Sklar. Chicago: Charles H. Kerr Publishing Co., 1986.

Kendrick, T. D. *The Lisbon Earthquake*. London: Methuen, 1956.

Kennedy, Paul. *The Rise and Fall of the Great Powers: Economic Change and Military Conflict from 1500 to 2000*. New York: Random House, 1989.

Kimari, Wangui. "'Under Construction': Everyday Anxieties and the Proliferating Social Meanings of China in Kenya." *Africa* 91.1 (2021): 135–152.

Klinenberg, Eric. *Palaces for the People: How Social Infrastructure Can Help Fight Inequality, Polarization, and the Decline of Civic Life*. New York: Crown Publishing Group, 2018.

Koeppel, Gerard. *City on a Grid: How New York Became New York*. Boston: Da Capo Press, 2015.

Koolhaas, Rem. *Delirious New York*. New York: Monacelli Press, 1997.

Koolhas, Rem, with Edgar Cleijne and Ademide Adelusi-Adeluyi. *Lagos: How It Works*. Baden: Lars Muller Publishers, 2007.

Koselleck, Reinhart. *Futures Past: On the Semantics of Historical Time*. New York: Columbia University Press, 2004.

Kostof, Spiro. *The City Shaped: Urban Patterns and Meanings through History*. Boston: Little, Brown and Co., 1991.

Krieger, Alex. *City on a Hill: Urban Idealism in America from the Puritans to the Present*. Cambridge, MA: Harvard University Press, 2019.

Laitinen, Riitta, and Thomas V. Cohen, eds. *Cultural History of Early Modern European Streets*. Leiden: Brill, 2009.

Lamarão, Sérgio Tadeu. *Dos Trapiches ao Porto: um estudo sobre a área portuária do Rio de Janeiro*. Rio de Janeiro: Departamento Geral de Documentação e Informação Cultural, 1991.

"La razón en la ciudad: el Plan Cerdà. Cuaderno central." In *Barcelona Metropolis: Revista de información y pensamiento urbanos* 76 (2009): 43–110.

Laugier, Marc-Antoine. *Essai sur l'architecture*. Paris: Chez Duchesne, 1953.

Les Cités de Chemins de Fer (Éd. 1857). Paris: Hachette, 2018.

Le Corbusier. *Aircraft*. New York: Studio Ltd., 1935.

Le Corbusier. *The City of Tomorrow and Its Planning*. New York: Dover, 1987.

Le Corbusier. *La Ville Radieuse*. Boulogne: Editions de l'Architecture d'aujourd'hui, 1935.

Le Corbusier. *Oeuvre Compléte, 1938–1946*. Edited by Willy Boesiger. Basel: Birkhäuser, 2015.

Le Corbusier. *Précisions sur un État Présent de l'Architecture et de l'Urbanisme*. Paris: Crès et Cie., 1930.

Le Corbusier. *Urbanisme*. Paris: G. Crès et Cie., 1924.

Le Corbusier and Pierre Jeanneret. *Oeuvre Complète 1910–1929*. Zurich: Éditions Dr. H. Girsberger, 1943.

Lecouvreur, Frank. *From East Prussia to the Golden Gate by Frank Lecouvreur*. Translated and compiled by Julius C. Behnke. New York; Los Angeles: Angelina Book Concern, 1906.

Lefebvre, Henri. *La Production de L'Espace*. Paris: Éditions Anthropos, 1981.

Leibniz, Gottfried Wilhelm. *Theodicy: Essays on the Goodness of God, the Freedom of Man, and the Origin of Evil*. Translated by E. M. Huggard. Lasalle, IL: Open Court, 1985.

Lejeune, Jean-François, ed. *Cruelty and Utopia: Cities and Landscapes of Latin America*. Princeton, NJ: Princeton Architectural Press, 2005.

Lenzi, Maria Isabel Ribeiro. "Francisco Pereira Passos—Possibilidade de um outro olhar." *Revista Rio de Janeiro* 10 (2003): 133–141.

Lepore, Jill. *If Then: How the Simulmatics Corporation Invented the Future*. New York: Liveright, 2020.

Levy, Jonathan. *Ages of American Capitalism: A History of the United States*. New York: Penguin Random House, 2021.

L'Exposition Universelle de 1867 Illustrée: Publication Internationale Autorisée par la Commission Impériale. Paris: Commission Impériale, 1867.

Liernur, Jorge Francisco, and Pablo Pschepiurca. *La Red Austral: Obras y Proyectos de Le Corbusier y sus Discípulos en la Argentina (1924–1965)*. Buenos Aires: Prometo Libros, 2008.

Lindbergh, Anne Morrow. *The Wave of the Future, Confession of Faith*. New York: Harcourt, Brace and Company, 1940.

Link, Stefan J. *Forging Global Fordism: Nazi Germany, Soviet Russia, and the Contest over the Industrial Order*. Princeton, NJ: Princeton University Press, 2020.

Lispector, Claire. *Complete Stories*. Translated by Katrina Dodson. New York: New Directions, 2015.

Lispector, Clarice. *Um sopro de vida*. Rio de Janeiro: Rocco, 2019.

Lomnitz, Claudio. *Deep Mexico, Silent Mexico: An Anthropology of Nationalism*. Minneapolis: University of Minnesota Press, 2001.

Longchamps, Pierre de. *Malagrida: tragédie en trois actes.* Lisbon [?]: De l'imprimerie de l'inquisition, 1763.

López-Durán, Fabiola. *Eugenics in the Garden: Transatlantic Architecture and the Crafting of Modernity.* Austin: University of Texas Press, 2018.

Loyer, François. *Paris XIXe Siècle.* Paris: Hazan, 1987.

Lynch, Kenneth, Etienne Nel, and Tony Binns. "'Transforming Freetown': Dilemmas of Planning and Development in a West African City." *Cities* 101 (2020): 102694.

Macoun, Thomas, Ulrich Leth, and Harald Frey. "Effects of the Internal Constraints of Transportation Systems on the Reliability of Forecasts." *12th World Conference on Transport Research Society.* Lisbon, 2010.

Maddison, Angus. *Contours of the World Economy, 1–2030 AD: Essays in Macro-Economic History.* Oxford: Oxford University Press, 2007.

Malagrida, Gabriel. *Juizo da verdadeira causa do terremoto, que padeceo a corte de Lisboa, no primeiro de novembro de 1755 [. . .].* Lisboa: Na officina de Manoel Soares, 1756.

Maneglier, Hervé. *Paris Impérial: La Vie Quotidienne sous le Second Empire.* Paris: Armand Colin, 1990.

Manning, Patrick. "African Population, 1650–2000: Comparisons and Implications of New Estimates." In *Africa's Development in Historical Perspective.* Edited by Emmanuel Akyeampong, Robert H. Bates, Nathan Nunn, and James Robinson. Cambridge: Cambridge University Press, 2014.

Mansfield, Howard. *Cosmopolis: Yesterday's Cities of the Future.* New Brunswick, NJ: Center for Urban Policy Research, 1990.

Manso, Juana Paula. *Los Misterios del Plata: episodios históricos de la época de Rosas, escritos en 1846.* Buenos Aires: J. Menéndez, 1936.

Marcuse, Peter. "The Grid as City Plan: New York City and Laissez-Faire Planning in the Nineteenth Century." *Planning Perspectives* 2.3 (1987): 287–310.

Marques, José. "The Paths of Providence." *Cadernos de História e Filosofia da Ciência* 3, 15.1 (2005): 33–57.

Marx, Karl, and Friedrich Engels. *The Marx-Engels Reader.* Edited by Robert Tucker. New York: Norton, 1978.

Maxwell, Kenneth. "Lisbon: The Earthquake of 1755 and Urban Recovery under the Marquês de Pombal." *Out of Ground Zero: Case Studies in Urban Reinvention.* Edited by Joan Ockman. New York: Temple Hoyne Buell Center for the Study of American Architecture, Columbia University, 2002.

Maxwell, Kenneth. *Pombal: Paradox of the Enlightenment.* Cambridge: Cambridge University Press, 1995.

Mayhew, Henry. *London Labour and the London Poor.* London: Griffin, Bohn, and Company, Stationers' Hall Court, 1861–1862.

Mays, Kyle. *City of Dispossessions: Indigenous Peoples, African Americans, and the Creation of Modern Detroit.* Philadelphia: University of Pennsylvania Press, 2022.

Mbembe, Achille. "The Society of Enmity." Translated by Giovanni Menegalle. *Radical Philosophy* 200 (2016): 23–35.

McAuliffe, Mary. *Paris, City of Dreams: Napoleon III, Baron Haussmann, and the Creation of Paris.* Lanham: Rowman & Littlefield, 2020.

Meade, Teresa A. *"Civilizing Rio": Reform and Resistance in a Brazilian City, 1889–1930*. University Park: Pennsylvania State University Press, 1997.

Meadows, Donella H., Dennis L. Meadows, Jørgen Randers, and William W. Behrens III. *The Limits to Growth: A Report for the Club of Rome's Project on the Predicament of Mankind*. New York: Universe Books, 1972.

Melly, Caroline. *Bottleneck: Moving, Building, and Belonging in an African City*. Chicago: University of Chicago Press, 2017.

Melville, Herman. *Billy Budd, Bartleby, and Other Stories*. Edited by Peter Coviello. New York: Penguin Books, 2016.

Mercier, Louis-Sébastien. *Astræa's return: or, the halcyon days of France in the year 2440: a dream*. Translated by Harriot Augusta Freeman. London: Hookham and Carpenter, 1797.

Mercier, Louis-Sébastien. *L'An 2440: Rêve s'il en fut jamais*. London: [n.p.], 1772.

Mercier, Louis-Sébastien. *Memoirs of the year two thousand five hundred*. Translated by W. Hooper. London: Printed for G. Robinson, 1772.

Merrifield, Andy. *The New Urban Question*. London: Pluto Press, 2014.

Merriman, John. *Massacre: The Life and Death of the Paris Commune*. New York: Basic Books, 2014.

Meyer, Esther da Costa. *Dividing Paris: Urban Renewal and Social Inequality, 1852–1870*. Princeton, NJ: Princeton University Press, 2022.

Meyer, William. *The Environmental Advantages of Cities: Countering Commonsense Antiurbanism*. Cambridge, MA: MIT Press, 2013.

Miller, Sara Cedar. *Before Central Park*. New York: Columbia University Press, 2022.

Milza, Pierre. *L'Année Terrible: La Commune (Mars–Juin 1871)*. Paris: Perrin, 2009.

Minois, Georges. *L'Âge d'Or: Histoire de la Poursuite du Bonheur*. Paris: Fayard, 2009.

Moncan, Patrice de, and Claude Heurteux. *Le Paris d'Haussmann*. Paris: Les Editions du Mécène, 2002.

Mujica, Francisco. *History of the Skyscraper*. Paris: Archaeology and Architecture Press, 1929.

Mumford, Eric. *Designing the Modern City: Urbanism since 1850*. New Haven, CT: Yale University Press, 2018.

Mumford, Lewis. "American Architecture Today." *Architecture* 58 (1928): 181–188.

Mumford, Lewis. *The City in History: Its Origins, Its Transformations, and Its Prospects*. New York: Harcourt, 1961.

Mumford, Lewis. *The Lewis Mumford Reader*. Edited by Donald Miller. New York: Pantheon Books, 1986.

Murger, Henri. *Scènes de la vie de bohème*. Paris: M. Levy, 1851.

Murray-Miller, Gavin. *Revolutionary Europe: Politics, Community and Culture in Transnational Context, 1775–1922*. London: Bloomsbury Academic, 2020.

Muzaffar, Ijlal. *Modernism's Magic Hat: Architecture and the Illusion of Development without Capital*. Austin: University of Texas Press, 2024.

Nabuco, Joaquim. *Essencial Joaquim Nabuco*. Organized by Evaldo Cabral de Mello. São Paulo: Companhia das Letras, 2010.

Nabuco, Joaquim. *Minha Formação*. Brasília: Senado Federal, 1998.

Nabuco, Joaquim. *O Abolicionismo*. London: Typographia de Abraham Kingdon e ca., 1883.

Needell, Jeffrey D. *A Tropical Belle Epoque: Elite Culture and Society in Turn-of-the-Century Rio de Janeiro*. Cambridge: Cambridge University Press, 1987.

Neiman, Susan. *Evil in Modern Thought: An Alternative History of Philosophy*. Princeton, NJ: Princeton University Press, 2002.

Nelson, David. "Defining the Urban: The Construction of French-Dominated Colonial Dakar, 1857–1940." *Historical Reflections / Réflexions Historiques* 33.2 (2007): 225–255.

Nelson, William Max. *The Time of Enlightenment: Constructing the Future in France, 1750 to Year One*. Toronto: Toronto University Press, 2021.

Newman, William A., and Wilfred E. Holton. *Boston's Back Bay: The Story of America's Greatest Nineteenth-Century Landfill Project*. Lebanon, NH: University Press of New England, 2006.

Nicolini, Alberto. "Le Corbusier, Utopía y Buenos Aires." *Documentos de Arquitectura Nacional y Americana* 37/38 (1995): 106–113.

Nicoloso, Paolo. *Mussolini Architetto: Propaganda e Paesaggio Urbano nell'Italia Fascista*. Torino: G. Einaudi, 2008.

Nightingale, Carl. *Segregation: A Global History of Divided Cities*. Chicago: University of Chicago Press, 2012.

Nilsen, Micheline. *Railways and the Western European Capitals: Studies of Implantation in London, Paris, Berlin, and Brussels*. New York: Palgrave Macmillan, 2008.

Nixon, Rob. *Slow Violence and the Environmentalism of the Poor*. Cambridge, MA: Harvard University Press, 2011.

Norton, Peter D. *Fighting Traffic: The Dawn of the Motor Age in the American City*. Cambridge, MA: MIT Press, 2011.

Nuitter, Charles. *La Nouvel Opéra*. Paris: Librairie Hachette, 1875.

Núñez, Rafael E., Eve Sweetser. "With the Future behind Them: Convergent Evidence from Aymara Language and Gesture in the Crosslinguistic Comparison of Spatial Construals of Time." *Cognitive Science* 30.3 (2006): 401–450.

Obiadi, Bons, and Aloysius Osita Onochie. "Abuja, Nigeria Urban Actors, Master Plan, Development Laws and Their Roles in the Design and Shaping of Abuja Federal Territory and Their Urban Environments." *International Journal of Geography and Environmental Management* 4.4 (2018): 23–43.

Official descriptive and illustrated catalogue of the Great Exhibition of the Works of Industry of All Nations, 1851. London: Spicer Brothers, 1851.

Ogle, Vanessa. *The Global Transformation of Time: 1870–1950*. Cambridge, MA: Harvard University Press, 2015.

Okorafor, Nnedi. *Lagoon*. London: Hodder and Stoughton, 2014.

Olajide, Oluwafemi, and Taibat Lawanson. "Urban Paradox and the Rise of the Neoliberal City: Case Study of Lagos, Nigeria." *Urban Studies* 59.9 (2022): 1763–1781.

Oliveira, Carmen. *Flores raras e banalíssimas: a História de Lota de Macedo Soares e Elizabeth Bishop*. Rio de Janeiro: Rocco, 1995.

Oliveira, Patrick de. "Imagining an Old City in Nineteenth-Century France: Urban Renovation, Civil Society, and the Making of Vieux Lyon." *Journal of Urban History* 45.1 (2019): 67–98.

Oliveira, Vicente Carlos de. *Lisboa Restaurada*. Lisbon: Fernando Jozé dos Santos, 1784.

Olmsted, Frederick Law. *Frederick Law Olmsted: Essential Texts*. Edited by Robert Twombly. New York: W. W. Norton, 2010.

Olmsted, Frederick Law. *Frederick Law Olmsted, Landscape Architect, 1822–1903*. Edited by Frederick Law Olmsted Jr. and Theodora Kimball. New York, London: G. P. Putnam's Sons, 1922–1928.

Olmsted, Frederick Law. *The Papers of Frederick Law Olmsted: Creating Central Park, 1857–1861*. Edited by Charles E. Beveridge and David Schuyler. Baltimore, MD: Johns Hopkins University Press, 1983.

Orwell, George. *1984*. London: Secker & Warburg, 1949.

O'Shea, Lizzie. *Future Histories: What Ada Lovelace, Tom Paine, and the Paris Commune Can Teach Us about Digital Technology*. London: Verso, 2019.

Osterhammel, Jürgen. *The Transformation of the World: A Global History of the Nineteenth Century*. Translated by Patrick Camiller. Princeton, NJ: Princeton University Press, 2009.

Owen, Robert. *A New View of Society*. London: Printed for Longman, Hurst, Rees, Orme, and Brown, 1816.

Paccoud, Antoine. "Planning Law, Power, and Practice." *Planning Perspectives* 31.3 (2015): 341–361.

Paccoud, Antoine. *A Politics of Regulation: Haussmann's Planning Practice and Badiou's Philosophy*. PhD diss., London School of Economics and Political Science, 2012.

Page, Max. *The City's End: Two Centuries of Fantasies, Fears, and Premonitions of New York's Destruction*. New Haven, CT: Yale University Press, 2008.

Paice, Edward. *Youthquake: Why African Demography Should Matter to the World*. London: Apollo, 2021.

Pappe, Silvia. *Estridentópolis: Urbanización y Montaje*. México, D.F.: Universidad Autónoma Metropolitana, Unidad Azcapotzalco, 2006.

Paquette, Gabriel. *Imperial Portugal in the Age of Atlantic Revolutions: The Luso-Brazilian World, c. 1770–1850*. Cambridge: Cambridge University Press, 2013.

Páramo, Martha Susana. *Un Fracaso Hecho Historia: la Corporación de Transportes de la Ciudad de Buenos Aires*. Mendoza: Universidad Nacional de Cuyo, 1991.

Patte, Pierre. *Mémoires sur les Objets les plus Importans de l'architecture*. Paris: Rozet, 1769.

Patte, Pierre. *Monuments érigés en France à la gloire de Louis XV, précédés d'un tableau du progrès des arts & des sciences sous ce règne [. . .]*. Paris: [n.p.], 1767.

Petit, Catherine. "Notice inédite sur Lisbonne en 1781." *Bulletin des Etudes Portugaises et Brésiliennes* 35–36 (1974–1975): 93–120.

Phillips, Leigh. *Austerity Ecology and the Collapse-Porn Addicts: A Defence of Growth, Progress, Industry and Stuff*. Washington, DC: Zero Books, 2015.

Picon, Antoine. *Les Saint-Simoniens: Raison, Imaginaire et Utopie*. Paris: Belin, 2002.

Pieterse, Edgar. *City Futures: Confronting the Crisis of Urban Development*. London: Zed Books, 2008.

Pinkney, David H. *Napoleon III and the Rebuilding of Paris*. Princeton, NJ: Princeton University Press, 1958.

Pinto, Virgílio Noya. *O Ouro Brasileiro e o Comércio Anglo-Português*. São Paulo: Companhia Editora Nacional, 1979.

Poe, Edgar Allan. *The Gift: A Christmas and New Year's Present 1845*. Philadelphia: Cary and Hart, 1845.

Prendergast, Christopher. *For the People by the People? Eugène Sue's Les Mystères de Paris*. Oxford: Legenda, 2003.

The Proceedings and Sentence of the Spiritual Court of Inquisition of Portugal, against Gabriel Malagrida, Jesuit, for Heresy, Hypocrisy, False Prophecies, Impostures, and Various Other Heinous Crimes. Lisbon; London: C. Marsh, at Cicero's Head, Charing-Cross, 1762.

Proceedings of the First National Conference on City Planning. Chicago: American Society of Planning Officials, 1967.

Puchner, Martin. *Poetry of the Revolution: Marx, Manifestos, and the Avant-Gardes*. Princeton, NJ: Princeton University Press, 2006.

Rama, Angel. *La Ciudad Letrada*. Hanover, NH: Ediciones del Norte, 1984.

Ramalho, Maurício Miguel. *Lisboa Reedificada, poema épico*. Lisbon: Na Regia officina typografica, 1780.

Rawson, Michael. *The Nature of Tomorrow: A History of the Environmental Future*. New Haven, CT: Yale University Press, 2021.

Recopilación de leyes de los reynos de las Indias. Madrid: Centro de Estudios Políticos y Constitucionales, 1998.

Reese, Carol McMichael. "The Urban Development of Mexico City, 1850–1930." In *Planning Latin America's Capital Cities, 1850–1950*. Edited by Artur Almandoz. London: Routledge, 2002.

Reis, João José. "African Nations in Nineteenth-Century Salvador, Bahia." In *The Black Urban Atlantic in the Age of the Slave Trade*. Edited by Jorge Canizares-Esguerra, Matt D. Childs, and James Sidbury. Philadelphia: University of Pennsylvania Press, 2013.

Reis, João José. *Rebelião Escrava no Brasil: A História do Levante dos Malês (1835)*. São Paulo: Companhia das Letras, 2003.

Report from the Select Committee on Metropolitan Communications [. . .]. London: Parliament, House of Commons, 1855.

Reynolds, George. *The Mysteries of London*. London: Milner, 1980.

Reynolds, George. *The Mysteries of the Court of London*. London: J. Dicks, 1850–1856.

Rice, Shelley. *Parisian Views*. Cambridge, MA: MIT Press, 1999.

Riis, Jacob A. *How the Other Half Lives: Studies among the Tenements of New York*. New York: Charles Scribner's Sons, 1890.

Rio, João do. *Vida Vertiginosa*. Rio de Janeiro: H. Garnier, 1911.

Robespierre, Maximilien. *Oeuvres de Maximilien Robespierre*. Volume 9. Paris: E. Leroux, 1957.

Robida, Albert. *La Vie Électrique: le vingtième siècle*. Paris: Librairie illustrée, 1892.

Roemer, Kenneth M. "Contexts and Texts: The Influence of Looking Backward." *Centennial Review* 27.3 (1983): 204–223.

Rosenbaum, Samuel. *A Voyage to America Ninety Years Ago: The Diary of a Bohemian Jew on His Voyage to New York in 1847*. San Bernardino, CA: Borgo Press, 1995.

Rosenberg, Daniel. "An Eighteenth-Century Time Machine: The 'Encyclopedia' of Denis Diderot." *Historical Reflections / Réflexions Historiques* 25.2 (1999): 227–250.

Rosenzweig, Roy, and Elizabeth Blackmar. *The Park and the People: A History of Central Park*. Ithaca, NY: Cornell University Press, 1992.

Rose-Redwood, Reuben. "Mythologies of the Grid in the Empire City, 1811–2011." In *Gridded Worlds: An Urban Anthology*. Edited by Liora Bigon and Reuben Rose-Redwood. Heidelberg: Springer International Publishing, 2018.

Rossa, Walter. *Além da Baixa*. Lisboa: Ministério da Cultura, 1998.

Rothschild, Emma. *An Infinite History: The Story of a Family in France over Three Centuries*. Princeton, NJ: Princeton University Press, 2021.

Rothstein, Richard. *The Color of Law: A Forgotten History of How Our Government Segregated America*. New York: Liveright, 2017.

Rousseau, Jean-Jacques. *Emile*. Translation by Barbara Foxley. London: E. P. Dutton & Co., 1911.

Rousseau, Jean-Jacques. *Émile, Or, De L'education*. Netherlands: [n.p], 1762.

Rousseau, Jean-Jacques. *Julie, or, The New Heloise*. Translation by Philip Stewart and Jean Vaché. Hanover, NH: University Press of New England, 190, 192, 193.

Russell-Wood, A.J.R. *The Portuguese Empire, 1415–1808*. Baltimore, MD: Johns Hopkins University Press, 1998.

Rybczynski, Witold. *City Life: Urban Expectations in a New World*. New York: Scribner, 1995.

Rydell, Robert, ed. *The Reason Why the Colored American Is Not in the World's Columbian Exposition: The Afro-American's Contribution to Columbian Literature*. Urbana: University of Illinois Press, 1999.

Sadighian, David. *The World Is a Composition: Beaux-Arts Design and Internationalism in the Age of Empire, 1867–1914*. PhD diss., Harvard University, 2023.

Safier, Neil. "The Confines on the Colony." In *The Imperial Map: Cartography and the Mastery of Empire*. Edited by James Akerman. Chicago: University of Chicago Press, 2009.

Saint-Amour, Paul K. *Tense Future: Modernism, Total War, Encyclopedic Form*. Oxford: Oxford University Press, 2015.

San-Antonio-Gómez, Carlos, Cristina Velilla Lucini, and Francisco Manzano-Agugliaro. "Similarities between L'Enfant's Urban Plan for Washington, DC, and the Royal Site of Aranjuez, Spain." *Journal of Urban Planning and Development* 145.2 (2019).

Sanches, Antonio Ribeiro. *Tratado da Conservação da Saúde dos Povos*. Paris; Lisboa: Bonardel e Du Beux, 1756.

Sand, George. *Correspondance entre George Sand et Gustave Flaubert*. Paris: Calmann-Lévy, 1916.

Sand, George. "Rêverie à Paris." Translated by Gideon Fink Shapiro in "Luxury for All." *Places Journal*, January 2022.

Sandoval-Strausz, A. K. *Barrio America: How Latino Immigrants Saved the American City*. New York: Basic Books, 2019.

Sarkis, Hashim, Roi Salgueiro Barrio, and Gabriel Kozlowski. *The World as an Architectural Project*. Cambridge, MA: MIT Press, 2019.

Sarlo, Beatriz. "Buenos Aires: el exilio de Europa." *Letra Internacional* 126 (2018): 5–22.

Sarlo, Beatriz. "Los Debates sobre Modernidad Periférica, Escenas de la Vida Posmoderna y la Cuestión del Valor Estético." In *Mapas Culturales para América Latina: Culturas Híbridas, No Simultaneidad, Modernidad Periférica*. Edited by Sarah de Mojica. Bogotá: Centro Editorial Javeriano, 2001.

Sarmiento, Domingo Faustino. *Civilización y Barbarie*. Santiago: Imprenta del Progresso, 1845.

Schaffer, Daniel. *Garden Cities for America: The Radburn Experience*. Philadelphia: Temple University Press, 1982.

Schley, David. *Steam City: Railroads, Urban Space, and Corporate Capitalism in Nineteenth-Century Baltimore*. Chicago: University of Chicago Press, 2020.

Schorske, Carl E. *Fin-de-Siecle Vienna: Politics and Culture*. New York: Alfred A. Knopf, 1980.

Schrad, Mark Lawrence. *Smashing the Liquor Machine: A Global History of Prohibition.* Oxford: Oxford University Press, 2021.

Schuyler, Montgomery. "The Art of City Making." *Architectural Record* 12.5 (1902): 1–26.

Schwarcz, Lilia Moritz, and Heloisa Murgel Starling. *Brasil: Uma Biografia.* São Paulo: Companhia das Letras, 2015.

Scobie, James. *Buenos Aires: From Plaza to Suburb, 1870–1910.* New York: Oxford University Press, 1974.

Scott, James C. *Seeing Like a State: How Certain Schemes to Improve the Human Condition Have Failed.* New Haven, CT: Yale University Press, 1998.

Scruggs, William. "Restriction of the Suffrage." *North American Review* 139 (1884): 492–502.

Seiler, Cotten. *Republic of Drivers: A Cultural History of Automobility in America.* Chicago: University of Chicago Press, 2008.

Seligman, Martin E. P., Peter Railton, Roy F. Baumeister, and Chandra Sripada. *Homo Prospectus.* Oxford: Oxford University Press, 2016.

Sennett, Richard. "American Cities: The Grid Plan and the Protestant Ethic." In *Gridded Worlds: An Urban Anthology.* Edited by Liora Bigon and Reuben Rose-Redwood. Heidelberg: Springer International Publishing, 2018.

Sennett, Richard. *Building and Dwelling.* New York: Farrar, Straus, and Giroux, 2018.

Sevcenko, Nicolau. *A Revolta da Vacina: Mentes Insanas em Corpos Rebeldes.* São Paulo: Brasiliense, 1984.

Sevilla-Buitrago, Álvaro. *Against the Commons: A Radical History of Urban Planning.* Minneapolis: University of Minnesota Press, 2022.

Shapiro, Ann-Louise. *Housing the Poor of Paris, 1850–1902.* Madison: University of Wisconsin Press, 1985.

Shaw, Matthew. *Time and the French Revolution: The Republican Calendar, 1789–Year XIV.* Woodbridge: Boydell Press, 2011.

Sheller, Mimi. *Aluminum Dreams: The Making of Light Modernity.* Cambridge, MA: MIT Press, 2014.

Simone, AbdouMaliq, and Edgar Pieterse. *New Urban Worlds: Inhabiting Dissonant Times.* Cambridge, UK: Polity, 2017.

Singh, Dhan Zunino. "City of Tomorrow: The Representations of Buenos Aires in the Future through Imagined Mobility c. 1880–1914." In *Cultural Histories of Sociabilities, Spaces and Mobilities.* Edited by Colin Divall. Brookfield, VT: Pickering & Chatto, 2015.

Sklar, Kathryn. *Florence Kelley and the Nation's Work.* New Haven, CT: Yale University Press, 1995.

Slater, Michael. *Charles Dickens.* New Haven, CT: Yale University Press, 2009.

Smethurst, Paul. *The Bicycle: Towards a Global History.* London: Palgrave Macmillan, 2015.

Smil, Vaclav. *Invention and Innovation: A Brief History of Hype and Failure.* Cambridge, MA: MIT Press, 2023.

Smiles, Samuel. *Self-Help: with Illustrations of Character and Conduct.* London: Ward Lock, 1859.

Sorkin, Michael. *What Goes Up: The Right and Wrongs to the City.* Brooklyn: Verso, 2018.

Spengler, Oswald. *The Decline of the West: Perspectives of World History.* Translated by Charles F. Atkinson. New York: Knopf, 1926.

Stacy, Christina, Chris Davis, Yonah Slifkin Freemark, Lydia Lo, Graham MacDonald, Vivian Zheng, and Rolf Pendall. "Land-Use Reforms and Housing Costs: Does Allowing for Increased Density Lead to Greater Affordability?" *Urban Studies* 60.14 (2023): 2919–2940.

Stovall, Tyler. *White Freedom: The Racial History of an Idea*. Princeton, NJ: Princeton University Press, 2020.

Strachan, Hew. *The First World War*. New York: Viking, 2004.

Streeby, Shelley. *American Sensations: Class, Empire, and the Production of Popular Culture*. Berkeley: University of California Press, 2002.

Subin, Zachary, Jackie Lombardi, Raghav Muralidharan, Jacob Korn, Jeetika Malik, Tyler Pullen, Max Wei, Tianzhen Hong. "US Urban Land-Use Reform: A Strategy for Energy Sufficiency." *Buildings and Cities* 5.1 (2024): 400–417.

Sue, Eugène. *The Mysteries of Paris: A Novel*. Translated by Charles H. Town. New York: Harper, 1843.

Sugrue, Thomas J. *The Origins of the Urban Crisis: Race and Inequality in Postwar Detroit*. Princeton, NJ: Princeton University Press, 1996.

Sutcliffe, Anthony. *The Autumn of Central Paris*. London: Arnold, 1971.

Sutton, Robert P. *Les Icariens: The Utopian Dream in Europe and America*. Urbana: University of Illinois Press, 1994.

Tafuri, Manfredo. *Architecture and Utopia: Design and Capitalist Development*. Translated by Barbara Luigia La Penta. Cambridge, MA: MIT Press, 1976.

Tallon, Andrew. "The Portuguese Precedent for Pierre Patte's Street Section." *Journal of the Society of Architectural Historians* 63.3 (2004): 370–377.

Tavares, Rui. *O pequeno livro do grande terramoto: ensaio sobre 1755*. Lisbon: Tinta-da-china, 2005.

Taylor, Keeanga-Yamahtta. *Race for Profit: How Banks and the Real Estate Industry Undermined Black Homeownership*. Chapel Hill: University of North Carolina Press, 2019.

Tenorio-Trillo, Mauricio. *I Speak of the City: Mexico City at the Turn of the Twentieth Century*. Chicago: University of Chicago Press, 2015.

Tinhorão, José Ramos. *Domingos Caldas Barbosa: o poeta da viola, da modinha e do lundú, 1740–1800*. Lisboa: Editorial Caminho, 2004.

Tocqueville, Alexis de. *Democracy in America*. New York: G. Adlard, 1839.

Tocqueville, Alexis de. *The Recollections of Alexis de Tocqueville*. New York: Macmillan, 1896.

Toffler, Alvin. *Future Shock*. New York: Random House, 1970.

Tomasi di Lampedusa, Giuseppe. *Il gattopardo*. Milan: G. Feltrinelli, 1959.

Torpey, John. *The Invention of the Passport: Surveillance, Citizenship and the State*. Cambridge: Cambridge University Press, 2018.

Tsey, Komla. *From Head-Loading to the Iron Horse: Railway Building in Colonial Ghana and the Origins of Tropical Development*. Oxford: Langaa RPCIG, 2012.

Tsing, Anna Lowenhaupt. *The Mushroom at the End of the World: On the Possibility of Life in Capitalist Ruins*. Princeton, NJ: Princeton University Press, 2015.

Tuana, Nancy. "Climate Apartheid: The Forgetting of Race in the Anthropocene." *Critical Philosophy of Race* 7.1 (2019): 1–31.

Turner, Frederick Jackson. *The Frontier in American History*. New York: Henry Holt & Company, 1920.

Twain, Mark, and Charles Warner. *The Gilded Age: A Tale of To-day*. Hartford, CT: American Publishing Company, 1874.

Upton, Dell. *Another City: Urban Life and Urban Spaces in the New American Republic*. New Haven, CT: Yale University Press, 2008.

Urry, John. *What Is the Future?* Cambridge, UK: Polity, 2016.

Valle, Luisa. *The Beehive, the Favela, the Castle, and the Ministry: Race and Modern Architecture in Rio de Janeiro, 1811 to 1945*. PhD diss., CUNY, 2022.

Vance, James E. *The Continuing City: Urban Morphology in Western Civilization*. Baltimore, MD: Johns Hopkins University Press, 1990.

Van Zanten, David. *Building Paris: Architectural Institutions and the Transformation of the French Capital, 1830–1870*. Cambridge: Cambridge University Press, 1994.

Vasconcelos, José. *La Raza Cosmica*. México: Espasa-Calpe Mexicana, 1948.

Vaz, Lilian Fessler. *Contribuição ao Estudo da Produção e Transformação do Espaço da Habitação Popular*. PhD diss., Universidade Federal do Rio de Janeiro, 1985.

Vera y González, Enrique. *La Estrella del Sur: a través del porvenir*. Buenos Aires: Instituto Histórico de la Ciudad de Buenos Aires, 2000.

Verne, Jules. *Paris in the Twentieth Century: The Lost Novel*. Translated by Richard Howard. New York: Del Rey, 1997.

Vitz, Matthew. *A City on a Lake: Urban Political Ecology and the Growth of Mexico City*. Durham, NC: Duke University Press, 2018.

Voltaire [Jean-François-Marie Arouet]. *Candide, ou l'Optimisme*. Geneva: Cramer, 1759.

Voltaire [Jean-François-Marie Arouet]. "Des embellissemens de Paris." In *Recueil de pièces en vers et en prose*. Amsterdam: Lambert, 1750.

Voltaire [Jean-François-Marie Arouet]. *Poèmes sur la religion naturelle et sur la destruction de Lisbonne*. [Paris?: s.n.]: 1756.

Wagner-Conzelmann, Sandra. *Die Interbau 1957 in Berlin*. Petersberg: M. Imhof, 2007.

Walker, Nathaniel. "Lost in the City of Light: Dystopia and Utopia in the Wake of Haussmann's Paris." *Utopian Studies* 25.1 (2014): 24–51.

Walker, Nathaniel. *Victorian Visions of Suburban Utopia: Abandoning Babylon*. Oxford: Oxford University Press, 2021.

Walker, Timothy. "Enlightened Absolutism and the Lisbon Earthquake." *Eighteenth-Century Studies* 48 (2015): 307–328.

Wallace, Max. *The American Axis: Henry Ford, Charles Lindbergh, and the Rise of the Third Reich*. New York: St. Martin's Press, 2003.

Washington, Booker T. *The Future of the American Negro*. Boston: Small, Maynard & Company, 1899.

Weekley, Ernest. *An Etymological Dictionary of Modern English*. London: J. Murray, 1921.

Weiss, Joaquín E. *El rascacielos, su génesis, evolución y significación en la arquitectura contemporánes*. Havana: Tipos-Molina y cía, 1934.

Wells, H. G. *The Shape of Things to Come*. New York: Macmillan Company, 1933.

Wells, H. G. *The Sleeper Awakes*. New York: Harper & Brothers, 1910.

Wells, H. G. *The War That Will End War*. New York: Duffield & Company, 1914.

Westenhöfer, Joachim, Elham Nouri, Merle Linn Reschke, Fabian Seebach, and Johanna Buch-cik. "Walkability and Urban Built Environments—A Systematic Review of Health Impact Assessments (HIA)." *BMC Public Health* 23.518 (2023): 1–19.

Weyland, Kurt. "The Diffusion of Revolution: '1848' in Europe and Latin America." *International Organization* 63.3 (2009): 391–423.

White, Lucia, and Morton White. *The Intellectual versus the City: From Thomas Jefferson to Frank Lloyd Wright.* Cambridge, MA: Harvard University Press, 1962.

Whitman, James. *Hitler's American Model: The United States and the Making of Nazi Race Law.* Princeton, NJ: Princeton University Press, 2017.

Wilkerson, Isabel. *The Warmth of Other Suns: The Epic Story of America's Great Migration.* New York: Random House, 2010.

Wilkie Jr., Everett C. "Mercier's *L'An 2440:* Its Publishing History during the Author's Lifetime." *Harvard Library Bulletin* XXXII 1(1984): 5–35.

Williams, Eric. *Capitalism and Slavery.* Chapel Hill: University of North Carolina Press, 2021.

Williams, Raymond. *The Country and the City.* Oxford: Oxford University Press, 1973.

Wilson, Thomas. *The Ashley Cooper Plan: The Founding of Carolina and the Origins of Southern Political Culture.* Chapel Hill: University of North Carolina Press, 2016.

Wilson, William E. *The Angel and the Serpent: The Story of New Harmony.* Bloomington: Indiana University Press, 1967.

Wright, Frank Lloyd. "Broadacre City: A New Community Plan: Architectural Record (1935)." In the *City Reader.* Edited by Richard T. LeGates and Frederic Stout. New York: Routledge, 2020.

Wright, Gwendolyn. *The Politics of Design in French Colonial Urbanism.* Chicago: University of Chicago Press, 1991.

Wynn, Martin. "Barcelona: Planning and Change 1854–1977." *Town Planning Review* 50.2 (1979): 185–203.

Yates, Alexia. *Selling Paris: Property and Commercial Culture in the Fin-de-siècle Capital.* Cambridge, MA: Harvard University Press, 2015.

Zamyatin, Yevgeny. *We.* Translated by Gregory Zilboorg. New York: E. P. Dutton, 1924.

Zola, Émile. *La Curée.* Paris: Le livre de poche, 1984.

Zweig, Stefan. *Brasilien: Ein Land der Zukunft.* Stockholm: Bermann-Fischer, 1941.

ILLUSTRATION CREDITS

Fig. 1.1, Biblioteca Nacional de Portugal; Fig. 1.2, Oeiras City Hall (Portugal) / Wikimedia Commons; Figs. 2.1, 2.2, Wellcome Collection; Figs. 2.3, 3.4, 4.7, Library of Congress Geography and Map Division; Fig. 2.4, Brigham Young University-Idaho, David O. McKay Library; Fig. 2.5, Bibliothèque nationale de France; Figs. 3.1, 3.3, 3.5, 5.1, Library of Congress Prints and Photographs Division; Fig. 3.2, © Victoria and Albert Museum, London; Fig. 3.6, Philadelphia Museum of Art: Gift of Helen Tyson Madeira, 1991; Fig. 3.7, Musée Carnavalet, Histoire de Paris; Fig. 3.8, Museu d'Historia de la Ciutat de Barcelona; Fig. 3.9, Lionel Pincus and Princess Firyal Map Division, The New York Public Library; Figs. 4.1, 5.3, 5.7, Wikimedia Commons; Fig. 4.2, México en Fotos, A.C.; Fig. 4.3, Yale University Art Gallery, Everett V. Meeks, B.A. 1901, Fund; Fig. 4.4, Author's Collection; Figs. 4.5, 4.6, Harvard Fine Arts Library; Figs. 4.8, 4.11, Instituto Moreira Salles Collection; Figs. 4.9, 4.10, Fundação Biblioteca Nacional (Brazil); Fig. 5.2, Smithsonian Libraries and Archives; Fig. 5.4, Russell Sage Foundation records (FA015) Series 3: Early Office Files, City Housing Corporation— Reports, Clippings 1924–1936, Rockefeller Archive Center; Fig. 5.5, Beinecke Rare Book and Manuscript Library, Yale University; Fig. 5.6, Courtesy of Margarita Gutman; University of Illinois at Urbana-Champaign; Figs. 5.9, 5.10, 5.19, 5.20 © F.L.C. / ADAGP, Paris / Artists Rights Society (ARS), New York 2024, Fig. 5.11, Moviestore Collection Ltd / Alamy Stock Photo; Fig. 5.12, Cooper Hewitt, Gift of Mrs. Hugh Ferriss; Fig. 5.13, The Ohio State University; Fig. 5.14, Album / Alamy Stock Photo; Fig. 5.15, Houghton Library, Harvard University; Fig. 5.16, Pictorial Press Ltd / Alamy Stock Photo; Fig. 5.17, Getty Research Institute, Los Angeles (88-B34645); Fig. 5.18, Francis Loeb Library, Harvard Graduate School of Design, Special Collections; Fig. 5.21, Francis Loeb Library, Harvard Graduate School of Design, Special Collections, Ferrari Hardoy Archives; Fig. 5.22, CPA Media Pte Ltd / Alamy Stock Photo; Fig. 6.1, Archives and Special Collections, UC Davis Library; Fig. 6.2, Arquivo Nacional Collection (Brazil); Fig. 6.3, rafastockbr / Shutterstock.com; Figs. 6.4, 6.5, 6.6, 6.7, Retro AdArchives / Alamy Stock Photo; Fig. 6.8, Amsterdam City Archives; Fig. 6.9, Tolu Owoeye / Shutterstock.com; Fig. 6.10, Fela Sanu / Shutterstock.com.

INDEX

Page numbers in *italics* refer to illustrations.

Abidjan, Ivory Coast, 325

Abuja, Nigeria, 320

Accra, Ghana, 325

Adams, John, 66

Adeyemi, Kunlé, 323

Adorno, Theodor, 289

Aircraft (Le Corbusier), 278

Alberti, Leon Battista, 31, 123, 275

Alcoa Corporation, 264

Algiers, 122, 292

Alphand, Adolphe, 127, 137, 173, 270, 322

aluminum, 264, 302

Alves, Rodrigues, 202–203

Amaral, Crispim do, 207, *208*, 209

Amazon region, 34, 224, 286, 298; forced
 labor in, 214; Ford Motor plant in, 247;
 gridded settlements in, 33; rubber
 plantations in, 214, 225

America First movement, 288

American Revolution, 22, 63, 64

America's Independent Electric Light and
 Power Companies, 303, *305*

Amsterdam, 112, 310, 336

L'An 2440 (Mercier), 43–51, 56, 71, 87, 96,
 100, 330

Angola, 162, 321

annexation, 119, 220

Anthropocene, 17, 19

antisemitism, 42, 84, 187, 225, 247, 252

Archigram collective, 299

Architectural Association, 299

Arendt, Hannah, 289

Argentina, 104, 170, 238, 239, 245, 267, 269,
 272, 283

Arrhenius, Svante, 15–16

Arts and Crafts movement, 230

Astor, John Jacob, 82–83, 85, 108

Astor Place riots (1849), 104

astrology, 32, 38, 44

automobiles, 155, 219, 230, 241, 243, 246, 300,
 327; in cinema, 255; environmental costs
 of, 315, 331–332; freedom equated with,
 307; in Latin America, 330–331; as novelty,
 218, 225, 245; politics of, 251–252; sprawl
 linked to, 258; in United States, 248, 266,
 294; utopianism linked to, 218, 301

autonomous vehicles, 303, 333

autos-da-fé, 41–42

aviation, 219, 237, 241, 253, 256, 260, 264, 275

Aymara people, 9

Azagaia (rapper), 326

Azevedo, Aluísio, 188–190, 192

Babeuf, Gracchus, 57

Baixa, Lisbon, 46, 51, 52; earthquake damage
 to, 27; rebuilding of, 27, *28*, 29, 34, 36, 39,
 41, 42, 73; tenements and decay in, 49–50

Baltard, Victor, *119*

Baltimore, 93, 111

Balzac, Honoré de, 86, 89, 90, 91

Bandeira, Manuel, 312

Banham, Reyner, 300

Barbosa, Orestes, 216

Barcelona, 107, 138, 139, 140–141, 152, 153, 336

"Bartleby, the Scrivener" (Melville),
108–112, 142–143, 158, 166, 262

Baudelaire, Charles, 117, 132, 193

Bauhaus, 254, 281

Bazalgette, Joseph, 99

Beijing, 45, 78, 86, 160, 221, 335

Bel Geddes, Norman, 13, 264, 265, 266

Bellamy, Edward, 194–195, 230, 234

Belle Époque, 224, 235

Benjamin, Walter, 10, 16, 17

Berardi, Franco, 17

Berlin, 87, 137, 219, 220, 231, 281, 286, 295

Berlin Wall, 316

bicycles, 245–246, 316, 330, 333, 336

biodiversity, 19, 300, 331

Black Lives Matter, 334

Blade Runner (film), 335

Blake, William, 63

Bleak House (Dickens), 114

Bogotá, 290, 331

bohemianism, 156

Bohn Aluminum and Brass Corporation,
302–303

Bosque, Luis Yboleon, 172

Boston, 50, 87; abolitionism in, 93; in
colonial period, 70; industrialization in,
144; Irish migration to, 98, 151; Olmsted's
plans for, 146, 149; in utopian writings,
194, 195, 230

bottlenecks, 327, 337

Brasília, 71, 296, 297, 298–299, 312–313,
314, 320

Brazil, 8, 170, 245, 270, 283; boundaries
within, 68; coffee production in, 172; gold
mining in, 23, 25, 26, 62, 166; highway
construction in, 313; independence
movement in, 49, 163, 168; medical
advances in, 210; racial hierarchy in, 215;
as semidemocratic republic, 204; slavery
abolished in, 163; slavery in, 91, 92–93, 94,
164–165, 170, 180–181, 199, 215; sugar
exports from, 104; in World War I, 238

Brooklyn, N.Y., 79, 148

Brown, Lester R., 315

Brussels, 31

Buenos Aires, 3, 177, 183, 219, 231, 234, 240,
247; under dictatorship, 280; electricity
in, 270; Le Corbusier's plans for, 3, 273–275,
278–279; as model city, 202; Plan Noel in,
269, 272–273; in the popular imagination,
212, 239, 243, 267–268; population growth
in, 163, 173, 221, 238, 267; sprawl in, 271;
suburbs of, 270, 273, 274; transportation
links to, 199

Buffon, Georges Louis Leclerc, comte
de, 51

Buntline, Ned, 88–89, 105

Burnham Daniel, 197–198

Bury, J. B., 102

Cabet, Étienne, 142–144

Cairo, 121, 220, 337

Caldas Barbosa, Domingos, 53–54, 212

calendar reform, 22, 23, 57, 134

California, 86, 111, 148, 233, 334, 335

Calvino, Italo, 342

Cambodia, 121

Campanella, Tommaso, 32

Canada, 221, 267, 283, 316

Candide (Voltaire), 41–42

carbon capture, 334

Carolina, Province of, 31

Carson, Rachel, 331–332

Central Park, New York, 8, 82, 146–151,
153, 197

Cerdá, Ildefons, 106, 138, 140–144, 152–153,
227, 272

Chandigarh, India, 298, 301

Charles II, king of England, 30, 34

ChatGPT, 337

Chicago, 85, 98, 145, 191, 229, 238, 239, 243,
282, 285, 309; Columbian Exposition in,
195, 196, 197–198, 199, 335

China, 45, 245, 337; automobile manufacture
in, 317; exports from, 25; global ambitions of, 321; gridded cities in, 73; high

technology in, 5; population growth in, 221, 335

cholera, 98, 140, 184

Churchill, Winston, 341

Cidade Nova, Rio de Janeiro, 339

City Beautiful movement, 171, 198, 226, 233, 272

The City in History (Mumford), 330

"City of the Future" (Krutikov), 260

Civil War, US, 128, 148, 150, 151

climate change, 2, 15–19, 317, 328, 332, 337, 338, 340

Clinton, Bill, 319–320

Clinton, DeWitt, 76

Club of Rome, 314

Cobden-Chevalier Treaty (1860), 121

coffee, 91, 166, 172, 204, 218

Colbert, Jean-Baptiste, 30

Cold War, 11, 296, 309, 313

Colombia, 104, 170

colonization, 4, 22, 52, 60; of Africa, 68, 160; of Asia, 160; by Britain, 226, 230, 313, 318; criticisms of, 57; by France, 121–122, 128, 154, 157, 230; difficulties of, 224; idealization of, 62, 146, 197; of the Spanish Americas, 33, 63

Columbian Exposition (Chicago, 1893), 195, 196, 197–198, 199, 335

Columbus, Christopher, 175, 195

Commissioners' Plan (New York City, 1811), 55, 56, 71, 75, 79–82, 147, 153, 172, 184, 319; authors of, 76–77, 78; Central Park's reshaping of, 147; criticisms of, 80, 100, 144; as historical anomaly, 103; openendedness of, 3, 55, 74, 77–78, 82; origins of, 73; speculation aided by, 81; verticalized, 85, 232

The Communist Manifesto (Marx and Engels), 101–102

computing, 9, 289–290

Comte, Auguste, 178, 179, 216

concrete, 235, 246, 250, 256, 281, 302, 315

Conselheiro, Antônio, 199–200

Copenhagen, 336

Copernicus, Nicolaus, 22

Cork, Ireland, 112

Correia da Serra, José Francisco, 42, 64

Costa, Lúcio, 296

Cotonou, Benin, 325

cotton, 7, 60, 91, 95, 98, 104, 172

Counter-Reformation, 38

Crane, Stephen, 192–193

Crimean War (1853–1856), 121

"Crystal Palace," Detroit, 246

Crystal Palace, London, *113*, 115, 116, 188, *302*; Great Exhibition in (1851), 112

Crystal Palace, New York City, 112

Cuauhtémoc, emperor of Mexico, 176

Cuba, 91, 94, 172–173, 187

Curitiba, Brazil, 112

Dakar, Senegal, 230, 327, 328

Danowski, Déborah, 17

Dante Alighieri, 341

Dar es Salaam, Tanzania, 326

Darwin, Charles, 8

The Death and Life of Great American Cities (Jacobs), 299, 332

decarbonization, 336, 338

Declaration of the Rights of Man and of the Citizen (1789), 48

Declaration of the Rights of Women and of the Female Citizen (1791), 49

The Decline of the West (Spengler), 252–255

decolonization, 22, 290

deconcentration, 248, 272, 301

Delirious New York (Koolhaas), 78, 319

dependency theory, 299–300

Detroit, 198, 246, 247, 249, 262

De Witt, Simeon, 76, 78, 80

Díaz, Porfirio, 175, 176, 179

Dickens, Charles, 73, 87, 89, 114

Diggers, 57

diphtheria, 98

Disraeli, Benjamin, 97–98

Dittrich, Julio, 239

Dostoevsky, Fyodor, 114–115

Douglass, Frederick, 93–94, 150, 168, 195

Dubai, 290, 324, 328
Dublin, 112
Dunbar, Paul Laurence, 285
Dylan, Bob, 1

e-bikes, 334, 336, 337
Edison, Thomas, 247
Eiffel Tower, 85, 106–107, 157, 195, 225
Eisenhower, Dwight D., 301, 309
Eixample, Barcelona, 138, 140–141, 144,
    152–153
Eko Atlantic (Lagos development project),
    319–321, 323, 328
electricity, 121, 176, 220, 311; in Buenos Aires,
    270; in industry, 229, 247; for lighting,
    118, 160, 197, 206; in speculative fiction,
    157; for streetcars, 152, 181, 184, 245
electric vehicles, 181, 182, 239, 246, 333
elevators, 85, 112, 160
Elgozy, Georges, 314
Émile (Rousseau), 46, 50, 63
Empire State Building, 85, 232, 263–264
The End of History and the Last Man
    (Fukuyama), 317
The Ends of the World (Viveiros de Castro
    and Danowski), 17
Engels, Friedrich, 98, 101–102, 191
engineering, 44, 115, 340; infrastructure
    development linked to, 239; military, 38
Enlightenment, 21, 24, 37, 41, 42, 49, 50, 71,
    166, 168, 171, 198, 224; stadial theories in,
    32; in urban settings, 22
Erie Canal, 78, 79, 111
La Estrella del Sur (Vera y González), 239, 266
Etzler, John, 99
eugenics, 282, 286
Exposición Universal (Barcelona, 1888), 152
Exposition Universelle (Paris, 1889), 157,
    195, 224, 225, 270

Fanon, Frantz, 295
Fauset, Jessie Redmon, 285
Federal-Aid Highway Act (1956), 301, 303, 307
Federal Housing Administration, 308

Federalist Party, 67, 70, 100
Ferriss, Hugh, 256–258, 262–263, 264
Filarete, 31–32
Firestone Tire Company, 303, 304
First International (International Working
    Men's Association), 125, 134
Five Weeks in a Balloon (Verne), 156
Flaubert, Gustave, 126, 136
Florence, 137
flux: in ecosystems, 69; fixity vs., 5, 13, 54, 55,
    57, 62, 92, 110, 112, 117, 152, 230, 249, 300, 312,
    337; of modern culture, 91; in New York
    City, 55; social status linked to, 88, 327
Ford, Henry, 246–249, 251, 272, 279
Ford Motor Company, 246–247, 251
Forestier, Jean-Claude Nicolas, 173, 270
Forty-Eighters, 104
Fourier, Charles, 96–97
France, 50, 58, 62, 81, 91, 92, 102, 270, 283; as
    colonial power, 121–122, 128, 154, 157, 230;
    political turmoil in (1970s), 314
Franco-Prussian War (1870–1871), 132, 137
Franklin, Benjamin, 64, 68
Franz Ferdinand, archduke of Austria, 235
French Revolution, 22, 48–49, 134, 178, 288
French Society of Urbanists, 225, 232
Frontin, André Gustavo Paulo de, 203, 204
Fukuyama, Francis, 316–317
Fuller, Buckminster, 308, 309, 310
Futurama (General Motors exhibit), 268,
    300–301, 303, 326
Future Shock (Toffler), 314
Futurism, 234–235, 237, 249, 268

Gama, Luís, 165–168, 171, 182, 191, 203, 215
Gama, Vasco da, 52
Garden Cities, 219, 227–231, 249, 253, 260,
    272, 276, 283
Garlic, Delia, 94
Garnier, Charles, 129, 130, 142, 158
Garrison, William Lloyd, 93
Gaudí, Antoni, 152
Gautier, Théophile, 128
General Motors, 251, 266, 300–301

gentrification, 18, 330

Germany, 219, 238, 243, 247, 281, 283, 289, 291, 301

Gibson, William, 327

Giedion, Siegfried, 155

Gladney, Ida Mae, 285

Glaeser, Edward, 335

glass, 1, 14, 45, 111–112, 115, 122, 195, 235, 246, 250, 256, 262–264, 296, 303, 308, 314

Glissant, Édouard, 319

gold mining, 23, 25, 26, 62, 86, 166

Goncourt, Edmond de, 128, 136

Goncourt, Jules de, 128, 136

Gore, Al, 332

Gouges, Olympe de, 49

Gramsci, Antonio, 247

Gratz, Benjamin, 83

Gratz, Maria, 83

Gratz, Rebecca, 83

Great Britain, 283, 300; as colonial power, 226, 230, 318; land management in, 67, 98; slavery abolished in, 92; textile manufacturing in, 91

Great Depression, 16, 244, 248, 261, 264, 266, 285

Great Fire (London, 1666), 30–31, 115

Great Migration, 282, 284, 309

Greeley, Horace, 146

grids, 30; in antiquity, 73; in Barcelona, 138; churches diminished by, 35–36; closed vs. open, 81; developers' avoidance of, 307; efficiency of, 69, 127; in Lagos, 319–320; in Lisbon, 28, 29, 31, 34, 42, 122, 308; in literature, 52; modernity linked to, 13, 32, 149; in New York City, 3, 55, 56, 71–82, 85, 100, 103, 144, 147, 153, 172, 184, 232; in Northwest Ordinance, 66; in Paris, 118, 122; in Philadelphia plans, 77; in Portuguese colonies, 33; in post-colonial Africa, 322; in post-disaster rebuilding, 31; in Spain and its colonies, 33, 172–174, 221, 267, 271–273, 275; suburbanization and, 307; in United States, 68–70; utopian, 142–143; virtue and rectitude

linked to, 80, 198, 206–207; in Washington plans, 70–71, 72, 77

Griffith, Mary, 100

Grimké, Angelina Emily, 95

Grimké, Sarah Moore, 95

Gruen, Victor, 298

Grund, Francis, 67, 86

Haiti, 50, 92

Haitian Revolution, 22, 23, 64, 65–66, 94

Hamilton, Alexander, 100

Hangzhou, China, 335

Hankou, China, 221

Hanoi, 224, 225–226

Hardoy, Jorge Ferrari, 278, 279

Harlem Renaissance, 339

Harrison, Wallace, 292

Haussmann, Georges-Eugène, 129, 131, 133, 152, 227; as autocrat, 107, 122, 125; Cerdá contrasted with, 138, 148; conservatism of, 125, 135; dismissal of, 132; eclecticism of, 118; influence of, 121, 122, 125, 128, 137, 144, 153, 195, 280; Olmsted contrasted with, 138, 147; Passos inspired by, 203; Pombal likened to, 122–123; as prefect, 117, 123, 125, 126, 147; resistance to, 127, 136; Roman influence on, 118; transportation planning by, 118–119; urban development viewed by, 123–124; utopianism linked to, 143

Havana, 170, 172–173, 202

Havens, Nicodemus, 76

Heath, William, 58, 59, 60, 61

Her (film), 335

History of the Skyscraper (Mujica), 268

Hitler, Adolf, 253, 281, 282, 286, 288, 291

Hobrecht, James, 137, 272

Hobsbawm, Eric, 115

homelessness, 322, 334, 340

Homestead Act (1862), 230

Hong Kong, 319, 335

Hoover, Herbert, 247–248

Housing Act (1949), 307

Howard, Ebenezer, 219, 227–232, 253, 272, 276

How the Other Half Lives (Riis), 183–188, 193
Hughes, Minrod, 76
Hugo, Victor, 126, 156
Hutton, James, 68
Hyperloop, 333–334

Icarians, 142–143
Immigration Act (1924), 282, 283
India, 25, 91, 245, 298
Inferno (Dante), 341
informal settlements, 8, 202, 211, 291–292, 295, 313, 320, 322–323, 340
Inquisition, 37
International Congress of Modern Architecture (CIAM), 275, 296, 298, 299
International Working Men's Association (First International), 125, 134
Invisible Cities (Calvino), 342
Iraq invasion, 317
Ireland, 94, 98, 144
Istanbul, 220, 337
Italy, 88, 137, 235, 280–281
Ivanaj, Drita, 294

Jackson, Andrew, 67
Jacobs, Jane, 299, 301, 308, 332
Japan, 73, 299, 335
Jefferson, Thomas, 63, 65, 66, 70, 71, 100, 103; cities despised by, 67, 146; Erie Canal viewed by, 111
Jesus, 66
The Jetsons (television program), 10, 11, 311, 338
João V, king of Portugal, 25, 27
Johnson, Lyndon B., 11, 309
Jokinen Plan, *310*
Jonathan, Goodluck, 320
Jordan, June, 310
José I, king of Portugal, 26, 34, 36, 39, 41, 52
Juarez, Benito, 175, 176
Julie; or, The New Heloise (Rousseau), 46–47, 48, 259
July Revolution (1830), 81, 91, 117

Kant, Immanuel, 21
Kelley, Florence, 190–191, 197
Kent, James, 80
Kerouac, Jack, 303
Khidekel, Lazar, 260
King, Moses, 241, 253, 267, 302
King's Dream of New York, 241, 242, 253, 267
Kinshasa, 322
Koestler, Arthur, 294
Koolhaas, Rem, 78, 318–319
Koselleck, Reinhart, 21, 22–23, 48, 64, 65
Kostof, Spiro, 69, 81
Krutikov, Georgii, 260
Kubitschek, Juscelino, 206, 313
Ku Klux Klan, 197, 282
Kurchan, Juan, 278

Lagoon (Okorafor), 326–327
Lagos, 3, 7, 290–291, 317–329
Lamarckism, 283
Lang, Fritz, 253–254, 258–259
Laugier, Marc-Antoine, 30
Law of the Meander, 275
Laws of the Indies, 32, 34, 37–38
Le Corbusier, 12, 219, 221, 232, 248–250, 251, 252, 264, 299, 322; Buenos Aires plans of, 3, 273–275, 278–279; centralized planning embraced by, 276–278; Punjab plans of, 298; United Nations project sought by, 291–292
Lecouvreur, Frank, 86
Leibniz, Gottfried Wilhelm, 24
L'Enfant, Pierre Charles, 70–71, 73, 74, 117, 198
The Leopard (Tomasi di Lampedusa), 102
The Limits to Growth (1972), 314
Lindbergh, Anne Morrow, 288
Lindbergh, Charles, 288
Lisbon: earthquake in (1755), 2, 3, 20–24, 35, 53; Napoleonic invasion of, 162; rebuilding of, 24–29, 31, 33–40, 46, 49–50, 52, 70, 77, 122, 154
Lispector, Clarice, 14, 312, 314
Liverpool, 60, 92, 98, 157

Lloyd, Harold, 255
Logue, Edward, 308
Lomé, Togo, 325
London, 232; in apocalyptic writings, 76; automobiles in, 245, 295; in fiction, 87–89, 239, 241; as financial and mercantile capital, 35, 60, 115; Great Fire in (1666), 30–31, 115; inequality in, 43; leftist politics in, 124–125; migration to, 58; Paris contrasted with, 179; population growth and density in, 86, 226; rebuilding of, 31, 35; sanitation in, 99, 226, 227; urban planning influenced by, 220
"London" (Blake), 63
Looking Backward (Bellamy), 194–195, 230, 234
Los Angeles, 252, 293, 335
Lost Illusions (Balzac), 86, 90, 91
Louisiana Purchase (1803), 65–66
Louis Philippe I, king of the French, 81–82
Louvre, Musée du, 30, 44
Luanda, Angola, 291, 321
lundús, 53
Luther, Martin, 23

Macedo, Miguel, 176–177, 178, 180
Machado de Assis, Joaquim Maria, 181–182, 200–201, 209
Madrid, 87, 112, 140, 337
Mafra, Portugal, 25–27, 35, 38
MAGA (Make America Great Again), 334
Maggie: A Girl of the Streets (Crane), 192–193
magical realism, 13
Magic Motorways (Bel Geddes), 13
The Magnificent Ambersons (Welles), 255–256
Mahin, Luísa, 165–167, 211
Maia, Manuel de, 27, 29, 30, 35
Makoko (Lagos settlement), 323–325, 328
Malagrida, Gabriel, 36–37, 42, 51
malaria, 73, 98
Manaus, 224, 225
Manchester, England, 98, 221
Manet, Édouard, 126
Mangin, Joseph François, 79

Manifest Destiny, 146
Manila, 198
Manso, Juana, 88
Mardel, Carlos, 29
Maria I, queen of Portugal, 51–52
Marinetti, Filippo, 234–235, 280
Marx, Karl, 8, 101–102, 135, 191
mass transit, 244, 246, 251, 323, 331, 334, 336–337; beginnings of, 115; in East Asia, 316; federal support for, 309; futuristic views of, 185, 241, 244, 303; in Latin America, 272, 331; in London, 115, 226; low emissions from, 17; opposition to, 307
Maximilian, emperor of Mexico, 122, 173
measles, 98
Mein Kampf (Hitler), 253
Melville, Herman, 108–110, 111–112
Mendelianism, 283
Mercier, Ernest, 276
Mercier, Louis-Sébastien, 54, 56, 96, 100, 194, 330, 331; literary culture championed by, 51; new secular order envisioned by, 46, 51, 71; Old Regime attacked by, 44–45, 50; uncertainty dismissed by, 47–48, 87, 156; Verne compared to, 158
Mérida, Spain, 33
Metabolism movement, 299
Metropolis (Lang), 253–254, 258–259
The Metropolis of Tomorrow (Ferriss), 256–258
Mexican Revolution, 176–177
Mexico, 64, 104, 121, 128, 170, 175, 238
Mexico City, 33, 79, 163, 173–179, 183, 202, 313, 314
Meza, Guillermo, 313
military engineering, 38
Minas Gerais, Brazil, 23, 49, 62, 166
miscegenation, 215, 268, 286
Les Misérables (Hugo), 156
Los Misterios del Plata (Manso), 88
Mitchell, Joni, 299
mixed-use development, 18, 152, 276, 308, 332, 337
modinhas, 53–54
Moilin, Tony, 156, 157

monorails, 241, 243, 244, 253, 264

Monroe, James, 65, 211

Montesquieu, Charles de Secondat, baron
de, 51

Montreal, 112, 316

Morales, Carlos Maria, 270

More, Thomas, 31, 43

Morocco, 230–231

Morris, Gouverneur, 77, 78, 80

Moscow, 294, 337

Moses, Robert, 302, 308–309, 322

Mourenx, France, 295

Mozambique, 162

"Mrs. Manstey's View" (Wharton), 232–234,
256–257

Mujica, Francisco, 268

Mumford, Lewis, 31, 38, 71, 154, 238, 299, 330

Munich, 112

Murger, Henri, 156

Musk, Elon, 333

Mussolini, Benito, 237, 280, 281

The Mysteries and Miseries of New York
(Buntline), 88–89, 105

The Mysteries of London (Reynolds), 88, 89

The Mysteries of Paris (Sue), 87–88, 126

Nabuco, Joaquim, 162, 163–165, 179–181,
193, 195

Nadar, Félix, 14

Napoleon I, emperor of France, 64, 102, 118

Napoleon III, emperor of France, 122, 123,
129, 138, 154; ancient Rome invoked by,
117, 118; as autocrat, 121, 125–126; Bois
de Boulogne envisioned by, 126–127;
Cerdá likened to, 141; as colonialist,
121; criticisms of, 124; death of, 136;
Emperor Maximilian backed by, 121, 173;
Haussmann appointed by, 117; Haussmann dismissed by, 132; influence of,
102–103, 116; subsidized housing backed
by, 125

National Association for the Advancement
of Colored People (NAACP), 191

National Theater of Nigeria, 323–324, 325

Nazis, 246, 247, 249, 252–253, 281–283, 286,
288

Nehru, Jawaharlal, 298

Netherlands, 92

New Caledonia, 121, 135

New Delhi, 226

New Harmony, Ind., 96

New Orleans, 66, 69

New York City, 1, 293, 294; as city of the
future, 219, 235, 241, 244, 256, 270; civil
disorder in, 104; Crystal Palace
exhibition in (1853), 112, 114; in film and
fiction, 192, 252, 255, 285; Irish migration
to, 98, 151; Latin American views of, 180,
238–239, 267–268; Le Corbusier's view
of, 249–250, 274; mass transit in, 152,
245; Mexico City compared to, 173, 177;
Moses's plans for, 308; Olmsted's plans for,
146–149; perpetual change in, 84–85;
poverty and inequality in, 183–184, 186,
193; racism in, 8, 94, 150–151; rapid growth
of, 78–79, 232, 267, 291; skyscrapers in, 85,
157, 232, 238, 253, 267; zoning in, 257–258.
See also Commissioners' Plan (New York
City, 1811)

Niemeyer, Oscar, 292, 296

Nigeria, 318–325

Nigerian Civil War (1967–1970), 324

NIMBY (Not In My Backyard), 234,
332, 334

9/11 attacks, 1, 317

Nineteen Eighty-Four (Orwell), 314–315,
316

Nixon, Richard, 307, 308

Noel, Carlos, 272, 273

Northwest Ordinance (1787), 68

Notes from Underground (Dostoevsky),
114–115

Occupy (political movement), 334

O Cortiço (Azevedo), 188–190, 192, 193

oil, 13, 19, 246, 252, 264, 276, 290, 296, 314,
316, 317, 318, 319, 321, 326

Okorafor, Nnedi, 318, 327

Oliver Twist (Dickens), 87
Olmsted, Frederick Law, 107, 138, 144–153, 197, 219, 270, 322
Olympic Games, 211, 252, 335
On the Art of Building (Alberti), 31
Orwell, George, 314–315
Osaka, Japan, 335
Otis, Elisha, 112
Owen, Robert, 96, 142
Oyo Empire, 318

"The Painter of Modern Life" (Baudelaire), 117
Palace of Westminster, 115–116
Pantagruel (Rabelais), 187
Pantheon, Rome, 288
Paris, 14, 73, 112, *120*, 141; automobile industry in, 225; city planning influenced by, 137, 178, 195, 226; civil disorder in, 101–102; Colbert's plans for, 30; Commune in, 8, 132–136, 149, 154, 156, 198, 200–201, 202–203; Francophone migrants in, 295; growing pains of, 237; high-rise development opposed in, 238; Le Corbusier's plans for, 249–250; leftist politics in, 62, 314; London contrasted with, 179; mass transit in, 245, 336; modernity embodied by, 107, 117–118, 153–156, 202, 224; opera house in, 129–131; population growth in, 21, 58, 86, 119–120; redevelopment of, 107, 115–132, 149, 152, 212, 332; in speculative fiction, 43–48, 50, 51, 96, 158, 330; women's rights in, 48–49
Paris in the Twentieth Century (Verne), 156–158
Paris in the Year 2000 (Moilin), 156
Parker, Barry, 230
Passos, Pereira, 161, 202–214, 217, 273, 307
Patte, Pierre, 39
Paxton, Joseph, 112, 115–116, 142
Pedro I, king of Portugal, 65
Peñalosa, Enrique, 331
Penn, William, 69–70
Perón, Juan, 278

Peru, 49, 64
Peter I ("the Great"), emperor of Russia, 31
Petrópolis, Brazil, 112
Philadelphia, 77, 79, 83, 100, 128, 259; grid design in, 69–70, 71; Quakers in, 95; rebuilt London's influence on, 31
Philippines, 187
Philip V, king of Spain, 39
phones, 160, 194, 222, 290, 311, 317, 327, 328, 333
photography, 160, 184
Piacentini, Marcello, 281
Picabia, Francis, 235
Poe, Edgar Allan, 331
pollution, 12, 19, 145, 157, 247, 326, 331, 332, 338
Pombal, Sebastião José de Carvalho e Melo, marquis de, 26–27, 29, 33–41, 50, 52, 122–123, 308
The Population Bomb (1968), 315
Porto, 112
Portugal, 36; Brazilian gold and, 25, 26; clergy in, 25; as colonial power, 41, 162, 168; emigration to Brazil from, 198–199; Inquisition in, 42; Jesuits expelled by, 37, 50; religious holidays in, 20; slavery abolished in, 39, 92
Portuguese America, 33, 58, 64, 68
positivism, 159, 178–179, 190, 216, 225, 286
"Positivism" (Rosa and Barbosa), 216–217
Praça do Comércio (Terreiro do Paço), 35, 36, 310
preservationism, 85, 285–286, 311, 339
printing, 23, 25–26, 50, 58
Progressive Era, 187, 190, 198
Protestant Reformation, 26
Pruitt-Igoe (public housing), 300
Prussia, 137
Prussian Planning Act (1875), 137
public transit. *See* mass transit
Puritans, 66–67, 81
Pyramid of Giza, 85, 106, 111, 320

Rabelais, François, 187

racism, 163, 311; among abolitionists, 164; antiurbanism linked to, 67; in geopolitics, 65; in Latin America, 286; in New York City, 8, 94, 150–151; "scientific," 171, 179, 187, 189, 192, 225, 281–282; suburbanization linked to, 284

The Radiant City (Le Corbusier), 275–278

railroads, 106, 107, 142, 144, 184, 194, 203, 214, 221, 241, 248, 255, 318; in France, 121; in garden cities, 229; in literature, 157; in London plans, 115; in Mexico, 175; Rio's neglect of, 205; in United States, 248; urbanization linked to, 106, 110–111, 146; in West Africa, 326

Recife, Brazil, 104, 105, 163

Reconstruction, US, 151, 168, 182

rectilinearity. *See* grids

redlining, 284, 341

Red Scare, 191

Reformation, 23

Regional Planning Association, 231

Rennes, 31

Revolt of the Vaccine (1904), 212–214

Reynolds, George, 88, 89

Ribeiro Sanches, António, 42

ride-hailing apps, 334

Riis, Jacob, 183–188, 191, 193

Rio, João do, 218–219

Rio de Janeiro, 3, 177, 311–312; anarchist rebellion in (1918), 259; Black women in, 190; conflicting development aims in, 162; cultural life in, 339; *favelas* in, 202; in fiction, 181; inequality in, 193; high-rise construction in, 238; Le Corbusier's plans for, 275; mass transit in, 183; Passos's surban reforms for, 198–199, 202–215, 217, 273, 307; population growth in, 161, 163, 172, 173; Portuguese migrants in, 189, 198–199; poverty in, 189, 201; in speculative fiction, 218; topography of, 209

Risanamento, 137

Robespierre, Maximilien, 22, 23, 36, 48, 49

Robida, Albert, 222

Rockefeller, Nelson, 292

Romanticism, 156, 332

Rome, 4, 38, 58, 73, 117, 118, 124, 179, 280–281, 286

Roosevelt, Franklin D., 285

Roosevelt, Theodore, 186

Rosa, Noel, 216

Rosas, Juan Manuel de, 88, 104

Rosenbaum, Samuel, 83

Rousseau, Jean-Jacques, 21, 46–48, 51, 63, 96, 97, 217, 234

rubber, 114, 214, 225, 247

Rush, Benjamin, 67

Russian Revolution, 8, 225, 259, 260, 266

Rutherfurd, John, 76–77

Sage, Russell, 182

Saint-Simon, Henri de, 96, 142, 178

Salvador, Brazil, 94, 165, 170

samba, 54, 215, 216, 217, 255

Sand, George, 131–132, 136, 179

San Francisco, 198, 334

sanitation, 29, 162, 171, 220, 283; in Brazil, 210–211, 214; in British colonies, 318; in Cerdá's Barcelona, 140; in France, 118, 124, 155; in London, 99, 226, 227; miasma theory and, 98; in New York City, 184; in self-built neighborhoods, 323

Sant'Elia, Antonio, 235, 236, 238

Santos, Eugénio dos, 29

São Paulo, 166, 198, 199, 202, 238, 275, 281, 337

Sarmiento, Domingo Faustino, 271

Savannah, Ga., 69

Scandinavia, 31

scarlet fever, 98

Scenes of Bohemian Life (Murger), 156

Schuyler, Montgomery, 80

scientific racism, 171, 179, 187, 189, 192, 225, 281–282

Second World Black and African Festival of Arts and Culture (1977), 324

segregation, 88, 182, 214, 226, 230, 282, 307, 309, 318, 320, 341; class-based, 117, 130, 141, 157, 194, 240; nationalism linked to, 281;

social Darwinism linked to, 8; suburban-
ization linked to, 284
self-building, 8, 202, 211, 291–292, 295, 313,
320, 322–323, 240
Seneca Falls Convention (1848), 104
Seneca Village, Manhattan, 8, 150–151
Seoul, 220, 290, 335
Sermon on the Mount, 66
Sert, Josep Lluis, 299
setbacks, 247, 256, 258, 326
Seven Sleepers, 43
sewage, 2, 18, 220, 290, 340; in Barcelona,
140; in Buenos Aires, 270; in Lisbon, 49;
in London, 99, 115, 226; in New York City,
184; in Paris, 118; in Rio, 210
Sex Pistols, 314
Shanghai, 335
Shenzhen, 335
Shell Motor Oil, 264–265
Silent Spring (Carson), 331–332
Silicon Valley, 334
silver mining, 64
Singapore, 333
Singer Manufacturing Company, 85, 91
Situationist International, 299
Sixtus V, Pope, 38, 280
skyscrapers, 184, 335; in the Americas vs.
Europe, 268, 269, 281; in Chicago, 195,
282; grid designs compatible with, 78; in
futuristic writings, 218, 239, 241, 243, 249,
256, 257; in Latin America, 177, 183, 259,
278; in New York City, 85, 157, 232, 238,
253, 267; as symbols, 14, 174; technology
of, 112, 222
slavery, 7, 13, 23, 56, 60, 341; abolition of, 39,
62, 92, 95, 102, 150, 151, 160, 168, 172, 318; in
Brazil, 91, 92–93, 94, 164–165, 170, 180–181,
199, 215; in Mexico, 175; modernity in
conflict with, 171; taxation and, 26;
technological advances linked to, 24; in
United States, 93; in West Africa, 91–92
The Sleeper Awakes (Wells), 239–240
"The Sleeper Wakes" (Fauset), 285
smallpox, 98, 210, 213

smart cities, 322, 337
Smith, Al, 248
Soares, Lota de Macedo, 298–299
social Darwinism, 8, 159, 179, 180, 187, 207
South Africa, 245
Soviet Union, 247, 259–262, 289, 290,
294–295, 301, 316
Spain, 33, 92
Spanish America, 22, 32–33, 63–65, 68,
163, 168
Speedy (film), 255
Speer, Albert, 286
Spencer, Herbert, 179, 180
Spengler, Oswald, 252–255, 268, 286
The Sport of the Gods (Dunbar), 285
sprawl, 222, 226, 260, 284, 295, 340; in the
American Sunbelt, 252; in Buenos Aires,
271; in the developing world, 290, 326;
environmental damage from, 17, 18,
258, 331; fear of cities linked to, 99; futuristic visions of, 10, 11, 247, 300, 311; inequality linked to, 174; in Le Corbusier's
Parisian plans, 250; tax policy linked to,
11, 301
Staël, Madame de, 64–65, 103
Stalin, Joseph, 260, 262
steam power, 114, 169, 204, 241; in agriculture, 164; in construction, 144; Futurists'
celebration of, 234; in manufacturing,
247; in the military, 160–161; in printing,
58; for ships, 56, 106, 141, 151; for trains,
98, 106, 110–111, 142
steel, 1, 141, 194, 315; in automobile manufacture, 331; in building construction, 85,
112, 161, 184, 195, 256, 263–264; in landfill
construction, 144; in military technology,
160–161; in modernist planning, 249–250;
in trains and rails, 111, 142, 172; urbanization linked to, 17, 106, 141, 235
Stevenson, Adlai, 301
St. Louis, 69, 212, 300
Stockholm, 333
St. Paul's Cathedral, 35, 112
St. Petersburg, 31, 35, 128

streetcars, 255, 309; decline of, 329; in Detroit, 246; electric, 152, 181, 184, 245; foreign investments in, 272; horse-drawn, 16, 245; in Latin America, 183, 205; revival of, 215; suburbanization linked to, 146, 182, 258
streetlights, 118, 212, 226
suburbs, 8, 252, 253, 258, 290, 296, 313; in Africa, 327; automobile industry linked to, 246, 293–294; in Berlin, 219; in Brazil, 209, 214, 215, 221; in Buenos Aires, 270, 273, 274; commuting from, 146; criticisms of, 298, 307; energy use linked to, 17–18; garden cities linked to, 230, 231; glorification of, 99, 144, 145, 150, 295, 302–303; highway construction linked to, 293, 301, 307; in Mexico City, 174; in Morocco, 230–231; in New York City, 150; Olmsted's design of, 144–145; in Paris, 119; in popular culture, 303, 311; population growth in, 308; in Portugal, 39; racial segregation linked to, 284, 301, 307–308, 309; zoning's stranglehold in, 338
Sue, Eugène, 87–88, 126
Suez Canal, 121, 157
sugar, 79, 91, 104, 166, 172
sunlight, 118, 140, 184, 250, 256, 258
surdo de Exu (musical instrument), 216–217
swamps, 70, 73, 331, 334
Sydney, 112

Tafuri, Manfredo, 77, 81, 84
Tasso, Torquato, 130
Távora family, 36, 42
taxation, 204, 251; French voting rights linked to, 81; of imports, 199; in Portugal, 39, 49; of real property, 339; slavery and, 26; sprawl linked to, 11, 301
Team Ten, 299
Tea Party (political movement), 334
Teatro Colón, 221
telegraphy, 114, 121, 122, 157, 159, 169, 237
Tenochtitlan, 33, 175
Teoría general de la urbanizacion (Cerdá), 141–142

Teotihuacán, 33, 175
textiles, 7, 60, 62, 79, 91, 96, 138, 190, 201
Thatcher, Margaret, 300, 316
Thays, Charles, 270
Things to Come (film), 264
third spaces, 340
Three Hundred Years Hence (Griffith), 100
Thunberg, Greta, 332
timekeeping, 4, 108, 200; calendric, 22, 23, 57, 134
Tlateloco Massacre (1968), 314
tobacco, 160
Tocqueville, Alexis de, 73, 100–101, 102
Toffler, Alvin, 314
Tokyo, 220, 335, 336
Tomasi di Lampedusa, Giuseppe, 102
To-Morrow (Howard), 227–228
Toronto, 112, 316
Treaty of Madrid (1750), 33, 37
Treaty of Tordesillas (1494), 68
Triumph of the City (Glaeser), 335
Truman, Harry, 291
Tsing, Anna, 17
tuberculosis, 98
Turin, 30, 31
typhoid, 98, 178

Uniform Vehicle Code (1926), 246
United Nations, 291–292
Universal Exhibition (Paris, 1855), 121
Unwin, Raymond, 230
Urbanisme (Le Corbusier), 274–275
Uruguay, 283
Utopia (More), 43

Vancouver, B.C., 316
van Loo, Louis-Michel, 39, 41
Vasconcelos, José, 286
Vaux, Calvert, 147
Veloso, Caetano, 162
Venezuela, 13, 170
Venice, 32
ventilation, 98–99, 140, 143, 184, 186, 206
Vera y González, Enrique, 239, 266, 267

Verne, Jules, 156–157, 194, 237, 239

Vienna, 4, 26, 137–138, 336

Vietnam, 121, 157, 225

Vila Rica (Ouro Preto), 49, 50

Viveiros de Castro, Eduardo, 17

Voltaire, 21, 24, 30, 41–42, 51, 171

Voyage en Icarie (Cabet), 142–143

walkability, 18, 215, 250, 266, 298–299, 326, 331–332, 335, 337

War of Canudos (1896–1897), 200, 202, 213

Warsaw, 224

The War That Will End War (Wells), 236

Washington, Booker T., 168

Washington, D.C., 70–71, 72, 77, 80, 117, 141, 169, 170

Washington, George, 71

Washington Consensus, 316

water supply, 4, 18, 44, 99, 220, 340; in Barcelona, 140; in Buenos Aires, 270; in Lisbon, 27; in New York City, 74, 184; in Paris, 118, 124; in Rio, 210

The Wave of the Future (Anne Morrow Lindbergh), 288

We (Zamyatin), 262

Weber, Max, 81

Welles, Orson, 255

Wells, H. G., 227, 236, 237, 239–240, 264

Wells, Ida B., 195

Wharton, Edith, 153, 232–234

whooping cough, 98

Williams, Raymond, 109

Wilson, Woodrow, 247

Winthrop, John, 66, 70

women's rights, 97, 104, 151, 216–217; abolitionism linked to, 95; bicycles and, 245; in fiction, 100, 189–190, 195; in Paris, 48–49; in Latin America, 94; in Progressive Era, 190–191; utopians' disregard of, 45

women's suffrage, 13, 257, 283

World's Columbian Exposition (Chicago, 1893), 195, *196*, 197–198, 199, 335

world's fairs, 183, 211, 235, 266, 281; in Barcelona, 152; in Chicago (Columbian Exposition, 1893), 195, *196*, 197–198, 199, 335; colonialism linked to, 224–225; in East Asia, 335; in Paris, 157, 195, 224, 225, 249, 270; race among nations linked to, 114, 180; sites selected for, 197

World's Fair on Modern Decorative and Industrial Arts (Paris, 1925), 249

World Trade Center, 1, 264

World War I, 8, 16, 224, 225, 243, 244, 245, 252, 266, 281; aviation in, 219, 237; optimism shattered by, 235, 237, 252, 266; technology in, 237

World War II, 116, 219, 236, 281, 282, 283, 288, 289, 291, 295

Wren, Christopher, 30, 35, 115

Wright, Frank Lloyd, 231

Wuhan, 221, 335

yellow fever, 67, 98, 140, 210, 318

Yu, Kongjian, 335–336

Zamyatin, Yevgeny, 262

Zaragoza, Spain, 33

Zócalo, Mexico City, 33, 175

Zola, Émile, 14, 126, 127, 188

zoning, 2, 257, 277, 278, 292, 333, 334; in Brasília, 297; in Buenos Aires, 272; in New York City, 257–258; obstruction linked to, 311, 338; precursors of, 119, 231; racial discrimination linked to, 258; in Tokyo, 336

Zweig, Stefan, 298

A NOTE ON THE TYPE

This book has been composed in Arno, an Old-style serif typeface in the classic Venetian tradition, designed by Robert Slimbach at Adobe.